Ethnobotany

Ethnobotany

A Reader

Edited by Paul E. Minnis

University of Oklahoma Press : Norman

Also by Paul E. Minnis

Social Adaptation to Food Stress: A Prehistoric Southwestern Example (Chicago, 1985)
(ed., with Charles L. Redman) *Perspectives on Southwestern Prehistory* (Boulder, 1995)
(ed., with Wayne J. Elisens) *Biodiversity and Native America* (Norman, 2000)
(with Michael Whalen) *Casas Grandes and It's Hinterland* (Tucson, 2001)
ed., *People and Plants in Ancient Eastern North America* (Washington, D.C., 2003)
ed., *People and Plants in Ancient Western North America* (Washington, D.C., 2004)

With the exception of the five Introductory articles, the essays in this book were all previously published in the *Journal of Ethnobiology* and are used here with permission of the Society of Ethnobiology.

Library of Congress Cataloging-in-Publication Data

Ethnobotany : a reader / edited by Paul E. Minnis.
    p.   cm.
  Includes bibliographical references and index.
  ISBN 978-0-8061-3180-1 (paper)
    1. Ethnobotany.   2. Human ecology.   3. Folk classification.   4. Traditional medicine.
  5. Traditional Farming.   I. Minnis, Paul E.

GN476.73.E83 2000
306.4 5—dc21

                                                          99–047294
                                                              CIP

Contents

Ethnobotany

Introduction

PAUL E. MINNIS

All people are dependent on plants. Every morsel of our food, most medicines, much cloth and fiber, many other material needs, and, for most groups of people in the world, even the majority of our fuels are derived from plants. Similarly, the idea of the natural world is a potent image and central theme in the beliefs and actions of many cultures. As much as some would like to believe otherwise, industrial and postindustrial societies have not broken their intimate links with plants. Rather, coadaptation between plants and humans has changed and perhaps even intensified with the growth of urbanism and increasingly international economies. The consequences of maladaptive ecological relationships may now be greater than in the past, because the margin of error is so much smaller. Anthropogenic environmental effects have increased greatly in the twentieth century, as a result of a vastly larger population in a closely integrated and energy-intensive industrialized world economy [see Baskin (1997) and Wilson (1992) for readable introductions on modern environmental issues]. In fact, there is little question that throughout the world humans have become the keystone species—organisms that have a disproportionally large impact on environments. Therefore, the study of the relationships between people and plants—the domain of ethnobotany—has a central role in understanding humanity and its place in the environment.

People tend to think of ethnobotany as only the study of plant uses by "primitive" peoples in exotic locations; how people of tribe X use plant Y for purpose Z. This view is limiting in two ways. First, people do more than simply "use" plants; any interaction between people and plants occurs within intricate cultural and environmental contexts. Humans imbue some plants with great meaning and organize their understanding and use of the botanical world in culturally specific ways. A meal of peanut butter and fried worms on lettuce topped off with chiles may be very nutritious, but it would be unacceptable to most North Americans because the foods are combined in culturally, not biologically, inappropriate ways.

The second common misconception about ethnobotany is that it applies to only nonindustrialized and nonurbanized societies. Ethnobotanists study human and plant interrelationships among all peoples. Yet working with the people of indigenous, non-Western cultures, who comprise the vast majority of humanity now and in the past, holds a special place in ethnobotanical inquiry, because the contributions of these peoples have been previously undervalued in academia and industry. In fact, most universities have more courses on the literature of European authors than on all the indigenous peoples in the rest of the world. But aboriginal peoples have developed sophisticated understandings of local ecology—an indigenous science—through centuries and even millennia of intense interaction with their biotic environments, and the need to understand other cultures and to share information so that all peoples can thrive in a sustainable and just future is a compelling reason for ethnobotanical research.

WHY ETHNOBOTANY?

The world truly is becoming smaller. People in regions that for millennia had minimal direct contact with the outside world are now increasingly interdependent with the economics, communications, politics, culture, education, and tourism of other countries. These changes create problems as well as offering opportunities. One of the greatest advantages of contact is the increased facility for learning from others. Humans and cultures gain knowledge by their experiences, which results in a cumulative fund of information. The tens of thousands of cultures that have existed, containing the wisdom of billions of people adapting to thousands of environmental settings, surely comprise a tremendous store of expertise.

Ethnobotanical knowledge can be used to help find solutions for pressing problems, such as increasing food production while improving agricultural sustainability, developing new medicines, and finding environmental conservation strategies that are well articulated with new economic development and with cultural survival. It is dangerous to believe that only one's own culture has all the answers to contemporary problems; ignorance is a poor foundation for human adaptation. We can learn from the successes of traditional peoples, and learning from their errors can help us avoid similar mistakes. Human adaptation is not perfect and never has been; the landscapes throughout the world are littered with the remains of extinct cultures. For instance, salinization of arid croplands, caused by poor irrigation systems, has occurred for thousands of years, and today important producing areas, such as some wheat-growing areas of Australia, face similar problems. Ethnobotanical information can be a vital part of the efforts to correct these problems.

Ethnobotany is of immediate use in two broad ways. The first is exploration for economically useful plants—the economic botany tradition—and the second concerns the quest for indigenous ecological knowledge. Recent popular works (e.g., Plotkin 1993; Schultes and Von Reis 1995) have familiarized the public with the search for new medicines known by traditional healers, and pharmaceutical companies are intensifying their drug prospecting efforts among indigenous peoples. Modern medicine is still heavily dependent on drugs derived from plants, and the number of plants used as medicines is staggering. For example, Moerman (1986) lists over two thousand plant species known to have been used as medicines by native North Americans. Recent research has shown that groups in less intensively studied areas still rely on many medicinal plants unknown to outsiders. There are many drugs still to be discovered.

Similarly, humans throughout the millennia have used thousands of food plants, both wild and domesticated. Some of the wild plants may be useful worldwide in environmentally nondestructive ways. For example, there has been much effort to find markets for tropical rainforest resources that are renewable in order to stop or reduce the replacement of the forests with livestock pasturage and fields. One contribution of ten thousand years of human agriculture is thousands of domesticated plant species and tens of thousands of crop varieties. At the very time that this genetic diversity is needed to maintain food production, the spread of industrial-scale agriculture threatens it (Fowler and Mooney 1990). Consequently, governments and private organizations are trying to preserve as much traditional crop diversity as possible. To effectively preserve diversity and to understand how this diversity came into existence and has been maintained, one needs to understand the cultural context of indigenous food production.

Concern for loss of biological diversity, and calls for a greater understanding of tropical rain forests and other poorly known areas of high biodiversity, are increasing. Yet in many of these regions and in fact in nearly all areas of the world, indigenous peoples are keen observers of their environments; they have to be because they make their living from the local environment. The recognition that native peoples are ecologists is not new. More than a century ago, Powers (1873–1874: 373) suggested: "But it is not for a moment to be supposed that the Indian is a superficial observer; he takes a note of the forms and qualities of everything that grows on the face of the earth." More and more, the vital role of indigenous peoples in understanding and conserving environments is being recognized (e.g., Minnis and Elisens 2000; Oldfield and Alcorn 1991; Orlove and Brush 1996).

As many note, biodiversity is related to cultural diversity; preservation of the former requires concern for the latter (e.g., Brush and Stabinsky 1996; Kemf 1993; Johnson 1994; Oldfield and Alcorn 1991; Orlove and Brush 1996). Not only are cultures repositories of past experiences and knowledge, but they are also the frameworks for future human adaptation. Human adaptation, in turn, requires choice or self-determination. Thus, preservation of cultural diversity requires self-determination. Ethnobotany could become only the study of static relationships if peoples of the world do not have the self-determination to choose, as much as possible, their own solutions to the problems that they face. And it is quite likely that we all can appreciate and learn from the choices that others make.

The new context of ethnobotany that recognizes indigenous peoples as partners who deserve respect and self-determination has also changed the ethical and legal issues entailed in ethnobotanical research at the beginning of the twenty-first century. In the past, researchers simply "mined" ethnobotanical knowledge of a particular group and published the results. Traditional peoples were too often assumed to be passive participants in research and scholars believed that data were free for the taking. Ethnobotanists and others now recognize that indigenous peoples should also benefit from research, especially when their ethnobotanical knowledge, which is a form of intellectual property, has economic value. Who owns ethnobotanical knowledge and exactly how should traditional peoples profit from marketing their cultural tradition [see, for example, Brush and Stablinsky (1996); Downs (1996)]? If pharmaceutical manufacturers make money from drugs first noted by indigenous people, should not the original discoverers of the drug be enriched too? The value of indigenous ethnobotanical knowledge needs to be factored into ecosystem value estimations, that is, attempts to calculate the monetary and nonmonetary value of natural environments (Daily 1997).

HISTORICAL ROOTS OF ETHNOBOTANY

The current state of ethnobotany is shaped in part by its historical roots. There is no obvious point in time at which we can say ethnobotany began, because all peoples have noted with some interest how members of their own culture, as well as other peoples, relate to the natural world. The most obvious expression of cross-cultural interest in plant use is the spread of various agricultural crops throughout the world. For thousands of years, farmers have acquired new crops from their neighbors and from faraway places. New World crops, such as maize, cassava, and potato, are staples today for many Old World groups, and Old World crops, such as wheat, sorghum, and rice, are essential foods for most New World peoples.

Systematic investigation of what we would now call ethnobotany has a long history in the Western tradition. Early interest in ethnobotany was built on Greek, Roman, and Islamic foundations and intensified by colonialism and geographic exploration. The establishment of botanical gardens and the publication of herbals and botanical treatises in Renaissance Europe began in the sixteenth century and spread rapidly (Ambrosoli 1997).

But the systematic study of the natural world, which has been so widely associated with the Western world, has equals elsewhere. For example, the Incas of South America maintained botanical gardens (Niles 1987; Yacovleff and Herrera 1934), as did the Aztecs of Mesoamerica (Coe 1994). The ancient Egyptian queen Hatshepsut commissioned a botanical expedition to what is now Somalia in 1495 B.C., and her nephew Thutmosis III brought back plants from his military expedition to Syria (Coats 1969). There is also a long history of ancient ethnobotanical exploration in China (Anderson 1988). In the early fifteenth century, Chou Ting-Wang compiled the *Chiu-Huang Pen-ts'ao,* an extraordinary treatise describing 414 native foods used in Hunan Province, China (Read 1946). Curiosity about plants and their relationships with humans is not uniquely Western, nor is it solely a product of the modern era. But the exponential growth of ethnobotanical research is a product of the modern world.

While it is not possible to identify one specific point at which ethnobotanical research began, its modern history is clearer [for fuller treatments of the history of ethnobotany see Cotton (1996); Ford (1978a, 1986); Reed (1942); Schultes and Von Reis (1995)]. The term *ethnobotany* was coined a little over one hundred years ago by J. M. Harshberger, a botanist at the University of Pennsylvania, who examined ancient plant remains from cliff dwellings in southwestern North America. While reporting his discoveries, he described his study as "ethnobotany" (Harshberger 1896). Harshberger was not the only scholar working in the American West at the time (Whiting 1967).

Others included Fewkes (1896), Palmer (1871), Powers (1873–1874), and Hough (1898); Powers termed his study "aboriginal botany." Some of the early studies were surprisingly sophisticated, because the researchers studied more than simple plant uses; they often recorded beliefs about the plants and human ecological relationships as well. Barrows's (1900) study of the Cahuilla ethnobotany in California is a remarkable early example of high-quality ethnobotanical research. This initial work was soon followed by ethnobotanical research by many scholars and in notable early North American centers of study at the University of New Mexico under Edward F. Castetter, at the University of Michigan with Melvin Gilmore and Volney H. Jones, and at Harvard University with Oakes Ames.

The amount of ethnobotanical research in the American West is unusually great. For example, Ford (1978a: Table 1) tabulated that there had been at least 904 North American ethnobotanical reports up to 1977. Reports on the Southwest accounted for a little over 21 percent, whereas reports on the next most intensively studied area, the Plains, accounted for a little less than 10 percent. Although unusually well documented, the American West is still only one small area of the world. Scholars working in Africa, Asia, Australia, the Pacific, Central and South America, and Europe have long conducted ethnobotanical investigations, and these regions have become important centers of research [see Cotton (1996: Figure 1.1) for a simple statistical comparison of the geographic diversity of ethnobotanical research]. India, Mexico, and China, in particular, have recently trained strong cadres of ethnobotanical scholars.

From its modest beginnings, ethnobotany has grown in size and importance. Today scholars from many disciplines, such as anthropology, botany, archaeology, geography, medicine, linguistics, economics, landscape architecture, and pharmacology, are rekindling a new renaissance in ethnobotanical research. Each discipline brings its own perspective, while at the same time interdisciplinary research creates a stimulating and diverse field of study. More popular books and movies, scholarly publications, and textbooks are now available for ethnobotany than at any time in the past. Throughout the world, academic societies and nongovernmental organizations devoted to ethnobotany sustain this intellectual renaissance.

ABOUT THIS VOLUME

Ethnobotany: A Reader contains original ethnobotanical studies by scholars presenting the results of their own studies in their own words, and it can be used with one of a number of textbooks (e.g., Alexiades 1996; Balick and Cox 1996; Cotton 1996; Ford 1978b; Heiser 1990; Martin 1995; Roddick 1990). Students reading original reports, rather than secondary summaries, clearly see that research is an exciting process of discovery. The articles chosen include classic studies and samples of ethnobotanical research being conducted today, and the selections are organized so that students of ethnobotany can cover a great deal of the broad range of research in this field.

To provide structure for this diverse research, the readings are grouped into four themes: ethnoecology, folk classification, food and medicines, and agriculture. Each section is introduced by a noted scholar who is an active researcher in that field.

"Ethnoecology," introduced by Catherine S. Fowler, has been proposed as an over-arching term to subsume ethnobotany, ethnozoology, and similar disciplines that recognize human-environment interactions as ecological. "Folk Classification," intro-duced by Cecil H. Brown, has been a significant part of ethnobotany for decades, because it deals with the central issue of how people view their environment. The historical heart of ethnobotany is economic botany—the study of new food plants and medicines; the section, "Food and Medicines," introduced by Timothy Johns, focuses on this aspect. The section on "Agriculture," introduced by Richard I. Ford, deals with the especially intricate ecological relationships involved in plant domestication.

Unfortunately, a single volume cannot cover all aspects of ethnobotany. None of the articles in this book deals with the ethnobiology of the ancient past, the study of archaeobotany or paleoethnobotany. Since most human-environmental interactions occurred before the advent of writing about five thousand years ago and among groups lacking a written record of their history, archaeobotany is an integral part of ethno-botany. And it is difficult to understand the ecology of modern environments without taking into account environmental history that often involves prehistoric human inter-ventions (Stahl 1996). For example, the study of ancient crops and agricultural tech-niques holds promise for the modern world; prehistoric Tiwanaku farming techniques have been reintroduced in South America (Kolata 1996). One volume could not do justice to both ethnobotany and archaeobotany, but fortunately there are several archaeobotanical books available at various levels of sophistication (e.g., Dimbleby 1978; Gremillion 1997; Hastorf and Popper 1988; Pearsall 1989; Reitz, Newson, and Scudder 1996).

The readings in this book are from the *Journal of Ethnobiology,* the official publi-cation of the Society of Ethnobiology. Although a relatively new society, publishing its first journal issue about two decades ago, members of the SEB are on the forefront of ethnobiology. We invite you to examine recent issues of the journal and join the Society.

ACKNOWLEDGMENTS

The article authors whose innovative and high quality work made this volume possible and who generously gave their permission to have their work reprinted deserve thanks. The four authors who introduce each section—Cecil Brown, Richard Ford, Catherine Fowler, and Timothy Johns—are also thanked for their contributions. The many colleagues who suggested articles for this reader provided essential advice. Patricia Gilman, Gordon Uno, and several anonymous reviewers commented on the introductory chapters. University of Oklahoma Press staff, particularly John Drayton and Randolph Lewis, are thanked for expediting this book's publication.

LITERATURE CITED

Alexiades, Miguel N. 1996. Selected Guidelines for Ethnobotanical Research: a Field Manual. New York Botanical Gardens, New York.
Anderson, E. N. 1988. The Food of China. Yale University Press, New Haven.

Ambrosoli, Mauro. 1997. The Wild and the Sown: Botany and Agriculture in Western Europe, 1350–1850. Cambridge University Press, Cambridge.

Balick, Michael J. and Paul Alan Cox. 1996. Plants, People, and Culture: the Science of Ethnobotany. Scientific American Library, New York.

Barrows, David P. 1900. The Ethno-botany of the Coahuilla Indians of Southern California. University of Chicago Press, Chicago.

Baskin, Yvonne. 1997. The Work of Nature. Island Press, Washington, D.C.

Brush, Stephen B. and Doreen Stabinsky. 1996. Valuing Local Knowledge: Indigenous People and Intellectual Property Rights. Island Press, Washington, D.C.

Coats, Alice M. 1969. The Plant Hunters. McGraw-Hill, New York.

Coe, Sophie D. 1994. America's First Cuisine. Yale University Press, New Haven.

Cotton, C. M. 1996. Ethnobotany: Principles and Application. John Wiley and Sons, Chichester, England.

Daily, Gretchen C. 1997. Nature's Services: Societal Dependence on Natural Ecosystems. Island Press, Washington, D.C.

Dimbleby, Geoffrey. 1978. Plants and Archaeology. Granada Publishing, London.

Downs, David R. 1996. Global trade, local economies, and the biodiversity convention. Pp. 202–16 in Biodiversity and the Law, edited by William J. Snape, III. Island Press, Washington, D.C.

Fewkes, J. Walter. 1896. A contribution to ethnobotany. American Anthropologist 9: 14–21.

Ford, Richard I. 1978a. Ethnobotany: historical diversity and synthesis. Pp. 33–50 in The Nature and Status of Ethnobotany, edited by Richard I. Ford. University of Michigan Museum of Anthropology Anthropological Papers No. 67. Ann Arbor.

————. 1978b. The Nature and Status of Ethnobotany. University of Michigan Museum of Anthropology Anthropological Papers No. 67. Ann Arbor.

————. 1986. An Ethnobiology Source Book: The Use of Plants and Animals by American Indians. Garland Publishing, New York.

Fowler, Cary and Pat Mooney. 1990. Shattering: Food, Politics, and the Loss of Genetic Diversity. University of Arizona Press, Tucson.

Gremillion, Kristen J. 1997. People, Plants, and Landscapes: Studies in Ethnobotany. University of Alabama Press, Tuscaloosa, Ala.

Harshberger, J. W. 1896. The purposes of ethno-botany. American Antiquarian 17: 73–81.

Hastorf, Christine A. and Virginia S. Popper. 1988. Current Paleoethnobotany. University of Chicago Press, Chicago.

Heiser, Charles B. 1990. Seeds to Civilization. W. H. Freeman, San Francisco.

Hough, Walter. 1898. Environmental interrelationships in Arizona. American Anthropologist 11(os): 133–55.

Johnson, B. A. 1994. Who Pays the Price?: the Sociocultural Context of Environmental Crisis. Island Press, Washington, D.C.

Kemf, Elizabeth. 1993. The Law of the Mother: Protecting Indigenous Peoples in Protected Areas. Sierra Club Books, San Francisco.

Kolata, Alan L. 1996. Tiwanaku and its Hinterland: Archaeology and Paleoecology: Agroecology, Vol. 1. Smithsonian Institution Press, Washington, D.C.

Martin, Gary J. 1995. Ethnobotany: a Methods Manual. Chapman and Hall, London.

Minnis, Paul E. and Wayne J. Elisens. 2000. Biodiversity and Native America. University of Oklahoma Press, Norman.

Moerman, Daniel E. 1986. Medicinal Plants of Native America. University of Michigan, Museum of Anthropology Research Reports in Ethnobotany No 2. Ann Arbor.

Niles, Susan A. 1987. Callachaca: Style and Status in an Inca Community. University of Iowa Press, Iowa City.

Oldfield, Margary L. and Janis B. Alcorn. 1991. Biodiversity: Culture, Conservation, and Ecodevelopment. Westview Press, Boulder.

Orlove, Benjamin S. and Stephen B. Brush. 1996. Anthropology and the conservation of biodiversity. Annual Review of Anthropology 25: 329–52.

Palmer, Edward. 1871. Food products of the North American Indians. Report of the Commission for 1870, pp. 404–28. U.S. Department of Agriculture, Washington, D.C.

Pearsall, Deborah M. 1989. Paleoethnobotany, a Handbook of Procedures. Academic Press, San Diego.

Plotkin, Mark. 1993. Tales of a Shaman's Apprentice. Viking, New York.

Powers, Stephen. 1873–1874. Aboriginal botany. Proceedings of the California Academy of Sciences 5: 373–379.

Read, Bernard E. 1946. Famine Foods Listed in the Chiu Huang Pen Ts'ao. Southern Material Center, Taipei, Taiwan.

Reed, Howard S. 1942. A Short History of the Plant Sciences. Chronica Botanica, Waltham, Mass.

Reitz, Elizabeth J., Lee A. Newson, and Sylvia J. Scudder, eds. 1996. Case Studies in Environmental Archaeology. Plenum Press, New York.

Roddick, Anita. 1990. Plants for People. Natural History Museum Publications, London.

Schultes, Richard E. and Siri Von Reis. 1995. Ethnobotany: the Evolution of a Discipline. Timber Press, Portland.

Stahl, Peter W. 1996. Holocene biodiversity: an archaeological perspective from the Americas. Annual Review of Anthropology 25: 105–26.

Whiting, Alfred F. 1967. The present status of ethnobotany in the Southwest. Economic Botany 21: 316–25.

Wilson, E. O. 1992. The Diversity of Life. Belknap Press of the Harvard University Press, Cambridge, Mass.

Yacovleff, E. and F. L. Herrera. 1934. El Mundo Vegetal de los Antiguos Peruanos. Museo Nacional, Lima.

Part One

Ethnoecology

Ethnoecology

An Introduction

CATHERINE S. FOWLER

Ethnoecology, as an approach to human ecology, was first proposed in the mid-1950s and early 1960s in a series of thought-provoking papers by Harold Conklin (1954, 1957) and Charles Frake (1962). As Frake (1962: 55) noted, a field worker "cannot be satisfied with a mere cataloging of the components of a cultural ecosystem according to the categories of Western science. He must also describe the environment as the people themselves construe it according to the categories of their ethnoscience." Only in that way, Frake continues, can one hope to determine "the extent to which ecological considerations, in contrast, say, to sociological ones, enter into a person's decision of what to do" (Frake 1962: 55).

Although with earlier roots in the cultural ecology of the 1940s as promoted by Julian Steward, and with certain alternative expressions in the 1960s and since [see, for example, Rappaport's (1963) "cognized environment"], ethnoecology has continued to guide and influence ethnobotanical methodology since its inception. Gary Martin (1995: xx) sees the term *ethnoecology* as "increasingly used to encompass all studies which describe local people's interaction with the natural environment," making it the parent of subdisciplines such as ethnobotany and ethnozoology. This expanded view of ethnoecology has been responsible for taking ethnobotany (and other areas of ethnoscience) beyond the stage of cataloging uses and into many other facets of human-environment interrelationships. The interests of some of its practitioners have developed into concerns with folk classification (see Brown's Introduction in this volume), while those of others have led to explorations of indigenous environmental perceptions or systems of knowledge (Johnson 1992). Some ethnoecologists look at issues of sustainability in both natural product harvesting and agriculture (see Ford's Introduction in this volume). And most recently still others have become involved in broader issues of conservation and indigenous land-management systems (Blackburn and Anderson 1992).

The prefix *ethno* as in ethnoecology, ethnoscience, and ethnobotany is used with two meanings. In the meaning originally intended in *ethnobotany* (see Minnis's and Ford's Introductions in this volume), it refers to *ethnic,* thus meaning the studies of the botany, science, or ecology of a particular ethnic group—something unique to the history of that group. However, in the sense in which it was originally used when the words *ethnoscience* and *ethnoecology* were coined in the 1950s and 1960s, *ethno* referred to the perceptions or views by the indigenous group of the phenomena in question. Here the meaning indicated by *ethno* was more a concept involving the cultural insider's cognition, than an outsider's observations. Conklin and Frake, as well as many since, were seeking what they felt would be a more complete understanding of ecology by exploring and including insider's views (see also Johns's Introduction in this volume). The methods of ethnoscience that they and others suggested should be applied to the task depended on a combination of linguistic tools that were to be used to get at what indigenous people have to say about these matters, along with observational tools to see what they indeed did about them in ordinary behavior (Fowler 1977). While contemporary ethnoecology still applies these tools and methods and does indeed attempt to assess the views of the cultural insider, it also depends on the tools and methods of Western science to measure a whole host of environmental situations, changes, and effects (see Martin 1995). Ethnoecology has become a much more holistic and thorough approach by combining insider and outsider views and both senses of the prefix *ethno*.

Because ethnobotanists and ethnoecologists are willing to listen to and carefully observe the practices of indigenous or traditional peoples (those who have been on the land and working with systems for many years and over generations), they have learned much of value. They have learned that decision making is often a complex process that involves many factors not obvious at first glance to the outsider, no matter how well trained. As C. M. Cotton (1996:61) notes, one can easily misconstrue evidence observed in the field as the result of a lack of knowledge on the part of traditional peoples of an ecologically more worthwhile approach, when indeed what they know and how they do things is the more correct, if complicated, solution. This is not to say that indigenous peoples do not make ecological mistakes at times, but often these are self-correcting, and a deeper probing of activities may indeed show that their so-called mistakes provided long-term gains over short-term goals. Given that indigenous decision making is often holistically based, or inclusive of many cultural as well as environmental parameters, superficial examination rarely leads to understanding. Only a more thorough and complex set of research techniques and methods involving careful analyses will give good results. Full integration of indigenous knowledge systems, such as traditional ecological knowledge (TEK) [but also others (see Cotton 1996: 61–62)], with other ways of knowing and observing should be the goal, although indigenous knowledge systems also stand on their own merits.

The three articles that follow, two from the early 1980s and one from 1991, reflect to a significant degree both pioneering thinking within ethnoecology as well as present-day trends. None of the articles is particularly "dated" by the use of terminology or concepts; rather, the topics they discuss are still important and the subjects of continuing fieldwork and theoretical insights. Each chapter can serve as supplementary reading or as the focus of discussion of general topics in ethnoecology as well as specific ones.

The article by Janis Alcorn provides an overview of some of the many concepts of ethnoecology, such as botanical resource perception, plant management, and discovering and defining the impact of human activities on plants and plant communities. The focus of her investigations are the Huastec peoples of east-central Mexico. She stresses that their ethnobotanical knowledge has adaptive functions, that it is culturally driven and motivated, and that what is perceived, or better reported, by any one person—let alone a group of people—varies with specific contexts: environmental, economic, social, familial, and ideological. This knowledge is constantly subject to reevaluation, and thus it changes, but while serving immediate needs. Alcorn speaks of the need to consider a "grammar of human ecological relations," most likely in the sense of a grammar as a structured set of relations that, when operationalized, is capable of generating old as well as new patterns. Without a knowledge of the overarching cultural patterns, the truly adaptive nature of ethnobotanical knowledge would be less obvious to the outside observer and less functional for the participant.

Gary Nabhan and colleagues take up a more specific theme within ethnoecology, that of the impact of indigenous people on biodiversity through their diversification of habitats. This team effort compares the biotic diversity of two Sonoran Desert oases, one still farmed by descendants of mixed O'odham populations (mostly former Sand Papago people), and the other formerly farmed but now "recovering" as part of a national monument. Although not conclusive for all biota investigated, the study seems to show that the oasis remaining under native management (with agriculture) is biotically the richer. The anthropogenic environment supports more botanical species (including cultigens and weeds) than the other, and this diversity appears to benefit various other biotic groups (such as birds and mammals) as well. Thus, the hand of humans does not always have a devastating or destructive impact on species or landscapes, an idea once prevalent among environmentalists and even conservation biologists, but one that should be carefully considered and evaluated in each situation. What appears at first examination to be disturbed may indeed be richer for that disturbance.

Kat Anderson carries forward the theme of anthropogenic environments in her article on the management of redbud by the Southern Sierra Miwok of California. Although the data she reports are preliminary and in need of additional verification and expansion, she points out how indigenous management systems that include such practices as pruning, coppicing, and burning can create environments that benefit not only people but plants. They also often go unrecognized by contemporary land managers, who are unaware of the long history of environmental manipulation by indigenous peoples. Anderson cautions land managers to carefully investigate and consider the long-term effects of new forms of management on present-day ecosystems. Although native Californians have been prevented from practicing traditional management techniques for fifty or more years, some have persistent knowledge of former practices. And they are willing to share the knowledge if it benefits the plants, and if they in turn can be given a share in the results. This is a powerful message to all of us in a world made smaller and less healthy by insufficient willingness to share power and decision making to mutual benefit.

Collectively as well as individually, these articles provide a good introduction to the concerns as well as some of the techniques of contemporary ethnoecology. The persons reporting their work in this section are still active in research on these and related areas, as students of ethnobotany will undoubtedly discover. They have remained firm in their commitments to the geographic areas on which they are reporting, as well as to the themes here explored.

LITERATURE CITED

Blackburn, Thomas C. and Kat Anderson. 1992. Before the Wilderness: Environmental Management by Native Californians. Ballena Press, Menlo Park, Calif.

Conklin, Harold C. 1954. An ecological approach to shifting agriculture. New York Academy of Sciences Transactions 172: 133–44.

————. 1957. Hanunoo Agriculture: a Report on an Integral System of Shifting Cultivation in the Philippines. Food and Agricultural Organization, United Nations, Rome.

Cotton, C. M. 1996. Ethnobotany: Principles and Applications. John Wiley and Sons Ltd., Chichester, England.

Fowler, Catherine S. 1977. Ethnoecology. Pp. 215–43 in Ecological Anthropology by Donald L. Hardesty. John Wiley and Sons, New York.

Frake, Charles O. 1962. Cultural ecology and ethnography. American Anthropologist 63(1): 113–32.

Johnson, M., ed. 1992. Lore: Capturing Traditional Environmental Knowledge. Dene Cultural Institute, Fort Hay, Canada.

Martin, Gary J. 1995. Ethnobotany: a Methods Manual. Chapman and Hall, London.

Rappaport, Roy. 1963. Aspects of man's influence on island ecosystems: alternation and control. Pp. 155–74 in Man's Place in Island Ecosystems, edited by F. R. Fosberg. Bishop Museum Press, Honolulu.

FURTHER SUGGESTED SOURCES

Balée, William. 1994. Footprints of the Forest: Kalapor Ethnobotany—the Historical Ecology of Plant Utilization by an Amazonian People. Columbia University Press, New York.

Ellen, Roy F. and K. Fukei, eds. 1994. Beyond Nature and Culture: Cognition, Ecology and Domestication. Berg, London.

Posey, Darrel A. and William Balée, eds. 1989. Resource Management in Amazonia: Indigenous and Folk Strategies. Advances in Economic Botany 7. New York Botanical Garden, New York.

Warren, D. M., L. J. Sikkerveer, and D. Brokensha, eds. 1995. The Cultural Dimension of Development: Indigenous Knowledge Systems. Intermediate Technological Publications, London.

CHAPTER ONE

Factors Influencing Botanical Resource Perception Among the Huastec

Suggestions for Future Ethnobotanical Inquiry

JANIS B. ALCORN

INTRODUCTION

This paper focuses on the botanical resource perception of individual human actors who sustain themselves in a moist tropical northeastern Mexican environment emicly understood on Huastec terms. The questions to be addressed are: What makes a given plant a particular kind of resource? What kinds of needs do resources fill? What factors influence the perception and choice of resources to fulfill these needs? In order to answer the questions I have raised, my discussion will develop the meaning of "resource" and "need" in the context of action-related decisions made by individual Huastec actors. Before the discussion is begun, however, I will briefly delimit the term "resource perception." As it is used here, "resource perception" refers to the process of assigning a particular resource role, or "use" to a plant by evaluating that plant's possible utility and the consequences of using it.

By elucidating the factors influencing resource perception, I hope to accomplish two things. First I hope to provide a new perspective for interpreting the data in useful plant lists, and secondly, I hope to contribute to the development of appropriate methods for evaluating the adaptive functions of ethnobotanical knowledge. Useful plant lists collected from indigenous people are often touted as the empirically valuable results of millennia of native experimentation designed to fine-tune the human to his environment. It is generally felt that, unless a "superstitious" basis for a plant's use is clear, the plants are listed as specific kinds of resources because they have the physical properties which answer standard human needs and would very likely serve these purposes well in any context where they are available. In most cases, no further criteria beyond the folklore vs. functional distinction are applied for understanding the value or meaning of a plant's use. The Huastec data suggest that the value of the information in these useful plant lists, so long associated with the term ethnobotany, has been both under and over estimated.

In addition to containing "uses", ethnobotanical lists usually include native plant names. During the past few decades cognitive and linguistic anthropologists have focused on the plant names in these lists to the *de facto* exclusion of their accompanying uses. Investigators (Berlin et al. 1973; D'Andrade 1976; Hunn 1977; Randall 1976), however, have debated the value, structure and functioning of classification systems generated using ethnoscientific methods. Randall (1976) has stressed that the motive for classification must be examined in the context of real-life situations if classification behavior and the underlying mental organization of the information relevant to the classification are to be understood; i.e., plant names and plant uses need to be tied back together and studied within real contexts where plant names are signs for information about more than just the plant's morphology. Hays (1981) has called for testing of assumptions that folk biological classification systems are adaptive. If "uses" are to be interpreted as "behavioral responses" as Hays (1974; 1981) suggests, then we must learn to recognize and understand these responses by developing a deeper understanding of the real-life contexts in which the responses occur. The following consideration of Huastec resource perception suggests the complexity pursuant to developing appropriate methods for evaluating the adaptive functions of ethnobiological knowledge and folk biological classification systems.

RESEARCH SETTING AND METHODS

The Huastec are Mayan language speakers who in pre-Conquest times controlled a large ecologically diverse area including most of San Luis Potosi and large areas of Hidalgo, Tamaulipas, Queretaro, and Veracruz states (Laughlin 1969). Today approximately 60,000 Huastec speakers live southwest of Tampico in the Sierra Madre Oriental foothills of southeastern San Luis Potosi and northern Veracruz, primarily a climax vegetation zone of tropical rainforest, Bosque Tropical Perrenifolio (Rzedowski 1966). The vegetation today, however, consists almost entirely of successional communities that reflect human management (henceforth referred to as anthropogenic vegetation zones).

Huastec resources labeling decisions occur within the context of the natural and social ecosystems in which they participate. The Huastec live as Indians within the mestizo (i.e., national cultural identity) dominated politico-economic setting of Mexico. Families generally live in dispersed household units within corporate communities and receive their subsistence from the products of their land, cash cropping and wage labor. Anthropogenic vegetation zones usually maintained by a Huastec family include cash producing sugarcane, managed forest plots, and cornfield-fallow cycling fields managed as *milpa* by slash and burn methods. The details of Huastec botanical resource management within these anthropogenic zones have been discussed elsewhere (Alcorn 1981). Land use patterns are affected by individual and community concerns, local interpretation of government regulations about using available land, and locally administered government loan policies. Cash cropping centers around sugarcane which is processed into raw sugar by individual family operations and sold at low prices into a mestizo controlled market. Henequen and coffee are also important cash crops in some areas.

Research was designed to identify Huastec botanical resources, to investigate the methods and impact of Huastec resource management, and to construct and integrate cognized and operational models of the Huastec natural and social environment in order to generate hypotheses about the impact of Huastec world view on ethnobotanical processes influencing elements of the Huastec vegetational environment. Methods used during 13 months of fieldwork included structured and informal discussions, the administration of interview schedules, the drawing of land use maps in consultation with Huastec land holders, and participant observation. Interviews were conducted in Spanish and Huastec. Extensive data about plant uses, plant names, and plant management were provided by 50 informants from 20 communities. Eighty-four individuals were formally interviewed but many more people provided valuable insights. One Huastec collaborated with me throughout the entire project and participated in most interview sessions.

To date, 2000 plant specimens have been collected in scientifically identifiable condition (i.e, flowering or fruiting specimens). I have identified the majority by using pertinent floras, monographs, and the University of Texas herbarium. Specimens that were difficult to identify were sent to appropriate specialists for determination. Different botanical taxa collected and identified from the Huastec habitat during this project now total 910. Vouchers will be deposited in the following herbaria: CHAPA, INIF, MEXU, TEX, and the Instituto Nacional de Investigaciones sobre Recursos Bioticos in Jalapa, Veracruz.

RESULTS

The Huastec depend on the plant world for many raw materials. Men, women and children quickly discriminate between plant resources and nonresources every hour of the day. Specific uses have been recorded for 65% of the botanical taxa I collected. Plant utility is reflected in three of the four Huastec botanical life-form cover terms. The word for tree, *te'*[1], also means a branch, a pole, or a piece of wood, be it a loom, a housepost, or a quickly fashioned hook for retrieving a desired fruit. *Ts'a:h*, the cover term for vine, also refers to any lashing material, be it vine or rope. *Ts'oho:l*, the cover term for herbaceous plant, is also used to mean medicine derived from any plant source (tree, vine, bark, root, etc.). Today *to:m* only refers to grass. Grass is rarely used for thatch in the Huasteca today but in Tzeltal, a related Maya language, *tom* refers to the grass bundles prepared for thatching a house. A term for grass thatch bundles was not elicited in Huastec.

When presented with a fresh vegetative shoot, Huastec informants attempted to recognize and identify the specimen by evaluating characteristics which would make it useful. Leaves were usually crushed and smelled (chemical evaluation). Questions were asked about the fruit, habit and habitat. Knowledge of all these characteristics has potential value for resource assessment as well as for identification. Unless they were large and showy, edible, or otherwise useful, flowers were rarely discussed. Once identification was made, the informant usually volunteered uses for the plant and added qualifying statements about preparation, value, and problems involved in its use. The resource value of a particular plant for a particular use often hinged upon the context of the use and the user. Although "resource" means something which is used to satisfy social, biological, and physical needs, the Huastec acknowledge that trade-offs are inherent in the use of any resource.

Plants are clearly resources for the Huastec. But what kinds of resources are necessary and what makes "plant X" a specific kind of resource? When a Huastec informant was asked, for example, "Is 'plant X' a resource for 'use Y,'" a wide range of responses were given. "Yes" and "no" answers were rare. Characteristic answers included:

"My ancestors needed it, I don't."

"Only other people know."

"I can't use it, people are too invidious."

"I've heard that it can be used, but I've never tried it so I don't know."

"I don't know. Maybe that's why mestizo merchants buy it from us in the market."

"No, well yes. It could be used, but I use 'plant Z' because I have it here by the house."

The range of answers to this question gives us some clues about the Huastec resource labeling process. The utility of a resource is assessed by the individual from a shared Huastec bias and a personal idiosyncratic bias. Respondents' replies indicate a personal consideration of actions implicit in the choice, the appropriateness of the action, and the constraints limiting the action. Nonetheless, a given respondent's answer is not necessarily optimally adaptive. His decision obtains from his calculation of the interplay effects of factors which also shape that context.

Patterns abstracted from conversation, interview sessions, and observed behavior suggest some of the factors shaping the context of Huastec resource perception. Based on the investigative focus necessary to study them in further detail, I have chosen to lump the factors into four general categories: biological and physical; cultural; economic; and personal and social.

Basic to the Huastec resource evaluation process are the empirically measurable physical or chemical qualities which qualify or disqualify a plant from the use in question. Huastec, however, not only assess the physical and chemical attributes of "plant X" but also consider its spatial and temporal position in their vegetational environment. The plant's ecological requirements, its membership in a particular community, its life cycle, its reproductive biology, its speed of growth as well as other aspects of the plant's biology are considered, as far as they are known to the individual, within the context of the existing time and space investment patterns which characterize his land management system. Because his existing land management system is designed to meet many other needs apart from the one under question, the consideration of the changes necessary for the integration of "plant X" into that system is critical to his decision. Ecological changes potentially caused by the integration of "plant X", the scarcity of "plant X", and the scarcity of resources necessary to maintain "plant X" are also considered and compared to similar criteria for available substitutes. Other empirically measurable variables considered include the biological needs of the individual, his household, and his domestic animals.

There are also, however, less easily measurable factors that are important in the resource perception process. Culturally generated needs create the requirement for certain resources (e.g., specific ritual items). The perceived context for plant use is shaped by Huastec world view. Native inquiries into a plant's properties and the interpretation of the results are shaped by native epistemological biases. Cultural sanctions against the use of "plant X" in a given way may remove it from the resource category of "use Y." In some cases a use or a plant may be identified with a particular cultural identity and thus appropriate or inappropriate for the person being questioned. For example, some plants are identified with mestizo as opposed to Indian identity. Other plants/uses are identified with a particular role within Huastec society. For example, the use of short, hollow lengths of carrizo [*Arundo donax* L., *Pennisetum bambusiforme* (Fourn.) Hemsl. (*paka:b*)] is associated with curers.

Other considerations are economic. Allocation of time and space necessary for the maintenance, acquisition and/or use of the possible resource is considered within the context of the individual's present life strategy and against the value assigned free time. The known "opportunity costs" of opting for a "new" resource are evaluated against the probable gains. The risks and uncertainties that surround the maintenance of "plant X" were it to be acknowledged as a resource are considered within the context of the land management system presently in operation. Risks are also evaluated in a social context. Some resources are more easily appropriated by other people, and the individual must assess the ease of appropriation as well as the losses and benefits which might attend such a transaction. Limitations on the individual's land management system may leave particular needs unfilled and transactional resources become necessary to fulfill these needs. The cash generating potential of a resource, the labor investment necessary, and the stability of the market for "plant X" may also be considered in this context.

A final category of considerations are those peculiar to each individual. The individual's household demography affects the household's needs and resources, and, of course, changes over time. The individual's personal knowledge of "plant X" and alternatives, as well as his knowledge of particular resource categories, clearly affects his answer to our question. His knowledge depends upon the form of existing information networks and the person's participation in them in order to gain other's knowledge. It also depends on the individual's own investigations of the plant. Age, personality, experience, and status affect the individual's knowledge as these factors change with time. The individual's particular management skills and his personality also affect the decision to perceive "plant X" to be a resource. For example, an individual's definition of plant resources is affected by his personal response to the traditional wealth leveling pressures of the community, his personal desire for power and the paths he chooses to achieve it. The individual may rely on others for certain services/products and have no need to know about resources necessary to them. The factors considered by the individual in resource labeling decisions reflect the fact that the Huastec derive their plant resources from two sources: directly from the natural environment to which they have access, or indirectly through transactions with other people. Resources maintenance activities include the management and cultivation of social relationships as well as the management and cultivation of vegetation. Methods open to the individual for attaining goods indirectly through other people influence his resource perception and vegetation management.

The factors which I have listed here clearly do not exist in isolation. My isolation and classification of them can only be heuristic because these and other interrelated factors interact in shaping resource perception. The individual's answer will vary over time as any of the factors mentioned above, and thus the interrelationship between factors, is altered. In addition, past interactions have created historical trends of resource definition and "use" that shape the possible present-day choices. Huastec plant resource "needs" and "uses" are restricted to those that are part of particular present-day Huastec strategies (including existing technological patterns such as raw sugar production practices, the "invisible technology" of Huastec agroecosystem management, etc.) designed to operate in today's Huastec habitat and within Huastec social organization. At the same time, however, "needs" and "uses" bear marks of the historical strategies out of which they developed.

Conflicts and constraints limit the use of available resources. Needs and the choices of certain resources may conflict with the choice of others. Such conflict imposes constraints on the use of particular plants. Other constraints are generated by peculiar intracommunal resource access regulation. For example, while each family has a specific, often inadequate, land holding, other people may request loan of the land without payment of rent, or demand part of a harvest in exchange for volunteered labor. Thus, individuals are forced to juggle their household operations both to avoid being taken advantage of by others while at the same time attempting to get as much as possible from others. Finally, the politico-economic environment of the individual as an Indian within the Mexican sector of the world economic system limits and shapes his decisions. His choices can only be made within the context created by the decisions of those of higher authority.

The ethnobotanical list of Huastec plants and their uses generated by my research reflects the interaction of factors influencing Huastec resource perception. A brief treatment of a few selected species in each of three "use" categories important for survival (firewood, construction materials, and medicine[2]) will illustrate this interaction.

The species commonly recognized as firewood include: *Acacia angustissima* (Mill.) Kuntze *(shi:shit)*, *Acacia cornigera* (L.) Willd. *(thobem)*, *Adelia barbinervis* Schlecht. & Cham. *(ata')*, *Calliandra houstoniana* (Mill.) Standl. *(wi:t'ot')*, *Callicarpa acuminata* H.B.K. *(et te')*, *Conostegia xalapensis* (Bonpl.) D. Don. *(chikab te')*, *Croton reflexifolius* H.B.K. *(olih)*, *Cupania dentata* DC. *(ts'aw')*, *Guazuma ulmifolia* Iam. *(akich)*, *Leucaena pulverulenta* (Schlecht.) Benth. *(thuk')*, *Lippia myriocephala* Schlecht. & Cham. *(anam te')*, *Nectandra loeseneri* Mez. *(oh te')*, and *Sapindus saponoria* L. *(walul)*. Although one might expect the firewood designation to be awarded to heavy wood which burns slowly to produce long lasting, hot coals, some of these species produce firewood of a very poor quality. What these species do share in common is their membership in the fast growing successional community of fallow cornfields. Depending on its age and structure, the vegetation which covers the fallow can be a resource to be burned, grazed, or kept for future use. If the decision is made to slash and burn the vegetation, then the option is where to burn it and for the production of what. It can either be burned in the field to provide ash for fertilizing the corn to be planted or it can be collected and burned in the hearth to provide heat for cooking.

Fig. 1. Planting milpa after firewood harvest. Stacked between the new milpa and the stand of flowering corn in the background is the firewood collected before burning the slash. Light burning left more firewood to be gathered later. Also visible are spared palms for thatch production and developing housepost trees that were pollarded for firewood during preparations for planting corn.

My preliminary data suggest that the amount of land devoted to the cornfield-fallow cycled fields depends more on the amount of firewood needed than on the amount of corn needed.[3] Management practices often emphasize firewood production over corn production. Deliberate light burning of fields and removal of wood before burning increases the firewood yields but cuts the yield of corn (Fig. 1). Pollarding of firewood-producing trees and opting not to carry out the traditional one-time weeding of the milpa speed up firewood production. Thus, factors influencing agricultural patterns, the availability of alternate firewood resources, species' response to the agriculture regime, and species' representation in the successional fallow vegetation are reflected in the labeling of these species as firewood resources.

The species commonly used for the main houseposts in house construction include: *Cordia alliodora* (R. & P.) Oken *(wish te'), Diphysa robinoides* Benth. *(chichath), Harpalyce arborescens* A. Gray *(k'an te'), Nectandra loeseneri* Mez. *(oh te'),* and *Piscidia piscipula* L. Sarg. *(tsi:hoi).* The physical requirements for houseposts strictly limits the species that could potentially fulfill this resource role. The species listed share strong wood, a straight bole, and decay resistance. They also share the ability to grow well on agriculturally poor ridgetop soils or as isolated individuals spared in the sugarcane or milpa-fallow cycle fields.

The species used for roofing materials are: *Imperata brasiliensis* Trin. *(ata: to:m), Licaria capitata* (Schlecht. & Cham.) Kosterm. *(sholim te'), Sabal mexicana* Martius *(oto: mal, apats')* and *Saccharum officinarum* L. *(pakab)*. The superior material is the thatch of *Licaria capitata* leaves. A *Licaria* leaf roof is said to last for 30 or more years, keep the house cool, and be impervious to rain. Today, however, few people recognize or use *Licaria capitata* as a roofing resource ostensibly because increasingly intensive land use has caused *Licaria capitata* to become a scarce forest tree in many places. Palm thatch from *Sabal mexicana* has largely displaced *Licaria* and *Imperata brasiliense* thatch. *Sabal mexicana* is a multipurpose species that has been purposefully introduced into many local areas in the past 50 years. Palms neatly fit into existing patterns of land use because, once established, they can be spared during milpa clearing or integrated into sugarcane fields. People who are really pressed for land and can't afford to devote space in their fields to palms or those who can't afford to get palm leaves from others choose to use the inferior thatch of sugarcane leaves, instead of using the sugarcane leaves as a resource to mulch and fertilize their cane fields. Thus, the list of thatch resources is not a list of four functionally equivalent species but rather a list that reflects a trade-off between land use and utilitarian considerations.

The list of Huastec medicinals can not simply be viewed as a list of drug plants used to treat biomedical diseases. Medicines, as a Huastec category, have the innate power to transform, or to be empowered by a curer or witch to transform a person's state of being. They may be used to poison or to sicken someone as well as to cure a person of an illness, or to prevent illness from striking. An illness, moreover, is not just a biomedical malfunction but also an event within a social field, and both of these aspects of illness are treated by curative medicines. Medicines may do their work by direct application, by ingestion, by merely being swept over a person, or by burning at midnight in the pathway to a person's home. Huastec illness etiologies include such agencies as embedded foreign objects sent by witches, interference by dead spirits, the action of stars, and soul loss by fright.

While knowledge of the same construction and firewood resources is shared by most adult Huastec, the knowledge of many medicinal plants is not. Over half of the 900 plants I collected had medicinal uses but agreement on the use and the means of application varied widely. There are many reasons for this. A person may learn about medicines from treatments applied by relatives, neighbors, and curers. Visible signs of use (e.g., seeing scars on a tree's trunk) might lead the individual to ask someone what kind of resource the tree is. At the same time, however, a person may also have a plant's use revealed to him or her in a dream. Some people also experiment with plants to determine their effects on the body, and the information derived is then processed according to Huastec beliefs. Such individually derived information is not freely shared. Another factor influencing medicinal plant resource recognition is the increasing availability of manufactured medicines which substitute for some herbal remedies. People may know that a given plant has a given medicinal use but not perceive it to be resource for themselves because they prefer some other plant or because they prefer to get injections or take pills instead.

In order to illustrate briefly the complexity of evaluating Huastec medicinal plants, I will discuss one commonly used species. *Cissampelos pareira* L. *(k'on k'ach)*, a pantropical vine found in a variety of habitats, is used to treat *ichich* in the Huasteca. *Ichich* is similar to the concept of "evil eye", but rather than referring to eyes, it refers to hearts. The heart of an older, more serious person, for example, naturally saps energy from the heart of a younger, more lighthearted person, causing *ichich*. Children are especially vulnerable to this malady, but adults and even pigs also suffer from it. *Ichich* is often the initial diagnosis made when someone feels ill, especially from gastro-intestinal problems. The patient who is suspected to be suffering from *ichich* may be swept with the leaves of *k'on k'ach* or a number of other plants. In the case of *k'on k'ach*, the leaves are then crushed in a small amount of water by rubbing between the hands. If the liquid gels, as it invariably does, it is seen as a positive diagnosis of *ichich* detected and removed by the sage, omniscient plant. Of the 34 people questioned about *k'on k'ach*, only three stated that this diagnostic procedure could be followed by the ingestion of a root decoction made from the same plant. *K'on k'ach* is a relative of the South American plant *Chondrodendron tomentosum* Ruiz & Pav. from which tubocurarine and other alkaloids that paralyze voluntary muscles are extracted for biomedical use. The roots of *k'on k'ach* contain some of the same alkaloids and have been exported as substitutes for *Chondrodendron tomentosum* (Morton 1977). In other parts of the world, native people have taken advantage of the muscle relaxant properties of *k'on k'ach* for a number of purposes including the expulsion of intestinal worms (Uphof 1968). But, although the root is pharmacologically active, the Huastec primarily perceive the plant to be a medicinal resource because of its predictable, diagnostically valuable (as culturally defined) gelling properties. Huastec who have chosen to identify themselves as mestizos assert their new identity by denying the existence of *ichich* and the resource value of *ichich* treatment plants like *k'on k'ach*.

Change in the resource status of a plant can alter its management and thereby the ethnobotanical process to which it is subjected. Huastec informants assign resource value to plants not only while acting to use particular plants but also while making plant management decisions. Twenty-five percent of native non-crop plants available to the Huastec are currently "managed for" by some individuals, and resource status is an important determinant of how a particular plant is managed (Alcorn 1981). Resource designation, then, potentially affects at least two types of "behavioral responses": the usage of a plant and the management of a plant.

DISCUSSION

The Huastec data fulfill the expectation that indigenous people know a great deal about their environment. But the Huastec data also demonstrate that the specific "uses" to which plants are put at any given time derive from a complex plant resource evaluation process operating from a well developed knowledge base that includes contextually related/dependent data. Resource evaluation is not an objective consideration of a plant's material qualities abstract from context, and resource perception is influenced not only by the individual's context but also by his understanding of that context.

The "needs" whose fulfillment is being sought include biological needs of the individual and household, as well as cultural needs, both of which vary over time. The use of one particular resource, be it plant or human, may in turn create the need for other specific resources. Consideration of "costs" of recognizing a particular resource include the assessment of the energy expenditure to fulfill the "need" and the possibility of losing this investment to others with or without compensation. The interpretation of what "fulfills" a need also depends on biological and cultural factors. Because of culturally determined preferences, a particular food, a particular style of house, or a particular kind of medical treatment may "fulfill" needs better than other available items of equal or better functional value.

Useful plants lists isolated from their context may be of limited value to economic botanists seeking empirically valuable data about the useful characteristics of particular species. On the other hand, these lists provide an indispensable vocabulary for studying the grammar of human ecological relations. For example, once resources are known, studies of the management of these plant resources can contribute to the evaluation of human impact on plant evolution and the structure of plant communities (Alcorn 1981; Bye 1979). Furthermore, investigation into the context of plant use not only contributes to the interpretation of plant uses, but also, in turn contributes to the understanding of humans' adaptation to their environment. Plant "use" is an integral part of the mental and physical life of people who live in direct contact with their natural resources. Any attempt to understand the adaptive value of the structure and functioning of human cognition as evidenced in ethnobiological classification systems must come to grips with the fact that the "uses" or "behavioral responses" to plants are not so simple as they have been understood by many investigators. Assigning "functional equivalence" (Hays 1974; 1981) to plants is problematic when "use" and appropriateness of use may vary depending on specific contexts.

CONCLUSION

Ethnobiology is a rich, relatively unexploited domain that could yield important information on human ecology. But if the adaptive value of ethnobotanical knowledge is to be tested in any meaningful way, plant "use" must be analyzed as a text that derives part of its meaning from the cultural, natural and social context in which it occurs and serves its function. The complex of factors influencing resource perception described here forces us to recognize that meaningful investigation into the adaptive value of botanical resource use requires not only the collaborative efforts of botanical, ecological, biomedical, pharmacological, economic, and nutritional approaches, but also anthropological study of potentially adaptive functions of resources used in the social and politicoeconomic aspects of the human's ecosystem.

Despite recent redefinitions of ethnobotany to include linguistic, epistemological, and evolutionary approaches to plant-human interrelationships, ethnobotany quixotically remains an ill-defined discourse without a unifying theme (Ford 1978). More workers are bringing the techniques of their particular disciplines to bear on different aspects of plant-human interrelationships, but their fragmentary contributions are not being synthesized in a way that makes their results useful or meaningful to workers in other disciplines. A renewed focus on the useful plant lists that traditionally defined ethnobotany may provide the important and necessary starting point for the systematic, multidisciplinary inquiry that is the unrealized potential of ethnobotany. Understanding the dynamic process leading to the inclusion of plants in useful plant lists provides the blueprint for work to flesh out the bare bones of these lists so that their potential contribution to human ecology can be fulfilled. Knowledge of the factors important to individuals' resource perception and the interrelationships between those factors structures a juncture about which multidisciplinary inquiry can articulate by coordinating the collection, interpretation, and integration of data gathered by workers using the approaches of their diverse disciplines. Such a multidisciplinary approach would mutually enrich the participating disciplines and add new depth for archaeological and linguistic interpretation of plant-related data.

On the applied level, the integration of such ethnobotanical inquiry with current efforts in peasant agricultural decision-making research (e.g., Barlett 1980) could make a significant contribution to the development of locally adapted sustained yield agroecosystems that provide appropriate resources to meet the needs generated by the physical, biological, social and politico-economic realities of the local ecosystem.

ACKNOWLEDGMENTS

Special thanks are given to the people of *Te:nek Tsaba:l* for their participation in Huastec ethnobotanical research. The collaboration of Candido Hernandez Vidales and Alphonsa Rodriguez Orta is gratefully acknowledged. I also wish to thank Brian Stross and Terence Hays for commenting on the original paper presented at the 4th Ethnobiology Conference in Columbia, Missouri, and Barbara Edmonson for commenting on a later draft. For their continuing moral and intellectual support throughout this project, I would like to express my appreciation to Marshall Alcorn, Robert Bye, Richard I. Ford, Alcinda Lewis, Marshall C. Johnston, Brian Stross, and Molly Whalen. Support for field research August 1978–1979 was provided by a Social Science Research Council International Doctoral Research Fellowship, National Science Foundation Dissertation Improvement Grant (DEB 78-05968), an E.D. Farmer International Fellowship, and grants from the University of Texas Institute of Latin American Studies and the Office of Graduate Studies. An International Summer Fellowship from the International Student and Faculty Exchange Office at the University of Texas supported fieldwork during June 1980. The Huastec ethnobotany project is being done in association with Instituto Nacional de Investigaciones sobre Recursos Bioticos (INIREB) and the Flora of Mexico project. The conclusions of this paper, however, remain my own responsibility.

LITERATURE CITED

Alcorn, J. B. 1981. Huastec non-crop resource management: implications for prehistoric rain forest management. Human Ecol. 9: 395–417.

Bartlett, P. F., ed. 1980. Agricultural Decision Making: Anthropological Contributions to Rural Development. Academic Press, New York.

Berlin, B., D. E. Breedlove, and P. H. Raven. 1973. General principles of classification and nomenclature in folk biology. Amer. Anthropol. 75: 214–42.

Bye, R. A. 1979. Incipient domestication of mustards in Northwest Mexico. Kiva 44: 237–56.

D'Andrade, R. G. 1976. A propositional analysis of U.S. American beliefs about illness. Pp. 155–80, in Meaning in Anthropology edited K. H. Basso and H. A. Selby. Univ. New Mexico Press, Albuquerque.

Ford, R. I., ed. 1978. The nature and status of ethnobotany. Anthropol. Papers No. 67, Museum of Anthropology, Univ. Michigan, Ann Arbor.

Hays, T. E. 1974. Mauna: Explorations in Ndumba ethnobotany. Unpubl. Ph.D. dissert. Univ. Washington, Seattle.

Hays, T. E. 1981. Utilitarian/adaptationist explanations of folk biological classification: Some cautionary notes. Paper presented at Fourth Ethnobiology Conference, Columbia, Mo.

Hunn, E. S. 1977. Tzeltal Folk Zoology: The Classification of Discontinuities in Nature. Academic Press, New York.

Laughlin, R. M. 1969. The Huastec. Pp. 298–311, in Handbook of Middle American Indians, Ethnology Part One, edited by E. Vogt. Univ. Texas Press, Austin.

Morton, J. F. 1977. Major medicinal plants. Charles C. Thomas, Springfield, Ill.

Randall, R. A. 1976. How tall is a taxonomic tree? Some evidence for dwarfism. Amer. Ethnol. 3: 543–53.

Rzedowski, J. 1966. Vegetación del estado de San Luis Potosí. Actas Científicas Potosinas 5: 1–291.

Uphof, J. C. Th. 1968. Dictionary of Economic Plants. Verlag Von J. Cramer. Lehre, Germany.

NOTES

1. For the general reader, Huastec words are spelled here as they would be in English. Vowel sounds are approximately those of Spanish. In addition, the colon (:) indicates an extended or lengthened vowel, and glottal stops after vowels and glottalized consonants are signified by the vertical apostrophe ('). Spelling relects pronunciation in the Potosino dialect of Huastec. Plant names given are those in most common usage.

2. The category of food resource was not chosen because food resource evaluation is very complex. Accurate measurements of food consumption by a representative sample of all age and sex groups of the population, reliable nutrient analysis of the food as it is prepared and served, and knowledge of the nutrient requirements of all sectors of the population would be necessary to make any meaningful statements about the empirical food value of particular species and species combinations. Furthermore food classification, dietary rules defining culturally appropriate meals, and the symbolic values of foods would require extensive investigation.

3. Quantitive evaluation of the amount of firewood available and the amount of firewood used is difficult, however. The amount of firewood used varies according to the size of the family and the food being prepared. In addition, non-cooking usage of firewood (raw sugar production, pottery firing, charcoal making, heat, etc.) also varies widely. Because people can collect firewood from land not their own, it is difficult to circumscribe the area producing firewood to meet the needs of a given set of firewood users. In addition, firewood production per hectare varies according to the stand's age and management.

CHAPTER TWO

California Indian Horticulture
Management and Use of Redbud by the Southern Sierra Miwok

M. KAT ANDERSON

INTRODUCTION

Found in five plant communities, redbud is a widely distributed native shrub in California. Before Anglo contact, Native American weavers used redbud branches and ground stems in the construction and decoration of baskets (Merrill 1923). At least 20 different tribes utilized the branches and ground stems of redbud, spanning 22 California counties. The horticultural techniques used historically by Indians to manage redbud were burning, pruning and coppicing (Anderson 1988–1989). Coppicing is severe pruning of plants just above ground level. Knowledge of the uses and management of redbud persist in some parts of California today, having been passed down from earlier basketmakers. Southern Sierra Miwok perceived effects of coppicing on redbud are that it "strengthens the shrub."

This paper reports results from a study conducted in Sierra National Forest which quantifies the regeneration of redbud in response to simulated management practices of the Southern Sierra Miwok. A goal of the study was to test to what extent the Indians' cultural knowledge of redbud can assist scientists in their understanding of ecological systems, and also increase their appreciation of native cultures and horticultural practices. Indian horticultural practices may prove to be a valuable source of knowledge for managing noncommercial native plant species on public lands; yet the effects of many of these cultural techniques (i.e., burning, pruning, or digging) on the vegetation have never been accurately measured by plant ecologists or resource managers.

METHODS

A series of ethnographic interviews were conducted with selected families in the Sierra Nevada at their homes and in the field during the period 1986–89. These informants totaled 32 persons and are of Southern Sierra Miwok, Central Sierra Miwok, North Fork Mono, Chukchansi Yokuts, Mono Lake Paiute, and Western Mono ethnic backgrounds. Questions were asked regarding memory and current use of specific horticultural techniques (burning, pruning, coppicing, tillage, etc.) employed to manipulate shrub species and the frequency, time of year, and intensity of these practices. The cultural purposes (i.e., straighter branches, bark color, branch length, branch diameter) for using these techniques were recorded as well as any information regarding the former abundance and distribution of native plant species. Ethnographers have published detailed accounts of California Indian plant material culture. From 1986–89 I've attempted to locate and document vegetation management information through extensive ethnohistoric research in various government, university, and private libraries.

MORPHOLOGICAL CHARACTERISTICS OF REDBUD

There are in all seven species of redbud native to North America, southern Europe and Asia, but only one, *Cercis occidentalis* is native to California (Synge 1956). The Southern Sierra Miwok Indians called the California species, Tap-pah-tap-pah (Merriam 1902).

Western redbud is a leguminous shrub that grows from 2 to 5 m tall with a dense rounded crown that almost reaches the ground. The leaves are simple, thick, round or reniform, and cordate at the base, and have from seven to nine prominent veins. They are deciduous (Sudworth 1967); their autumn display of yellow turning to red and brown rivaling that of some eastern hardwoods. Similar to riparian trees, this species loses its leaves and bears the strain of complete spring refoliation, if the substrate retains some moisture throughout the warm season (Bakker 1971).

The striking pea-shaped flowers appear before the leaves, in small fascicles along the branches (Peterson 1966). Each flower has five petals that range in color from magenta pink to reddish purple (Weeden 1981). Pollination is by bees (Dr. Herbert Baker, pers. comm. 1988).[1] Although the pink sprays can be seen from February through April, any one shrub will remain in flower only about two weeks (Munz and Keck 1973).

In autumn the branches often bear many clusters of pointed, flat, very thin pods, the upper suture with a conspicuous winged margin (Hopkins 1942). In ripening, the pods are first purple and then russet-brown, each containing an average of seven hard, bean-like seeds (Sudworth 1967). The mature pods persist into the next winter (Storer and Usinger 1963).

RANGE AND DISTRIBUTION OF REDBUD

Redbud grows in 22 counties of California and is a component of five plant communities in the state: the oak woodland, the chaparral, the yellow pine forest, the riparian woodland and the closed cone forest (Barbour *et al.* 1980; Munz 1974). It grows at elevations of 4,000 feet or less, in canyons and on rather steep slopes, in gravelly, and rocky soils along streams, where it is never flooded (Sudworth 1967). It also grows in the bottom of ephemeral streambeds in little pockets, benches or crannies of boulder outcroppings. The plant is drought tolerant and grows in a wide variety of soils, but it is usually found in rather harsh environments with depauperate, nutrient-poor soils (Stewart Winchester pers. comm. 1988).[2] It grows mostly singly, but some-times, in sheltered situations, in shrubby clumps (Sudworth 1967).

THE VALUE AND USES OF REDBUD TO CALIFORNIA INDIANS

Redbud is of little economic importance to foresters and range managers, for it has no value as timber and receives a poor rating as browse for livestock (Sampson and Jespersen n.d.). However, horticulturalists have planted it in informal and formal gardens and landscapes since 1886 and it has been called one of California's most attractive flowering shrubs in gardeners' manuals and horticultural guides (Peterson 1966).

Although some Indian groups used other plant species (e.g., chain fern *Wood-wardia fimbriata;* greenbriar *Smilax californica;* Joshua tree *Yucca brevifolia;* and rush *Juncus textilis*) to create red patterns in baskets, redbud bark was the most widely used fiber for red designs in California. In the past, at least twenty California Indian tribes utilized redbud as basketry material (Barrett and Gifford 1933; Kroeber 1976; Merrill 1923; Margaret Mathewson pers. comm. 1988).[3] Today, Indian people (i.e., Southern Sierra Miwok, Maidu, Pomo, Washo, Western Mono, Chukchansi Yokuts) still harvest these plants and use their rich red color in special patterns in their baskets (Anderson 1988–1989). The Miwok like other California Indian peoples valued redbud particularly for its branches and ground stems, which they used for structural as well as design purposes in making baskets. The plant is used in both the warp (the rods or foundation) and the weft which are structural elements of coiled and twined baskets (Fig. 1).

If used for the weft, redbud branches are split immediately after collecting or up to one month after harvesting. Branches are split in half from the thick to the thin end (Bev Ortiz pers. comm. 1987)[4] through the buds. The halves are then split again more finely to remove the pith. The material is coiled and stored for at least one year in a dry place. Later, it is soaked in water for several hours, and reshaped and cleaned before use.

Redbud is still gathered at least twice a year for different purposes. In the fall or winter, after its leaves have fallen, it is harvested for the red bark, the split fibers of which are to be used as wine-red sewing strands in decorative designs or the whole branches are used as the foundations of twined baskets. In the spring or summer redbud is harvested and the bark removed and the branch split, to be used as a white sewing strand (Anderson 1988).

THE HORTICULTURAL MANAGEMENT OF REDBUD BY THE SOUTHERN SIERRA MIWOK

Many material culture items manufactured by California Indian tribes for domestic use (e.g., looped stirring sticks, arrows, baskets) required special types of branches and ground stems. Because such branches and stems seldom occurred naturally on mature "wild" shrubs, manipulation of the plants by burning or pruning was necessary to obtain shoots of the desired characteristics in sufficient quantity.

Burning as a Management Tool.—Redbud has morphological and physiological characteristics that allow it to survive disturbances and, in the case of fire, even thrive in the reduced competition of its new habitat. Experimentation in botanical gardens has shown that redbud seeds are adapted for prolonged periods of dryness and cold and that they require special treatment to germinate, owing to an impervious seed coat plus a dormant embryo (Everett 1957). These characteristics suggest that germination of redbud seed is favored by fire, which cracks the seed coat and generates the heat needed to stimulate germination (Spurr and Barnes 1980).

Purposeful burning by Native Americans of chapparral and foothill woodland plant communities, where redbud commonly occurs, has often been reported in the ethnohistoric literature (Aginsky 1943; Driver 1937). This practice may have stimulated the germination of redbud and other species, increasing resources for basketry and other purposes.

There has been no scientific documentation of redbud's ability to sprout after fire. Yet in the Inner Coast Range, I have observed suckers from damaged boles vigorously resprouting after lightning fires. Indian informants affirm that this is indeed the case. In fact, burning was a traditional management practice of various tribes before the advent of modern pruning tools (Anderson 1989; Potts 1977; and Craig Bates, pers. comm. 1988).[5]

Prior to Anglo settlement, the initial management of large redbud shrubs required the use of fire. A sharp piece of chert or basalt was used for harvesting redbud ground stems and branches up to one centimeter diameter with ease, and up to two and one-half centimeters with more effort and time (Margaret Mathewson, pers. comm. 1989).[2] But the boles of large redbud shrubs often reach 10 or 12 cm. in diameter, and in such cases fire was used to reduce the shrub to a manageable stature. Thereafter, the resprouting stems could be kept small and straight with yearly harvesting with a basalt or chert tool or by tearing the branches from the boles (Anderson 1989).

Redbud occurs in large numbers around archaeological sites in the Sierra foothills. The shrubs decrease outward from the center of some of these archaeological sites, suggesting that the Southern Sierra Miwok utilized and maintained semi-wild redbud populations adjacent to villages. Studies are needed to interpret archaeological, ecological and historical data to determine if there is a correlation between redbud distribution and the occurrence of Indian village sites.

In the Sierra foothills, I have observed a lack of redbud regeneration, reflected in the absence of smaller size classes. Seedlings and saplings are scanty whereas most of the redbuds are mature and of tree size. The greatest number of immature redbuds are found along roadcuts. Furthermore, there are dying redbud shrubs under oak canopies. The shrub is not very shade tolerant and is outcompeted in such situations, by other species (Stewart Winchester, pers. comm. 1988).[5] Perhaps the current status of redbud reflects the absence of intense fires due to fire exclusion practices by public lands agencies, and the lack of Indian management of redbud at these sites.

Fig. 1. A Miwok coiled basket. The dark designs are made with split redbud bark.

Pruning and Coppicing as Management Tools.—At least two types of pruning of redbud were practiced by different tribes after Anglo contact. One technique was coppicing where the whole plant was cut within several inches of the ground (Fig. 2). The other was selective pruning within the canopy to direct the growth of the plant (Chestnut 1974; Anderson 1988). Today the Southern Miwok use both techniques to manage redbud. The shrubs are coppiced or selectively pruned one full growing season before harvest using tools such as hand saws or pruning shears (Fig. 4).

Redbud responds to pruning as it does to fire, by vigorously sprouting new shoots. The result is increased numbers of long, straight, slender switches with inconspicuous leaf scars, wine-red bark and no lateral branching. These are the characteristics most valued by the Southern Sierra Miwok and other California Indian peoples for basketry material (Fig. 3). Consistent, frequent pruning also keeps redbud shrubs of a smaller stature, with many slender boles that are easy to reach and cut, saving the basketweaver harvesting effort and time. In contrast, wild redbud has grey bark and twisted branches that are forked and often brittle; where the branches fork there is a notably more fragile area, making this section unsuitable for basketry.

Anthropologists and travelers, having spent little time in redbud habitat with California basketmakers, did not discern the difference between a "wild" plant and a "coppiced" plant, even though the shrubs display different architectures and vary in colors of bark. These observers probably did not perceive the breaking or cutting of

Fig. 2. Coppicing redbud to induce rapid elongation of sprouts the following year.

plant parts as "management" *per se,* but rather as a destructive practice. Consequently, seldom in the ethnohistoric literature is there mention of pruning or coppicing of redbud by California Indians to meet cultural needs.

The type of sprouting that occurs on redbud after severe pruning is probably epicormic branching, which is defined as the release of suppressed buds along the bole. These suppressed buds are normal branches but submerged (Zimmermann and Brown 1980). Sprouting from the roots apparently does not occur. However, further studies are needed to understand the sprouting process fully.

The wine-red color of the redbud bark, so valuable in Indian basketry designs, appears only in juvenile wood tissue, and is the result of anthocyanin pigments. These chemical substances are stored in the plastids in the cells of the cortical tissue just below the epidermis. As the branch ages it loses the color in either of two ways: (1) as the shoot expands it sheds the red bark and the cells in the mature tissue lose their ability to store or produce anthocyanins, or (2) the anthocyanins in the cortex cells are hidden by the production of bark (Richard Dodd, pers. comm. 1988).[6]

THE RESPONSE OF REDBUD TO COPPICING AND PRUNING

Most native shrubs and trees are not harmed by pruning (Schmidt 1980). In fact, many trees and shrubs, as they approach maturity, accumulate dead twigs and branches, which if not removed, may harbor pests and diseases (Brown 1972).

Fig. 3. Long, straight, slender switches of redbud with no lateral branches. These are the characteristics most valued by California basketweavers. (Switches harvested one year after initial pruning.)

Harvesting and horticultural methods used by the Southern Sierra Miwok are closely related to the annual growth cycle of redbud. The Indians are keenly aware of the dormancy period of redbud, referring to this period as the time "when the sap's down," and this is the preferred time for pruning. Harvesting redbud during this resting period usually is the least detrimental to its vital processes.

MIMICKING INDIAN HORTICULTURAL PRACTICES

To better understand the methods for collection and management of redbud by the Southern Sierra Miwok and to determine the shrub's response to coppicing practices, I conducted an ecological field experiment which simulated one of their horticultural techniques.

The objective of the experiment was to evaluate the effects of fall coppicing on the regeneration of redbud. Regeneration was estimated by determining the numbers of shoots, both ground stems and branches, produced after coppicing.

Two sites in the El Portal area at an elevation of approximately 640 m. were selected for the experiment: (1) Dry Gulch Creek in Sierra National Forest and (2) Merced River 19 kilometers west of El Portal in Sierra National Forest and on private property. I selected healthy, mature redbud plants for the experiment. Those with large amounts of dead material, symptoms of disease, or with flood damage were rejected. I chose plants in areas where the trees had never been pruned or coppiced, inspecting for evidence of previous cutting by thoroughly checking all basal stems. The sample size for the experiment was 15 coppiced and 15 non-coppiced redbuds per site. These 30 plants per site were randomly allocated a coppice or non-coppice treatment.

Before plants were cut, two measurements were taken: (1) number of ground stems; (2) number of "usable" branches. "Usable shoots" were defined as shoots with no lateral branching and a minimum length of twelve inches. These same variables were measured again after one growing season in October 1987.

Coppicing consisted of cutting the plants off at the ground level or immediately above the root crown with pruning shears or a small power saw. All shoots were removed to within a stub length of five inches.

Observations on post-coppicing growth were recorded in October 1987. The same measurements were taken (number of stems and the number of usable shoots) and any mortality noted. The differences between cut and uncut plants were assessed using a student's t-test for unpaired replicates (n = 30 each per site). An analysis of variance was performed with the data from both sites to determine the significance of differences in shoot production and ground stem production between coppiced and uncoppiced shrubs.

Numbers of usable shoots increased significantly with coppicing (Table 1) on the Merced River/private property site. Numbers of usable shoots increased ten-fold with coppicing on the Dry Gulch site (Table 2), but the increase was not statistically significant. Numbers of ground stems increased with coppicing, but the difference was not significant on either site (Tables 1 and 2).

An important outcome of this experiment was that none of the redbud shrubs that had been coppiced in 1986 died. Instead, coppicing was followed by vigorous re-sprouting on all 30 shrubs (15 per site). Rates of growth after coppicing were fairly uniform. In October 1987, eleven months after the cutting treatment, the general appearance of the coppiced plants was distinctly different from that of the uncoppiced ones: bark color had changed from grey to wine red, branches were much straighter, lateral branches were absent or in negligible quantity, and overall height of the shrubs was less (Fig. 4).

The results from the experiment suggest that the effects of one year of coppicing were not detrimental to the target plant species and were possibly beneficial. Furthermore, the coppicing treatment at the Merced River/private property site showed that significantly higher numbers of usable shoots could be produced by this practice.

Recommendations which incorporate Indian management practices cannot as yet be made based on these data. In order to maintain and manage redbud, the manager must know how the plant responds to repeated coppicing through several years. Frequency of manipulation could be an important factor influencing plant vigor and productivity, requiring a multi-year study. Questions which require further research include: (1) How does coppicing in several consecutive years affect the growth of a redbud shrub? and (2) What frequency of coppicing will result in maximal production of shoots of optimal quality over the normal lifespan of the plant?

TABLE 1. Effects of coppicing on plant variables of redbud *(Cercis occidentalis)* along the Merced River, Sierra National Forest and El Portal private property.

| Variable | No Treatment | | Coppiced | |
| | | Mean ± S.E. | | |
	1986	1987	1986	1987
Average no. of usable shoots per plant	9 ± 2*a	4 ± 1 a	21 ± 6 a	107 ± 15 b
Average no. of ground stems per plant	29 ± 5 a	26 ± 4 a	28 ± 4 a	32 ± 3 a

* Numbers for the same treatment in 1986 and 1987 followed by the same letter are not significantly different according to the student t-test (P<.05).

TABLE 2. Effects of coppicing on plant variables of redbud *(Cercis occidentalis)* at Dry Gulch Creek, Sierra National Forest.

| Variable | No Treatment | | Coppiced | |
| | | Mean ± S.E. | | |
	1986	1987	1986	1987
Average no of. usable shoots per plant	4 ± 1*a	2 ± 1 a	5 ± 2 a	49 ± 13 a
Average no. of ground stems per plant	8 ± 2 a	9 ± 2 a	18 ± 5 a	22 ± 4 a

* Numbers for the same treatment in 1986 and 1987 followed by the same letter are not significantly different according to the student t-test (P<.05).

CONCLUSIONS

The Southern Sierra Miwok and other California native peoples had an active role in manipulating the plant architecture of redbud with pruning, coppicing, and fire management. This offers further evidence that hunter-gatherers had the capabilities for effecting environmental changes in California plant communities. The extent to which aboriginal burning and pruning effected redbud distribution and abundance needs to be further investigated. The management of redbud for the production of branches and ground stems suitable for basketry is still practiced by members of the Southern Sierra Miwok and other California Indian tribes. The shrub remains integral to many modern tribal cultures. By repeated pruning or coppicing of redbud, Indians

Fig. 4. Vigorous sprouting of redbud in Sierra National Forest one year after experimental coppicing.

ensure a sustained yield of high quality shoots for basketry and simultaneously maintain the health of the plant. Public land managers, in managing redbud, should take into account this knowledge possessed by Indians.

Indian horticultural practices and resulting impacts on vegetation cannot be reliably assessed solely through the interpretation of ethnohistoric literature and ethnographic research. Vegetation productivity resulting from or related to Indian cultural practices must be measured by experiments using methods similar to those of specific Indian groups if the cultural needs of the Indian community are to be taken seriously by public lands agencies. Ecological field experiments, therefore, can provide new data to test hypotheses regarding the possible effects on plant communities of past and present California Indian vegetation management. Specifically designed experiments also could substantiate historical and ethnographic reports regarding certain Indian plant management techniques.

Land managers have to be better informed by becoming acquainted with Indians and understanding their current cultural needs, and by conducting studies to learn about Indian harvesting and management practices and their appropriateness for public lands. During this process, resource managers will have to weigh carefully conflicts with other values and redefine cultural preservation to include the concerns of living Indians.

ACKNOWLEDGMENTS

I am deeply indebted to the Indian families in the Sierra Nevada for sharing their memories, crafts, and horticultural knowledge. I wish to thank Scott Carpenter and Dr. Jan van Wagtendonk, Co-Directors of the Yosemite Research Center, for their moral and logistic support. Pat Schaefer, Bill Lester, and Pete McGee gave me permission to cut redbud plants on their property and helped me with the coppicing. I am grateful to Gregory Whipple, Dr. Miguel Altieri, and Dr. Steve Edwards for reviewing the draft manuscript. Drs. Bill Waters, Arnold Schultz, Bob Martin and Jim Anderson gave valuable advice during the project. The Yosemite Association, Yosemite National Park, and the California Native Plant Society provided financial support for this study.

LITERATURE CITED

Aginsky, B. W. 1943. Culture Element Distributions: XXIV Central Sierra. Anthropological Records Vol. 8:4.

Anderson, M. Kat. 1989. Unpublished Western Mono, Chuckchansi Yokuts, Southern Sierra Miwok and Central Sierra Miwok field notes.

———. 1988. Southern Sierra Miwok plant resource use and management of the Yosemite region. Master's Thesis. Department of Forestry and Resource Management. U.C. Berkeley.

Bakker, Ellen S. 1971. An island called California. Berkeley.

Barbour, Michael G., J. H. Bark and W. D. Pitts. 1980. Terrestrial plant ecology. Benjamin/ Cummings Publishing Co. Menlo Park.

Barrett, Samuel A., and Edward W. Gifford. 1933. Miwok material culture. Bulletin of the Public Museum of the City of Milwaukee 2(4): 117–376.

Brown, G. E. 1972. The pruning of trees, shrubs and conifers. Great Britain.

Chesnut, V. K. 1974. Plants Used by the Indians of Mendocino County, California. Mendocino County Historical Society. Mendocino, Calif.

Driver, P. 1937. Culture element distributions: VI Southern Sierra Nevada. Anthropological Records Vol. I:2. University of California Press, Berkeley.

Everett, T. H. 1957. A summary of the culture of California plants at the Rancho Santa Ana Botanic Garden 1927–1950. The Rancho Santa Ana Botanic Garden. Claremont, Calif.

Hopkins, M. 1942. *Cercis* in North America. Rhodora. Vol. 44.

Kroeber, Alfred L. 1976. Handbook of the Indians of California. Dover Publications, Inc. New York.

Merriam, C. H. 1900–1934 and n.d. Selected unpublished journals. Library of Congress. Washington D.C.

Merrill, Ruth E. 1923. Plants Used in Basketry by the California Indians. UCPAAE 20: 215–242. Berkeley.

Munz, Philip A. and David D. Keck. 1973. A California flora and supplement. Univ. of California Press, Berkeley.

Munz, Philip A.1974. A Flora of Southern California. Univ. of California Press. Berkeley.

Peterson, P. V. 1966. Native trees of Southern California. University of California Press. Berkeley.

Potts, Marie. 1977 The Northern Maidu. Naturegraph. Happy Camp, Calif.

Sampson, A. W. and B. S. Jespersen. n.d. California Range Brushlands and Browse Plants. California Agricultural Experiment Station. Manual 33.

Schmidt, M. G. 1980. Growing California native plants. California Natural History Guides: 45. University of California Press. Berkeley.

Spurr, S. H. and B. V. Barnes. 1980. Forest ecology. Third Edition. John Wiley and Sons. New York.

Storer, T. I. and R. Usinger. 1963. Sierra Nevada natural history. University of California Press, Berkeley.

Sudworth, G. B. 1967. Forest trees of the Pacific slope. U.S. Department of Agriculture, Washington, D.C.

Synge, P. M.1956. Dictionary of Gardening: A Practical and Scientific Encyclopedia of Horti-culture. Edited by F. J. Chittenden Second Edition. Vol. 1. Oxford at the Clarendon Press.

Weeden, N. F.1981. A Sierra Nevada flora. Wilderness Press. Berkeley.

Zimmermann, M. H. and C. L. Brown. 1980. Trees structure and function. Springer-Verlag. New York.

NOTES

1. Herbert Baker, Professor, Department of Integrative Biology, University of California at Berkeley.

2. Stewart Winchester, Professor, Department of Botany, Diablo Valley College, California.

3. Margaret Mathewson, Ph.D. student, Department of Anthropology, Kroeber Hall, University of California at Berkeley.

4. Bev Ortiz, San Francisco Bay Area Park Naturalist, and Ethnographic Consultant.

5. Craig Bates, National Park Service Curator at Yosemite, P. O. Box 218, Yosemite National Park, California.

6. Richard Dodd, Professor, Department of Forestry and Resource Management, University of California at Berkeley.

CHAPTER THREE

Papago (O'odham) Influences on Habitat and Biotic Diversity

Quitovac Oasis Ethnoecology

GARY P. NABHAN, AMADEO M. REA, KAREN L. REICHHARDT,
ERIC MELLINK, CHARLES F. HUTCHINSON

INTRODUCTION

Native American influences on habitats and associated biotic diversity have been the subject of several, recent provocative essays (Linares 1976; Rea 1979; Emslie 1981). It has been hypothesized that the diversification of habitats associated with native agriculture has had a beneficial effect on faunal species richness, due to edge effect phenomena, increased insect and seed availability.

The values of diversified farmland habitats to fauna, and the potential edible or economic return to farmers, were active topics of research among American ecologists earlier in this century (see Dambach 1948). However, as agriculture has become more mechanized, larger fields of single crops with clean borders have taken the place of diversified family farms where the maintenance of cover crop borders, hedgerows, or windbreaks was not only practical but advisable (Burger 1978; Sampson 1981).

Despite the renewed interest in this topic from agricultural ecologists and ethnographers, there are few data with which to compare directly the richness of species (useful or otherwise) associated with native subsistence agricultural habitats with that found in nearby, uncultivated or modern cash crop agricultural ecosystems.

Through the Man and the Biosphere program, we have attempted to document qualitatively and quantatively the plant and wildlife diversity associated with various agro-ecosystems and comparable, uncultivated ecosystems in the Sonoran Desert. The habitat complex, and seed plant, bird and mammal diversity were surveyed at the Papago farming oasis of Quitovac, Sonora and at the similar Quitobaquito, Arizona in Organ Pipe Cactus National Monument, where cultivation has not occurred for over 25 years (Fig. 1). There are considerable differences in the biota associated with the sites. Since the two sites differ more in their management history than their physical character, we focus on Papago land use and subsistence practices at Quitovac which influence habitat and biotic diversity. We hope that this ethnoecological perspective on the last Papago oasis will aid in the archaeological and "natural" historical interpretation of other Sonoran Desert oases, as well as in their management. This study is also the most comprehensive treatment of the folk biology of the western Papago

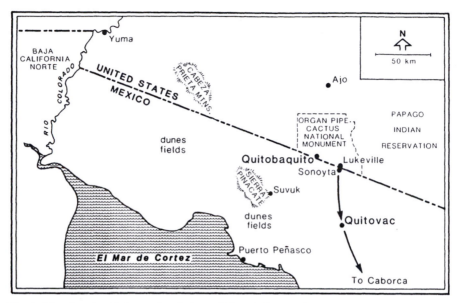

Fig. 1. Map showing Quitovac in relation to Western Papago Country.

of Sonora,[1] whose knowledge and uses of desert biota is in many ways different from the central Papago emphasized in Castetter and Underhill's (1935) classic work.

THE STUDY AREAS

Quitovac is a spring fed oasis, at an elevation of 350 m, in the *municipio* of Puerto Peñasco, Sonora. It is found 41 km south-southeast of the Sonoyta-Lukeville border crossing, and 54 km southeast of Quitobaquito. Hastings and Humphrey (1969) reported its mean annual rainfall as 21.9 cm; it lies within the transition between the Lower Colorado and Arizona Upland vegetation subdivisions of the Sonoran Desert (Shreve 1951).

The presence of water deposited tufa and marl sediments, some of which contain calcified Rancholabrean megafaunal fossils, indicates that the springs of Quitovac have flowed for millenia. When Juan Manje visited the Papago at the site in 1694, calling it *San Luis de Bacapa,* and *Moicaqui* ('Soft Wash' in Papago), he described it as "close to a high peaked mountain at whose foot were some springs of water and some lakes" (Bolton 1948). In 1774, Anza described the site as "one of the best of all the *Papagueria,* because it has five springs of water . . . which they gather and use to irrigate some small pieces of very sandy land where at most a half a *fanega* of maize can be planted . . ." (Bolton 1930). These observations indicate that Papago water control and agricultural management of Quitovac were well established prior to the introduction of Old World technology, draft animals, and crops.

Kino visited a Papago camp at another set of springs in 1698; his *San Serguio* is surely a site along the springs of the pre-Cambrian Quitobaquito Hills, on the present day U.S.-Mexico border. Kino did not explicitly mention a pond there, so some historians have assumed that one did not form until Anglos built a dam there in the 1860s. Others disagree, observing that the Papago improved springs and excavated basins elsewhere earlier; the Quitobaquito pupfish shows considerable divergence from Rio Sonoyta pupfish populations nearby, suggesting the antiquity of Quitobaquito pond habitat (Robert Rush Miller, pers. comm.). From the 1860s on, the presence of Papago pond-irrigated fields and orchards there are well known (Bell et al. 1980; Nabhan 1982). Organ Pipe National Monument was established in the 1930s, but the Papago continued farming and livestock raising there until 1957. The pond was then a 35 cm deep, swampy marsh edged by a grass flat, riparian trees and an orchard; it was ideal pupfish habitat (Robert Rush Miller, pers. comm.). In 1962, it was dredged to a 1–2 m depth, and has since been managed as a popular birdwatching area.

Not all Papago from the two oases consider themselves to be the distinctive Sand Papago—(*Hia C-eḍ O'odham,* 'In the Sand People'; *Hia Tadk Ku:mdam,* 'Sand Root Crushers'; or *S-'O'obmakam,* 'Apache-like Papago'). However, after an 1851 yellow fever epidemic, some surviving Sand Papago families moved out of the Pinacate region to these nearby oases, or to other western Papago settlements (Bell et al. 1980). At any rate, the Sand Papago regularly visited Quitovac historically, and shared with the people there the use of a number of plants and animals not found elsewhere in *Papagueria* (Nabhan 1980). Since the 1850s, a rain and cactus harvest ceremony called the *Vi'igita,* originally performed among Sand Papago in the Pinacate region to the west, has been observed at Quitovac (Davis 1920; Ives 1936; Bell et al. 1980). Within the following notes on the uses of biota, many of the religious uses are those associated with the *Vi'igita.*

Linguistically, the Quitovac Papago may be intermediate between the *Hia C-eḍ O'odham* and other *Tohono O'odham.* They regularly use the fricative [v] in certain sound environments where most Papagos make a sound closer to the English [w], and occasionally utilize [t] in place of the more commonly used [c] ([ch] in English). Both of these allophones are believed to be proto-Piman (Hale, pers. comm.). We are using the Alvarez and Hale (1970) orthography for *Tohono O'odham,* but are substituting [v] for [w] to reflect the above-mentioned dialect difference.

Currently, 16 houses are maintained by Papago and Papago-*mestizo* families at Quitovac, but not all are lived in year-round. Population has ranged from 27 to 38 individuals since 1960. Papago simply call the place *Vak,* and *Quitovac* is rapidly being replaced by *Bak* as the officially-recognized name for the oasis and the recently established indigenous land reserve there.

METHODS

Study of the plant and bird life, and ethnobiology of Quitovac began in November 1979, and has focused on a 10 ha area surrounding the oasis pond. Through July 1982, 12 visits to the area were made for 2–4 day periods, during which a number of data collecting activities were accomplished. In August, 1981, a more formal comparison of Quitobaquito and Quitovac was initiated, using a 5 ha study site centered on the pond. The study methodology also was used for Quitobaquito as well, with exceptions as noted. Agricultural clearing at Quitovac in autumn, 1981, destroyed the habitat on approximately 3 ha of the study site. Consequently, vegetation transects begun in one area were extended to adjacent areas within the same vegetation associations, and only half the original 5 ha area was sampled for mammals.

Habitat mapping utilized February 1982 hand-held aerial photos taken by Peter Kresan, July 1982 vertical aerial photos taken by Vern Palmer, and a sketched map based on paced distances drawn by Nabhan in September 1980. These three data sources were combined in an attempt to reconstruct the extent of habitat areas prior to the autumn 1981 clearing.

Each of these mappable habitat units was described in terms of plant species, vegetative cover, lifeform mixture, soils and land uses. The project's plant ecologist (K.L.R.) visually discerned discontinua in the vegetative cover of the site. Each unit was sampled for perennials, 75 cm tall or more, via five 30 m line transects placed randomly from a baseline, and via 250 point frame hits for annuals and perennials shorter than 75 cm. Following Karpiscak (1980), cover values from these two methods, including both August 1981 and May 1982 point frame samples, were combined to express a percent of sampled distance with vegetative cover within each habitat. If species were sampled using both methods or during both seasons, the highest value was used. These coverage values were used as indicators of species importance for calculating the diversity (i.e., heterogeneity) of each habitat's vegetation, utilizing both the Shannon-Weaver and Simpson indices as described by Peet (1974). To calculate a plant species heterogeneity value for the entire site, species values within each habitat unit were multiplied by the fraction of the total site area occupied by that habitat, and summed.

Within each habitat unit, either a soil or water sample was taken from a 30 cm column below the surface, and analyzed by the University of Arizona Soils, Water and Plant Tissue Testing Laboratory, from which methodological details may be obtained. Lifeform descriptions follow Shreve (1951). Land uses were observed during visits, and further documented by interviews with local informants. In addition to plants found on vegetation transects, an inventory was made of all seed plant species found within the 5 ha site. Over 300 voucher specimens were collected over a four year period during all seasons, and most have been deposited in the herbaria of the University of Arizona and San Diego Natural History Museum. Nomenclature follows Lehr (1978), to which nonbotanists are referred for common English names. Determination of species native or introduced to North America follows Shetler and Skog (1978).

Ethnobotanical interviews were made in Spanish, with Papago frames and lexemes occasionally used to reinforce questions. Although six Quitovac Papago and one Arizona Papago visitor contributed knowledge of plant names and uses, the bulk of the information was derived from the community elder, Luciano Noriego. Over a 3-year period, information was volunteered by Noriego while walking the site with us or while vouchers were being pressed. Additional plants observed directly in use by other residents were noted.

Birds found on the 5 ha site were surveyed during one two-day visit during each of four seasons, and the highest visual or audial count for each species over the two day

period taken as the best population estimate. Dawn and dusk surveys of 2–3 hour dura-
tions, with extended time spent in dense canopy areas, were sufficient for most identifications and population estimates. Dove population projections were based on half hour
morning counts. It was assumed that dove visitation to the lagoon occurred at a consistent rate, throughout the morning, with no more than one extended watering per bird
each half day. Thus, the half-hour count was multiplied by 8 to estimate the total dove
population. Linnaean taxonomy for birds includes recent revisions by Rea (in press).

Notes were taken regarding the habitats in which each bird species spent most of
its time, but since few species utilize space for foraging strictly upon the lines of our
mappable habitat units, certain habitats were combined (or collapsed) in our calculations. Simpson and Shannon-Weaver diversity indices were then calculated for these
revised habitat groupings more useful in discussing bird foraging, and for each 5 ha
site (Quitovac and Quitobaquito) as a whole.

Mammal data gathering included the nocturnal setting of Sherman live traps
baited with a commercial grain mixture (millet, oat and wheat), the diurnal setting of
snap gopher traps, and the visual counts of larger mammals. The Sherman live traps
were set in the evening to capture small nocturnal rodents; they were checked and
closed the next morning. Trapping took place one night each in December, 1981,
March, 1982, and two nights in May, 1982. Traps were set in a grid pattern with 12 m
between traps in the same line, and 20 m between lines. At Quitovac, 100 traps were
set on the irregularly shaped undisturbed half of the study area. At Quitobaquito, 200
traps were set each night. For each season, the sites and the habitats within the
Quitovac site were compared using the Simpson and Shannon-Weaver indices. The
comparisons utilize (a) animal numbers and (b) animal biomass based on individual
weights in grams at the time of trapping. Identifications were made in the field utilizing
Cockrum (1960), with vouchers collected and identifications confirmed for trapping
mortalities. Linnaean taxonomy for mammals follows Hall (1981), with the exception of *Dama,* for which we retain *Odocoileus.*

Interviews on bird and mammal knowledge and uses were occasional throughout
the study, but also included 3–4 hours of taped interviews in May 1982 with Luciano
Noriego and his grandchildren. A scrapbook of photos or drawings of most bird and
mammal species potentially present in the vicinity was shown to Noriego, with explanations of calls, behavior or eating habits discussed. Additional data on animal use
come from inspecting hunted carcasses gathered by Papago youth, and from attending
of the Papago *Vi'igita* ceremony.

RESULTS

Through autumn, 1981, Quitovac was a traditional Sonoran Desert farming oasis
which included eight large scale (mappable) vegetation associations, and two small scale
vegetational features worthy of note (Fig. 2). The mapped vegetation associations
provided one element of our descriptions of habitats. Soils, lifeform and seed plant species
diversity, and land uses were also noted (Table 1). The two small scale associations, were
(a) man-made ditches running into the orchard and field dominated by *Cyperus,*

Fig. 2. February 1982 oblique photo of Quitovac, four months after bulldozing (Pete Kresan, photo).

TABLE 1. Habitats at Quitovac, Sonora (5 ha study site).

Location and % of total area	Soil or water characteristics	Dominant plant species (highest cover first)	Lifeform mixture	Diversity Shannon-Weaver	Indices: Simpson	Land Uses
A. Open water of lagoon and springs; 10% of area	Spring water: pH. 7.6: soluble salts, 689 ppm; EC x 10³ 1.10; NH₄-N, 0.10 ppm; K.5.83 ppm	*Potamogeton pulvinatus* *Zannichellia palustris*	Submergent macrophytes and floating algae	—	—	Swimming; aquatic bird hunting; use of water for irrigation
B. Cultivated field of annual crops irrigated from pond and springs; 6.5% of area.	Sandy loam: pH. 8.4: soluble salts 2121 ppm; EC x 10³, 3.03; N, 3.75 ppm; P, 1.28 ppm; K; 1.15 meq/L	*Cynodon dactylon* *Cucurbita mixta* *Citrullus lanatus* *Ambrosia confertifolia*	Herbaceous weedy ephemerals, and perennials, plus crop annuals	.947	.856	Tillage, seed sowing, irrigating, and crop harvest, wild greens harvesting
C. Tufa mesa rimming the pond, and nearby scrubland, (including abandoned fields); 27.5% of area	Sandy loam: pH. 7.4: soluble salts, 994 ppm; EC x 10³, 100; N, 32.13 ppm; P, 11.82 ppm; K, 2.27 meq/L	*Suaeda torreyana* *Prosopis velutina* *Lycium andersoni*	Open, mixed spinescent. drought deciduous and evergreen shrubs and trees	.526	.670	Wild fruit gathering; woodcutting; hunting and trapping
D. Cultivated orchard of irrigated fruit trees. and adjacent fieldside hedge; 2.5% of area	Sandy loam same as (B) cultivated field of annual crops	*Ambrosia confertifolia* *Ficus carica* *Sarcostemma cynanchoides* *Cynodon dactylon*	Broadleaf deciduous tree canopy with broadleaf deciduous shrubs, ephemerals and vines	.831	.818	Cultivated fruit harvesting; irrigation: wild and cultivated perennial transplanting; hunting
E. Ephemeral watercourse (arroyo) and adjacent uncultivated floodplain: 4.5% of area	Loamy sand: pH. 7.6: soluble salts 504 ppm; EC x 10³, 0.72; N, 10.2 ppm, P, 8.47 ppm. K. 1.26 meq/L.	*Hymenoclea monogyra* *Lycium berlandieri* *Ambrosia ambrosioides*	Microphyllous shrubs, cacti, broadleaf shrubs, and few ephemerals	.514	.604	Grazing: hunting or trapping: cactus harvesting
F. Lagoon edge, shallow holding pond, and ditches, and spring to pond channels 15% of area	Silty loam: pH. 8.3: soluble salts, 6181 ppm; EC x 10³, 8.83; N. 5.35 ppm; P, 8.23 ppm; K. 2.51 meq/L.	*Typha domingensis* *Scirpus olneyi* *Distichlis spicata*	Emergent perennial reeds and grasses	.616	.736	Burning; grazing fiber gathering; medicinal plant gathering from ditches
G. Meadow-like flats with alkaline seeps; 34% of area	Sandy loam: pH. 9.1: soluble salts, 70,427 ppm; EC x 10³, 100.6: N. 6.32 ppm; P. 4.78 ppm; K.31.48 meq/L	*Distichlis spicata* *Wislizenia refracta* *Heliotropium curassavicum*	Perennial mat-forming grasses, few herbaceous root perennials and ephemerals	.089	.078	Grazing

Anemopsis, Heliotropium and *Rumex;* and (b) living, fieldside fence rows including intentionally planted *Salix, Tamarix, Sambucus, Opuntia* and *Prosopis,* which had associated with them piled brush and self-sown *Ambrosia, Bebbia, Olneya,* and *Parkinsonia.*

These small scale features are best considered part of the diverse field/orchard complex in the south-center of the study site. In both diversity indices based on plant coverage data, the cultivated field is the most heterogeneous vegetation association, and the orchard the second most. The Shannon-Weaver index is typically most sensitive to changes in the importance of rare species in the sample, and the Simpson index to common species (Peet 1974). These cultivated habitats make up less than 10% of the area of the study site, which is important in the interpretation of whole-site diversity index comparisons of Quitovac and Quitobaquito. Because each habitat's coverage values are "weighted" by the percentage of the 5 ha upon which that habitat exists, and Quitovac's cultivated habitats are so relatively small in area, their influence is "diluted" in our whole site calculations. The contrasts between Quitovac's whole-site plant diversity values (.971, Shannon-Weaver; .813, Simpson), and those for Quitobaquito (.822, Shannon-Weaver; .764, Simpson) nevertheless suggest that Quitovac has more diverse vegetation. (Note that the higher the diversity index value, the higher the diversity or heteroteneity).

Floristically, there are considerably more plant species, genera and families represented at Quitovac than at Quitobaquito, no matter how large the areas examined are (Table 2). This is due in part to the number of domesticated species (17) intentionally cultivated within the Quitovac site, but cultivation contributes more than just intentionally sown plants to a flora. There are an additional 59 species of plants found in the field/orchard complex. Many of these can be considered "biologically [as] weeds which are evolutionary and ecological products adapted to survival in habitats

TABLE 2. Floristic Richness at two Sonoran Desert oases.*

	5 hectare study site at oasis-pond	8–10 hectare plains around oasis-pond	oasis, plains and closest hills
Quitovac, Sonora			
plant families	45 (41)	49 (42)	55 (44)
genera	115 (100)	131 (106)	139 (114)
species	139 (122)	158 (131)	172 (143)
Quitobaquito, Ariz.			
plant families	32 (30)	37 (35)	38 (36)
genera	71 (69)	92 (90)	101 (99)
species	80 (78)	104 (102)	118 (116)

* Includes only seed plants. Data for Quitobaquito are from Adams (1971); Bowers (1980); and Nabhan and Reichhardt, field notes. Data for Quitovac are from Nabhan (in press). Values in parentheses represent adjusted totals that exclude intentionally planted domesticated species.

disturbed by human activity" (Bye 1981). We consider 18 of these species to be found at Quitovac only within the cultivated field/orchard complex. A complete flora of Quitovac is near completion, and will list each species by its habitats (Nabhan, in preparation). It is not surprising that more than 21 post-Columbian introduced species, in addition to 11 species of Old World domesticates, are part of the Quitovac flora, and are more numerous than at Quitobaquito today. These are primarily ephemerals that for millenia colonized fields, trails and roadsides in the Old World, before rapidly spreading through New World deserts (Naveh 1967; Young et al. 1972).

Table 3 lists the 78 taxa named by Quitovac Papago in their local dialect, as well as the uses of these plants. Over 40 of these utilized species can be found in the field/orchard complex. Even recently introduced species such as *Brassica tournefortii* are utilized in a similar manner to edible greens of considerable antiquity in the region. Terming such a species a "native" subsistence resource is somewhat of a misnomer. Numerous Old World crops and weeds are well-integrated into Papago cuisine even at the agricultural margins of Papagueria. A detailed discussion of how particular plants are used will be included in the Quitovac flora (Nabhan et al., in preparation), but from the data included here it is clear that named and utilized species are largely concentrated in and affect the management of three habitats more than the others: the field, the orchard and the adjacent scrubland. These three habitats are "off limits" to grazing animals most of the time. Such plant uses appear to parallel those which western Papago practiced at Quitobaquito earlier in this century (Bell et al. 1980).

Bird life at Quitovac includes 103 species observed on the 5 ha site during our eight days of survey in 1981–1982. Table 4 indicates that during every seasonal visit, species richness was higher at Quitovac than at Quitobaquito. The diversity indices for the two sites do not show such a clear picture; each site had a more heterogeneous avifauna in two of the seasons. Table 5 shows considerable seasonal variation in bird diversity within each habitat at Quitovac. It appears that the field-orchard complex, and the adjacent microphyllous shrubs in the wash provide the habitats with the most consistent diversity from season to season.

The open water (A) and pond fringe habitats (F and G) varied drastically from season to season. This was due in part to the autumn, 1981, draining and clearing of the lagoon. It was too shallow for any swimming waterfowl in January, 1982, and most pond fringe cover was removed. The pond was being utilized again by waterfowl by early spring and refilled to over 1.2 m deep by May.

Quitovac is attractive to a number of species of wading shorebirds in addition to waterfowl; these include some migrants and vagrants that have no muddy, open shoreline upon which to land at Quitobaquito. Quitovac also serves as a drinking place for much larger populations of columbiforms, particularly White-winged Doves, than does Quitobaquito. Both sites support a large number of "desert riparian" insectivores, including icterids, flycatchers, woodpeckers and wood warblers.

Table 6 presents data on 30 species of birds known to be named and/or utilized by the Papago at Quitovac. This is not a particularly large percentage of the local avifauna. The poor eyesight of our primary Papago consultant, as well as the limited time spent on interviews regarding birds, may contribute to this low number.

TABLE 3. Folk taxa and uses of plants at or near Quitovac, Sonora

Papago name	Scientific name	Common name	Uses	Wild Self-Sown	Wild Trans-plant	Domes-ticated & Sown	Habitats
'a'uḍ	Agave deserti	Desert Agave	food, (fiber?)	X			hills
'auppa	Populus fremontii	Cottonwood	(wood?)	X			C
'acĭ vipinoi	Opuntia leptocaulis	Desert Christmas Cactus	food, med.	X			E
'adavĭ	Cucurbita digitata	Finger-leaved gourd	(med.?)	X			E
babaḍ i:vakĭ	Heliotropium curassavicum	Heliotrope	med.	X			B,D$_2$,F,G
bahidaj	Carnegiea gigantea (fruit)	Saguaro	food, relig.	X			E, hills
ban manzanilla	Dyssodia concinna	Fetid Marigold		X			C
ban vi:v	Nicotiana trigonophylla	Desert Tobacco		X			E
bh:bhiag	Merremia dissecta	Ornamental Vine		X	?		D
ce:mĭ	Lophocereus schottii	Senita	food	X			E, hills
ce:'ul	Salix goodingii	Goodding Willow	relig.		X		D, F
ciolim	Opuntia acanthocarpa	Cholla	food	X			E
cucuvis	Stenocereus thurberi	Organpipe Cactus	food, wood	X			E, hills
cuhukkia	Amaranthus palmeri	Amaranth	food	X			B
cucud șosą	Phoenix dactylifera	Date Palm	wood			X	C
cuvi u:pĭ	Solanum nodiflorum	Nightshade		X			D$_2$, F
galnayu	Punica granatum	Pomegranate				X	C, D
gepĭ	Citrullus lanatus	Watermelon	food			X	B
gisokĭ	Opuntia violacea	Purple Prickly Pear	food	X			E
hadsetkam	Petalonyx thurberi	Sandpaper Plant		X			E
hakowaḍ	Phorandendron californicum	Desert Mistletoe		X			C, E
ha:l	Curcurbita argyrosperma	Cushaw Squash	food			X	B
ha:nam	Opuntia fulgida	Jumping Cholla	food	X			D$_1$, E
ha:sañ	Carnegiea gigantea (plant)	Saguaro	wood, util.	X	X		E, hills
hauk 'u'us	Bebbia juncea	Sweet Bush	med.	X			B, D
Heña hetam	Sapium biloculare	Mexican Jumping Bean	wood, util.	X			E, hills
hoi'idkam	Olneya tesota	Ironwood	food, relig.	X			E, hills
hu:ñ	Zea mays	Corn	food			X	E
'i:bhai	Opuntia phaecantha (fruit)	Prickly Pear	food	X			D$_1$, E
'i:hug	Proboscidea parviflora	Devil's Claw	(util.?)	X			B

O'odham name	Scientific name	Common name	Use				
'i:svig	*Echinocereus fasciculatus*	Hedgehog Cactus	food	X	?		C (off area)
'i:watod	*Hymenoclea monogyra*	Burro Brush	"wood"	X			E
jiavul	*Ferocactus covillei*	Barrel Cactus	food	X			E
kasvañ	*Trianthema portulacastrum*	Horse Purslane	food	X			B, C
kauk kuavul	*Condalia globosa*	Bitter Condalia	?	X			C
kek cehedagĭ	*Parkinsonia microphylla*	Foothill Palo Verde	food	X			E (off area)
komagĭ 'u'us	*Tessaria sericea*	Arroweed	fiber, util.	X			F (off area)
ko'okomaḍk.kalisp	*Parkinsonia florida*	Palo Verde	food	X			D_1, E
kotadopĭ	*Datura discolor*	Jimson Weed	(relig.?)	X			B, C
kuavul	*Lycium exsertum*	Wolfberry	food	X			C
	Lycium berlandieri		(food?)	X			E
	Lycium parishii		(food?)	X			E
	Celtis pallida	Hackberry	?	X			C
kui	*Prosopis velutina*	Mesquite	util., (med.?)	X	X?		C, D, E
	Prosopis glandulosa		food, wood	X	?		C (off area)
kujul	*Prosopis pubescens*	Screwbean Mesquite	food	X			B
ku'ukpalk	*Portulaca oleracea*	Purslane	food	X			B
milon	*Cucumis melo*	Melon	food	X		X	D_2
mo:stas	*Brassica tournefortii*	Mustard	food	X			B
mu:mṣam	*Plantago insularis*	Wooly Plantain	forage	X			B
mu:ñ	*Phaseolus vulgaris*	Bean	food			X	B
nav	*Opuntia phaecantha (pads)*	Prickly Pear	food	X	X		D_1, E
niatum	*Sphaeralcea coulteri*	Coulter Globe Mallow	food	X			C
nonakam	*Agave murpheyi*	Maguey	food, (fiber?)		X?		C (of area)
ñuñui je:j	*Ambrosia ambrosiodes*	Ragweed	(med.?)	X			D, E
'olas pilkañ	*Triticum aestivum*	Wheat	food, fiber	X		X	B
'onk i:vakĭ	*Atriplex elegans*	Saltbush	food	X			C
	Atriplex polycarpa		food	X			C
	Atriplex wrightii		food	X			B
	Chenopodium murale		food	X			C
'oñk 'u'us	*Tamarix aphylla*	Tamarisk	wood	X	X		C, D
'oñk vaşai	*Distichlis spicata*	Saltgrass	forage	X			D, G
pa:lma	*Washingtonia filifera*	Desert Palm	wood	X	?		C, D
pu:hl	*Trifolium repens*	White Clover	food	X			B, D
s-cuk' oñk	*Suaeda torreyana*	Desert seepweed	(food?)	X			C

TABLE 3. Folk taxa and uses of plants at or near Quitovac, Sonora (continued)

Papago name	Scientific name	Common name	Uses	Wild Self-Sown	Wild Trans-plant	Domes-ticated & Sown	Habitats
si:lantlo	*Coriandrum sativum*	Coriander	food			X	B
siwol	*Allium spp.*	Onion	food			X	B, D
s-toa baví	*Phaseolus acutifolium*	Tepary Bean	food			X	B
s-toa kuavul	*Lycium andersonii*	Wolfberry	food	X			C, D
su:na	*Ficus carica*	Fig	food			X	D
segai	*Larrea tridentata*	Creosote Bush	med.	X			C, E
tahapidam	*Sambucus mexicana*	Elderberry	food, med.		X		D, F
tohawes	*Encelia farinosa*	Brittlebush	relig.	X			B, C
toma:di	*Lycopersicon esculentum*	Tomato	food			X	B
'uduvaḍ	*Typha angustifolia*	Cattail	fiber, food	X			F
'u:dvis	*Vitis vinifera*	Grape	food			X	D (off area)
'u:paḍ	*Acacia greggii*	Catclaw	?	X			C, E
'u:spaḍ	*Zizyphus obtusifolia*	Graythorn	food	X			C
vak	*Scirpus olneya*	Bulrush	relig.	X			F
vakvandam	*Rumex crispus*	Dock	?	X			D_2, F
vapko	*Lagenaria siceraria*	Bottlegourd	util.			X	B (off area)
va:s	*Jatropha cinerea*	Limber Bush	fiber	X			E, hills
va:visa	*Anemopsis californica*	Yerba del Mango	med.	X			D_2, F
vi:bam	*Sarcostemma cynanchoides*	Climbing Milkweed	gum	X			C, D, E
vihol	*Pisum sativum*	Pea	food			X	B
vipinol	*Opuntia arbuscula*	Pencil Cholla	food	X			E
vipisimal	*Justicia californica*	Hummingbird Bush	food	X			C, E

A = open water; B = cultivated field; C = mesa scrubland; D = orchard; E = arroyo; F = lagoon edge and channels; G = alkaline flats. D_1 = fencerow. D_2 = irrigation ditches.

TABLE 4. Avian species richness and diversity at two Sonoran Desert oases.

Locality & Season	No. of species recorded (5 ha)	Diversity Indices	
		Simpson	Shannon-Weaver
Quitovac, Sonora			
August 81	52	.177	.238
Dec.-Jan. 81-2	21	.923	1.202
March 82	42	.960	1.523
May 82	70	.112	.174
Quitobaquito, Ariz			
August 81	42	.787	1.080
Dec.-Jan. 81-2	18	.870	1.048
March 82	39	.747	.909
May 82	53	.797	1.122

TABLE 5. Avian species diversity by habitat at Quitovac, Sonora.

Index & Habitat	August	Dec.-Jan.	March	May
Simpson				
A	.689	—	.759	.585
C	.924	.444	.790	.922
B&D	.772	.776	.925	.913
E	.747	.864	.840	.929
F&G	.137	.796	.881	.053
Shannon-Weaver				
A	.568	—	.721	.608
C	1.136	.276	.728	1.217
B&D	.878	.673	1.163	1.272
E	.670	.911	.881	1.203
F&G	.170	.826	1.020	.067

Waterfowl, doves and quail are the major bird foods utilized by Quitovac Papago. These are taken with .22 rifle, slingshot, or a trip-trigger deadfall box trap made of saguaro ribs, called a *kakast*. Feathers of several bird species are used ceremonially on staffs and prayersticks during the *Vi'igita*. These surely include Golden Eagle and turkey; probably Red-tailed Hawk and Great Horned Owl, and possibly raven. Unfortunately (for us!), some are painted bright colors, and others are old and mis-shapen from years of use, so that casual observation during the ceremony was not enough to confirm identifications noted in the literature (Cano-Avila 1979; Davis 1920).

The mammals which we consider to be present on Quitovac's 5 ha study site include the same four small rodent species live-trapped at Quitobaquito (see those marked with asterisks in Table 7); a trapped gopher; and nine other taxa observed during our visits. Five of these 14 species are domesticated mammals. The Papago

TABLE 6. Folk taxa and uses of birds at or near Quitovac, Sonora.

Papago Name	Scientific Name	Common Name	Food	Relig.	Documented On Site	Nearby
ba'ak	Aguila chrysaetos	Golden eagle		X		X
cem vahum	Micrathene whitneyi	Elf owl			X	X
ciwicuic	Charadrius vociferus	Kildeer			X	
cuhugam	Dendrocopos scalaris	Ladder-backed woodpecker			X	
cukud	Bubo virginianus	Great horned owl			X	
cuk vacuk	Fulica americana	American coot	X			
ge'e visag	Pandion haliaetus	Osprey				X
ge'e hawañ	Corvus corax	Common raven		?	X	
gi:dowal	Progne subis	Purple martin			X	
haupal	Buteo jamaicensis	Red-tailed hawk		X	X	
hewel mo:s	Sayornis saya	Say's Phoebe			X	
ho:hi	Zenaida macroura	Mourning dove	X			
ho:kud	Campylorhynchus brunneicapillus	Cactus wren				X
kakucu	Callipepla gambeli	Scaled quail	X		X	
kokova	Athene cunicularia	Burrowing owl			X	
ko:kud	Ardea herodias	Great Blue heron	X			
ko:logam	Phalaenoptilus nuttalli	Common Poor-will			X	X
ñui	Cathartes aura	Turkey vulture			X	
ñupud	Chordeiles acutipennis	Lesser night hawk			X	
si:pak	Cardinalis spp.	Cardinal, Pyrrhuloxia			X	
şaşañ	Agelaius phoeniceus	Red-winged blackbird			X	
	Xanthocephalus xanthocephalus	Yellow-headed blackbird			X	
	Quiscalus mexicanus	Common grackle			X	
	Molothrus ater	Brown-headed cowbird			X	
	Molothrus aeneus	Bronzed cowbird			X	
su:g	Mimus polyglottus	Mockingbird			X	
tadi	Geococcyx californianus	Roadrunner			X	
toa u'uwhik	Ardea alba	White heron			X	
	Ardea thula					
tova*	Meleagris gallopavo	Turkey	X	X	X	X
va'akek	Tyrannus spp.?	Kingbirds			X	
vacukek	Anatidae	Ducks	X		?	
vahum	sp. in Strigidae or Tytonidae	Owls			X	
vakokam	Icterus cucullatus	Hooded oriole			X	
	Icterus galbula	Baltimore oriole			X	
vipismal	Trochilidae	Hummingbirds			X	

* *Meleagris gallopavo* (turkey), though not now kept as a domesticated bird at Quitovac, is found at a nearby Sonoran Papago village.

TABLE 7. Folk taxa and uses of mammals at or near Quitovac, Sonora.

Papago Name	Scientific Name	Common Name	Food	Relig.	Wild	Domestic	Reported On Site	Reaching Nearby
('ali)'u:phia	Spilogale putoris	Spotted skunk			X			X
ban	Canis latrans	Coyote	X	X	X		X	
cekolĭ	Spermophilus variegatus	Rock squirrel			X			X
cuavĭ	Vulpes velox	Kit fox			X			X
cuk cu:vĭ	Lepus californicus	Black-tailed jackrabbit	X		X		X	X
ceşoiñ	Ovis canadensis	Bighorn sheep	X		X			
cuvho	Thomomys umbinus	Pocket gopher			X		X	
dahivo	Dipodomys merriami*	Merriam's kangaroo rat			X		X	
ge:vo	Lynx rufus	Bobcat	X		X		X	
ge'eju koson	Bassariscus astutus	Ringtail	X	X	X			X
gogs	Canis familiaris	Dog				X		
havañ	Bos taurus	Cattle	X			X		
hoho'i	Erethizon dorsatum	Porcupine			X			X
huavĭ	Odocoileus hemionus	Mule deer	X	X	X			X
kaşo	Urocyon cinereoargenteus	Gray fox			X			X
ka:vĭ	Taxidea taxus	Badger	X	X	X			X
kaviyu	Equus caballus	Horse			X	X	X	
kiñs, misciñ ko:ji	Dicotyles tajacu	Javelina	X		X		X	X
ko:ji	Sus scrofa	Pig	X			X	X	
koson	Neotoma albigula*	White-throated woodrat	X		X		X	
ku'wid	Antilocapra americana	Pronghorn	X	X	X			X
mavit	Felis concolor	Mountain lion			X			X
mu:la	Equus caballus x E. asinus	Mule				X		
nahaggiu	Peromyscus eremicus*	Cactus mouse			X		X	
	Perognathus intermedius*	Desert pocket mouse			X		X	
nanakam	Phyllostomatidae	Leaf-nosed bats			X		?	
	Vespertilionidae	Vespertilionid bats			X		?	
şelik	Spermophilus tereticaudus	Round-tailed ground squirrel			X		X	
si:kĭ	Odocoileus virginianus	White-tailed deer	X		X		X	X
toa cu:vĭ	Lepus alleni	Antelope jackrabbit	X		X		X	
to:bĭ	Sylvilagus audobonii	Desert cottontail	X		X		X	
'u:phia	Mephitis mephitis	Striped skunk			X			X
vavuk	Procyon lotor	Racoon			X			X

* Live-trapped in study site.

report that 13 additional species can be found in nearby mountain ranges and valleys; particularly in times of drought, certain of these mammals may attempt to drink at the lagoon. Yet due to near-continuous human presence, we doubt whether mammals such as deer and javelina drink or browse at Quitovac as frequently as they do at Quitobaquito.

Although the same four rodent species were eventually trapped at both sites, trapping at Quitobaquito in December and March resulted in more species and individuals than at Quitovac (Table 8). Unfortunately, no trapping was done at Quitovac prior to the clearing; but mammal diversity was obviously less than at Quitobaquito in the first months following this habitat destruction. The May diversity indices based on mammal weights were higher for Quitovac, while those based on mammal numbers were higher for Quitobaquito. This is because packrats *(Neotoma)* contributed 70% of the weight of trapped mammals at Quitobaquito, but only 30% of the total number of individuals trapped.

Table 7 provides ethnozoological data on 31 mammal taxa occurring in the Quitovac vicinity which the Papago there name and/or utilize. Of the 15 taxa utilized for food, most are now shot with .22 rifle; it has been decades since bow hunting and on-foot drives were regularly used.

Of religious uses, the tail of the ringtail *(Bassaricus)* and many parts of the mule deer *(Odocoileus hemionus)* are apparently still utilized in the *Vi'igita*. We could neither confirm nor deny the *Vi'igita's* ceremonial enactment of killing other large mammals (such as pronghorn) in addition to mule deer, as Davis (1920) suggested.

Finally, dogs, horses, and cattle are ever-present at Quitovac, and in many ways limit the presence of other animals. Pigs and chickens as well as other domesticates are occassionally kept in the village, but their influence is not so obvious.

CONCLUSIONS

Recently, human ecologists have hypothesized that Native Americans formerly managed habitats in ways that encouraged diversity, resulting in benefits in environmental

TABLE 8. Mammal species richness and diversity at two Sonoran Desert oases (based on live-trapping).

Locality & Season	No. of species	Diversity Indices			
		Based on Weight		Based on Numbers	
		Simpson	Shannon-Weaver	Simpson	Shannon-Weaver
Quitovac, Sonora					
Dec. 81	0	—	—	—	—
March 82	1	0	0	0	0
May 82	4	.686	.545	.493	.410
Quitobaquito, Ariz.					
Dec. 81	1	0	0	0	0
March 82	4	.427	.332	.667	.477
May 82	4	.469	.393	.675	.532

stability or food abundance and reliability (Nabhan and Sheridan 1977; Brush et al. 1981; Emslie 1981). The meaning of diversity, the best ways to measure it, and its relationship to environmental stability are all controversial among theoretical ecologists (Peet 1974, Murdoch 1975). Nevertheless, Altieri (1980) has demonstrated that in agricultural situations, there is clearly a positive correlation between plant diversity in fields, and stability with regard to vulnerability to animal pests.

Utilizing several measures of diversity, we have compared two oases: Quitovac, a "traditional" agricultural setting until the autumn, 1981 clearing in preparation for modern mechanized groundwater agriculture; and Quitobaquito, formerly much like Quitovac, but managed as a wildlife sanctuary in a National Monument since the late 1950s. Because of the removal of cattle and certain introduced plants, as well as the earlier cessation of farming, most Park Service managers would consider that Quitobaquito is undergoing secondary succession "back" to a more natural, perhaps more diverse, condition.

Yet when compared to Quitobaquito, Quitovac is more diverse in terms of plants, somewhat more diverse in birds, and not nearly as diverse in mammals, despite recent habitat disruption. The richness of biota at Quitovac has provided its inhabitants with a diversity of foods, medicines and ceremonial paraphernalia, over and above any cash crops produced there. At Quitobaquito, only dying figs and pomegranates, a few field weeds, and voucher specimens persist to suggest that additional species (and habitats?) may have been present a few decades ago. Even when exotics are deleted from diversity analyses, Quitovac remains more diverse.

To fully explain the present differences between the two oases, it is necessary to consider Papago land use activities. Figure 4 illustrates subsistence-related land uses at Quitovac, some of which affect only target species, while others impact upon all species of one life-form, or a food chain based in a particular habitat. Since we feel

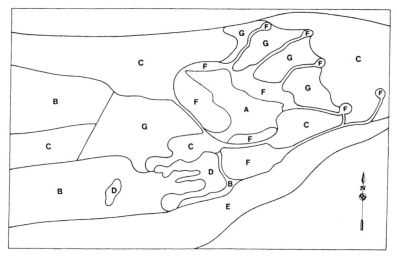

Fig. 3. Oblique map of habitats at Quitovac, reconstructing pre-August 1981 conditions, based on Figure 2.

that these activities account for the differences in biotic diversity between Quitovac and Quitobaquito more than do other historic or contemporary factors, we will discuss each activity in Figure 4 (according to its letters) in the context of both sites. The habitats in which these activities take place are shown in Figure 3 and described in Table 1. Some activities may take place in more than one habitat.

At Quitovac, wild plant gathering occurs in the field as well as on the pond fringe and in the arroyo (A). Humans compete with birds for saguaro and wolfberry *(Lycium)* fruit; Davis (1920) reported that 120 gallons (454 l) of cactus wine was consumed at the *Vi'igita* alone. Since only a small percentage of the seeds produced naturally germinate in favorable sites, it is unlikely that wild fruit gathering reduces plant population sizes. Likewise, the wild greens (eg., *Chenopodium*) harvested are so abundant in good years and produce so many propagules that whole plant harvesting probably does not diminish populations.

The mosaic of disturbed soil, low shrub cover (fence rows and pomegranate bushes) and generally the greater availability of fruits and seeds (and presumably insects, which we did not monitor) at Quitovac promote larger numbers of grackles, Northern Cardinals, Pyrrhuloxia, Canyon Towhees, White-crowned Sparrows and certain transients such as Black-headed and Blue Grosbeaks. However, mistletoe and wolfberry fruits are more abundant, in season, at Quitobaquito. These are utilized by mimids, bombycillids, and several other semi-frugivorous groups.

Although intentional burning could locally-extirpate fire-susceptible species, it is largely practiced on the pond fringe (B). Emergent *Scirpus* and *Typha* stands with much accumulated dead standing crop are annually "cleaned out" at low water, in part so that newer tender shoots will be available to livestock. The plants regenerate, but the temporary openings between them provide habitat for rails, herons, and other wading birds.

Livestock grazing and browsing probably eliminates certain palatable species from the area altogether (C). Along channels from the springs to the lagoon, Quitovac lacks the tender *Eustoma exaltam* and *Centaurium calycosum* found at Quitobaquito. Livestock disperse and "plant" seeds. They also compete with other mammals.

Plowing and other forms of periodic soil disturbance release the wild seed reservoir in the soil for germination (D). Some weed seeds, including *Amaranthus,* and *Proboscidea* have their dormancy broken by light exposure (Wiese and Davis 1967; Anderson 1968); a plow's superficial covering encourages germination. At Quitobaquito, due to lack of periodic soil disturbance, few ephemeral or weedy annuals germinate. Plowing also exposes invertebrates to blackbirds and grackles, that readily feed in open furrows (Carothers 1974).

The planting of living fence rows (E) provides field- and pond-edge borders that flycatchers (7 spp.) regularly utilize as perches from which to feed. The planting of *Salix, Prosopis* and *Tamarix* has provided some of the most intensively utilized habitat at Quitovac; at Quitobaquito, fewer Salix are regernating on their own. The brush woven between fieldside fence rows provides habitat for the few *Neotoma* at the Quitovac site.

Hunting and trapping, primarily of quail and dove, reduce population numbers only slightly today (F). Occasionally other, rarer bird species are killed with slingshots.

Fig. 4. Papago land uses affecting biotic diversity (see text for explanation). Illustration by Paul Mirocha.

Cottontails and jack rabbits are hunted around the fields, but their populations do not appear to be threatened.

Irrigation of selected areas (G) provides moisture to germinate and bring to seed numerous plant species. Plants such as *Anemopsis, Spergularia* and *Heliotropium* thrive in irrigation ditches. Flowing water, and increased humidity attract certain insects, and in turn attract birds (e.g., phoebes).

Transplanting and tending of domesticated perennials such as palms and figs provide Quitovac with its most diverse habitat (H). The shade, and multiple strata are heavily utilized by orioles, woodpeckers, cowbirds and migrating insectivores (flycatchers, vireos, and wood warblers). At Quitobaquito, the last dozen or so pomegranates and figs are dead or senescing, and palms have been removed.

Large carnivorous birds (families or flocks of Black Vultures, Turkey Vultures, Red-tailed Hawks, Harris' Hawks) were common and conspicuous throughout the day at Quitovac. They were attracted by several large dead or nearly dead cottonwoods formerly standing in open fields where the birds could drink and bathe. In spite of constant human activities, these large birds were quite at ease at Quitovac. In contrast, hawks and vultures only incidentally flew over the Quitobaquito oasis.

The large cottonwoods at Quitovac also attracted Purple Martins and several other swallow species. However, at Quitobaquito the immediate juxtaposition of open pond and mesquite bosque attracted much higher breeding and post-breeding populations of Phainopeplas than we found at Quitovac.

Finally, intentional seed sowing (I) provides grain, melons, legumes and forage utilized by humans and other animals. The only domesticated annual at Quitobaquito is safflower *(Carthamnus),* which is feral along roadsides in northern Mexico.

The dynamic habitats at Quitovac have provided food, water and shelter to humans and other lifeforms for centuries. Recently, however, much of this habitat was removed when 125 ha of land was cleared for groundwater irrigated agriculture. The project was promoted by governmental agencies to provide economic opportunities for Papagos. While Quitovac residents look forward to increased crop production in the future, to this date the development has not been completed due to political and economic problems. Residents clearly lament the unnecessary destruction of fence rows, abandoned houses, and other historic structures, as well as the disruption of the springs. Future pumping of groundwater will likely influence flow to the pond. Thus re-establishment of riparian habitat is questionable. As at Quitobaquito in the 1950s, sustainable, traditional agriculture, and the "wild" resources associated with it were not evaluated to any extent before a different course of management was initiated (Nabhan 1982).

Johnson et al. (1977) have argued that habitat destruction has contributed more to the post-1600 extinctions of 120 bird and mammal species than have hunting, trapping and other "direct causes." In doing so, Johnson and colleagues rightfully call for further efforts to protect "endangered" wild habitats. It may be worth considering that diverse agricultural habitats, including certain ones maintained by native American farmers for centuries, are also now endangered. It is unlikely that one could find environments more rare or more vulnerable than those found in desert oases like Quitovac or Quitobaquito. Their loss will affect not only the bird and mammal populations sustained by them, but may impoverish the life of the human community as well.

ACKNOWLEDGMENTS

We thank the Papago community of Quitovac, particularly Luciano Noriego, Hector Manuel and David Manuel, gobernador general del tribu Papago in Sonora. Other Papago, including Ofelia Zepeda and Delores Lewis, helped us appreciate and gain perspective on Quitovac, its people and their language. Several additional scientists cooperated with us in gathering field data: Larry Toolin, Janice Bowers, Richard Felger, Bryan Brown, Peter Warshall, Julian Hayden, John Sumner, Peter Kresan, Barney Burns and Takashi Ijichi. Malcolm Schmerl, Sue Moore and Paul Mirocha greatly assisted in manuscript preparation. We appreciate the cooperation of the National Park Service personnel at Organ Pipe Cactus National Monument, as well as R. Roy Johnson and Keith Anderson, in the study of Quitobaquito. This work was funded by the Consortium for the Study of Man's Relationship with the Global Environment, Man and the Biosphere program, and the Tinker Field Foundation.

LITERATURE CITED

Adams, W. G. 1971. A flora of Quitobaquito. Unpubl. Ms. deposited at Organ Pipe Cactus Natl. Mon.

Altieri, M. 1980. Diversification of corn agroecosystems as a means of regulating fall army-worm populations. Florida Entomologist 63(4): 450–56.

Alvarez, A. and K. Hale. 1970. Toward a manual of Papago grammar. Internatl. J. of Linguistics 36: 83–97.

Anderson, L. C. 1968. Effects of gibberellic acid on germination and continued growth of *Proboscidea lousianica*. Phytomorph. 18(1): 166–73.

Bell, R., K. M. Anderson and Y. G. Steward. 1980. The Quitobaquito cemetary and its history. Natl. Park Service Western Archaeol. Center, Tucson.

Bolton, H. E., ed. and trans. 1930. Anza's California expeditions. Univ. California Press, Berkeley.

———. 1948. Kino's historic memoir of Pimeria Alta. Univ. California Press, Berkeley.

Bowers, J. E. 1980. Flora of Organ Pipe Cactus National Monument. J. Arizona-Nevada Acad. Sci. 15: 1–11; 33–47.

Brush, S. B., H. J. Carney and Z. Huaman. 1981. Dynamics of Andean potato agriculture. Econ. Botany 35(1): 70–88.

Burger, G. V. 1978. Agriculture and wildlife. Pp. 88–107 *in* Wildlife and America, edited by H. P. Brokaw. Council of Environmental Quality, Washington, D.C.

Bye, R. A. 1981. Quelites—ethnoecology of edible greens—past, present and future. J. Ethnobiol. 1: 109–23.

Cano-Avila, G. 1979. La fiesta del Cuca, danza de la lluvia de los Papagos. Simposio de historio de Sonora, Memoria IV: 138–44.

Carothers, S. 1974. Unusual feeding habits in two species of blackbird. Wilson Bull. 86: 121.

Castetter, E. F. and R. M. Underhill. 1935. The ethnobiology of the Papago Indians. Univ. New Mexico Bull. 275, Biol. Ser. 4(3); Ethnobiol. Stud. Amer. Southwest 2.

Cockrum, E. L. 1960. The Recent Mammals of Arizona: Their Taxonomy and Distribution. Univ. Arizona Press, Tucson.

Dambach, C. A. 1948. A study of the ecology and economic value of crop field borders. Grad. School Stud., Biol. Series 2, Ohio State Univ. Press, Columbus.

Davis, E. H. 1920. The Papago ceremony of Vikita. Indian Notes and Monogr. 3(4). Mus. Amer. Indian, Heye Found., New York.

Emslie, S. D. 1981. Birds and prehistoric agriculture: the New Mexican pueblos. Human Ecol. 4: 331–49.

Hall, E. R. 1981. The Mammals of North America. Second Edition. Wiley-Interscience, New York.

Hastings, J. R. and R. R. Humphrey. 1969. Climatological data and statistics for Sonora and Northern Sinaloa. Univ. Arizona Inst. Atmospheric Physics, Tech. Reports on the meteorology and climatology of Arid Regions 19: 1–96.

Ives, R. L. 1936. Some Papago migrations in the Sonoyta Valley. Masterkey 10: 161–67.

Johnson, R. R., L. T. Haight, and J. M. Simpson. 1977. Endangered species vs. endangered habitats: a concept. Pp. 68–79, in Importance, preservation and management of riparian habitat: a symposium, edited by R. R. Johnson and D. A. Jones. USDA Forest Service General Tech. Report RM-43, Fort Collins.

Karpiscak, M. M. 1980. Secondary succession of abandoned field vegetation in southern Arizona. Unpubl. Ph.D. dissert., Univ. Arizona, Tucson.

Lehr, J. Harry. 1978. A catalogue of the flora of Arizona. Desert Botanical Garden, Phoenix.

Linares, O. F. 1976. "Garden hunting" in the American tropics. Human Ecol. 5: 97–111.

Murdoch, W. W. 1975. Diversity stability, complexity and pest control. J. Appl. Ecol. 12: 745–807.

Nabhan, G. P. and T. E. Sheridan. 1977. Living fencerows of the Rio San Miguel, Sonora, Mexico: traditional technology for floodplain management. Human Ecol. 5: 97–111.

Nabhan, G. P. 1980. *Ammobroma sonorae,* an endangered parasitic plant in extremely arid North America. Desert Plants 2: 188–96.

———. 1982. Where the birds are our friends—the tale of two oases. Pp. 87–98, in The Desert Smells Like Rain. North Point Press, San Francisco.

Nabhan, G. P. In prep. Flora of Quitovac, Sonora, with notes on vegetation and ethnobotany.

Naveh, Z. 1967. Mediterranean ecosystems and vegetation types in California and Israel. Ecology 48: 443–59.

Peet, R. K. 1974. The measurement of species diversity. Annu. Rev. Ecol. Syst. 5: 285–307.

Rea, A. M. 1979. The ecology of Pima fields. Environment Southwest 484: 1–6.

———. 1983. Once a river—bird life and habitat change on the middle Gila. Univ. Arizona Press, Tucson.

Sampson, R. N. 1981. Farmland or wasteland—a time to choose. Rodale Press, Emmaus.

Shetler, S. G. and L. E. Skog. 1978. A provisional checklist of species for flora North America. Monogr. in systematic botany. Missouri Botanical Garden, St. Louis.

Shreve, F. 1951. Vegetation of the Sonoran Desert. Carnegie Inst. Wash. Publ. 591.

Wiese, A. F. and R. G. Davis. 1967. Weed emergence from two soils at various moistures, temperatures, and depths. Weeds 15(1): 118–21.

Young, J. A., R. A. Evans and J. Major. 1972. Alien plants in the Great Basin. J. Range Manag.: 194–99.

NOTE

1. Since the original publication of this article, the Papago have legally changed their name to the preferred "O'odham."

Part Two

Folk Classification

Folk Classification

An Introduction

Cecil H. Brown

Folk classification refers to how members of a language community, the "folk," name and categorize plants and animals. The three articles in this section investigate folk classification of plants (and, in two instances, of animals as well) by speakers of Chewa, spoken in Malawi, of Thompson and Lillooet, two Salishan languages of British Columbia, and of Sahaptin, used in the Columbia Plateau region of the Pacific Northwest.

Discussion in each of the chapters alludes to general principles of folk biological classification as presented in the work of Brent Berlin (1992; Berlin, Breedlove, and Raven 1973, 1974). At the core of Berlin's proposals is the concept of *ethnobiological rank*. Each class within a system of folk biological classification, that is, a folk taxonomy, is associated with one of six such ranks. Ranks are systematically related to levels of hierarchic inclusion in folk taxonomies. Figure 1 presents a small fragment of an American English plant taxonomy illustrating levels and ethnobiological ranks.

LEVEL	CLASS		RANK
0	*plant*		unique beginner
1	*tree*	*plant*	life-form
2	*oak*	*maple*	generic
3	*white oak*	*black oak*	specific
4	*swamp white oak*	*northern white oak*	varietal

Figure 1. A fragment of an American English folk plant taxonomy showing hierarchic levels and ethnobiological ranks.

The most inclusive class of a folk taxonomy belongs to the "unique beginner" rank. For example, in figure 1 the unique beginner class in American English botanical taxonomy is *plant*. The rank of unique beginner is associated with the first level of hierarchic inclusion, which Berlin has designated "Level 0." He notes that unique beginners often are not labeled in taxonomies. In other words, languages rarely name biological classes comparable to those of English's *plant* and *animal*.

The next most inclusive rank is the "life-form," which occurs at Level 1, illustrated by *tree* and *plant* in figure 1. (In American English, *plant* has two botanical applications: first to botanical organisms in general [unique beginner], and second to most botanical organisms exclusive of trees [life-form].) Life-form classes always immediately include labeled classes at Level 2 (shown only for *tree* in figure 1). According to Berlin, life-form taxa are usually few in number, rarely exceeding ten in taxonomies of any language.

Classes of Level 2 that are immediately included in life-form categories (of Level 1) are affiliated with the "generic" rank as illustrated by *oak* and *maple* in figure 1. (Generic classes can also occur at Level 1 in folk taxonomies, but this is not depicted in figure 1.) Generic categories are by far the most numerous in folk biological taxonomies and, according to Berlin, constitute a level of abstraction that is psychologically basic or salient.

Generic classes may or may not immediately include other labeled categories. If they do, classes immediately included in generics are associated with the "specific" rank, illustrated by *white oak* and *black oak* in figure 1. Specific categories immediately included in Level 2 generics are found at Level 3. Like generics, specifics may or may not immediately include labeled categories. Classes immediately included in specific categories are affiliated with the "varietal" rank, illustrated by *northern white oak* and *swamp white oak* occurring at Level 4 in figure 1. Folk biological taxonomies rarely demonstrate more than a handful of varietal taxa.

Finally, there is a sixth ethnobiological rank not illustrated in figure 1. "Intermediate" classes occur between life-forms of Level 1 and generics of Level 2. An example in English is *evergreen tree*, which is immediately included in *tree* and itself immediately includes such generic classes as *pine, fir,* and *cedar.* Labeled intermediate categories are rare in most folk biological taxonomies.

Biological classes of the same rank exhibit nomenclatural, biological, taxonomic, and psychological characteristics that distinguish them from classes affiliated with other ranks. One feature, which involves nomenclature or, in other words, linguistic naming, requires elaboration. Classes of the unique beginner, life-form, and generic ranks are typically labeled by "primary lexemes." Primary lexemes are usually simple unitary words such as *plant, animal, tree, fish, oak,* and *trout.* On the other hand, labels for classes of the specific and varietal ranks are typically "secondary lexemes." A secondary lexeme is composed of the term for the class in which the plant or animal it labels is immediately included and a modifier, for example, *white oak,* a kind of *oak; cutthroat trout,* a kind of *trout;* and *swamp white oak,* a kind of *white oak.* Secondary lexemes are also known as "binomial labels."

Since Berlin's initial formulation of principles of folk biological classification, other cross-language patterns have become apparent. For example, I have assembled evidence (Brown 1984) from a large number of globally distributed languages suggesting that both plant and animal life-form categories are typically added to languages (lexically encoded) in more or less fixed sequences. One of these encoding sequences, that for plants, is described in figure 2. This is interpreted as series of stages in the development of botanical life-form vocabularies, with one life-form class being added at each stage.

STAGE: 1   2   3   4–6

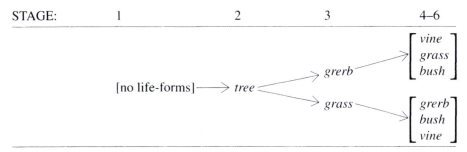

Figure 2. Plant life-form encoding sequence.

In the sequence of figure 2, Stage 1 languages lack terms for botanical life-form categories. Moving to Stage 2, a first botanical life-form class, which is always *tree*, is added to a language. *Tree* designates large plants with chiefly woody parts in a particular locale. At Stage 3, either *grerb* or *grass* is added as a second plant life-form. *Grerb* (grass + herb) denotes small plants of a particular locale with parts that are mainly leafy or herbaceous, a category labeled by *plant* in American English. At Stages 4–6, *vine*, *bush*, and *grass* or *grerb* are added but in no particular order. *Grass*, *vine*, and *bush* classes are more or less comparable to American English categories with those names.

Each of the chapters in this section evaluates findings for individual groups against these proposals. Brian Morris's treatment of Chewa folk biological classification challenges the implicit assumption of both Berlin's and my proposals that folk taxonomies are motivated by "intellectualist" rather than by "utilitarianist" considerations. Proponents of utilitarianism argue, in part, that folk classification of plants and animals is a means for human beings to adjust to their environments by classifying and assigning names to those species that have important, practical consequences for human existence (for example, those species that are eaten, used as fuel, used as medicine, or used for construction). In contrast, proponents of intellectualism propose that biological organisms are categorized and named by people independent of the practical uses species may possess for them. In the intellectualist view, folk biological knowledge is fundamentally intellectually motivated, entailing judgments of relative degrees of similarity and differences among species with little regard to their usefulness for humans.

Nancy Turner's study of Thompson and Lillooet ethnobotanical classification focuses on general plant categories. She judges whether or not these classes manifest features of life-forms as discussed in Berlin's work and my own. In her view, general plant categories in these two languages are fluid and ambiguous compared to the life-form classes described in our approaches. However, life-forms in both languages do appear to fit the plant life-form sequence since, as Turner notes, Lillooet is a Stage 3 language, having only two life-forms, *tree* and *grass,* and Thompson is a Stage 6 language with *tree, grass, grerb, bush,* and *vine* categories (see figure 2). The systems studied by Turner also lend some support to the utilitarianist position since some of their life-form categories appear to be at least partially motivated by utilitarian factors.

The chapter by Eugene Hunn and David French adds another dimension to principles of folk biological classification by indicating that systems of hunter-gatherers, such as that of Sahaptin speakers, differ in regular ways from systems of small-scale farmers. This is an observation that I have also made independently (Brown 1985), but this possibility was not initially considered by Berlin when developing his framework of principles since data from foraging groups were not available at that time. While folk taxonomies of small-scale agrarian peoples closely follow Berlin's original proposals by showing several levels of hierarchic inclusion (see figure 1), those of hunter-gatherers tend to have only one level, consisting almost entirely of generic classes. Because specific (and varietal) classes rarely pertain to taxonomies of foragers, these systems also exhibit very few if any categories denoted by secondary lexemes, a type of label common in taxonomies of farmers.

Findings reported by Hunn and French can be viewed as strongly suggestive of patterns in the development of folk biological taxonomies. A major thrust of human societal development over the last several millennia has been replacement of a foraging way of life with agriculture. As societies have shifted from hunting and gathering to farming, their folk taxonomies have tended to expand up and down, adding more-inclusive life-form and less-inclusive specific classes to preexisting generic categories. This developmental possibility was first speculatively advanced by Berlin (1972) some time before the nature of folk biological classification as it pertains to hunter-gatherer groups was first outlined by scholars such as Hunn and French.

Issues in folk biological classification may be pursued further by consulting the works referenced in this introduction, especially Berlin (1992).

LITERATURE CITED

Berlin, Brent. 1972. Speculations on the growth of ethnobotanical nomenclature. Language in Society 1: 51–86.

———. 1992. Ethnobiological Classification—Principles of Categorization of Plants and Animals in Traditional Societies. Princeton University Press, Princeton, N. J.

Berlin, Brent, Dennis E. Breedlove, and Peter H. Raven. 1973. General principles of classification and nomenclature in folk biology. American Anthropologist 75: 214–42.

———. 1974. Principles of Tzeltal Plant Classification. Academic Press, New York.

Brown, Cecil H. 1984. Language and Living Things: Uniformities in Folk Classification and Naming. Rutgers University Press, New Brunswick, N.J.

———. 1985. Mode of subsistence and folk biological taxonomy. Current Anthropology 26: 43–64.

CHAPTER FOUR

The Pragmatics of Folk Classification

BRIAN MORRIS

INTRODUCTION

In 1925, almost sixty years ago, Malinowski (1974: 44) wrote: "The road from the wilderness to the savage's belly and consequently to his mind is very short. For him the world is an indiscriminate background against which there stands out the useful, primarily the edible, species of animals and plants." There has been a justified, though perhaps unnecessarily harsh, reaction against this kind of pragmatism. No one has expressed this better than Levi-Strauss, who has argued that the outlook of pre-literate peoples towards the natural world is primarily intellectual, and that totemic symbols cannot be understood in terms of a naturalistic perspective. For Levi-Strauss (1966: 9) the "specific" character of the animal and plant world is the initial source or impulse for symbolic classifications, but the main purpose of these classifications is not a practical one: "It meets intellectual requirements rather than . . . satisfying needs."

Of equal interest, however, is the viewpoint of the ethnoscientists, such as Brent Berlin and his associates (1974). Although stemming from a different theoretical tradition—that of Anglo-Saxon empiricism—the latter share with the structuralists an interest in folk classifications. As with Levi-Strauss, folk knowledge is seen primarily in classificatory terms, and there is an equal stress on a logic of what Levi-Strauss (1969: 163) calls "oppositions and correlations, exclusions and inclusions . . . ," that is, on systematics and coherence. Furthermore, though focusing on specific semantic domains, they have other affinities with Levi-Strauss in their search for universals, reflecting a consistent and healthy opposition to cultural relativism. Similarly, like Levi-Strauss, ethnoscientists see folk classifications as expressing a purely intellectual interest in the natural world. Whereas for Malinowski (1925), pre-literate people appear to think through the stomach, Levi-Strauss and the ethnoscientists view the interest in the world of pre-literate people as cognitive and intellectual and, divorced from pragmatic concerns, as being related primarily to a "search for order." Neither tradition, of course, denies that animals and plants have a utilitarian significance, e.g., food or medicines, but both imply that this is largely unrelated to the way that people systematically classify the natural world.

Given the different philosophical perspectives of the ethnoscientists and the structuralists, the two traditions naturally advocate a different kind of intellectual and classificatory mode. For Levi-Strauss, pre-literate people are concerned with a mode of
thinking that unifies through symbolic logic diverse aspects of their culture; for Berlin
and his associates (1974), on the other hand, subjects are proto-botanists concerned
with ordering the natural world through criteria based on morphology and structure.
Both of these perspectives have been necessary, but they have also limited our understanding of folk classifications. The structuralist approach, by focusing on the
symbolic logic, over systematizes the social reality and tends to ignore the praxis of
human groups. The approach of the ethnoscientists, on the other hand, has tended to
underplay the relevance of practical interests in the structuring of folk taxonomies.
My aim in this paper is to focus on the latter issue and to show, through an examination of the natural taxonomies of the Chewa people of Malawi[1] that pragmatic
concerns are highly relevant in interpreting the nature and structure of folk classifications, echoing some of Bulmer's (1974) early misgivings about ethnoscience.

TWO ILLUSTRATIONS OF FUNCTIONAL CATEGORIES

In an article on the uses of succulent plants in Malawi, one biologist, Hargreaves
(1976: 190), admitted that he found local plant nomenclature somewhat confusing.
He wrote:

> I found, for example, that a small herbaceous mint, a shrub, a grass and the large
> tree *Acacia albida* were all referred to as *'Mbeya.'* These plants were totally unre-
> lated and showed no resemblance to each other. I was therefore puzzled until an
> informant told me to taste them. Then it became clear. *'Mbeya'* means 'salt'! I
> soon learned to overcome my own taxonomic prejudice and look at plants
> according to their uses. Many plants in Chitipa, in fact, have no local name
> because they have no use.

And he goes on to state that "Botany grew from herbals listing useful plants and did
not arise out of the objectivity which modern scientists like to pretend to."

It would be easy, of course, to dismiss these suggestions as untenable. Some
plants in Malawi, as elsewhere, have names but no apparent utility, e.g. the parasitic
Kamfiti, *Striga asiatica*. Clearly there is no simple correlation, as Hargreaves seems
to imply, between utility and nomenclature. Nonetheless, it is important to realize, as
Brokensha and Riley (1980: 121) write of the Mbeere, that utility is a major factor in
the classification of plants.

One could also perhaps question Hargreaves on his knowledge of the local
language, and suggest that **Mbeya** is not a plant name at all, since it means salt; the
term, significantly, is not in the Malawi 'Dictionary of Plant Names' (Binns 1972).
Indeed, some have thought it important to indicate the semantic confusions that appear
to have crept into local floras, when terms were discovered which meant 'medicine'
or 'poison' or are the name of some local disease or complaint (cf. Carrington 1981).

These, it is suggested, cannot possibly be taxonomic labels! Although offered as criticisms of botanists, such suggestions indicate a stringent taxonomic outlook. After all, no one disputes that such English terms as "heartsease," "eyebright," "sanicle" (from Latin verb *sano,* heal), "gum," "rubber," "wormwood" and "liverwort" are valid plant names—not to mention those terms that have long since disappeared from our vocabulary, e.g., "nosebleed" (yarrow). It is therefore somewhat misleading to assume that terms like "poison" or "salt" or the name of some disease do not have taxonomic significance in folk classifications; indeed it is my contention that they do, which brings me to my second illustration.

Some years ago while studying the epiphytic orchids of Malawi (Morris 1970), I noticed that many of these plants were well-known to local people, and that the commoner species—*Angraecopsis parviflora, Cyrtorchis arcuata, Bulvophyllum sanderonii*—though morphologically quite distinct, were referred to by the collective term ***Mwana wa mphepo,*** meaning "child of the wind." Given my ecological bias, I thought it quite an appropriate term for epiphytic orchids, many of which grew high on the outer branches of trees. Many years later I discovered that this term was applied to several other plant life forms—herbs, shrubs and climbers—and was not restricted to epiphytic orchids. Focused on the family Vitaceae, the herbs *Cyphostemma junceum* and *Ampelocisus obtusa* being prototypical, many of these plants, but not all, are referred to by other generic terms (Table 1). Plants referred to as ***Mwana wa mphepo*** belong, therefore, to several distinct families, and each one is used as a medicine in the treatment of a disease which is called by the same term, and which is as complex as the plant taxon. The important point is that ***Mwana wa mphepo*** is a polysemic term, and it is quite contrary to Chewa thought to consider plants and diseases as somehow utterly distinct and exclusive domains (cf. Turner 1967: 299–358). Many plant categories do indicate their utility, and one herbalist I knew categorized the plants she used either by the term ***(Mtengo) Wazilengo*** (relating to misfortunes caused by medicines) or by the term ***(Mtengo) wa madzoka*** (of the spirit induced illness Madzoka). For these particular trees she never used, or indeed knew, any other term. To understand Chewa folk concepts, therefore, one has to accept that they have a pragmatic dimension, and that such taxonomies are not conceptually isolated, as a domain, from other aspects of Chewa culture.[2]

ZOOLOGICAL LIFE FORMS

As with many other cultures, there are no terms in Chewa that can be considered equivalent to the English terms 'animal' and 'plant,' which derive from Latin and were used widely only toward the end of the 16th Century (cf Morris 1980). The Chewa have a concept of life *(- Moyo)* and in many contexts use terms that imply a distinction between the two main types of living organisms. The noun-classes themselves to some extent reflect this distinction. Whereas many animals belong to the ***Munthu*** class ***A/Fisi, A/Nyalugwe, A/Mende*** (hyena, leopard, creek rat), most of the ***Mtengo*** category—which includes the majority of the plants known to the Chewa—belong to a different noun class (typically referred to as the ***Mtengo*** class) such as ***Mkuyu,***

TABLE 1. Outline of the taxon mwana wa mphepo

Group	Subgroup	Species	Vernacular name
	CHIWAMASIKA	*Ampelocissus obtusata*	
		Cyphostemma crotalarioides	
		Cyphostemma zombensis	
	MPELESYA	*Rhoicissus tridentata*	MPESA MPETE
		Cissus cornifolia	
		Cissus integrifolia	
		Cissus quadrangularis (*Cissus rubiginosa*)	MTAMBE
	NDEMIKANGONO	*Cissus buchananji*	
		Cyphostemma junceum	MWINIMUNDA MWANANKALI
	NCHOFU	*Cyphostemma subciliatum*	
		Cayratia gracilis	NTEREVERE
MWANA WA MPHEPO		*Angraecopsis parviflora*	
		Cyphostemma gigantophyllum	
		Cyphostemma rhodesiae	
		Ampelocissus africana	
		Rhoicissus tomentosa	
		Cissus cucumerifolia	
		Cissus faucicola	
		Cissus producta	
		Cissus trothae	
		Cissus aristolochitolia	
		Rhoicissus revoilii	
		Jateorhiza bukobensis	KAMUTU
			NTUMTOMUKO
		Tinospora caffra	MDYAPUMBWA
		Bulbophyllum sandersonii	NJOKA
		Crystorchis arcuata	KASANA
			CHIDYAKAMBA
		Adenia gummifera	KALISACHI
			KALISACHI
		Elephantorrhiza goetzei	MWANAMVULA
			MKUTA
		Paullinia pinnata	MLOZI
		Pyrenacantha kaurabassana	CHITETE
			CHALIMA
			MKANDANKHUKU
			CHITUPA
			NAKULUNGUNDI

Mkundi, Msopa, Mlombwa (all taking the plural prefix Mi-). As in other languages, there are a host of terms referring both to plant morphology and usage and to plant growth that would imply a distinction between plants and other organisms, but whether such distinctions warrant the label of "covert" category (Berlin et al 1968, 1974; Brown 1974) is difficult to say.

The main life-form categories of the Chewa are as follows:

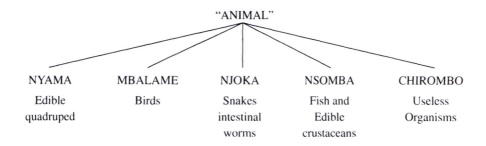

"ANIMAL"

NYAMA	MBALAME	NJOKA	NSOMBA	CHIROMBO
Edible	Birds	Snakes	Fish and	Useless
quadruped		intestinal	Edible	Organisms
		worms	crustaceans	

Nyama is a polysemic term referring both to meat and to any edible species of mammal. It can include edible reptiles and amphibians but it excludes *Nsomba* (fish and edible freshwater crustaceans), *Mbalame* (birds) and *Njoka* (snakes). *Nyama* has a complex meaning: and in normal contexts it excludes the larger predatory mammals, e.g., hyena, leopard, and lion, as well as those smaller animals not usually eaten, like the mongoose and jackal. It also has a great ritual significance to the Chewa because of its association with hunting. Schoffeleers (1968) suggests that besides meaning "edible quadruped," it refers to the spirit or power released by the blood of a slain person—thus giving the concept a mystical quality. Significantly the "flesh" of a bird, snake or a vegetable substance is not referred to as *Nyama* but as *Mnofo.* Besides these four main life forms—to call them zoological drastically narrows their meaning—there is a kind of residual category *Chirombo,* which refers to any hostile wild animal: *Nyalugwe* (leopard) and *Fisi* (hyena) are prototypical. Essentially however, *Chirombo,* means any useless living thing, and also includes weeds and most invertebrates; like *Nyama,* the term also has important symbolic connotations, being associated with evil spirits and with the masked dancers (who impersonate spirit animals) at certain ceremonies.

"Within" these categories a distinction is made between wild and domesticated species. Domesticated animals are referred to as *Chiweto* or *Chifuyo;* the latter terms include chickens, ducks and dog, as well as the larger livestock like goats and cattle. For example *Bakha* refers to the domestic duck, and besides being seen as outside the *Mbalame* (bird) category, is considered quite distinct from wild species such as *Chipweyo,* the fulvous tree duck and *Kalanga,* the Hottentot teal. Europeans often use *Bakha* as a generic term, but Chewa-speakers around Lake Chilwa were adamant that the term *Bakha* applied *only* to the domesticated species.[3] This conceptual demarcation is common amongst the Chewa; *Nkhumba* and *Nguluwe,* for example, refer to the domestic and wild pig respectively and **Nkhunda** and **Njiwa** to the domestic and wild pigeon. The distinction between the village *(Mudzi)* and woodland *(Thengo)* is indeed an important ecological and symbolic demarcation amongst the Chewa, and it is a division that has wide cross cultural reference (cf. Strathern 1980).

In an important sense, then, three of the five life form categories which I have briefly discussed above are largely functional categories that cannot be understood simply in terms of morphological criteria. The polysemous nature of the main category **Nyama** suggests, as Bulmer remarked, that such 'life-forms,' "may be defined as much by cultural evaluation . . . as by their objective biological characteristics" (1974: 23). Needless to say, in Chewa thought people *(Anthu)* form a separate and unique category. [4]

BOTANICAL LIFE FORMS

There is no term in Chewa for "plant" although literate speakers of the language often try to find or make one. Thus the terms **Chomera** or **Chimerara** (derived from **Ku-mera,** to sprout or shoot) can be used to describe plants generally but their focus is essentially on cultivated species, especially those like the sweet potato which are propagated vegetatively. These terms have no general use. There are three basic terms in Chewa for what might loosely be described as the plant world: **Mtengo,** which, at a superficial level, is a general category for trees and woody plants, **Maudzu,** grasses, and grass-like herbaceous plants like the anthericum lilies, and **Bowa,** edible fungi.

The majority of plants known to the Chewa fall under the category **Mtengo,** and in addition to trees, it includes vines, creepers and small herbs. It also refers to a stick, the woody stem or a piece of wood; the allied concept **Thengo** is a general term for woodland dominated by the genera *Brachystegia* and *Uapaca* (not "bush" as it is usually translated), as distinct from evergreen forest **Nkhalango.** The term **Chire** is more frequently used to refer to regenerate bushland.

To understand the meaning of **Mtengo,** however, one has to shift one's perspective, and view the natural world not only in terms of morphology but also in terms of utility. Many small herbs that are utilized as food or medicines are referred to as **Mtengo,** although they are not trees in the European sense. In a program on Malawi radio on January 10, 1972, a professor of botany was interviewed in English about her work and writings. Part of the discussion was focused on the plant *Galinsoga parviflora* which has the quaint name **Mwamuna aligone** (literally 'My husband is sleeping') whose leaves form a useful relish dish. Throughout the discussion the Malawian interviewer described the plant as a 'tree' yet it is only a small slender herb, barely six inches high.

Many herbs, however, do not fit into the **Mtengo** category. If a local person is asked what sort of plant, say, a balsam is, or whether a generic category is a 'tree' **Mtengo** the informant may be hesitant, and may conclude that it is a **Maluwa** (flower), significantly using the plural. So in a sense **Duwa** or **Luwa** (flower—singular form) can take on the role of a general plant category, although many small herbs remain essentially unaffiliated. Many Europeans are surprised to discover, therefore, that many conspicuous plants such as *Gloriosa virescens, Crinum pedicellatum* and *Crocosmia aurea* have no name, and are virtually unnoticed and unrecognized by Chewa speakers (cf. Brokensha and Riley 1980; 121) who yet, somewhat paradoxically, have such a detailed and accurate knowledge of the plant world. The reason is that ***Mtengo*** is essentially, that is prototypically, a category of useful wild plants, and that *Crocosmia aurea* (for example), which has no evident uses, has no name and is not a 'tree.'

Two other words are often used almost interchangeably with that of ***Mtengo.*** The first is ***Mankhwala,*** which may be translated as "medicine," and includes both animal and plant material. Medicines and their uses permeate Chewa culture, and are utilized for protection against witchcraft *(Ufiti),* as good luck charms and in the treatment of illness and disease. I have often, in pointing to a shrub or tree, asked someone 'What's this?' *(Ichi ciani?)* only to get the reply *"Mankhwala,"* and many of my Yao informants in Malawi used the term ***Mtera*** which is a generic concept for both "medicine" and "tree." Such polysemy seems widespread in Africa, and in his classic study on the Azande Evans-Pritchard (1937: 440) notes:

> The Zande word which I have translated as 'medicine' or 'magic' according to context is ***Ngua. Ngua*** means 'tree' or 'wood' or 'plant' so when we ask a Zande what medicine is used for a certain activity we are asking him what tree or plant is used.

But if we concentrate, like Evans-Pritchard, on the magic, or like the ethnoscientists on the botany, we miss, I think, the essence of Chewa thought in which medicines and plants are intimately linked.[5] The second word which is used almost as a synonym for *Mtengo* is 'root.' The true Chewa term is ***Mezu*** (plural ***Mizu***) but I rarely heard this term used in the area where I did my research; the concept ***Mtsitsi*** was employed instead. It is difficult for us to understand or feel the significance that roots have for the Chewa. Although I am stressing the importance of utility in Chewa classifications I am not denying that they do not have an interest in plant morphology and structure— indeed they do—but this interest if focused to a large extent on leaves and roots. In asking what uses of specific plants were *(Ntchito ciani?)* the immediate response often was "You dig down" *(Mukumba Pansi),* and you were expected to realize the implications, i.e. that it had medicinal value as ***Mankhwala.*** Many times I have observed herbalists digging up roots to check or confirm the identification of a plant, and one woman to whom I showed a specimen (an *Albuca* lily) said to me "Bring me more leaves and the *root* and I'll tell you what it is!"

Many herbalists, in particular, have an amazing propensity for identifying plants by their roots. This is because many of the plants that are of crucial importance to the Chewa are neither trees, nor do they have conspicuous flowers; it is their utility as food or medicines that give them salience. Several members of the plant families Vitaceae, Asclepiadaceae and Menispermacceae are examples. Incidentally, the old Greek herbalists were called *Rhizotomoki,* the root gatherers.[6]

It is important, then, to realize that there are no concepts in Chewa which correspond to the broad morphological divisions of 'tree,' 'shrub,' 'herb' (noted by

Theophrastus, [Hort 1968]) or 'vine' (cf. Berlin et al 1974: 373). There are terms which are sometimes glossed as "shrub" or "bush" such as **Chitsamba** (*Tsamba*, leaf) or **Chipfutu**. Essentially these refer to the shrubby or tufted growth of either grasses or trees, on their regeneration after being cut back or burned and not to shrubs as such. The term **Chilambi** (Yao **Chisirisya**)—**Cissampelos Mucronata** is prototypical—is also used to cover several creepers, and like the term **Mtsitsi**, appears to mean, in some contexts, 'vine' or 'creeper.' However, cultivated vines and plants such as the creeper **Mondia Whytei**, because they are not used as cordage, are not considered 'vines' at all, although they ought to be on morphological pounds. Equally important is the fact that bamboos, bananas and many cultivated plants are considered outside (unaffiliated) to the two main categories. Thus millet, maize and sorghum are not **Mandzu**, although, again, they ought to be by morphological criteria, and indeed the pearl millet **Machewere** belongs to the same genus *Pennisetum* as does the grass **Nsenjere**. This division largely reflects what we have already noted, namely the important symbolic categorization in Chewa between the village and the woodland, and both **Mtengo** and **Maudzu** essentially refer to useful plants that are to be found in the woodland.

Although there is a pragmatic emphasis at both the life-form and generic levels of Chewa classifications there are also a number of intermediate categories that have a largely functional significance. I have already mentioned **Mwanawamphero**. Three other taxa are worth noting: (1) **Thelele** is a grouping of plants used in the preparation of a kind of mucilaginous relish, referred to by the same term. It is focused around the semicultivated *Hibiscus acetosella*. Other species in this category are, in addition, referred to by monotypic generic terms, such as **Denje** *(Corchorus trilocularis)* and **Chewe** *(Sesamum angolense)*. (2) **Mtibulo**, although probably of Yao derivation, this is a category that is widely applied to plants that are used by men as a potency medicine. The category is focused on the creeper *Mondia whytei*. (3) **Mpira** is usually translated as rubber, but it is employed as a taxonomic category for many latex-bearing plants like *Landolphia kirkii* and *Euphorbia geniculata*. Whether one considers these as generic or intermediate categories seems unimportant: what is essential to understand is that these taxa have both a functional and a taxonomic significance for the Chewa. And each of these categories—indeed almost all categories for the Chewa—have a prototypical member which virtually defines the class; for instance, *Hibiscus acetosella* is described as **Thelele Yeni-Yeni** (truly this plant) (cf. Berlin et al 1974: 34, Bulmer 1979: 58).

To further stress the close relationship between utility and classification I now outline, in some detail, the Chewa classification of fungi, a category that tends to be overlooked by cognitive anthropologists.

CLASSIFICATION OF FUNGI *(Bowa)*[7]

Around 500 species of the larger fungi have been described from the Shire Highlands of Malawi (Morris 1983). Around 14 percent (70) of these are known to have cultural significance for the Chewa. With the exception of two taxa, all are categorized as **Bowa** and are considered edible. Although it may be possible to speak of **Bowa**, like the English term mushroom, as a general concept for the larger fungi, in

Chewa it essentially refers only to edible species. Edibility is a defining characteristic of the taxon, and in everyday usage inedible and poisonous fungi are *not* considered **Bowa.** Any of the latter species when categorized at all, for they have no generic name, are usually referred to as **Chirombo.** This category, as we have noted, is complex; it essentially refers to any organism that is useless or harmful to mankind.

I have heard it suggested that the term **Chirombo** is not applicable to fungi or plants, but almost everyone I knew who collected fungi made a clear categorization between edible fungi or **Bowa,** and inedible species which were described as **Chirombo.** "It is not a **Bowa** but a useless thing *(Chirombo)* "was an expression that women often used. Interestingly, several species which are in fact edible, but which are not eaten (as far as I could ascertain) in Malawi have no common name. Examples are *Agaricus silvaticus,* and, in the Zomba district at least, *Suillus granulatus.*

In an early report on local foods Williamson (1941: 12) mentions that in the classification of fungi "each district seems to have its own distinct set of names." This is true, and what is significant is that not only is there wide agreement about common names within a specific locality, but there seems to be a common pattern of categorizing fungi throughout Malawi. The basic schema is denoted as follows:

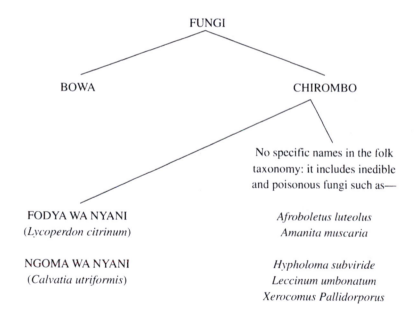

FUNGI

BOWA

CHIROMBO

No specific names in the folk taxonomy: it includes inedible and poisonous fungi such as—

FODYA WA NYANI
(Lycoperdon citrinum)

Afroboletus luteolus
Amanita muscaria

NGOMA WA NYANI
(Calvatia utriformis)

Hypholoma subviride
Leccinum umbonatum
Xerocomus Pallidorporus

ETHNOMYCOLOGY OF THE CHEWA

Most women in rural areas have an extensive knowledge of the identification and ecology of fungi. Although I recorded about seventy edible species, because of their varied geographical distribution, few women knew all of them. Most female informants could name, without difficulty, about 20 species. Knowledge about fungi, as with other wild vegetable foods, is largely confined to women, and there were few men who knew anything about fungi, except for the commoner species, which they normally referred to simply as **Bowa.** I asked the president of a herbalist association, a man with a deep and impressive knowledge of medicinal plants, what edible fungi he knew. He named four, and after a few minutes of thought, admitted that he could remember no more. This variability in folk knowledge according to age, sex, class or ritual affiliations tends to be overlooked in some discussions of folk classifications (cf. Hays 1976: 491).

Although there is a broad correspondence between folk terms and scientific nomenclature, several names are applied to species of quite diverse scientific genera. The grounds for doing so may be ecological. For example, many mushrooms are associated with the **Msuku** tree, *(Uapaca kirkiana)* and these bear names that indicate the association, **Kamsuka, Nakasuku, Ngunda Suku** (Pipe of the **Msuku**). Thus certain edible species of *Lactarius* are put in the same category as *Cantharellus,* although local people do not confuse them, for they usually treat the latex-bearing *Lactarius* to a more elaborate cooking procedure. Likewise the two species of *Lentinus* share the same term as the Bolete *Gyroporus Luteopurpureus,* **Kamchikuni (Nkhuni,** firewood), as all grow on or near dead timber.

Other groupings are based on texture or appearance. **Kanchombo** is a term derived from **Mchombo,** the navel, and is indicative of a pointed or unbonate cap. It is specifically applied to *Termitomyces eurrhizus* whose sharply pointed cap enables the fungus to push its way through the termite mound. But it is also applied to two common species of *Psathyrella,* one of which significantly bears the specific name **Atroumbonata (Atro,** dark, **Umbilicus,** navel). The mycologist, Pegler is clearly thinking along the same lines as the Chewa. Another widely used term is **Msongolo wa Nkhwali**—"the lower leg of the Francolin." This has been noted with reference to a number of very different fungi—*Cantharellus tenuis* and *Melanoleuca Melaleuca* for example, and alludes to the reddish color of the cap, which is reminiscent of the red legs of this common game bird.[8]

Like all good mycologists, Chewa women do not put much stress on color, but when handling and identifying fungi rely more on smell and texture. When discussing my specimens with women, I found great difficulty curbing their natural tendency to tear the fungus apart, as they always do in verifying the identification of a particular species. If one asks a woman to group a collection of fungi they invariably place the important species into two categories. Into one category they place *Russula schizoderma,* all the *Cantharellus* and *Termitomyces schimperi;* into the other they put the three main species of *Amanita,* and *Termitomyces eurrhizus.* If one asks about the rationale behind this 'covert' categorization it is suggested that the second grouping consists of those **Bowa** which have a slippery texture—"**Onse Lutelele.**" This is in accord with the folk classifications, for the taxon *Katelela* is virtually a generic term for the edible *Amanita.* Again this links with an important functional category within the **Mtengo** life-form, **Thelele** (discussed earlier).

Folk generics (see Table 2) can be roughly divided into two types: simple generics like **Manyame, Nakajeti** and **Nyonzwe,** and those which have metaphoric connotations, such as *Ngoma wa Nyani,* ("Drum of the Baboon"), *Mpafa ya Fulu,* ("Liver of the Tortoise") are examples. But significantly, this division corresponds to the cultural importance of the fungi; all those generic terms which are metaphorical are of secondary importance as a food source, or like *Fodya wa Nyani,* Baboon's Tobacco *(Lycoperdon citrinum)* are considered inedible.

Finally, it is worth noting that Chewa Women see a much closer association between mushrooms and meat *(Nyama)* than between fungi and either plants or vegetables. One woman categorized a basket of fungi by dividing them always into two piles, *Nyama* (edible) and *Chirombo* (inedible fungi). She used the term *Nyama* almost as a taxonomic category for the edible species. This association of fungi with animal life, rather than with plants *(Mtengo),* based as it is on texture and edibility rather than morphology, is probably widespread in traditional cultures. Gerard described fungi as "meates," and the tissue of fungi is normally spoken of by analogy as flesh (cf. The writings of Theophrastus in Hort 1968: 21). One anthropologist, writing of the Semai people of Malaysia, suggests that fleshy fungi are indeed grouped with animals as 'real' food (Dentan 1968: 34–35). The Chewa clearly see *Mtengo* and *Bowa* as quite distinct categories, and the general notion, accepted by Europeans and many past biologists, that all living things belong to one of two kingdoms, plants and animals (with "fungi" placed in the "plant" category) makes little sense to the majority of Chewa women. To suggest to a Chewa that a particular fungus belongs to the *Mtengo* category is rather like asking an English person whether a cabbage was a kind of tree. Thus the views of Chewa women are probably closer to those of the modern taxonomist than the ideas of the great botanist Linnaeus.

CONCLUSIONS

I have given above a broad outline of Chewa folk classification, and specifically the classification of fungi *(Bowa).* In the light of this discussion some broad conclusions can be made.

Firstly, although ethnoscience was motivated by a genuine desire to present the cognitive principles of a particular culture (and Sturtevant (1964) indeed defined ethnobotany as a "specific cultural conception of the plant world") an undue focus was put on morphology and classification. But folk taxonomic hierarchies are relatively shallow, and the term hierarchy is almost a misnomer when one considers, for instance, that about 20 percent of Tzeltal plant categories are unaffiliated to any life-form taxa, and that some 85 percent of the generics are monotypic. When Friedberg (1979: 85) suggests that plants in Bunaq taxonomy appear to be classified more according to a "complex" web of resemblances" rather than forming a neat hierarchy, she would seem closer to the ethnographic reality. Moreover, to suggest as do some ethnoscientists, that "a culture itself amounts to the sum of a given society's folk classifications " (Sturtevant 1964: 100) or that "natural phenomena may be said to be culturally relevant simply by virtue of their existence" (Hunn 1977) is to state both too little and too much. In the former regard, folk knowledge extends well beyond what is encapsulated in formal taxonomies, and many Chewa-speakers knew the medicinal

TABLE 2. Chewa classification of the Taxon Bowa

Cantharellus cibarius
CHIPATWE WAYERA
NAFUWANKHUKU
NGUNDASUKI

Cantharellus congolensis
CHIPATWE CHAKUDA
NAKAMBUZI

MANYAMA
CHIPATWE (Y)   MAKUNGUTA (Y)

Cantharellus longiporus
CHIPATWE WAFIRA
NGUNDASUKU
ANAKSUKU

Cantharellus densifolius
NGUNDASUKU WAYERA

MSONGOLO WANKHWALI   *Catharellus tenuis*

Melanoleuca melaleuca
KASANJALA
KANJALA

Lactarius gymnocarpus
KUNGULUKWETITI
KAMSUKI
NKWICHI

NAKASUKU

Lactarius sp. JW 563
KAMBWALO
KAMPHANDE

Lactarius sp. BM 131
NGUNDASUKU

Lactarius vellereus

Russula schizoderma
Russula sp. JW 578
LILANGWI
CHIPINDI   USINDA (Y)
MKADZADZULO

Russula sp. JW 593

Russula sp. JW 580
NAMALOBA

Russula cyanoxantha
TERENYA WAFIRA

TERENYA

Russula ochroleuca
TERENYA WAYERA

Macrolepiota diolichaula

TABLE 2. Chewa classification of the Taxon Bowa (continued)

		NAMANDADERENGWA
		Amanita hemibapha
		KALONGONDWA
		KATSOBOLA
	UTENGA (Y)	NDEZA
	TAMBALA	
NDELEMA		*Amanita rhodophylla*
KATELELA		
		Amanita zambiana
		SANDJI
		Amanita bingensis
		NAKAJONGOLO
		MSONGOLO WANKHWALI
		Aminita elegans
		BONGOLOLO
		NAKATOTOSI (Y)
		KATALESYA (Y)
		Amanita rubescens
NGODZI		*Amanita goossensiae*
NAKAJETI (Y)		MUSENDAIWA
		Amanita sp. JW 595
		Lepiota sp. JW 585
		NKOTWE
		Gyroporus luteopurpureus
KAMCHIKUNI		
		Lentinus cladopus
		Lentinus squarrosulus
		KAMSEMPHA
		CHINTSEMPHA
		NAKATASI (Y)
		Phlebopus colossus
		NGOMA WANYANI
MPAFA YAFULU		
MPHAMFA		*Russula nigricans*
		Phaeogyroporus portentosus
		Pulveroboletus aberrans
		Suillus granulatus
		Xerocomus soyeri
		Schizophyllum commune
KALISACHI		
		Clavaria cfr albiramea
		KABVISAZA
		KASANZA
		MUSANJALA
		NAKAMBI (Y)
		Termitomyces robusta

TABLE 2. Chewa classification of the Taxon Bowa (continued)

			Termitomyces eurrhizus
			KACHOFU
			NAKATERESYA (Y)
			UTEMBO (Y)
			UWUMBU
			MAZUMBUKIRA
			KAMBVI
NTANDO			
	KANCHOMBO		*Termitomyces microcarpus*
			MANDA
		UJONJO	
		NYONZWE	*Termitomyces clypeatus*
			NAKASUGULI

Micropsalliota brunneosperma
Psathyrella atroumbonata
Psathyrella candolleana
Mycena sp. JW 697
    CHAMASALA

Termitomyces schimperi
    NYONZWE WANKULU
    USINDA WANKULU (Y)
    LILANGWI
    MANANDARENGWA
    MAZUMBUKIRA
    NAKASOWU (Y)

Unaffiliated taxa
KASALE   *Termitomyces striatus*
CHANJIRA UPYA   *Termitomyces aurantiacus*
NAKATERESYA
UTALE   *Termitomyces* nr *titanicus*
BAMBOMULUZA
KATSOKOMOLE

NGUNDA NGULUWE   *Xerocomus pallidoporus*
MPANDO WAFISI   *Strobilomyces costatispora*
FISI
KASANGA   *Gyroporus castaneus*
KADYA M'LERO   *Lactarius* sp. JW 581
CHING 'AMBE
NYAME
BOWA WAFIRA   *Russula lepida*
KAFIDI   *Russula atropurpurea*
KAMWAZI
MKODZO WAGARU
KAMTHOVA   *Russula delica*
DEGADEGA   *Amanita baccata*
KACHITOSI   *Amanita* nr *calopus*
BONGOLOLO   *Amanita vaginata*
PEZUPEZU   *Amanita fulva*
CHADWALI   *Oudenmansiella radicata*

TABLE 2. Chewa classification of the Taxon Bowa (continued)

NKALANGANJI	*Serulina lachnocephala*
KANJADZA	*Stereopsis hiscens*
KANYAMA	*Cymatoderma dendriticum*
ULANDI (Y)	*Inocybe* sp. BM 74
NKOLAKOLA	*Agaricus campestris*
SMOLO WANKHWALI	*Agaricus* sp. JW 571
MATWE	*Auricularia auricula*
MAKUTUKUTU	
KHUTULANJOBVU	
MANGUNGULI	*Collybia dryophila*
KWASANGA	*Collybia* sp. JW 662

properties of plants for which they could not give a name, for much knowledge is memorate or unformalized. In the latter regard, to suggest that classification extends well beyond what has immediate utility, and that plants and animals have salience simply because they happen to be there within the human life-space, because "curiosity as well as hunger is a basic human drive" is to go to the opposite extreme.[9]

The Chewa do not "see," let alone know and classify most of the fungi which are to be found in their immediate environment, and the same might be said of most human communities. In addition Chewa folk concepts do not constitute logical or inclusive categories, for their folk classifications are inherently flexible, with many ambiguous or overlapping categories. While they do have a deep interest in the naming and categorization of plants (and in this they contrast significantly with the Hill Pandaram) their classifications largely focus *around* prototypical taxa. Hallpike's suggestion (1979: 169–235) that folk classifications are inherently complexive rather than hierarchic, and dominated by concrete associations and "functional entailment" are certainly confirmed by my own studies.

Secondly, although we can accept that there is no necessary one-to-one relationship between utility and nomenclature,[10] nevertheless it is important to recognize that functional criteria are intrinsically linked to taxonomic ordering. As I have tried to indicate above, many Chewa life-form categories cannot be understood in purely morphological terms, and functional categories like **Mwana wa Mphepo** also have a taxonomic relevance. Ethnoscientists have recognised that cultural significance has salience in the differentiation of folk generics (Berlin et al 1974: 99, Berlin 1976: 392–4) and they have recognized too that functional categories exist although these are seen rather misleadingly as nontaxonomic groupings (cf. Hays 1979: 257). But a true understanding of the nature of folk classifications, both in a culturally specific context and in terms of the evolution—the "encoding sequence"—of life-form categories demands that we incorporate into the analysis functional criteria. As anthropologists we should be concerned with systematically exploring the relationship between folk classifications and other aspects of cultural life. To view folk taxonomies simply as taxonomies, abstracted from utilitarian, ecological and cultural concerns, limits our understanding of how human groups related to the natural world.

LITERATURE CITED

Berlin, Brent, D. E. Breedlove and P. H. Raven. 1968. Covert categories and folk taxonomies. Amer. Anthro. 70: 290–99.

———. 1974. Principles of tzeltal plant classification. Academic Press, New York.

Berlin, Brent. 1974. Further notes on Covert Categories and Folk Taxonomies. Amer. Anthro. 76: 327–31.

———. 1976. The concept of rank in ethnobiological classification: some evidence from aguaruna folk botany. Amer. Ethnol. 3: 381–99.

Binns, Blodwen. 1972. Dictionary of plant names in Malawi. Govn. Print. Zomba.

Brokensha, David and W. Riley Bernard. 1980. Mbeere knowledge of their vegetation and its relevance for development. Pp. 113–129 in David Brokensha, D. M. Warren and Oswald Werner, Indigeous Knowledge Systems and Development. Univ. Press of America, Lanham, N.D.

Brown, Cecil H. 1974. Unique beginners and covert categories in folk biological taxonomies. Amer. Anthro. 76: 325–27.

———. 1977. Folk botanical life forms: their universality and growth. Amer. Anthr. 79... 317–42.

———. 1979a. Folk Zoological life-forms: their universality and growth. Amer. Anthro. 81: 791–817.

———. 1979b. Growth and development of folk botanical life forms in the Mayan language family. Amer. Ethnol. 6: 366–85.

Bulmer, Ralph. 1974. Folk Biology in the New Guinea Highlands, Soc. Sc. Inform. 13: 9–28.

———. 1979. Mystical and mundane in Kalam classification of birds, Pp. 57–79 in Roy F. Ellen and David Reason, Classifications in their social context. Academic Press, New York.

Carrington, J. F. 1981. Linguistic pitfalls in Upper Zairean folk taxonomy research. Unpubl. Mss. Nat. Univ. Zaire.

Dentan, Robert K. 1968. The Semai, Holt, Rinehart, New York.

Evans-Pritchard, E. E. 1937. Withcraft, Oracles and Magic amongst the Azande, Clarendon Press, Oxford.

Foley, Daniel J. 1974. Herbs for use and for delight. Dover Publ., New York.

Friedberg, Claudine. 1979. Socially significant plant species and their taxonomic position among the Bunaq of Central Timor, Pp. 81–100 in Roy F. Ellen and R. David Rason. Classification in their social context. Academic Press, New York.

Hallpike, C. R. 1979. The foundations of primitive though. Clarendon Press, Oxford.

Hargreaves, Bruce J. 1976. Killing and curing: succulent use in Chitipa. Cactus and Succulent J. 48: 190–196.

Hays, Terence E. 1976. An empirical method for the identification of covert categories in ethnobiology. Amer. Ethnol. 3: 489–507.

———. 1979. Plant classification and nomenclature in Ndumba, Papua, New Guinea Highlands. Ethnology 18: 253–70.

Hoeg, Ove A. 1983. Country People in Norway and their knowledge of plants. Paper delivered at Plants in Folklore Conference, Univ. Sussex, April 1983.

Hort, Arthur. 1968. Theophrastus: Enquiry into plants. Heinemann, London.

Hunn, Eugene S. 1977. Tzeltal folk zoology: the classification of discontinuities in nature. Academic Press, New York.

————. 1982. The Utilitarian Factor in Folk Biological Classification. Amer. Anthrop. 84: 830–47.

Levi-Strauss, C. 1966. The Savage Mind. Weidenfeld and Nicolson, London.

————. 1969. Totemism. Penguin Books, Harmondsworth.

————. 1972. Structural Anthropology. Penguin Books, Harmondsworth.

Malinowski, B. 1974. Magic, science and religion. Souvenir Press, London. Reprint of 1925 edition.

Mitchell, J. C. 1956. The Yao Village. Manchester Univ. Press, Manchester.

Morris, Brian. 1962. A denizen of the evergreen forest. African Wildlife 16: 117–21.

————. 1964. Mammals of Zoa Estate, Cholo, Nyasaland J. 17: 71–78.

————. 1967. Wild flowers of Mlanje Mountain. African Wildlife 21: 71–77, 152–57.

————. 1970. The Orchids of Malawi. Society of Malawi.

————. 1976. Whither the Savage Mind? Notes on the natural taxonomies of a hunting and gathering people. Man (NS) 11: 542–47.

————. 1980. Folk Classifications. Nyala 6: 83–93.

————. 1983. The Macrofungi of Malawi. Unpubl. Mss. on deposit with author.

Ngubane, Harriet. 1977. Body and Mind in Zulu Medicine. Academic Press, London.

Richards, Audrey I. 1969. Land, labour and diet in Northern Rhodesia (1939). Oxford Univ. Press.

Schoffeleers, J. M. 1968. Symbolic and social aspects of spirit worship among the Mang'anja. Unpubl. Ph.D. Thesis, Oxford Univ.

Strathern, Marilyn. 1980. No nature, no culture: The Hagen Case, Pp. 174–222 in C. P. MacCormack and M. Strathern Nature, Culture and Gender. Cambridge Univ. Press.

Sturtevant, W. C. 1964. Studies in Ethnoscience. Amer. Anthro. Pp. 39–61 in Culture and Cognition (1974) edited by J. W. Berry and P. R. Dasen. Methuen, London.

Tambiah, S. J. 1969. Animals are good to think and good to prohibit. Ethnology 8: 424–59.

Turner, Victor. 1967. The forest of symbols. Cornell Univ. Press, Ithaca, New York.

Williamson, Jessie. 1941. Nyasaland native foods. Nyasaland Times.

————. 1975. Useful plants of Malawi. Univ. Malawi, Zomba.

Witkowski, Stanley R. and Cecil H. Brown. 1978. Lexical Universals Ann. Rev. Anthro. 7: 427–51.

Witkowski, Stanley R., Cecil H. Brown and Paul K. Chase. 1981. Where do tree terms come from? Man (NS) 16: 1–14.

NOTES

1. Ethnobotanical research in Malawi was undertaken during the year 1979–80 and was supported by an SSRC grant for which I am grateful. My own ethnobiological researches in Malawi go back more than twenty years, for during seven years' residence in the Thyolo and Mulanje districts (1958–65) I collected a lot of data on the folk names and cultural uses of plants and small mammals. (cf. Morris 1962, 1964, 1967). I am thus fairly fluent in Chichewa. During my year's residence I became a student 'novitiate' to several *asinganga* (doctor-diviners) and market herbalists, and altogether I worked closely with about twenty-five informant friends, ten of whom were women. In the drafting of the present paper I am appreciative of the help given by Willard Van Asdall and Pat Caplan.

2. It is beyond the scope of this present paper to offer ethnographic material on the wider culture of the peasant communities of Malawi. For some useful background material on the Yao and Chewa-speaking peoples cf Mitchell 1956, Schoffeleers 1968.

3. Tambiah's (1969) interesting discussion of animal categories in Thailand notes that chickens and ducks are not considered to be birds *(Nog)*, and that many categories are almost defined in terms of edibility.

4. How these ethnographic facts fit into the encoding sequence in the evolution of zoological life forms, as postulated by Cecil Brown and his associates (Witkowski and Brown 1978: 437–8, Brown 1979a) it is difficult to assess. But clearly **Nyama** is a life-form category of the same taxonomic status as **Njoka** and **Mbalame** (under no circumstances would **Njoka** be described as a kind of **Nyama**), and it is defined by cultural criteria for which Brown's perspective finds no place, at least in his discussion of animal categories. Moreover, to situate 'animal' beyond or outside the schema obscures some interesting developments that have occurred in the evolution folk taxonomies, and the shift of focus from utility to morphology.

5. The polysemous nature of plant categories is widespread (cf Richards 1969: 232, Bulmer 1974: 20, Ngubane 1977: 22). In a recent paper, Witkowski and his associates (1981) note that the wood/tree polysemy is found in a variety of languages. Whether the loss of this polysemy is *directly* linked to increased societal complexity is difficult to say, for a hunter-gathering community like the Hill Pandaram has three morphological categories—**Maram** (trees and woody plants), **Valli** (creepers and lianas) and **Chedi** (ferns and herbaceous plants) (Morris 1976: 546), that are very similar to those described elsewhere (cf. Berlin et al 1974, Berlin 1976: 385, Hays 1979) while a much more technologically complex society like the Yao has but two life forms (excluding the fungi), the primary category **Mtera,** which like the Chewa **Mtengo,** is polysemous and extremely wide in scope. Brown's study of the development of Mayan botanical life-forms (1979) indicates that almost all life-form categories derive initially from functional polysemous concepts, and yet, surprisingly, in an earlier paper (1977: 320) he appears to *define* these categories as non-functional.

6. The Anglo-Saxon word "wort" originally meant 'root,' and was used to designated many plants that had medicinal properties. Many English plant names still carry the term, e.g., St. John's Wort, Figwort, Mugwort, Ragwort. It has been suggested that it was a virtual synonym for "herb," a concept that did not originally refer to small herbaceous plants, i.e., it was not a morphological category at all, but to any plant that had utility as medicine or for culinary purposes (Foley 1974: 187). Many common herbs, of course, are shrubs (Dogrose), trees (Wych Hazel) or climbers (Nightshade). Early English folk classifications also seem, therefore, to have a functional bias. In an interesting paper, Hoeg (1983) has described how country people in Norway are able to identify ferns by the feel of their rhizomes, and in Gerard's classic 'Herbal' (1597) the illustrations of the plants all show the structure of the roots, sometimes, as with the common arum, without the flowers.

7. With respect to the present paper I should particularly like to express my thanks to Chenitta Selemani and her sister Esmie, Benson Zuwani, Kitty Kunamano, Rosebey Mponda and Salimu Chinyangala for help and instruction on those aspects of Malawi cultural life relating to *bowa.* During the year—and in a subsequent short visit—I made water-color sketches, and collected data and specimens of over five hundred fungi. The specimens are deposited in herbaria located at Kew and Zomba. Material for this paper is based on these collections, and draws on my larger study on the Macrofungi of Malawi (in press). For the identification of my specimens I am grateful to Dr. David Pegler of the Herbarium, Royal Botanical Garden, Kew, England.

8. Importantly when categorizing and describing fungi reference is continually made to the three 'primary' colors, names *-era,* light or white, *-da,* dark or black, and *-fira,* covering all the fiery colours as well as yellow. These are basic to the Chewa and have important symbolic connotations.

9. In a recent paper, Hunn (1982) has modified his earlier views and has, like myself, although in a more substantive theoretical manner, come to stress the 'utilitarian factor' in folk classifications.

10. In a more recent study of the Aguaruna Indians of Peru, Berlin (1976: 393) suggests that about one third of the plants known to these people are conceptually recognized but lack cultural importance.

CHAPTER FIVE

General Plant Categories in Thompson (Nlaka'pamux) and Lillooet (Stl'atl'imx), Two Interior Salish Languages of British Columbia

NANCY J. TURNER

INTRODUCTION

Folk biological classification has been a major focus of research by ethnoscientists over the past two decades, stimulated largely by the pioneering investigations of Brent Berlin and his colleagues (cf. Berlin 1972; Berlin, Breedlove and Raven 1966, 1973, 1974). On the basis of their research in folk biotaxonomies they have identified five universal ethnobiological ranks arranged hierarchically and containing mutually exclusive taxa. The most general, all-inclusive category is the "unique beginner" (ie., "plant," in the case of folk plant taxonomies). Categories of "life form" rank are the next most inclusive. They are described as being ". . . invariably few in number, ranging from five to ten, and among them are included the majority of all named taxa of lesser rank . . . Life form taxa are labeled by linguistic expressions which are analyzed lexically as *primary lexemes* . . . and may be illustrated by the classes named by words such as *tree, vine, bird, grass, mammal,* and so forth." (Berlin, Breedlove and Raven 1974: 25–26).

Included within life form taxa are taxa of "generic" rank, and within some of these are contrast sets of "specific" taxa, which, in turn, may include "varietal" taxa. A sixth rank, comprised of "intermediate" taxa, is occasionally interposed between life form and generic taxa. However, these are said to be rare and not usually linguistically labeled (Berlin, Breedlove and Raven, 1974: 26). The various taxonomic ranks, as perceived by Berlin and his colleagues, are shown schematically in Fig. 1. "Lifeform" classes in folk biology have been further investigated by Cecil Brown and his co-workers (cf. Brown 1977; Witkowski, Brown and Chase 1981; Brown 1984; Brown 1986). From surveys of folk classification in 188 languages for plants and 144 languages for animals, Brown has postulated a number of cross-language uniformities in the linguistic encoding of life form taxa (Brown 1984).

Some problems with the "life forms" and other biological taxonomic categories as perceived by Berlin and Brown and their colleagues have been pointed out by Hunn (1982) and Randall and Hunn (1984). Hunn and Randall argue that neither Berlin nor Brown adequately accounts for the influence of cultural importance of organisms on

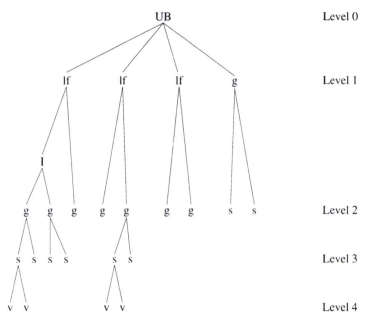

Fig. 1. Schematic diagram showing hierarchical arrangement of folk biological categories as described by Berlin and his co-workers (after Berlin, Breedlove and Raven 1974: 26). (UB - Unique Beginner; lf - life form; I - Intermediate; g - generic; s - specific; v - varietal.)

folk biological classifications. Furthermore, their descriptions, they maintain, do not reflect the real complexity of folk taxonomies, even at a general level.

In this paper I will describe and compare the most inclusive plant classes—those at the level of Berlin's "life form" and "unique beginner" ranks—within the linguistic and cognitive systems of Lillooet and Thompson, language groups of the Interior division of the Salish language family. Additionally, I will discuss the characteristics of Lillooet and Thompson general plant categories in relation to the universal features postulated by Berlin and Brown and their co-workers, with particular attention to the criticisms of these schemes made by Hunn and Randall.

This work is part of a broader study comparing many aspects of Lillooet and Thompson ethnobotany. These language groups are not only closely related linguistically, but also geographically, ecologically and culturally. Their geographical proximity is shown in Fig. 2. Their traditional territories extend over a broad and diverse area, encompassing the same range of biogeoclimatic zones. Hence, both groups have had access to the same, relatively diverse flora. Both languages are divided into "Upper" and "Lower" dialect regions, which correspond roughly with the ecological division between the hot, dry interior and the cooler, moister regions closer to the Pacific coast. Both groups are classed within the Plateau culture area, although both, especially their "Lower" divisions, exhibit influences of the adjacent Northwest Coast culture area. Both had traditional economies based on hunting, fishing and gathering.

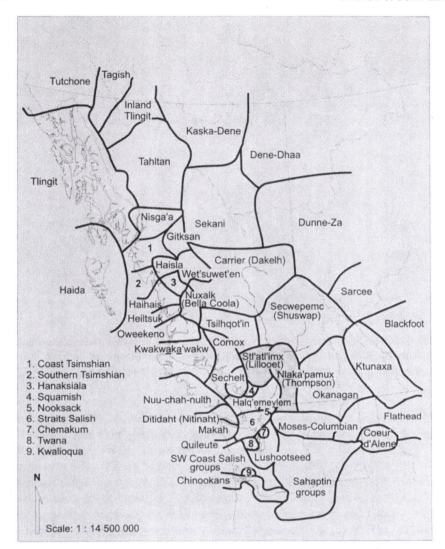

1. Coast Tsimshian
2. Southern Tsimshian
3. Hanaksiala
4. Squamish
5. Nooksack
6. Straits Salish
7. Chemakum
8. Twana
9. Kwalioqua

Scale: 1 : 14 500 000

Fig. 2. Map of First Nations of Northwestern North America showing Stl'atl'imx (Lillooet) and Nlaka'pamux (Thompson) traditional territories (Drawn by D. Loewen).

Except for native tobacco agriculture was not practiced until the advent of Europeans, although controlled burning for the maintenance of desirable habitats for certain food species was.

Data for this study were obtained through interviews with native speakers of Lillooet and Thompson conducted over a period of many years—since 1972 for Lillooet and 1973 for Thompson (see Appendix 1). A preliminary description of Lillooet folk plant taxa was included in Turner (1974). However, additional research and recent discussions of folk biological systems in the literature have contributed to an elaboration and refinement of the original descriptions of major plant categories in Lillooet in the present paper. Thompson folk plant classes were discussed in Turner *et al.* (1984).

Several linguists specializing in these native languages collaborated on this project, including Jan van Eijk, Randy Bouchard, Laurence C. Thompson, M. Terry Thompson and Steven Egesdal. Interviews were in English; virtually all the native elders speak English as well as their own language. However, plants were usually referred to by their native, rather than English, names, or simply by using growing or freshly picked specimens of various plants as samples to be discussed. General plant taxa were identified and inventoried by means of informal conversations about plants, and through discussions of applied terminology and more formal questions about the relationships and attributes of individual plant species and folk generic level taxa.[1]

The Lillooet and Thompson communities, like other native communities in British Columbia, have become largely assimilated linguistically and culturally to the dominant Euro-american English-speaking population. Though many aspects of native culture remain, these have been significantly influenced by the "White" culture. Few members of the younger generations of native people are able to speak their traditional languages fluently, and even elders may not recall some of the more obscure or specialized vocabulary. Inevitably, cognitive systems have changed. Nevertheless, their underlying structure, as reflected in language, remains. Furthermore, the changes themselves, and the ways in which new items and concepts have been incorporated, are also a valid and productive subject for research. In the case of folk plant taxonomies, studying how existing folk taxa have been altered and new taxa developed with the influx of exotic plants and plant products can reveal insights into the evolution of folk classification systems.

THE "PLANT" CONCEPT IN LILLOOET AND THOMPSON

Typical of northwestern North American languages (cf. Turner 1974; Turner and Bell 1971, 1973; Turner, Bouchard and Kennedy 1981; Turner and Efrat 1982; Turner *et al.* 1990) and in accord with Berlin's general principles (Berlin 1972: 78; Brown 1984: 4) neither Lillooet nor Thompson has a free-standing term denoting any and all members of the plant kingdom. "Plant" is nevertheless a psychologically valid category in Lillooet and Thompson. Our native consultants showed no hesitancy in discussing plants as a discrete group, to the exclusion of animals and inanimate objects. One might argue that the "plant" concept was acquired through contact with English-speaking peoples. However, the existence of suffixes and descriptive term in these languages with semantic ranges encompassing a broad spectrum of "plants" suggests otherwise.[2]

In both languages, there is a suffix which may be variously translated as "plant," "bush" or "tree." In Lillooet the suffix is -*aȝ́*, alternating with -*ɬəp* (var. -*ɬp*) or -*aɬp* in terms most likely borrowed from neighboring languages. This latter suffix is cognate with the Thompson suffix -*eɬp* and its variants. Examples of plant names containing these suffixes are shown in Table 1. In some instances, as with fruiting plants, the

TABLE 1. Examples of plant names in Lillooet and Thompson incorporating "plant" suffixes.

Lillooet*:

Plant name	English gloss	Corresponding species
pún-ɬəp		Rocky Mountain juniper
cíkcəkt-aż		common juniper
məlín-ɬəp		subalpine fir, grand fir
ćk-aż	'pine-seed plant'	whitebark pine
qʷlít-aż (P)	? 'pitch-plant'	lodgepole pine
ƛ̓əmq̓-áż		western yew
təx̌ʷʔac-áż/təx̌ʷʔac-áɬp	'bow-plant'	western yew
ləx̌-áż (F)		"cut-grass"
níx̌-nəx̌-aż (P)		'cutting-plant'
ƛ̓áqʷam-aż		"timbergrass"
síć-ɬəp		vine maple
káw-kw-aż		big sagebrush
t̓aqʔ-aż		salal
pácʔ-aż	'digging-stick-plant'	oceanspray

* Unless otherwise specified, names occur throughout the languages; in Lillooet, F denotes Fraser River dialect only, P, Pemberton dialect only.

Thompson:

Plant name	English gloss	Corresponding species
p̓əšk̓eʔ-éɬp	'hummingbird-plant'	Indian paintbrush, shrubby penstemon
məckʷ-éɬp	'blackcap-plant'	blackcap
s-q̓ʷoq̓ʷy̓ep-éɬp	'strawberry-plant'	wild strawberry
q̓ʷuys-éɬp	'silverberry-bark-plant'	silverberry
ʔik-eɬp-éɬp	'kinnikinnick-plant-plant'	twinflower
sćum̓-mn-éɬp	'sucking-substance-plant'	orange honeysuckle
y̓əɬyeti̓ʔtń-éɬp	'cough/cold-plant'	pussytoes
spećn-éɬp	'twine-plant'	Indian hemp
qʷn-éɬp		Indian hellebore
qʷiʔt-éɬp		lodgepole pine
p̓əp̓uʔń-éɬp	'flatulating-plant'	pasture wormwood, rabbit-brush
pún-ɬp		Rocky Mountain juniper, sometimes common juniper
ćq̓-áɬp	'sticky-plant'	Douglas-fir
xʷik̓ʷestn-éɬp	'scrubber-plant'	western hemlock
ƛ̓áqʷ-eɬp		pine grass

"plant" suffix is added to the name for the fruit or other culturally significant plant part to form the name for the whole plant [e.g. Lillooet *q̇an* - black hawthorn[3] fruit, *q̇án-aż*—black hawthorn bush; *(ṣ)pṣúṣ*—bitter cherry fruit, *pṣúṣ-aż*—bitter cherry tree; or, alternately *s*ʔ*íẇx*ʷ—bitter cherry bark (when removed from tree for use in wrapping implements and basket decoration), ʔ*íẇx*ʷ*-aż*—bitter cherry tree]. In other cases, the suffix is applied to a term which indicates an application of the plant or some other significant association (e.g. Lillooet *pác*ʔ*-aż*—oceanspray; cf. *páca*ʔ 'digging-stick'[4]). In a few terms, the stems are unanalysable (e.g., Lillooet *cátaw-aż*— red cedar, *cáx̌-aż*—Sitka spruce; Thompson *q*ʷ*n-éłp*—Indian hellebore). In Lillooet, about 50 percent of all plant names of generic rank include the "plant" suffix *-aż* or the equivalent borrowed suffixes, *-łap/-ałp* (Turner, 1974: 31). In Thompson, about 20 percent of the plant names incorporate the "plant" suffix *-ełp,* either optionally or mandatorily. It is notable that the names including this suffix pertain to a broad range of plants—mostly trees and shrubs, but also denoting some low herbaceous plants such as pine grass ("timbergrass") and wild strawberry. The existence of a "plant" suffix is widespread in northwestern North American languages.[5]

When additional terminological data are considered, the reality of the "plant" category is reinforced. For example, there are numerous morphological terms for different parts of plants that are exclusive to the domain. These include words for "leaf," "root," "branch," "stem," "shoot" and "seed" in both Lillooet and Thompson (J. van Eijk, pers. comm. 1985; Turner *et al.* 1990). These terms are applied to plant species the names of which include the "plant" suffix, to those which do not, and to plants which are unnamed. Hence, the existence of a covert "plant" category is implied by the range of application of anatomical terminology. Furthermore, as discussed later, many of the generic level plant names in Thompson which do not contain the "plant" suffix incorporate terms for major plant categories, especially those for "low herbaceous, broad-leaved plants" and "flowers." This reinforces at a basic level the notion of these plants belonging to larger groupings and ultimately, by virtue of overlapping major classes, to an all-inclusive category, "plant."

Are fungi and non-vascular plants such as mosses and lichens considered as "plants" in the traditional Lillooet and Thompson worldview? Contemporary native consultants have no difficulty in categorizing them as such, but in neither language is there any common linguistic element, such as the "plant" suffix, linking these organisms to other plants. Because they grow and do not move around, their "plantness" may have been perceived even in aboriginal times.

"LIFE FORM" LEVEL PLANT CATEGORIES

Below the "plant" class, the most inclusive labeled plant categories for Lillooet and Thompson are several roughly equivalent to the "life forms" of Berlin and Brown. These are listed in Tables 2 and 3. As might be expected, the names for and ranges of the major plant categories of Lillooet and Thompson are quite similar.

In Lillooet, the major named categories include: "trees (especially coniferous trees)," "grasses and grass-like plants" and/or "hay," "low, herbaceous broad-leaved

plants of little cultural significance," "flowers," "berries/fruits," "mosses and moss-
like plants" and "mushrooms and fungi." Additionally, "bushes" are generally recognized as a discrete category, but are not really named as such. Plants with culturally
significant (ie., edible) roots and underground parts are also conceptually discrete,
even though there is no inclusive Lillooet term for these (Turner 1974: 41).

In Thompson, the major named categories are: "large trees (especially coniferous
trees)," "tall bushes and small deciduous trees," "grasses and grass-like plants," "low
herbaceous broad-leaved plants of little cultural significance," "flowers," "berries/
fruits," "mosses and moss-like plants" and "mushrooms and fungi." "Vines" as a category in Thompson apparently originally included only two or three species, but has
been extended. A category, "roots and underground parts," though unnamed, is also
recognized. Each of these categories will be discussed in some detail, both in respect
to its counterparts in related languages and to its corresponding "universal life form"
status.

In both Lillooet and Thompson, the "tree" category comes closest to exhibiting
the features of a life form (cf. Brown 1982: 5–6). It is subordinate to the unique

TABLE 2. General plant classes in Lillooet.

Lillooet name	Approx. English equivalent	Examples of incl. taxa
s-ɣáp ('that which is upright')	"tree"	Douglas-fir; bitter cherry; cottonwood; ponderosa pine
(s)láqəm/s-cápəż	"hay"/"grass"	bunchgrass; timothy; giant wild rye
s-waʔp-úlṁəxʷ ('ground-growth/hair')	"low, herbaceous, broad-leaved plants of low cultural importance"	mullein; plantains; lambs' quarters; twinflower
s-p̓áq̓əm (cf. *p̓aq̓* 'white/light-coloured')	"flowers"	self-heal; wild rose; *Penstemon serrulatus*
s-q̓ʷəl ('ripe/cooked'); *-usaʔ* ('round/oval object')	"berries/fruits"	saskatoon; salal; black huckleberry; thimbleberry
páʔsəm	"mosses and moss-like plants"	*Rhytideadelphus triquetrus; Dicranum scoparium; Cladina* spp.; *Selaginella wallacei*
s-q̓əṁs (P);	"mushrooms and fungi"	pine mushroom; "cotton-wood mushroom"; shaggy mane; puffballs
unnamed	"edible roots and underground parts"	tiger lily; chocolate lily; water parsnip; wild onions

TABLE 3. General plant classes in Thompson.

Thompson name	Approx. English equivalent	Examples of incl. taxa
s-γép	"large trees"	Douglas-fir; red cedar; pines; cottonwood
múyx	"tall bushes and small deciduous trees"	mountain alder; Rocky Mountain maple; shrubby willows; oceanspray
s-yíqm	"grasses/hay and grass-like plants"	bunchgrass; reed canary grass; giant wild rye; "timbergrass"
*s-tuyt-úyṁx*ʷ ('ground-growth/hair')	"low, herbaceous, broad-leaved plants of low cultural importance"	stonecrops; plantains; vetch; lamb's quarters
s-ṗáq̓m	"flowers"	calypso; buttercup; arnica; garden flowers
s-q̓ʷíyt/ s-q̓ʷit-éłp/ -úseʔ ('round-object')	"berries/fruits"	huckleberries; saskatoon; soapberry; strawberry
qʷzém	"mosses and moss-like plants"	*Hylocomium splendens; Eurhynchium oreganum; Lobaria* spp.; *Lycopodium clavatum*
q̓áṁes (Lower)/ *məƛ̓qíʔ* (Nicola)	"mushrooms and fungi"	pine mushroom; "cottonwood mushroom"; shaggy mane; oyster mushroom
(q̓əc̓)q̓əc̓-usníni ('woven-as-it-grows')	"large vines"	white clematis; orange honeysuckle (sometimes); grape; English ivy
unnamed	"edible roots and underground parts"	wild onions; yellow avalance lily; spring beauty; bitterroot; balsamroot

beginner and is labeled by a "primary lexeme" (Berlin, Breedlove and Raven 1973: 215). This lexeme is complex, however, since it is analyzable, explicitly referring to the standing form of the class members (lit. 'that-which-is-put-upright') (J. van Eijk, pers. comm., 1985; Thompson and Thompson, 1996; see also Table 4). The "tree" class in each language is polytypic, including a substantial number of "generic" taxa which are mutually exclusive and mostly labeled by primary lexemes, many of which are analyzable. It is defined, apparently, by a small set of morphological features (ie., large, upright, woody), and can be said to be "general purpose" (Brown 1982: 14). However, the "tree" category in Thompson and Lillooet did not follow the most common development pattern as described by Berlin (1972: 71).

One might suppose, in looking at Lillooet in isolation, that the "tree" category developed through expansion of reference, since, in Lillooet, Douglas-fir (Fig. 3), a highly salient species, is called *s ɣap-ʔúl* 'real/original tree.' One could envision the development of the "life form" name from a generic based on the premises of Berlin (1972: 71) and Brown (1984: 60).

However, when terms for Douglas-fir in neighboring Interior Salish languages are considered, the development of the more general life form name through expansion of reference in Lillooet seems unlikely. The Thompson, Shuswap and Okanagan-Colville terms for "tree" are related, and in all three cases, as well as in Columbian, where the 'tree' term is unrelated, their names for Douglas-fir are different and unrelated to their terms for "tree" (see Table 4). In view of this, as well as the fact that the

Fig. 3. Douglas-fir, the "type" for the "tree" category in Lillooet.

TABLE 4. "Tree" terms and names for Douglas-fir in British Columbia Interior Salish Languages.*

Language	"Tree"	Douglas-fir	Reference
Lillooet	*s-γáp* ('that which is upright')**	*s-γap-ʔúl* ('real/original tree')	J. van Eijk, pers. comm. 1985
Thompson	*s-γép* ('upright/pole')	*c̓q̓-áɬp* ('sticky-plant')	Turner et al. 1984
Shuswap	*tsegáp* *(cəγə́p)*	*tsk'alhp* *(cq̓-éɬp)*	Palmer 1975: 44, 52
Okanagan-Colville	*tsegíp/tsiyíp* *(cəγíp/ciyíp)*	*tsk'ilhp* *(cq̓-iɬp)*	Turner, Bouchard and Kennedy 1981: 156

* Additionally, D. Kinkade (pers. comm., 1986) provides the following information for Columbian, an Interior Salish language of Washington. The singular term for tree is *ʔac-páx̌* ('single upright object'), the plural term is unrelated: *ʔas-c̓ə́lc̓əl* ('plural upright objects'). The latter also sometimes means 'brush, bushes.' The Columbian term for Douglas-fir is *c̓q̓-áɬp*, cognate with Thompson, Shuswap and Okanagan-Colville.

** Cf. root *γip* 'to grow,' *γəp* 'to stand up,"'; hence *s-γáp* means 'the grower,' or 'the standing-up one' (J. van Eijk, pers. comm. 1986).

term for "tree" in both Lillooet and Thompson is analyzable and implies an upright habit (as it does in Sahaptin, Flathead and Columbian, among other languages—Randall and Hunn 1984: 341; Hart 1974: 36; D. Kinkade, pers. comm., 1986), it seems more probable that the Lillooet term for Douglas-fir was derived from the "tree" term, through restriction of reference.[6] This would imply that the "life form" term "tree" is chronologically older than the "generic" term "Douglas-fir" in the Lillooet language. However, that does not mean that the category "tree" is older than the generic-level category "Douglas-fir." Rather, it is likely that Douglas-fir had an earlier name in Lillooet, perhaps cognate with the other Interior Salish terms, and the present name, 'real/original tree,' replaced the earlier name.

There is an additional piece of evidence to support the second supposition. Lillooet has a term, *c̓q̓áq̓ləp*, which is a reduplicated form of *c̓q̓-aɬp*, a form cognate to the Thompson name for Douglas-fir. While *c̓q̓-aɬp* itself does not occur in the Lillooet vocabulary, the presence of its diminutive form, meaning "young tree" and in particular "young Douglas-fir,"[7] implies the former existence of the more basic term (J. van Eijk, pers. comm. 1986). Van Eijk postulates that the term *c̓q̓-aɬp* may have fallen into disuse in Lillooet as a result of a word taboo, to be supplanted by the "real tree" epithet. Douglas-fir plays an important role in Lillooet and Thompson ritual and religious traditions (Turner 1986).

Incidentally, the Lillooet and Thompson application of "tree" has some ambiguity. Most of the core species in the taxon, those that would be exemplary, are large coniferous species, but on closer questioning most native speakers would include black cottonwood, which grows throughout Lillooet and Thompson territory, and red alder, trembling aspen and broad-leaved maple, where these occur. Marginal species would be Rocky Mountain maple and mountain alder, which might also be categorized as large bushes.

The "bushes and small deciduous trees" category in Thompson is perceptually more distinct than the corresponding Lillooet category. In the former it is named (*múyx*), whereas in the latter it is only implied by application of the cognate term *múlx* ("stick") (also applied to "trees"), and its reduplicated plural forms, *məl-múlx,* or *məl-məmləx,* ("bushes/woods/underbrush") to dense thickets of any type of bushes. The Thompson plural form, *mi-múyx,* also pertains to "woods/bushy places," but the Thompson *múyx,* unlike Lillooet *múlx,* seems to be used as a class name and is actually incorporated into the generic-level names for some shrubs. It is possible, however, that its meaning has simply tended to conform with "bush" within historical times, as a form of semantic convergence with English.[8] In a similar vein, there also may well be a tendency in Lillooet for the term *múlx* "stick" to assume the semantic role of a class name for "bush." Future speakers of Lillooet, if the language persists, may use it as such.

Like the "tree" category, the Thompson *múyx* category poses an interesting problem in the origin and evolution of general categories. In the Okanagan-Colville and Shuswap languages, the cognate terms, *múlx* and *múlux* (or *múlx*) respectively (Turner, Bouchard and Kennedy 1981: 134; Palmer 1975: 68; Kuipers 1974: 150), are generic names for black cottonwood. The term *múlx* is also used for cottonwood by the Nicola Valley Thompson, having been borrowed from Okanagan-Colville (Mabel Joe, pers. comm., 1984). In a number of southwestern American languages, the name for "cottonwood" is polysemous with the name for "tree" (cf. Trager 1939), but in Interior Salish, the relationship is more complicated because it transcends the boundaries of related but distinct languages, as well as the boundaries of two different major taxa, "tree" and "bush." Perhaps this situation reflects an original perceptual dichotomy between "evergreen woody plants" and "broad-leaved woody plants," rather than between "tree" and "bush." Expansion of reference—from "cottonwood" to "bush"— may well have occurred but if so, this semantic shift must have taken place in proto-Salish, while these languages were diverging. It seems equally plausible that the names for black cottonwood in Okanagen-Colville and Shuswap developed through restriction of reference from a proto-Salish term for "wood/stick" in the same manner as the Lillooet name for Douglas-fir must have been derived from the more general term of "tree." Brown (1984: 60) contends that in most languages the life-form name for "tree" derived historically from a term for "wood" or "firewood," which would have been more salient than "tree" in early cultures. In this case, "stick" may have had higher salience than "cottonwood" in a proto-Salish language, and the latter term have been derived from the former. Such a conjecture would be difficult to prove.

The "grasses and grass-like plants" categories in Lillooet and Thompson, like the "bush" classes, are subtly different, though roughly equivalent. They, too, seem to be diverging semantically. Most Lillooet speakers of the Fraser River dialect clearly distinguish *s-ləqəm* "hay" from *s-ċapəż* "grass" (J. van Eijk, pers. comm., 1985).[9] (In

Fig. 4. Bluebunch wheat grass, or "bunchgrass," the original "type" for "hay" and "grass/hay" in the interior dialects of Lillooet and Thompson respectively. Today its role is largely supplanted by sweet-clovers, alfalfa and hay crop grasses.

Fraser River Lillooet, *ləqm-am* means 'to make hay.') However, in the Pemberton Lillooet dialect, though *s-ləqəm* is glossed primarily as "hay," it is used for "any grass/grass-like plant" since no other term for "grass" is known. Still, *s-ləqəm* is now exemplified by introduced hay crop species such as timothy and red-top, as viewed by at least one Pemberton speaker (A. Peters, pers. comm., 1984). In Thompson, the cognate term *syíq-m* applies to "grass" or "hay" interchangeably.[10]

Bluebunch wheat grass ("bunchgrass"), a species of high salience in the dry Interior of British Columbia, is usually considered the prototype for "hay" and "grass/hay" respectively in Fraser River Lillooet and Thompson (Fig. 4). Traditionally it is known as excellent fodder for deer, and in historic times, has been valued as a hay crop and grazing species for horses and cattle (Steedman 1930: 515; Turner, Bouchard and Kennedy 1981: 53). It has been called *s-ləqəm-ʔúl* ('real/typical hay') in Fraser River Lillooet, but younger speakers of the language today (eg., Desmond Peters, pers. comm., 1985) apply this term to alfalfa and the sweet-clovers, which are not grass-like at all; both are in the legume family. In Thompson, the cognate form *s-yíqmʔúy* ('real/typical grass/hay') also refers to bluebunch wheat grass. This species does not occur in the coastward parts of the Lillooet and Thompson territories and was not known to the Pemberton Lillooet people.

"Bunchgrass" is also known as 'real hay' to some Shuswap speakers (Deadman's Creek) (Kuipers 1974: 166), and in Okanagan-Colville it has two names, one cognate with Shuswap "hay/grass," and the other polysemous with the general Okanagan-

TABLE 5. "Grass" and "hay" terms and names for bunchgrass in British Columbia Interior Salish Languages.*

Language	"Grass"/"Hay"	Bluebunch wheat grass	Reference
Lillooet	"hay" - *s-lə́qəm* "grass" *s-čəpáž*	*s-ləqəm-ʔúl* (F) ('real hay')	J. van Eijk, pers. comm. 1985
Thompson	"grass/hay" - *s-yíqm*	*s-yíqm ʔúy*	Turner et al. 1984
Shuswap	"hay/grass" - *s-t'yéʔ*; or *-ést'ye* (suffix)	*s-t'yeʔ-úʔy* (DC)	Kuipers 1974: 63, 166
Okanagan-Colville	"grass/hay" *swupúla7xw* ('ground' growth/ hair')	*st'iyí7;* or sometimes *swupúla7xw*	Turner, Bouchard and Kennedy 1981: 52

* F = Fraser River Lillooet dialect; DC - Deadman's Creek Shuswap dialect.

Colville term for "grass, hay or grass-like plant," (see later discussion on "low . . . broad-leaved plants . . .") (Turner, Bouchard and Kennedy 1981: 52–53). The various names for "grass," "hay," and "bluebunch wheat grass" in the four British Columbia Interior Salish languages are shown in Table 5.

What is the origin of the general class names for "hay" in Lillooet and "grass/hay" in Thompson? Have they developed in the manner proposed by Berlin (1972: 71) as a common method for derivation of general taxon names, through expansion of reference from the "generic" name of a highly salient species (ie., "bluebunch wheat grass")? Or, conversely, did they exist prior to the name for the generic "type"? In this case, I would suggest the former developmental sequence, based on the existence of the name 'real/typical grass/hay' for bluebunch wheat grass in three out of four of the British Columbia Interior Salish languages, and on the specific application of the cognate term for Shuswap 'grass/hay' to bluebunch wheat grass in the fourth language, Okanagan-Colville. A tentative sequence of encoding is proposed in Fig. 5.

In Fraser River Lillooet, both the "hay" and "grass" categories are largely "empty," since each includes only a very few members named at the generic level. Hence, neither would qualify as a *bona fide* life form according to the criteria of Berlin and Brown. In Thompson, there are several (approximately ten) named terminal taxa incorporated in "grass/hay," hence it qualifies as a true life form.

The category, "low, herbaceous, broad-leaved plants of little cultural importance," is more or less equivalent in Lillooet and Thompson, although in Lillooet the term *s-waʔp-úlmex*ʷ is used only in a general way, while in Thompson the corresponding term, *stuyt-úymx*ʷ, is often incorporated in the names for particular kinds of plants (see Table 6 for examples).

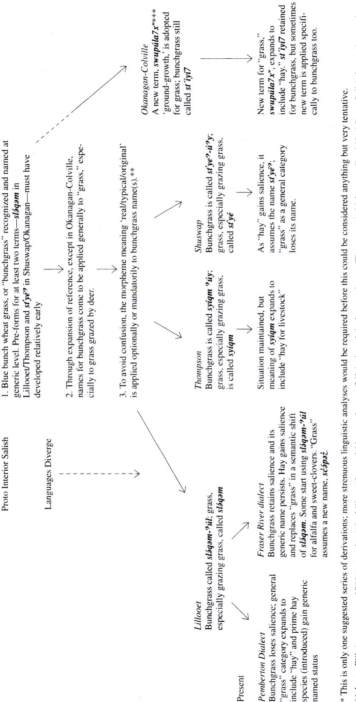

Proto Interior Salish

Languages Diverge

1. Blue bunch wheat grass, or "bunchgrass" recognized and named at generic level. Pre-forms for at least two terms—sɬáqəm in Lillooet/Thompson and sƛ'ye? in Shuswap/Okanagan—must have developed relatively early

2. Through expansion of reference, except in Okanagan-Colville, names for bunchgrass come to be applied generally to "grass," especially to grass grazed by deer.

3. To avoid confusion, the morpheme meaning 'real/typical/original' is applied optionally or mandatorily to bunchgrass name(s).**

Okanagan-Colville
A new term, **swupúla7x*****, 'ground-growth,' is adopted for grass; bunchgrass still called st'íyi7

New term for "grass," **swupúla7x***, expands to include "hay." **sƛ'íyi7** retained for bunchgrass, but sometimes new term is applied specifically to bunchgrass too.

Shuswap
Bunchgrass is called **sƛ'ye?-ú?y**; grass, especially grazing grass, called **sƛ'yé**

As "hay" gains salience, it assumes the name **sƛ'ye?**. "grass" as a general category loses its name.

Thompson
Bunchgrass is called **sγíqəm·?úy**; grass, especially grazing grass, is called **sγíqəm**

Situation maintained, but meaning of **sγíqəm** expands to include "hay for livestock"

Lillooet
Bunchgrass called **sɬáqəm-?úl**; grass, especially grazing grass, called **sɬáqəm**

Fraser River dialect
Bunchgrass retains salience and its generic name persists. Hay gains salience and replaces "grass" in a semantic shift of **sɬáqəm**. Some start using **sɬáqəm-?úl** for alfalfa and sweet-clovers. "Grass" assumes a new name, **scápəɬ.**

Present

Pemberton Dialect
Bunchgrass loses salience; general "grass" category expands to include "hay," and prime hay species (introduced) gain generic named status

* This is only one suggested series of derivations; more strenuous linguistic analyses would be required before this could be considered anything but very tentative.

** J. van Eijk (pers. comm. 1986) notes that "the Lillooet form of this morpheme, **-?úl**, is the original one, whereas Thompson (which generally shifted Proto-Salish *l* to *y*) shows a later development. Shuswap, which like Lillooet generally retained Proto-Salish *l*, has unexpectedly **-?úy**. The Shuswap form is thus possibly a borrowing from Thompson. The problem of development of plant taxonomies thus intersects with the problem of phonological developments and borrowing. It is also difficult to say whether in Thompson the suffix **-?úy** was added to s-**ɬáqəm** (the ancestor of **sγíqəm**) and that the entire form s-**ɬaqəm-?úl** shifted to **sγíqəm-?úy** . . . or whether **-?úy** was added to bunchgrass' after this form had already changed to **sγíqəm**."

*** D. Kinkade (pers. comm. 1986) notes that in Columbian Interior Salish, the related form, **swpúlaxʷ**, also pertains to "grass," and is generally glossed 'short grass,' although one speaker said it was particularly 'bunchgrass.' It has also been glossed as 'wild hay.' The Columbian term **sƛ'íya?** refers to 'hay, tall grass.'

Fig. 5. Proposed sequence of encoding of the Lillooet and Thompson general terms for "grass" and/or "hay."

In each language, this category appears to be a residual taxon, encompassing a wide variety of relatively short, non-woody, leafy species of low cultural significance. It is tempting to equate this category with the English folk taxon, "weed," as did the early ethnographer James Teit, who in his unpublished field notes on Thompson (1896–1918), recorded under lamb's quarters: *"stuwitu´imax . . ."* or *"stuwitu´imax a sáma"* ['whiteman's *stuyt—úyṁx*ʷ'] . . . weeds introduced by whites with no particular name or use especially annuals . . . " Contemporary native elders also generally translate *s-waʔp-úlṁəx*ʷ (Lillooet) and *stuyt-úyṁx*ʷ (Thompson) as "weed." Indeed, one Lillooet speaker defined the term *s-waʔp-úlṁəx*ʷ as ". . . just any weed in a garden . . . any type of mixed plants, or low plants, it's just like [that] speargrass[11] . . . whatever comes in the garden." (Desmond Peters, pers. comm., 1985). However, the term did not, at least originally, have the same negative connotation that "weed" has to many non-Indians,[12] or that the GRERB ["grass-plus-herb"] category has in some other languages where its name derives from "rotten," "litter," "garbage" or "filth" (Brown 1984: 63). Here, it is more a term of convenience, defined linguistically by physiognomic characteristics (ie., 'ground-growth') and applied as a sort of "catch-all" mostly for plants not important enough to have special generic-level names.

In each language, but especially in Thompson, the category encompasses many indigenous plants; originally, of course, it would have applied only to indigenous species. Teit's application of the modifer "whiteman's" to the category is indicative of a recognition in Thompson of both native and introduced *stuyt-úyṁx*ʷ. With the advent of gardening, farming and ranching among the Lillooet and Thompson, coupled with a reduction of wilderness activities such as hunting and gathering, introduced "weeds" have certainly gained in salience and wild 'ground-growth' became less salient, so that there has been a tendency for the class to conform with our "weed" class. Even today, though, the conformity is not exact, at least among the more traditionally minded native speakers. Annie York, a major Thompson consultant, for example, refers to *stuyt-úyṁx*ʷ very often in her discussions of low, herbaceous plants. She sometimes applies descriptive names such as *ʔes-wəlwíwl tək stuyt-úyṁx*ʷ ('having-little-fringe ground-growth'—for parsley fern) to such plants. She even incorporates the term in names for plants which are useful medicines, such as two varieties of rattlesnake plantain [e.g. *ʔes-n-cəlcl-ílkn (tək stuyt-úyṁx*ʷ) 'little-humpbacked (ground-growth')—for a wide-leaved variety].[13]

It is notable that in Okanagan-Colville and Flathead, the equivalent "ground-growth" terms have assumed the semantic role of "grasses" (cf. Okanagan-Colville *"swupúla7xw"* (*swupúlaʔx*ʷ) 'ground-hair/growth' for "grass, general" and Flathead *supúʔlex*ʷ 'hair on the earth' for "grass"—Turner, Bouchard and Kennedy 1981: 52; Hart 1974: 34). In the latter language, however, a "weed" category exists which was derived from the "grass" category: *ċes.upúʔlex*ʷ 'bad hair on the earth' (Hart 1974: 38). In Shuswap, the "weed" connotation for the equivalent term, *"swupúlexw"* (*swupúləx*ʷ), is retained (Palmer 1975: 44).

The "flowers" category in each language is similar to the "ground-growth" category. It is somewhat of a "catch-all," generally applying to herbaceous species with conspicuous blossoms. It seems more or less equivalent to the English folk category

TABLE 6. Some examples of generic-level names incorporating general class terms in Thompson (after Turner et al. 1984).

Thompson Term	English gloss	Species referred to
ʔes-ɬəqláq tək stuyt-úyṁxʷ	'clumped-here-and-there ground-growth'	licorice fern
ʔesnċəlċl-ílkn (tək stuyt-úyṁxʷ)	'little-humpbacked ground-growth'	rattlesnake plantain (wide-leaved variety)
ƛ̓əxʷƛ̓xʷə́p peɬ stuyt-úyṁxʷ	'paralysed-person's ground-growth'	Canada goldenrod
(ʔe)s-pəspás peɬ s-yíqm	'swamp grass'	Carex sp.
qəpqép tək sṗáq̓m	'soft flower'	western anemone
scẇéẇxʷ peɬ sṗáq̓m	'creek flower'	rein orchid
q̓əṗq̓əpkʷlé peɬ múyx (OR q̓əṗq̓əpkʷleh-éɬp)	'"click-click" bush' (OR '. . .-plant')	highbush cranberry
xʔ-úyṁxʷ peɬ múyx (a descriptive name)	'upland bush'	white-flowered rhododendron

"wild flowers," but with garden flowers also being included at the present time. If plants in the "flower" category are named more specifically, it is usually by some descriptive term (e.g., Thompson 'blue flower' for wild blue violet; 'creek flower' for rein orchid). The only "wild flower" in either language which has its own primary lexemic name is wild rose, called *(s-)qəlq̓* (bush—*s-qəlq̓-áẑ*) in Lillooet, but this term also applies to wild rose hips, and some apply it exclusively to the latter, calling rose flowers *ṗáq̓əm s-qəlq̓-áẑ* (lit. 'flowers of the rose bush') (Edith O'Donaghey, pers. comm., 1985).

The "flowers" category actually overlaps somewhat with the "ground-growth" category, as can be seen by the optional application of the general terms in the names of some plants in Thompson. For example, in several instances, Annie York used *stuyt-úyṁxʷ* and *s-ṗáq̓m* interchangeably in naming some herbaceous plants that also had conspicuous flowers. Not knowing a "real" name for wild bleeding-heart, for instance, she applied a translation borrowing from the English name. She used both *s-xʷakʷ xʷákʷ kʷukʷ tək stuyt-úyṁxʷ* (lit. 'heart ground-growth') and *s-xʷakʷxʷákʷ kʷukʷ tək sṗáq̓m* (lit. 'heart flower'). In one case, for an alternate name for buttercup, she applied these two general terms simultaneously: *ʔes-kʷəlkʷlóʔ tək stuyt-úyṁxʷ e s-ṗáq̓ms* (lit. 'little-yellow ground-growth flower'). This overlapping does not seem to be a case of ambiguity about category boundaries, but simply an acceptance of cross referencing of taxa, depending on which feature of a plant is being stressed. I found a similar overlapping of general categories in Haida (an unrelated language), where plants were referable to either a "leaf/medicine" category or a "flowers" category depending on context, and on which aspect of a plant was being stressed (Turner 1974: 36).

The "flowers" category, like the "ground-growth" class in each language, includes as primary members plants which were little used for food or as a source of materials. This is not to say that the blossoms of important food species such as spring beauty, yellow avalanche lily or chocolate lily were not called "flowers," but perceptually, they are not within the core of species which comprise this class. They are not normally given as examples of "flowers." There is, at least in Thompson, a utilitarian aspect of many, but not all, members of the "flowers" category that is apparent only on close scrutiny. Various types of flowers were used, more than members of any other class of plants, as charms, to bring luck in love, gambling and the acquisition of wealth. Flowering species such as red columbine, calypso, blue harebell, delphinium, large-leaved avens, bog orchid, alpine bitterroot, red monkeyflower, forget-me-not, night-flowering catchfly, campion and starflower were used for little else, but all were used as charms of some sort (Turner *et al.* 1990: Table 7).

Brown (1984: 10) argues that English "flower" is a special-purpose class, ". . . since its membership is not based on several clustering morphological features, but rather simply on the presence of prominent or ornamental blossoms." According to his view, the Lillooet and Thompson "flower" classes would not qualify as "life forms" because they would be attributed the same special-purpose status. However, Randall and Hunn (1984: 341) maintain that in both English and Sahaptin "having" a flower is not the only attribute of plants that are "flowers." Most are herbaceous with a showy inflorescence. Part of the confusion is that there is a polysemy between the plant "part" and the plant "class." The distinction is evident in the words of one of my relatives, describing a particular plant to my daughter: "It *has* a flower, but it's *not* a flower." Thus, Randall and Hunn suggest that "flower" should qualify as a life form as much as "grass," "tree" or "vine."

The "berries/fruits" category, as a special purpose utilitarian class, does not fit into Berlin's or Brown's concept of a "life form" at all, but it does exist as a named, psychologically valid general plant class in the various northwestern North American native languages I have studied (cf. Turner 1974: 36, 39, 41, 79; Turner and Efrat 1982: 21; Turner *et al.* 1984: 48). Randall and Hunn (1984: 340) have also recognized "edible fruit" as a major inclusive class in Sahaptin. In both Lillooet and Thompson, not only is it recognized with a general class name but additionally, a suffix, *-úse?* (lit. 'round-object') in Thompson and *-usa?* (lit. 'round-object'; also 'fruit/potato/money'; cf. also *-us* 'face/eye') in Lillooet, is applied in the names of many different types of berries, e.g.:

Lillooet
  cac?-úsa? (cf. *s-cicá?* 'crow')—blackcap
  swəłkʷa?ú?sa?—saskatoon, red variety
  q̇ʷ?x̌-q̇ʷíq̇ʷx̌-usa? 'black (redupl.) fruit'—northern black currant

Thompson
  cəqʷ- c̣iqʷ-úse? 'red-berries'—red huckleberry
  səxʷ-suxʷ-úse? 'grizzly-bear-berry'—black twinberry
  sc̣ól-se? 'sour/tart-berry'—Oregon-grape
  si?h-ús(e?) 'good-fruit'—saskatoon, "good" variety.

TABLE 7. Correspondence of Lillooet and Thompson major plant taxa described in this study with the criteria for life form recognition as defined by Berlin, Breedlove and Raven (1973) and Brown (1984).

General plant classes**	Life form Criteria*							Qualifies
	1	2	3	3A	4	5	6	
Lillooet:								
"tree"	X	X	X	—	X	X	X	YES
"hay"	X	X	—	E	X	—	—	NO
"grass"	X	X	—	E	X	X	—	NO
"low . . . plants . . ."	X	X	—	E	X	—	—	NO
"flowers"	X	X	—	E	(X)	—	—	NO
"berries/fruits"	X	X	X	—	(X)	—	—	NO
"mosses . . ."	X	X	—	E	X	X	X	NO
"mushrooms and fungi"	?X	X	X	—	X	X	X	YES
"edible roots . . ."	X	—	X	—	(X)	—	—	NO
Thompson:								
"large trees"	X	X	X	—	X	X	X	YES
"tall bushes . . ."	X	X	X	—	X	X	X	YES
"grasses/hay"	X	X	X	—	X	X	X	YES
"low . . . plants . . ."	X	X	X	—	X	—	—	YES
"flowers"	X	X	X	—	(X)	—	—	NO
"berries/fruits"	X	X	X	—	(X)	—	—	NO
"mosses . . ."	X	X	—	E	X	X	X	NO
"mushrooms and fungi"	?X	X	X	—	X	X	X	YES
"large vines"	X	X	—	—	X	X	X	YES (recent)
"edible roots . . ."	X	—	X	—	(X)	—	—	NO

* Criteria for life form recognition are as follows (after Berlin, Breedlove and Raven, 1973: 215) and Brown (1984: 18–21): **1.** occur at rank Level 1, immediately below unique beginner; **2.** are labelled by primary lexemes; **3.** are polytypic, including many [ten or more] labelled taxa (usually labelled by primary lexemes, although Brown cites examples where all included classes are labeled by secondary, or composite, lexemes); **3A.** are "Empty" (E), including few [under ten] or no named members but many unlabelled taxa. (Such categories are classified as "not full-fledged" life forms, but "incipient" life forms by Brown 1984: 21); **4.** reflect natural morphological discontinuities; **5.** are general purpose, not special purpose (ie., are not defined largely by a single utilitarian attribute); **6.** are mutually exclusive (although Brown cites instances where dual life form membership is evident). "X" indicates conformity with life form features. (X) indicates partial conformity. "—" indicates non-conformity. In **3A**, evaluation as an "Empty" category (E) is contrary to the characteristics of a true life form; in this case, a negative assessment (—) implies conformity with life form characteristics.

** See Tables 2 and 3 for native designations and more detailed descriptions of these classes.

Fig. 6. Black huckleberry, called simply *ʔusaʔ* 'berry/round object' in Fraser River Lillooet.

In the Fraser River dialect of Lillooet, *ʔúsaʔ* is applied specifically to black huckleberry (Fig. 6), although in Pemberton Lillooet, a different term, **mexáƛ̓**, is used for this species. In Thompson, black huckleberries, though not called "berries" as they are in Fraser River Lillooet, were nevertheless considered "special." Annie York called them "the head of all the fruits . . . an official fruit" and said that if one was given black huckleberries as a gift, he was expected to give a gift in return. In Okanagan-Colville, at least one speaker, Selina Timoyakin, called them the "chief" of the fruits. In another Salish language, Bella Coola, as with Fraser River Lillooet, their name is polysemous with the general name for fruit (Turner 1974: 79, 37). This is true also in Sahaptin (E. Hunn, pers. comm. 1986). The berries seem to have the equivalent status among native fruits that bluebunch wheat grass does among grasses in the Interior Salish area.

Obviously, the "berries/fruits" category is an overlapping one, especially with the "tall bushes . . ." taxon. It depends upon context, for example, whether one refers to saskatoon as a "bush" or as a "fruit." The majority of "fruits" (ie., "fruit-bearing plants") are, in fact, bushes, but "berries/fruits" could not be said to be a sub-taxon of "bushes" because there are some, such as strawberries and kinnikinnick, that do not fit into the "bush" category.

"Mosses and moss-like plants" is another ubiquitous general plant category in northwestern North American languages, although it is not discussed by Brown (1984) except in a passing reference to "lichens" (p. 14).[14] In Lillooet and Thompson, as with other northwestern North American languages, mosses and lichens are generally classed together (along with liverworts and other moss-like plants such as club-mosses), although differences in color and form are often given recognition. Some rather important or unique lichens, such as black tree lichen, wolf lichen and lung lichen, are called by more specific names, and may not even be perceptually included in the residual "mosses . . ." category by some individuals. In Thompson, lichens, especially the broad, thallose species, are sometimes called *papéẏłe tak q"zém* ('frog moss'). Some native speakers consider them to be "a kind of moss," whereas others say they are "similar to mosses."

Habitat and growth form seem to be the overriding factors in distinguishing among various types of mosses and lichens. In Lillooet, for example, various thallose lichens growing on the ground (e.g. *Peltigera aphthosa*) are called *X̌an²-úlṁax"* 'ground/earth-ear'; those growing in trees (e.g., lung lichen) are called *X̌an²-álq"* ('wood/tree-ear'). In Thompson, mosses and lichens growing on trees are called *q"zem-éyq"* ('wood/tree-moss') and those on the ground, *n-q"zem-úyṁx"* ('ground-moss'). Additionally, Annie York recognized several other loosely defined categories: "long moss," "short moss," "rock moss," "water moss" and "swamp moss." She, as a native botanical specialist, could distinguish many different types of mosses and lichens within these categories, but many of the people consulted, like most non-native people in the region, did not perceive many different kinds. As Alec Peters, a Pemberton Lillooet speaker, remarked when shown a variety of different mosses and lichens, "They're all *pá²sams* to me!"

In both languages, the "mushrooms and fungi" category is an important one, including several named species of high cultural significance and a large number of residual unnamed types of little cultural significance. The class names themselves certainly must have derived, or are in the process of deriving, through expansion of reference, from the generic-level names of the most salient types of mushroom. Towards the coast—in Lower Lillooet and Lower Thompson—as well as in the Thompson dialect spoken around Lytton, it is the name for pine mushroom [Lillooet—*(s)-q̓aṁs;* Thompson—*q̓áṁes*] that is elevated to the general class name, at least optionally. For the Nicola Valley Thompson, the "cottonwood" mushroom (Fig. 7) has become the "type" for mushrooms in general, and its name, *maX̌-qi²*, is used, at least by some, for mushrooms generally, including commercial fresh or canned mushrooms (Mabel Joe, pers. comm., 1985). In the Fraser River dialect of Lillooet, the term *maX̌-qín,* (said to be borrowed from Shuswap; lit. 'cottonwood/stick-head/top') pertains to "cottonwood" mushroom specifically and a cognate form of the Thompson term, *maX̌-qi², (s)-maX̌-áqa²* is applied as a general name for "any mushroom" (e.g. Desmond Peters, Bill Edwards, pers. comm., 1985; cf. also Turner, Kuhnlein and Egger, 1987).[15]

"Vine" is considered to be one of the five "universal life form" categories by Brown (1984). However, there are very few indigenous vine species in northwestern North America. Hence "vine" as a major plant category has low salience in Lillooet and Thompson. One outstanding vine species is white clematis, called *q̓aċusnínina* (cf. *q̓aċp* 'tangled/hard to untie') in Lillooet and *q̓aċ-q̓aċ-usnínus* ('woven-as-it-grows') in Thompson. Another vine, orange honeysuckle, is sometimes called by the

Fig. 7. "Cottonwood" mushroon, the "type" for mushrooms in general in Nicola Valley Thompson.

same name in Thompson[16] and could be considered as belonging to the same general class. The less common blue clematis, apparently not known to contemporary Thompson people, was formerly called by the folk specific name, *q̓ə́c-usnínes e x̓-úymx̌ʷ* ('high-country woven-as-it-grows') in Thompson (Steedman 1930: 459). These three species, therefore, would have been the only members of an original "vine" class in Thompson; it could hardly be called a major life form category. Now, however, with the introduction of various cultivated vines, such as grape, Virginia creeper and English ivy, the "vine" class has expanded, and the name *q̓ə́c-q̓ə́c-usnínus* now has, to some people but not to others, broader application as a general term for "vine" in Thompson. In Lillooet, however there is no real evidence to indicate the existence of a "vine" class, past or present.[17]

Randall and Hunn (1984: 340) report that in Sahaptin there is a named, highly inclusive "edible root" class. In Lillooet and Thompson "edible roots [and other under-ground parts]" were also of high importance in the traditional economy, but in neither language is there a term which refers to any and all edible underground parts, or to plants which bear them. Nevertheless, plants such as spring beauty, avalanche lily, bitterroot, tiger lily, chocolate lily, and wild onions do seem to form a discrete percep-tual unit. Most Lillooet and Thompson speakers discuss them as a group, one after the other. For example, Annie York, in talking about combinations of foods, noted: ". . . The food that goes with meat is avalanche lily[18] corms, bitterroot, tiger lily bulbs, chocolate lily bulbs, spring beauty corms . . . and if you can get balsamroot . . . you eat it with meat, and that wapato . . . and the other kind, "wild carrot" . . . they don't mix that with anything . . . and the silverweed . . . they just cook that by itself . . ." Within the course of the conversation she had mentioned, consecutively, nine "root" foods. If the languages had continued to develop without European influence, I would speculate that names would evolve for the incipient "roots" categories in Lillooet and Thompson, probably, as happened for Nitinaht (Turner *et al.* 1983: 48), by a process of expansion of reference of the name of one of the most important types of edible roots, perhaps bitterroot or yellow avalanche lily.

Some Lillooet and Thompson taxa do not fit within any of the major "life form" level categories mentioned here. Fireweed, for example, seems to fall conceptually between the "tall bushes" and "low herbaceous plants" categories, but not actually within either. Cow-parsnip, too, is not generally incorporated within any of these major classes, nor are the large fern species, although Annie York used the term *stuyt-úymx*[w] for two small ferns, parsley fern and licorice fern.

Other plant classes in Lillooet and Thompson could well be considered that are comparable to some of those already described. These include "medicines" and "water plants." These classes are less rigorously defined and overlap broadly with other major categories. Thus, their relationship with other major plant classes is not hierarchical. I will discuss them in a future paper along with a whole range of other heterogenous "intermediate" level plant classes existing in these two languages.

DISCUSSION

Lillooet and Thompson conform with many other pre-industrial language groups in having no single free-standing term denoting "plant," but they and a number of other northwestern Salishan and Wakashan languages do incorporate "plant" suffixes in many of their generic-level plant names. This phenomenon is somewhat comparable to the use of "plant" in "eggplant" or "spiderplant" but is more pervasive. Many generic level names are developed by adding the "plant" suffix to the term for the most salient part of the plant. This would be as if, in English, the use of "potato *plant*, "'strawberry *plant*, "globe artichoke *plant*" were more or less mandatory when referring to these plants in an abstract context.

The origin of this suffix is still subject to speculation, but because it is so widespread in the Salishan and Wakashan languages, it must have great antiquity. Possibly it derived from a free-standing word for "tree" or "tree/bush," whose meaning expanded to "plant, general" but whose form was reduced to a suffix. A similar situation exists with body part terms (C. Brown, pers. comm., 1985). It would be interesting to know how many other languages of pre-industrial societies have concise linguistic means of recognizing "plantness" without actually having in evidence a free-standing term for "plant."

Only the "tree" category in each language and the Thompson "bush . . ." category conform with virtually all the criteria of "life form" classes as prescribed by Berlin and his colleagues (cf. Berlin, Breedlove and Raven 1974: 26; Brown 1984: 4). The other general categories differ in various ways (see Table 7). However, the "tree" and possibly Thompson "bush . . ." class names appear not to have originated by the most common means (Berlin 1972: 71), through expansion of reference from generic-level terms.

Several other general categories in Lillooet and Thompson differ from the Berlin "life form" by incorporating very few named generic level taxa, while at the same time encompassing a large number of recognizably distinct but unnamed terminal taxa. In all cases the named plants within these categories are highly salient, being very common or distinctive and/or culturally significant, whereas the unnamed plants are generally low in cultural importance. In Thompson, for example, there are only about ten named kinds of plants that fit into the *s-yíqm* ("grasses") category, yet *s-yíqm* could be applied by Thompson speakers to at least 25 kinds of plants that can be distinguished by native botanical specialists. A similar situation exists for the "low, herbaceous broad-leaved plant," "flower," "moss . . ." and "mushroom" categories in both languages. I have termed these "empty" categories because they include few or no named subtaxa while incorporating a large number of covert types. These "empty" categories also exist in Haida, Bella Coola, Nitinaht and other northwestern North American languages (Turner 1974: 35; Turner *et al.* 1983: 47). They also occur in Sahaptin, but, in this language, the "grass" and "flower" categories exclude the more salient, named kinds altogether, and incorporate only unnamed types of no cultural significance (Hunn 1982: 834).

Lillooet and Thompson general categories are not all defined solely by morphological features. As Hunn (1982) observes, there is a utilitarian factor in plant classification which is not accounted for in the scheme of Berlin, Breedlove and Raven (1973: 215,1974: 26), although Brown (1984: 10) gives some recognition to categories defined by cultural importance in describing "life form" classes. The "berries/fruits" categories in Lillooet and Thompson are the most obvious examples of utilitarian major plant classes. However, the "low, herbaceous broad-leaved plants" taxa also reflect cultural significance. In this case, plants are generally incorporated on the basis of non-use. The utilitarian factor is also evident in the "grasses" category, where a nomenclatural and perceptual distinction is made in Lillooet between "grass" and "hay." Even many members of the "flowers" category in Thompson are attributed characteristics which are not solely morphological—namely some magical power that makes them good for charms.

As these examples show, there is sometimes no clearcut distinction between morphological and utilitarian features of plants. The essence of "treeness" is the woody xylem tissues (and to a lesser extent, the phloem tissues of the bark) that support the tree and allow it to attain its large size. The woody tissue, because of its chemical composition and physical attributes, also makes a good fuel and an ideal construction material. It is not surprising, therefore, that "wood" and "tree" are synonymous in many languages, or that the name for "tree" often derives historically from the name for "wood" (Witkowski, Brown and Chase 1981: 3). Another example of the dualism of certain taxa is seen in the Haida term *xil,* which means both 'leaf' and 'medicine' and is the name of a major class of leafy, herbaceous plants, even being incorporated mandatorily in the generic-level names of many members of this class (Turner 1974: 31). Van Eijk (pers. comm. 1986) points out that the Salish general plant suffix itself has a utilitarian bias because it most often applies to plants having culturally significant products.

Finally, whereas the Berlin and Brown "life form" classes are mutually exclusive (cf. Berlin, Breedlove and Raven 1974: 25), I have found, in conversations with native speakers of Thompson, Lillooet and other northwestern languages, that the structure of taxonomic categories for plants is not rigid, and that, depending on the context of conversation, a particular plant could be assigned to two or even three different major classes. Just as in English our class of "wild flowers" might sometimes incorporate wild rose, and at other times wild rose would be called a "bush," so in Thompson, wild rose might be included as a "bush," a "flower" or a "fruit," depending on context. In English folk classification, "vine maple" might be termed under various circumstances a "shrub" or a "tree" (but not usually a "vine"), so it might in Lillooet or Thompson he assigned to the "bush" or "tree" class. The overlap between "flowers" and "groundgrowth" has already been demonstrated. There is, of course, individual variation too, as to which plants are perceived as belonging to a particular class, just as in English, different people may have different ideas about which plants are classed as "weeds."

There is no way of knowing, without further study of all the Salish languages and a reconstruction of proto-Salish, whether Lillooet and Thompson major plant categories follow the lexical encoding sequence for folk botanical life-forms proposed by Brown (1984: 24). Brown (1984: 143) classes Lillooet as a "Stage 3" language, having only two life-forms, "tree" and "grass," with an incipient "grerb" class, based on his interpretation of information in Turner (1974). Thompson was not included in Brown's survey. If it were, it would qualify as a "Stage 6" language, since it has named classes for "tree," "grass," "grerb," "bush" and "vine." It seems strange that two closely related languages, which must surely have evolved within the same time frame, should be shown by this scheme to be so different. Perhaps if other major classes were included, such as "mosses . . ." and "mushrooms," which are probably more relevant to peoples of northwestern North America than "vines," there would not be such a discrepancy. Additionally, the differences would diminish if the Lillooet "grerb" class were given real status, equivalent in its scope and application to "tree," even though it has few or no named members.

SUMMARY AND CONCLUSIONS

Lillooet and Thompson, two closely related Salish languages of northwestern North America, are similar, though not identical, in their perception and encoding of major plant classes. Both lack free form terms for "plant," but have suffixes on many of their generic-level plant names which denote "plantness." Both have named categories of "trees," "grasses," "low, herbaceous, broad-leaved plants," "mosses," "mushrooms" and "berries." Thompson also has a named category of "bushes," whereas this class is only incipient in Lillooet. In both languages there is an incipient, but unnamed class of "edible roots."

The historical derivation of the category names is still subject to question. The term for "trees" may well have originated in a manner contrary to the most common derivation pattern suggested by Berlin (1972: 71), as may have the Thompson name for "bushes." Names for "grasses," and/or "hay" on the other hand, probably originated through expansion of reference of the generic-level name for bluebunch wheat grass.

A number of the major categories are at least partially defined by utilitarian, rather than solely morphological features. These categories are not necessarily mutually exclusive. Most are residual, having a few highly salient named terminal taxa and many recognizably distinct, but unnamed, members. Most of the named taxa have, or had in the past, a high level of cultural significance, particularly as foods, materials or medicines.

The major premise of folk classification systems appears to be convenience to the originator and user. There are no rules that must be adhered to, as developed in our modern scientific biological classification system. The famous linguist Edward Sapir once wrote: "Unfortunately, or luckily, no language is tyrannically consistent. All grammars leak." (Sapir 1921: 38). One might equally well say, "All folk taxonomies leak." The major criterion in folk systems is that they allow communication between members of a society. It is not surprising, therefore, that folk categories like those of Lillooet, Thompson or English are fluid and sometimes ambiguous. Context is of paramount importance. Intonation, gestures and the way words are used within a general topic of conversation, can convey as much as the actual words themselves. These can never adequately be incorporated into such a brief description by a non-speaker of a language. For almost any rule one tries to formulate concerning the attributes of terminology, whether it be the hierarchical nature of folk taxa or their historical encoding, there will be exceptions, probably many. Lillooet and Thompson major plant categories are good examples.

ACKNOWLEDGMENTS

I am indebted to many for information, help and criticism in this project. I am deeply grateful to the members of the Lillooet and Thompson speech communities, listed in Appendix 1, who shared their knowledge and experience with me. Salishan linguists Dr. Laurence C. Thompson, M. Terry Thompson, Dr. Jan van Eijk, Dr. M. Dale Kinkade, Randy Bouchard, and Dr. Steven Egesdal were immensely helpful in providing information and accurate transcriptions of plant names. Van Eijk and Kinkade also read the manuscript and offered valuable editorial comment. I would also like to thank Drs. Eugene Hunn, Cecil Brown, Brent Berlin, Eugene Anderson and Robert T. Ogilvie for their critical reading of the manuscript.

This work was funded by a grant from the Social Sciences and Humanities Research Council of Canada (No. 410-84-0146).

LITERATURE CITED

Berlin, B. 1972. Speculations on the growth of ethnobotanical nomenclature. Lang. Soc. 1: 51–86.

Berlin, B., D. Breedlove and P. Raven. 1966. Folk taxonomies and biological classification. Science 154: 273–75.

———. 1973. General principles of classification and nomenclature in folk biology. Amer. Anthropol. 75(1): 214–42.

———. 1974. Principles of Tzeltal Plant Classification. An introduction of the botanical ethnography of a Mayan-speaking people of Highland Chiapas. Academic Press, New York.

Brown, C. H. 1977. Folk botanical life-forms: their universality and growth. Amer. Anthropol. 79: 317–42.

———. 1984. Language and Living Things. Uniformities in Folk Classification and Naming. Rutgers Univ. Press, New Jersey.

———. 1986. The Growth of Ethnobiological Nomenclature. Current Anthro. 27(1): 1–19.

Galloway, B. 1982. Upper Stó:lo Ethnobotany. Coqualeetza Education Training Centre, Sardis, British Columbia.

Hill-Tout, C. 1905. Report on the Ethnology of the StlatlumH [Lillooet] of British Columbia. J. Anthropological Inst. Great Britain and Ireland. Vol. XXXV: 126–218. London.

Hart, J. 1974. Plant Taxonomy of the Salish and Kootenai Indians of Western Montana. Unpubl. M. A. dissert. Univ. Montana, Missoula.

Hunn, E. S. 1982. The utilitarian factor in folk biological classification. Amer. Anthropol. 84(4): 830–47.

——— and D. H. French. 1984. Alternatives to taxonomic hierarchy: the Sahaptin case. J. Ethnobiol. 4(1): 73–92.

Kuipers, A. 1974. The Shuswap Language, Part 1. Mouton, The Hague, Netherlands.

Palmer, G. 1975. Shuswap Indian ethnobotany. Syesis 8: 29–81.

Randall, R. A. and E. S. Hunn. 1984. Do life-forms evolve or do uses for life? Some doubts about Brown's universals hypothesis. Amer. Ethnol. 11(2): 329–49.

Sapir, E. 1921. Language. An Introduction to the Study of Speech. Harcourt, Brace & World, New York.

Steedman, E. V., ed. 1930. The ethnobotany of the Thompson Indians of British Columbia. Based on field notes by James A. Teit. U. S. Bur. Am. Ethnol. 45th Annu. Rep. 1927, 28: 443–522. (Facsimile reproduction 1973, The Shorey Bookstore, Seattle, Washington.)

Thompson, L. C. and M. T. Thompson. 1996. Thompson River Salish Dictionary: Nte?Kepmxcín. University of Montana Occasional Papers in Linguistics No. 12, Missoula.

Trager, G. 1939. "Cottonwood" = "Tree": a southwestern linguistic trait. Internat. J. Amer. Linguist 9: 117–18.

Turner, N. J. 1973. The ethnobotany of the Bella Coola Indians of British Columbia. Syesis 6: 193–220.

———. 1974. Plant Taxonomic Systems and Ethnobotany of Three Contemporary Indian Groups of the Pacific Northwest (Haida, Bella Coola and Lillooet). Syesis Vol. 7, Suppl. 1.

———. 1986. The importance of a rose; evaluating cultural significance of plants in Thompson and Lillooet Interior Salish. Unpubl. ms., British Columbia Prov. Museum, Victoria.

——— and M. A. M. Bell. 1971. The ethnobotany of the Coast Salish Indians of Vancouver Island. Econ. Botany 25: 63–104.

———. 1973. The ethnobotany of the Southern Kwakiutl Indians of British Columbia. Econ. Botany 27: 257–310.

———, R. Bouchard and D. I. D. Kennedy. 1981. Ethnobotany of the Okanagan-Colville Indians of British Columbia and Washington. Occas. Paper No. 21. British Columbia Prov. Museum, Victoria.

———— and B. S. Efrat. 1982. Ethnobotany of the Hesquiat people of the west coast of Vancouver Island. British Columbia Prov. Mus. Cultural Recovery Pap. No. 2, Victoria.

————, H. V. Kuhnlein and K. N. Egger. In press. The cottonwood mushroom (*Tricholoma populinum* Lange): a food resource of the Interior Salish Indian Peoples of British Columbia, Can. J. Bot.

————, J. Thomas, R. T. Ogilvie and B. F. Carlson. 1983. Ethnobotany of the Nitinaht Indians of Vancouver Island. Occas. paper No. 28. British Columbia Prov. Museum, Victoria.

————, L. C. Thompson, M. T. Thompson and A. York. 1990. Thompson Ethnobotany. Memoir No. 3, Royal British Columbia Museum, Victoria.

Van Eijk, J. P. 1985. The Lillooet Language. phonology—morphology—syntax. Unpubl. doctoral dissert., University of Amsterdam, The Netherlands.

Whittaker, R. D. 1969. New concepts of the kingdoms of organisms. Science 163: 150–59.

Witkowski, S. R., C. H. Brown and P. K. Chase. 1981. Where do tree terms come from? Man (N.S.) 16: 1–14.

NOTES

1. These peoples are now properly referred to by the names Nlaka'pamux (formerly Thompson) and Stl'atl'imx (formerly Lillooet). In later papers I will discuss less inclusive plant categories in Lillooet and Thompson—those at the "intermediate" and "generic" ranks.

2. There is still some question among scientists whether fungi should be considered plants, or whether they are different enough from other botanical organisms that they should be considered as belonging to a separate "kingdom." Even Algae are now frequently classed in their own "kingdom." Blue-green algae and related bacteria are generally classed in a separate "kingdom." Slime molds, once considered close to fungi, are now usually included in a "kingdom" with simple, often one-celled organisms (cf. Whittaker 1969).

3. Scientific names are provided in Appendix 2. Throughout this paper, native terms cited are written in the orthographies of the original sources, except in Lillooet, where symbols and forms are from Van Eijk (1985). In Thompson, the orthography is standardized after L. C. and M. T. Thompson. However, note that here, *x* is written as *x̌* throughout, and, for simplicity, not all of the Thompson's symbols indicating underlying analyses of Thompson terms are shown. These may be seen in Turner *et al.* (1990).

4. In this paper, in reference to translations of native terms, single quotation marks are used for literal translations, and double quotation marks for general English glosses or interpretations of application.

5. Examples of similar suffixes in neighbouring Salish and Wakashan languages include (transcription as in original sources; note *ł = lh* = λ): Shuswap— *-álhp/-eλp* (Palmer 1975: 65; Kuipers 1974: 64); Okanagan-Colville— *-ilhp* (Turner, Bouchard and Kennedy 1981: 120); Columbian— *-ałp* (D. Kinkade, pers. comm. 1986); Halkomelem— *-elhp/-lhp* (Galloway 1982: 5); Straits Salish— *-iłč* (Turner and Bell, 1971: 87); Squamish— *-ay/-aẏ* (R. Bouchard, pers. comm. 1976); Sechelt— *-ay* (J. Timmers, pers. comm. 1972); Comox— *-ay* (R. Bouchard, pers. comm. 1973); Upper Chehalis— *-inił/-inł* (D. Kinkade, pers. comm. 1986); Bella Coola— *-lhp* (Turner 1973: 209); Nitinaht— *-ápt* (Turner et al. 1983: 90); Hesquiat Nootka— *-mapt* (Turner and Efrat 1982: 68); Kwakwala— *-ṁes/-7ems* (Turner and Bell 1973: 288). (The last three languages are Wakashan, a language family distantly related to the Salish Family; hence the suffixes are possibly cognate with the Salishan suffixes.)

6. Kinkade (pers. comm. 1986) cites further evidence for an original meaning of 'upright object' (singular) rather than 'tree': in both Thompson and Columbian, the plural form for 'tree' has a completely different stem than the singular, and in Columbian the plural means 'bushes, brush' as well as 'plural upright objects.'

7. Van Eijk (pers. comm. 1986) notes that some Lillooet speakers identify *čḡáḡłəp* with *qʷəla-qin/qʷəlaqə́qən* "young tree, sapling," whereas one of the most knowledgeable speakers describes the former as an older, but still not mature, growth stage and the latter as a younger stage.

8. Randall and Hunn (1984: 333) describe such a situation in the Sinama language, where originally there was a "bird-and-moth" class, which has come to conform with folk English "bird."

9. Hill-tout (1905: 213) defines these terms as "long" and "short" grass respectively. Perhaps this reflects their original dichotomy.

10. For some Lillooet and Thompson speakers the so-called "swamp grasses" are not really "grasses" at all. These "non-grasses" include a number of *Carex* species, one *Scirpus* species (*S. microcarpus*), both in the sedge family, and even some true grasses that grow in standing water. Other speakers, however, include these as a subcategory of "grasses."

11. Here is a case of overlapping of general categories, since "speargrass," cited as an example of *s-waʔp-úlmxʷ* "weed," is also classed as *s-čepeż,* "grass."

12. Webster's Dictionary defines "weed" as "any useless troublesome plant," although its derivation from Old English *weod,* "an herb," is indicative that it did not always have such a negative connotation. Many English folk names for plants not necessarily "useless" or "troublesome" (e.g., fireweed, gumweed) incorporate the term.

13. One of the Nicola Valley Thompson speakers recalled that there was also a special meaning for the term, *stuyt-úymxʷ,* more specific than the general category name. She said, "I heard a lot of another [plant], they call that *stuyt-úymxʷ* too . . . high up in the mountains, you have to find a special plant, ask the plant for good luck. See, there's a male and a female plant, and you name that plant . . . the woman's name and the man's name [if you want to use the plant as a love charm] . . . and you put them together and you tell them to live together . . . That's what they call *stuyt-úymxʷ,* I think." She went on to say that it was a plant that one might dream about, that would give you luck or success (Mabel Joe, pers. comm., 1984).

14. Hunn (pers. comm. 1986) is inclined to categorize "moss" as a polytypic generic taxon (like Tzeltal "butterfly"). It is true that most, if not all, of the labelled taxa encompassed by this class have names that are secondary, or composite, lexemes. However, the native speakers with whom I have discussed this class seem to accord it the same status as "tree" or "grass," and the specialists among them recognize many different types, even if not all are named. Hence I have included it here as a general class. If it is a generic, it is perceptually at rank level 1 in Berlin, Breedlove and Raven's (1973) folk taxonomic hierarchy.

15. There is a general nomenclatural and perceptual division in Lillooet and Thompson reflecting the natural discontinuity between the soft, fleshy "mushrooms" growing on the ground, and the tough, leathery shelf, or bracket fungi, mostly in Polyporaceae, growing on trees and stumps. The latter are all called *ḡəms-álqʷ* ('wood/tree mushroom') in Lillooet and *skel-ule -éyqʷ* ('great-horned-owl-wood/tree') in Thompson. It is debatable whether these bracket fungi are considered to be "kinds of" mushrooms, or only "like mushrooms."

16. Orange honeysuckle is also sometimes called *(n)-təł./tł-úymxʷ* (lit. 'trailing-over-the-ground'), a term also sometimes applied to twinflower, and to other low, creeping plants such as *Lathyrus* and *Vicia* species, both indigenous and introduced. This term could thus constitute

another general category name, but is more likely an intermediate-level class included within the general **stuyt-úym̓x^w** category in Thompson.

17. Hunn (pers. comm. 1986) notes that in Sahaptin there is only a generic term **tam-qiks-kula** for the white clematis; apparently neither orange honeysuckle nor blue clematis is recognized.

18. Annie York used the Thompson names for these plants in her conversation.

APPENDIX 1. Native language speakers consulted in this study (in alphabetical order of their last names, with year(s) interviewed)

Lillooet

Bill Edwards, Pavilion - 1985
Martina LaRochelle (late), Lillooet - 1972
Margaret Lester, Mount Currie - 1984, 1985
Charlie Mack, Mount Currie - 1974, 1985
Sam Mitchell, Fountain (late) - 1972, 1973, 1974
Edith O'Donaghey, Lillooet (originally Shalalth) - 1985
Alec Peters, Mount Currie - 1984, 1985
Desmond Peters, Pavilion (originally Shalalth) - 1985
Baptiste Ritchie (late), Mount Currie - 1974
Nellie Wallace, Mount Currie - 1984, 1985

Thompson

Lizzie Aljam, Coldwater - 1984
Mary Anderson, Fourteen-Mile - 1980
Bernadette Antoine, Coldwater - 1984, 1985
Hilda Austin, Lytton - 1981, 1982
Janet Charters, Nooaitch - 1984
Nora Jimmie, Nooaitch - 1984
Mabel Joe, Shulus - 1984, 1985
Julia Kilroy ("Shuli"), Coldwater (late) - 1984, 1985
Louie Phillips, Lytton - 1974, 1981
Annie York, Spuzzum - 1973–1985

APPENDIX 2. Scientific names of plant species mentioned in this paper (in alphabetical order of English common names)

alder, mountain *(Alnus crispa)*
alfalfa *(Medicago sativa)*
anemone, western *(Pulsatilla occidentalis)*
arnica *(Arnica* spp.)
avalanche lily, yellow *(Erythronium grandi-florum)*
avens, large-leaved *(Geum macrophyllum)*
balsamroot *(Balsamorhiza sagittata)*
bitterroot *(Lewisia rediviva)*
bitterroot, alpine *(Lewisia columbiana)*
blackcap *(Rubus leucodermis)*
bleeding-heart, wild *(Dicentra formosa)*
bluebunch wheat grass *(Agropyron spicatum)*
bracken fern *(Pteridium aquilinum)*
"bunchgrass" (see bluebunch wheat grass)
buttercup *(Ranunculus* spp.)
calypso *(Calypso bulbosa)*
campion *(Silene* sp.)
catchfly, night-flowering *(Silene noctiflora)*
cedar, western red *(Thuja plicata)*
cherry, bitter *(Prunus emarginata)*

chocolate lily *(Fritillaria lanceolata)*
clematis, blue *(Clematis columbiana)*
clematis, white *(Clematis ligusticifolia)*
columbine, red *(Aquilegia formosa)*
cottonwood, black *(Populus balsamifera* ssp. *trichocarpa)*
"cottonwood mushroom" *(Tricholoma populinum)*
cow-parsnip *(Heracleum lanatum)*
cranberry, highbush *(Viburnum edule)*
currant, northern black *(Ribes hudsonianum)*
"cut-grass" *(Scirpus microcarpus)*
delphinium *(Delphinium* spp.)
Douglas-fir *(Pseudotsuga menziesii)*
fir, grand *(Abies grandis)*
fir, subalpine *(Abies lasiocarpa)*
fireweed *(Epilobium angustifolium)*
forget-me-not *(Myosotis laxa)*
fungi, bracket or shelf *(Polyporus* spp., *Fomes* spp., *Ganoderma* spp.)

goldenrod, Canada *(Solidago canadensis)*
harebell, blue *(Campanula rotundifolia)*
hawthorn, black *(Crataegus douglasii)*
hemlock, western *(Tsuga heterophylla)*
honeysuckle, orange *(Lonicera ciliosa)*
huckleberry, black *(Vaccinium membranaceum)*
huckleberry, red *(Vaccinium parvifolium)*
Indian hellebore *(Veratrum viride)*
Indian hemp *(Apocynum cannabinum)*
Indian paintbrush *(Castilleja* spp.)
juniper, common *(Juniperus communis)*
juniper, Rocky Mountain *(Juniperus scopulorum)*
lamb's quarters *(Chenopodium album)*
lichen, black tree *(Bryoria fremontii)*
lichen, lung *(Lobaria pulmonaria)*
lichen, wolf *(Letharia vulpina)*
licorice fern *(Polypodium glycyrrhiza)*
maple, Rocky Mountain *(Acer glabrum)*
maple, vine *(Acer circinatum)*
monkeyflower, red *(Mimulus lewisii)*
mullein *(Verbascum thapsus)*
oceanspray *(Holodiscus discolor)*
onion, nodding wild *(Allium cernuum)*
orchid, bog *(Habenaria dilatata)*
orchid, rein *(Habenaria stricta)*
Oregon-grape *(Mahonia nervosa)*
oyster mushroom *(Pleurotus ostreatus)*
penstemon, shrubby *(Penstemon fruticosus)*
pine, lodgepole *(Pinus contorta)*
pine, ponderosa *(Pinus ponderosa)*
pine, whitebark *(Pinus albicaulis)*
pine grass *(Calamagrostis rubescens)*
pine mushroom *(Tricholoma magnivelare;* syn. *Armillaria ponderosa)*
plantains *(Plantago* spp.)
puffballs *(Lycoperdon* spp.)
pussytoes *(Antennaria* spp.)

rabbitbrush *(Chrysothamnus nauseosus)*
rattlesnake plantain *(Goodyera oblongifolia)*
red-top grass *(Agrostis alba)*
reed canary grass *(Phalaris arundinacea)*
rose, wild *(Rosa* spp.)
rhododendron, white-flowered *(Rhododendron albiflorum)*
rye grass, giant wild *(Elymus cinereus)*
sagebrush, big *(Artemisia tridentata)*
salal *(Gaultheria shallon)*
saskatoon berry *(Amelanchier alnifolia)*
self-heal *(Prunella vulgaris)*
shaggy mane mushroom *(Coprinus comatus)*
silverberry *(Elaeagnus commutata)*
silverweed *(Potentilla anserina* ssp. *pacifica)*
soapberry *(Shepherdia canadensis)*
"speargrass" *(Hordeum jubatum)*
spring beauty *(Claytonia lanceolata)*
spruce, Sitka *(Picea sitchensis)*
starflower *(Trientalis latifolia)*
stonecrops *(Sedum* spp.)
strawberry, wild *(Fragaria* spp.)
sweet-clover, white *(Melilotus alba)*
sweet-clover, yellow *(Melilotus officinalis)*
thimbleberry *(Rubus parviflorus)*
tiger lily *(Lilium columbianum)*
"timbergrass" *(Calamagrostis rubescens)*
timothy grass *(Phleum pratense)*
tobacco, wild *(Nicotiana attenuata)*
twinberry, black *(Lonicera involucrata)*
twinflower *(Linnaea borealis)*
vetch *(Vicia* spp.)
violet, wild blue *(Viola adunca)*
water-parsnip *(Sium suave)*
"wild carrot" *(Lomatium macrocarpum)*
willows *(Salix* spp.)
wormwood, pasture *(Artemisia frigida)*
yew, western *(Taxus brevifolia)*

CHAPTER SIX

Alternatives to Taxonomic Hierarchy
The Sahaptin Case

EUGENE S. HUNN, DAVID H. FRENCH

INTRODUCTION

Studies of folk biological classification begin with the matching of names to corresponding segments of the biota. Since they do not end there, the next step is to seek to discover and analyze the organizing principles that structure these systems, which may then be compared cross-culturally.

Berlin's universal principles of folk biological classification and nomenclature (1973; Berlin, Breedlove, and Raven 1973), though based on limited comparative data, represent a pioneering effort at such cross-cultural analysis, and provide the framework for most subsequent studies of the structure of folk biological classification systems. His proposals have been supported (e.g., Brunel 1974; Hays 1974, 1983; Hunn 1975), extended (Brown 1977; Brown et al. 1976), criticized (e.g., Bulmer 1974; Hays 1983; Healey 1978–79; Hunn 1976, 1977; Randall 1976), and revised (Berlin 1976). This paper is intended as both critique and extension of Berlin's point of departure. We will argue that the taxonomic principle of inclusion by which taxa at one level or rank are subsumed by those of a higher level or rank—basic to Berlin's hierarchic scheme of folk biological classification, as it is to the Linnean—is but one way to organize a set of folk biological taxa. Furthermore, the associated binomial naming principle is one of several ways to indicate nomenclaturally structural relationships within folk biological classification systems (Fig. 1).

Our research with Sahaptin-speaking Indians of the Columbia Plateau region of the Pacific Northwest (Fig. 2) has shown Sahaptin to be an unusual case in comparison with folk biological classification systems previously described. Plant and animal classification by our Sahaptin-speaking consultants exhibits an extraordinary lack of hierarchic structure (French 1981). In fact, the system closely approximates the null point of taxonomic hierarchy, the single level system. Berlin has postulated that such a system should represent the initial stage in an evolutionary sequence of development of folk taxonomies (1972).

Following Berlin's lead, Brown (1977, 1979) sought to demonstrate that named life form taxa, i.e., inclusive taxa at a level above that of the basic folk taxonomic

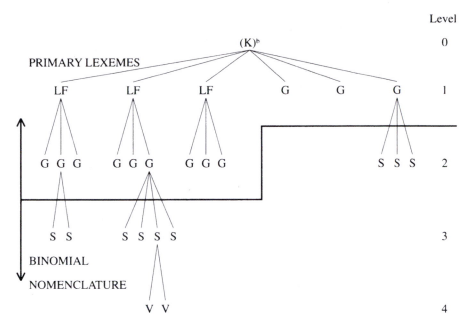

^a LF = life forms, G = folk generics or basic level taxa, S = folk specifics, V = folk varietals, based on Berlin, Breedlove, and Raven (1973).

^b The kingdom (K) rank is typically not named.

Fig. 1. Idealized taxonomic structure indicating the relationship between taxonomic levels and ranks and showing the distribution of binomial nomenclature.^a

level (the "folk generic" rank of Berlin), are added progressively to the folk biological inventories of the world's languages. Sahaptin is at an early stage of development, according to Brown's analysis, having a single botanical and a single zoological life form named, i.e., 'tree' and 'bird.' Of 217 cases sampled by Brown, only six are judged to have as few (5 cases) or fewer (one case) life forms (1977: 324, 1979: 796).

The minimal degree of hierarchic development in Sahaptin is even more apparent when Berlin's folk specific taxonomic level is considered. Berlin has compared a number of well documented folk botanical and zoological systems in terms of the percent of "folk generic" taxa subdivided by subordinate "folk specific" taxa, to which binomial names are characteristically applied (1976: 389). These and an additional case are summarized in Table 1. There is a surprising degree of consistency to these statistics, with all except the Hanunóo falling in the range of 11% to 18% of basic level taxa being polytypic. Sahaptin stands in sharp contrast. The frequency of basic level polytypy for plant taxa is 1% (excluding recent coinages), with only two cases known, while that for animals is 2%, with four cases known.

It is misleading, however, to conclude that Sahaptin-speakers fail to perceive structure within their biological domains. Furthermore, they use nomenclatural means

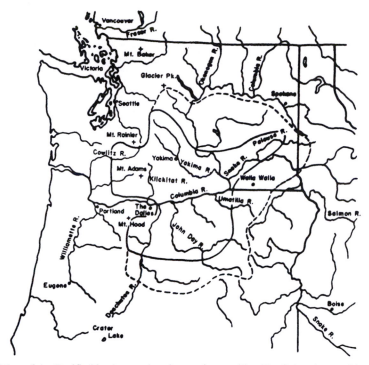

Fig. 2. Map of the Pacific Northwest showing territory utilized by Sahaptin-speaking peoples. The central area indicates territory used primarily by Sahaptin-speaking peoples and under their control. The peripheral area indicates territory used annually by Sahaptin speaking peoples but in common with neighboring groups of other linguistic affiliations. Both areas are approximate. Reproduced from page 22 of Eugene S. Hunn, "Mobility as a Factor Limiting Resource Use in the Columbia Plateau of North America," pp. 17–43 in *Resource Managers: North American and Australian Hunter-Gatherers*, A.A.A.S. Symposium Volume 67, Westview Press, Boulder, Colorado.

to indicate the structure they perceive, just as the use of binomial names may indicate relations of taxonomic hierarchy. We will describe two regular nomenclatural patterns employed in Sahaptin to indicate relationships among folk biological taxa. Both are more frequently employed than is binomial naming in Sahaptin folk biology. Both patterns reflect perceived resemblance or "kinship" among taxa. These relations *coordinate* taxa in direct contrast (cf. Lancy and Strathern 1981) rather than *subordinate* less inclusive taxa to those more inclusive.

Sahaptin speakers are much less likely to name a taxon by reference to its relationship to some other taxon—whatever the nature of that relationship—than speakers of other well known languages. The percentage of basic taxa named by reference to such relations in Sahaptin is substantially less than the percentage of binomially named taxa alone in comparable systems.

TABLE 1. Degree of basic level polytypy in folk biological systems.

System	Polytypy %	Number of Basic Level Taxa	Source
Sahaptin plants	1	213	Hunn 1980
Sahaptin animals	2	236	Hunn 1980
Chacan Quechua plants	11	n.a.	Brunel 1974
Ndumba plants	14	385	Hays 1974a
Ndumba animals	16	186	Hays 1983a
Tzeltal Mayan plants	16	471	Berlin, et al. 1974
Tzeltal Mayan animals	17	335	Hunn 1977
Aguaruna Jivaro plants	18	566	Berlin 1976
Hanunóo plants	36	n.a.	Conklin 1954

[a] These numbers represent the "shared" inventory, i.e., shared by nine of Hays' 10 informants. His totals are thus conservative compared with those reported by other researchers, who list a collective inventory.

METHODS OF DATA COLLECTION AND ANALYSIS

In the Sahaptin case, we have consulted a variety of sources: 1) the naming responses of Sahaptin-speaking consultants to individual plants and animals examined *in situ* or as pressed specimens, 2) discussions with consultants (conducted in English) of the characteristics of plants and animals (named in Sahaptin), and 3) comparable data reported by colleagues (K. French, V. Hymes, B. Rigsby, H. Schuster) and earlier ethnographers and linguists (M. Jacobs, E. Curtis, M. Pandosy, W. Everette). These data are of diverse quality. However, in the aggregate they represent several thousand instances of the naming of plant and animal taxa.

The key methodological issue is the operational definition of a *name*. In particular, names must be distinguished from more ephemeral constructions such as descriptive phrases, nonce forms, and idiosyncratic labels. Though a name may be constructed of two or more words, it is a single *lexeme* (Conklin 1962), that is, the referential meaning of the lexeme is not readily inferred from the referential meanings of its component morphemes or words. Thus, "silverfish" is not a silver fish and a "blackbird" is not just any bird which is black. For present purposes, a name must also reflect some degree of *consistency* of application across individuals and naming events. We have established the criterion for our data that to be considered a name a lexical expression must be employed consistently by at least two individuals on at least two independent occasions with the same referential meaning. This criterion is conservative in that it no doubt has led to the exclusion of some names from the corpus here considered. However, it provides a systematic means to exclude many (perhaps not all) nonce forms. This criterion is a necessary but not a sufficient condition for a lexical response to be considered a name. Expressions must also be considered appropriate responses to the query, "What is the name of X?" In Sahaptin this is *tun i-wanik-ša.*[2]

Sahaptin speakers are quite emphatic in denying the status of "name" (*waník-t*) to responses considered to be transparently descriptive. It seems to us that this emic distinction is identical to or closely parallel to the linguists' distinction between noun lexemes and polylexemic expressions (Lyon 1977: Vol. 1, 18–25; Taylor 1982). We have also queried consultants about each named taxon concerning uses, distributional patterns, and morphological and behavioral features. When consultants are able to provide detailed ancillary information about a named organism, we feel justified in concluding that the name indeed refers to a distinct concept, a "semantically primitive" kind of living thing.

We are also concerned here with a particular class of names, that is, those which indicate syntactically a formal or structural relationship between the taxon named and some related folk biological taxon. Such *structure-defining names* necessarily will be morphologically compound and thus particularly difficult to distinguish from lexically compound expressions of parallel syntactic composition. English structure-defining names are typically (if not exclusively) of binomial form, as for example, "big-leaf maple" and "hammer-head shark." The binomial form of these names consistently indicates that the taxon so named is subordinate to the taxon named by the head constituent of the name. Such names must be carefully distinguished from descriptive phrases, such as "moss-draped maple" and "man-eating shark," and from metaphorical look alikes such as "poolshark," "poison oak," and "silverfish," already mentioned.

Parallel naming conventions have been described for a number of languages unrelated to English, and the binomial pattern may be universal (Berlin, Breedlove, and Raven 1973). The lexemic typology devised by Conklin (1962), since refined by Berlin (1973), recognizes the binomial name form as of privileged status, and the class inclusion relations indicated thereby have come to be seen as *the* fundamental structural principle of folk biological classification. The generality of binomial naming in folk biological nomenclatural systems, plus its incorporation as the basis of scientific biological nomenclature, has obscured the fact that this naming convention is just one of several naming patterns indicative of structural relations among taxa.

In Sahaptin there are *three* nomenclatural patterns commonly used to reflect *two* distinct types of formal relations among taxa. Binomial nomenclature used to indicate class inclusion is one of these. More frequently used in Sahaptin are two other naming patterns. These latter indicate relations of coordination—a relationship sometimes referred to metaphorically by Sahaptin consultants in terms of human social or kinship relations, as for example, dog, coyote, and wolf are said to be *náymu* 'relative/friend' of one another.

One of these coordinating naming patterns is superficially binomial, in that the name is formed of the modified name of a second taxon, which remains unaltered as the head constituent. The attributive constituent is the bound suffix-*wáakuł*, which may be glossed 'resembling' or, simple '-like'. For example, *c'iiławáakuł* is used to name Belding's ground squirrel (*Citellus beldingi*), while *c'iiłá* [*c'ii* (onomatopoetic) + *-ła* (agentive)] names Townsend's and Washington ground squirrels (*C. townsendii, C. washingtoni*). Consultants who used this name (one each from the John Day and

Umatilla dialects) distinguish Belding's on the basis of size, calls, and range. The suffix **-wáakuł** is also frequently employed to indicate similarity in a descriptive context, as when the color of a horse is described as **wiwnuwáakuł** 'huckleberry-like'.

The second Sahaptin syntactic convention used in coordinate naming is reduplication, often combined with sound symbolism. This is a highly productive syntactic feature of Sahaptin (Jacobs 1931: 135–140; Rigsby n.d.) indicating variously diminution, distributive plurality, and—as here—the status of "younger sibling," i.e., the resemblance of a conceptually peripheral taxon to the more central or salient prototype. For example, **k'usík'usi** 'dog' is derived by this process from **k'úsi** 'horse.' This naming process is not restricted to recently introduced species such as the horse; it is also used, for example, in naming a species of *Vaccinium* that is a traditionally favored food item, **wiwlúwiwlu** 'grouseberry' (*'Vaccinium scoparium* Leiberg),[3] derived from **wíwnu** 'black mountain huckleberry' (*V. membranaceum* Dougl. ex Hook.), the arche-typical fruit for Sahaptin speakers.

Such relations of coordination of similar plants and animals may be *described* in English (or in other languages including Tzeltal), but such descriptive expressions as "dog-like" in English or *"kol pahaluk sok šuš"* 'almost the same as wasp' in Tzeltal are never used as names. The status of the parallel Sahaptin forms as true names is suggested by the fact that the nonce form **wiwluwiwluwáakuł** has been recorded (in response to an ambiguous *Vaccinium* specimen), as has the binomial **tanán sit'x̌ʷswáakuł**, literally, 'Indian corn,' from **tanán** 'Indian,' plus **sít'x̌ʷs** *'Brodiaea hyacinthina* (Lindl.) Baker,' plus **-wáakuł** '-like.'

A DISCUSSION OF THE SAHAPTIN CASES

Binomial Names.—The Sahaptin use of binomial nomenclature is sporadic, at best, and at times appears to be actively avoided. One simple case of binomial nomenclature involves the recognition of two species of raspberry:

(1) *šáx̌at*

čmúk šáx̌at, lit. 'black raspberry'

luc'á šáx̌at, lit. 'red raspberry'

Since the red raspberry (*Rubus idaeus* L.) is rare in the Sahaptin range, the unmodified generic term *šáx̌at* is normally used to label the common blackcap raspberry (*R. leucodermis* Dougl.) (cf. Curtis 1911: 175).

The naming and classification of willows (*Salix* spp.) in Sahaptin is complex. The general term is **ttáx̌š** (**táx̌š** in NW dialects). However, the large, erect peachleaf willow (*S. amygdaloides* Anderss.) is singled out as **haháw.** It is unique among the willows in its straight, nearly branchless bole (Peattie 1950: 346–347), and thus is favored for longhouse framing. The categories **haháw** and **ttáx̌š** are seen as closely related but distinct taxa. Other native willows (e.g., *Salix exigua* Nutt. ssp. *exigua* var. *exigua, S. rigida* Muhl. var. *mackenzieana* (Hook.) Cronq., *S. scouleriana* Barratt, *S. lasiandra* Benth. var. *caudata* (Nutt.) Sudw.) as well as the introduced willows (*S. alba* L. var. *vitellina* (L.) Stokes, *S. babylonica* L.) are *ttáx̣š*. This term may be modified, though without great consistency, as *pu²úxpu²ux̣ ttáx̣š* 'gray willow,' often used to refer to the shrubby, gray leaved coyote willow *(S. exigua)*, and *pt'x̣anupamá ttáx̣š* 'mountain-forest willow' for Scouler willow *(S. scouleriana)*, the typical large willow of the montane zone. Other willows are "just" *ttáx̣š* 'willow,' which creates a "residual category" (Hunn 1977: 57–58), labeled [R] in the diagram below.

(2) *haháw* 'peachleaf willow'

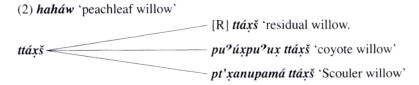

ttáx̣š ⎯⎯⎯⎯⎯ [R] *ttáx̣š* 'residual willow.

pu²úxpu²ux̣ ttáx̣š 'coyote willow'

pt'x̣anupamá ttáx̣š 'Scouler willow'

Chokecherry (*Prunus virginiana* L. var. *demissa* (Nutt.) Torr.) provides an interesting comparison. Chokecherries are an important traditional food. The cherries vary in color from red to black, but discontinuously so that three color types are readily recognized. Modern-day Sahaptins are aware of this variation but refused to apply binomials to label the variants, even when prodded to do so. Several consultants rejected **čmúk tmíš*, literally 'black chokecherry,' and **luc'á tmíš* 'red chokecherry,' while accepting the parallel raspberry names. They asserted that this variation among chokecherries is of no significance .

The four acceptable examples of binomial naming applied to animals are neither very widely nor very consistently used. Two informants distinguished the rare snowy owl *(Nyctea scandiaca)* as *qúyx̣ miimánu,* literally, 'white large owl.' Unmodified *miimánu* calls to mind as prototype the great horned owl (*Bubo virginianus*), the most common and the most powerful owl in the region. This is attested by consultants' descriptions of *miimánu* vocalizations, appearance, and habits. The term *miimánu* is now also extended to other medium to large owls, such as the barn owl *(Tyto alba)* and short-eared owl *(Asio flammeus),* when examples of these species are presented for naming. This may indicate that contemporary speakers have never learned the "proper" names for these owls. Although this naming pattern might suggest that the snowy owl is considered a *kind of* great horned owl, such is not the case. The snowy owl is seen as a related, but coordinate form, on the same taxonomic level as *miimánu.* The situation might be interpreted taxonomically if we were to posit two polysemous senses of *miimánu* (cf. Berlin 1976: 391–392), as follows:

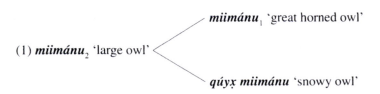

*miimánu*₁ 'great horned owl'

(1) *miimánu*₂ 'large owl'

qúyx̣ miimánu 'snowy owl'

However, this interpretation is hypothetical, snowy owl illustrations were never identified as unmodified **miimánu** (and their rarity prevented evaluation of naming responses in more realistic settings), and in the single myth recorded in which snowy owl is a character the binomial expression was used exclusively. Thus it is not possible to determine if **qúyx̱ miimánu** is more like the English "pack rat" (a kind of rat) than "musk rat" (which is not a kind of rat).

   Several consultants distinguish black-tailed jackrabbits *(Lepus californicus)* from their white-tailed cousins *(L. townsendii).*

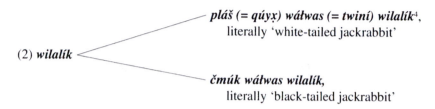

(2) **wilalík**

   pláš (= qúyx̱) wátwas (= twiní) wilalík[4],
   literally 'white-tailed jackrabbit'

   čmúk wátwas wilalík,
   literally 'black-tailed jackrabbit'

State of Washington consultants are quick to note that the black-tailed species is a modern-day intruder, having expanded its range north of the Columbia River in the past 60 years. In Oregon, where both species are longtime residents, Sahaptin speakers "mark" the less common white-tailed jackrabbit as **qúyx̱ twiní wilalík** in contrast to the black-tailed jackrabbit, known simply as **wilalík.**

   Typical lizards are called **watik'ásas,** a name which applies with equal force and without modification to fence lizards (two species of *Sceloporus*), and the side-blotched lizard *(Uta stansburiana)* [and possibly alligator lizards (two species of *Gerrhonotus*)]. The western skink *(Eumeces skiltonianus)* was singled out as **lámt wátwas watik'ásas,** literally, 'blue-tailed lizard,' by two consultants from contrasting dialect groups. The skink's tail is used as a good luck charm in gambling. Two lizards are not included in **watik'ásas,** but are contrasting basic level taxa: **x̱litáwit,** literally 'of root diggers,' is the shorthorned lizard *(Phrynosoma douglassi),* and **t'uulnawatá,** literally 'jumper,' is of uncertain identity.[5] Both are morphologically divergent species. Though **t'uulnawatá** is clearly thought of as a lizard-like creature, the horned lizard (n.b., "horned toad" in colloquial English) is not. The horned lizard is in addition considered to be an "Indian doctor" worthy of special respect and protection.

(3) **x̱litáwit** 'horned lizard'

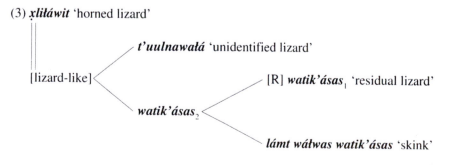

[lizard-like]

   t'uulnawatá 'unidentified lizard'

   [R] **watik'ásas**₁ 'residual lizard'

   watik'ásas₂

   lámt wátwas watik'ásas 'skink'

Typical snakes are called *pyúš*, with the abundant garter snakes (three species of *Thamnophis*) considered unexceptional examples. This name also may be applied unmodified to the racer *(Coluber constrictor)* and the gopher snake *(Pituophis melanoleucus)*, two other common species. However, the gopher snake was named *nč'í pyúš*, literally, 'big snake,' by at least three consultants of as many dialects. Others apply a contrasting basic level term, *ppáw,* to this species (Johnson-O'Malley 1977), perhaps reflecting a more differentiated nomenclature before Euro-American settlement. Individual consultants have on occasion used additional binomials to distinguish garter snakes and racers, but such usages failed to meet our nomenclatural standard for consistency of application. The western rattlesnake *(Crotalus viridus)*—like the horned lizard, an "Indian doctor"—is not considered to be a kind of *pyúš*, though its name, *wáxpuš,* clearly suggests an etymological link with *pyúš* now obscure to native speakers. Thus 'snake,' as we understand it, remains a covert category in Sahaptin.

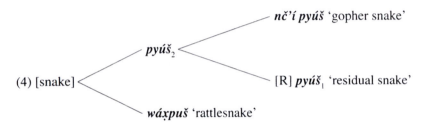

All four cases of binomial nomenclature among animals involve a minimal development of the specific contrast set. In three cases a binomial name is applied to one exceptional "species" within a folk "genus"—or possibly to a coordinate form in the case of the snowy owl—while the other member(s) of the genus is (are) not distinguished by a parallel binomial. Thus it would be necessary to postulate an unmarked polysemous type specific category in three of four cases in order to preserve the hierarchic form of the taxonomic model.

Expressions of Binomial Form which are not Valid Specific Names.—Binomial names in which the head component of the name refers to a taxon superordinate to the basic level were not treated above (very few cases are known for Sahaptin). This accords with Berlin's distinction (1973: 217) between "primary" names such as "mockingbird," which contrast with such names as "robin" (*not* "robinbird"), and "secondary" names, the true binomials, such as "bald eagle," which contrasts with "golden eagle," a name with parallel structure. One example of a "binomial name" at the basic level in Sahaptin is the form *tkʷínat núsuẋ* 'Chinook salmon,' more usually and simply rendered *tkʷínat* (for *Oncorhynchus tschawytscha*). The taxon *núsuẋ* 'anadromous salmonid' includes up to seven basic level categories (Hunn 1979), but spontaneous binomial combinations have been recorded only for *tkʷínat,* the prototype of *núsuẋ*.

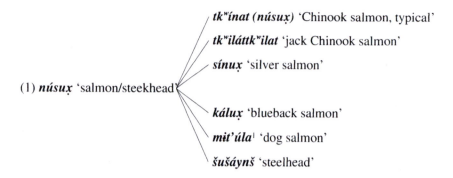

(1) *núsux̣* 'salmon/steekhead'

tkʷínat (núsux̣) 'Chinook salmon, typical'

tkʷiláttkʷilat 'jack Chinook salmon'

sínux̣ 'silver salmon'

kálux̣ 'blueback salmon'

*mit'úla*¹ 'dog salmon'

šušáynš 'steelhead'

The category *núsux̣* may be considered a small "life form" (as there is no general term for 'fish' in Sahaptin) or a named intermediate level taxon (see Berlin, Breedlove, and Raven 1973), as it includes several basic level taxa. A similar situation holds among names for coniferous trees, at least as Sahaptin is spoken today. Spruce trees (*Picea engelmannii* Parry ex Engelm.) may be called *qutqút patátwi* 'prickly fir.' However, *patátwi* also includes a number of trees known by primary names, e.g., *waqutqút* 'hemlock,' *táp'aš* 'Ponderosa pine,' and *naníkaaš* 'white-bark pine.' The occasional use of a primary name for spruce, *mic'ípaas,* literally, 'itchy tree/shrub,' suggests that the binomial term is a recent replacement for the "true name" now forgotten.

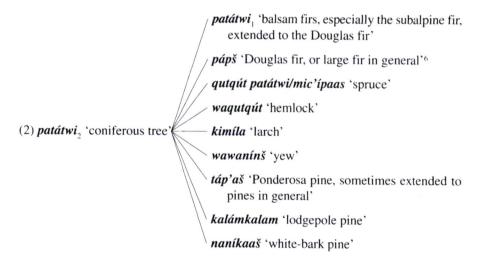

(2) *patátwi₂* 'coniferous tree'

patátwi₁ 'balsam firs, especially the subalpine fir, extended to the Douglas fir'

pápš 'Douglas fir, or large fir in general'⁶

qutqút patátwi/mic'ípaas 'spruce'

waqutqút 'hemlock'

kimíla 'larch'

wawanínš 'yew'

táp'aš 'Ponderosa pine, sometimes extended to pines in general'

kalámkalam 'lodgepole pine'

naníkaaš 'white-bark pine'

More than 20 varieties of *k'úsi* 'horse' are recognized nomenclaturally by contemporary consultants (a more exact count is not possible due to the productivity of binomial labeling used to describe horses). These varieties are labeled as in the following examples: *máamin* 'appaloosa,' *kawxkáwx* 'palomino,' *luč'á* 'bay' (from *luč'á* 'red'), and *wiwnuwáakuɬ* 'huckleberry roan' (literally 'huckleberry-like'). It is acceptable to say *máamin k'úsi* 'appaloosa horse,' but such a binomial variant is rarely noted in normal naming contexts or in conversation, even when the modifier is a widely used adjective such as *čmúk* 'black,' which thus may also mean 'black horse,' according to context. In a few instances there is a further subdivision of specific horse names into varieties which may be named binomially, as for example, *čmúk šiwíwšiwiw* 'black roan.' Sahaptin horse classification illustrates an unusual elaboration of Sahaptin nomenclature that is a consequence of a recently introduced biological phenomenon, a domesticated, and thus extremely variable organism. We have thus excluded horse varietal terms from present consideration. The very large number of recognized horse varieties is also anomalous with respect to the expected distribution of polytypy (Geoghegan 1976), a pattern consistent with the recent incorporation of the horse in Sahaptin culture.

We have also excluded cases in which a heterogeneous basic level taxon is frequently but idiosyncratically or inconsistently further specified binomially. Examples include *išáy* 'worm/caterpillar/maggot' and *kliwisá* 'ant.' Variation within these broad categories may be noted by reference to color, behavior, habitat, or host organism, but the forms seem clearly to be on-the-spot inventions to entertain the ethnographer. Finally, we have excluded cases involving recently introduced species. The binomial expression *tanán X,* literally 'Indian X,' is used by a few consultants to distinguish native forms from related introduced forms. For example, one consultant contrasted *tanán šáak* 'Indian onion,' the wild species of *Allium,* with *šáak* proper, which this consultant restricted to garden onions. Another individual referred to an ear of varicolored "Indian corn" as *tanán sit'xʷswáakuł,* literally 'Indian corn.' These usages, besides being recent, are idiosyncratic and sporadic.

The Suffix -wáakuł '-like.'—This naming convention is much more frequently used in botanical names than in the zoological. Our single animal case is the ground squirrel example cited above.

(1) *c'iiłá* 'Townsend's/Washington ground squirrel'

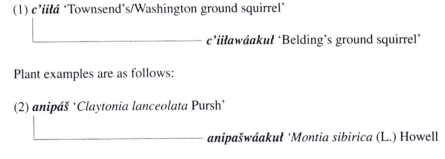

          c'iiławáakuł 'Belding's ground squirrel'

Plant examples are as follows:

(2) *anipáš* '*Claytonia lanceolata* Pursh'

          anipašwáakuł '*Montia sibirica* (L.) Howell

The first named is an "Indian potato"; the second is a striking look-alike and close relative, lacking underground tubers. In fact, the presence of a tuberous root is a trait used by certain botanists to distinguish *Claytonia* from *Montia.* This use of *anipašwaakuł* was recorded by Gunther during a 1935 ethnobotanical survey in western Washington (1973: 29) and is current on the Warm Springs Reservation in eastern Oregon.

(3) *č'iší* '*Purshia tridentata* (Pursh) DC.'

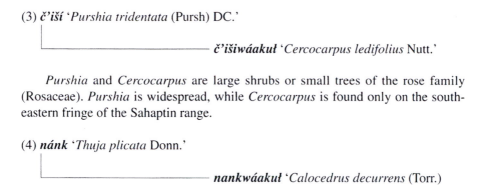

                                č'išiwáakuł '*Cercocarpus ledifolius* Nutt.'

Purshia and *Cercocarpus* are large shrubs or small trees of the rose family (Rosaceae). *Purshia* is widespread, while *Cercocarpus* is found only on the southeastern fringe of the Sahaptin range.

(4) *nánk* '*Thuja plicata* Donn.'

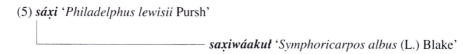

                                nankwáakuł '*Calocedrus decurrens* (Torr.) Florin.'

This Warm Springs case is precisely parallel to the preceding but involves two large tree species of the cypress family (Cupressaceae); *Thuja* is common and widely used, while *Calocedrus* is known only from the southwestern corner of the Sahaptin range.

(5) *sáx̣i* '*Philadelphus lewisii* Pursh'

                                sax̣iwáakuł '*Symphoricarpos albus* (L.) Blake'

Here two shrubs, though not closely related, share the characteristic of opposite leaves. Both are common, widespread, and useful; *Philadelphus,* in the rose family, as a durable wood and source of soap; *Symphoricarpos,* in the honeysuckle family (Caprifoliaceae), as a medicine. The "junior status" of *Symphoricarpos* may be because of its shorter stature and smaller leaves and flowers.

(6) *suspán* '*Fragaria* spp.'

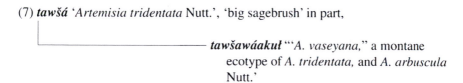

                                suspanwáakuł '*Geum triflorum* Pursh'

Here the strawberry *(Fragaria)* is compared to another herbaceous species of the same family (Rosaceae). The strawberry is a favorite though incidentally important food; *Geum triflorum* is used medicinally.

(7) *tawšá* '*Artemisia tridentata* Nutt.', 'big sagebrush' in part,

                                tawšawáakuł '"*A. vaseyana*," a montane ecotype of *A. tridentata,* and *A. arbuscula* Nutt.'

Tawšá is abundant at lower elevations, occasionally attaining the stature of a small tree. It has incidental technological applications and is a medicine. *Tawšawáakuł* is a form dwarfed by high elevation *("A. vaseyana")* or impoverished soils *(A. arbuscula).*

(8) **tmíš** 'Prunus virginiana L.'

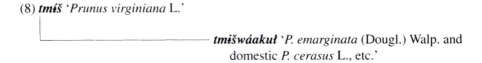

                       tmišwáakuł 'P. emarginata (Dougl.) Walp. and
domestic P. cerasus L., etc.'

The conceptual priority of the chokecherry (P. virginiana) presumably is because of
its value as a highly regarded food. Bitter cherry (P. emarginata) is not eaten here but
has technological and medicine value. The inclusion of the domestic cherries (P.
cerasus, etc.) gives the derived category a residual quality, that is, we might gloss
tmišwáakuł as 'any cherry but the chokecherry.'

(9) **wák'amu** 'Camassia quamash (Pursh) Greene'

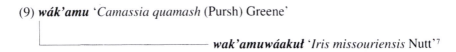

                       wak'amuwáakuł 'Iris missouriensis Nutt'[7]

Camas (Camassia), in the Liliaceae, is a staple root food while the iris, Iridaceae, is
not used. Both are showy monocots with grass-like leaves.

    The terms for corn and tomatoes provide two additional examples of the use of
plant names modified in this way. Both are introduced domesticates, though corn may
have been known to Sahaptins before Euro-American contact. Corn is almost universally known as **sit'x^{w}swáakuł;** its namesake **sit'x^{w}s** is Brodiaea hyacinthina (Lindl.)
Baker in the lily family, valued for its edible corms. The resemblance perceived,
however, is not between corn and the lily as plants, but in the form of the edible
portions of each, the kernel of corn fancied to resemble the corm of the Brodiaea. Our
second example is precisely comparable. The introduced tomato is often called **šč'a-
pawáakuł** 'rosehip-like,' and indeed a tomato's fruit bears a substantial superficial
resemblance to the fruit (hip) of the native roses. These two cases are intermediate
between the instances described above in which two taxa are closely related conceptually on the basis of overall morphological resemblance, and instances in which the
perceived resemblance is based on some single characteristic shared by the "prototype" and the form compared to it, as when a "huckleberry roan" is called
wiwnuwáakuł 'huckleberry-like' based on shared color.

Reduplication.—This naming pattern is less frequent than the preceding, but it is used
in the same way to link a simply named prototype to a derivatively named form (or
forms) perceived to be closely related. It usually carries the additional implication of
relatively smaller size. Botanical examples include the huckleberry case already cited:

(1) **wíwnu** 'Vaccinium membranaceum Dougl. ex Hook'

                       wiwlúwiwlu 'V. scoparium Leiberg'

The prototype in this case is a highly valued staple food; V. scoparium is also eaten,
but more as an incidental treat. Both the shrub and fruit of V. scoparium are dwarfed.

In some Sahaptin dialects taller native onions are called *šáak,* while low-growing species are *saaksáak:*

(2) *šáak* 'taller wild onions'

└─────────────────────────── *saaksáak* 'low-growing wild onions'

A similar (or identical?) contrast is handled differently in other dialects, in which the taller onions of wet meadows are called *qʷláwi* and the low-growing rock onions are *šámamwi.*

Zoological examples include the following:

(3) *tkʷínat* 'typical *Oncorhynchus tschawytschwa*'

└─────────────────────────── *tkʷiláttkʷilat* '"jack" *Oncorhynchus tschawytscha*'

The "jack" of the Chinook salmon is a form of that species that returns to spawn a year earlier than is typical. They are identifiable by their smaller size. The "jack" is not considered a kind of *tkʷínat,* but a "species" of salmon in its own right. The next two cases are close parallels.

(4) *apín* 'head louse'

└─────────────────────────── *apílapíl* 'small swarming invertebrates'

Examples of the latter include aphids and the larvae of mosquitoes.

(5) *ištxní* 'horse fly, typically, extended to include other large biting flies'

└─────────────────────────── *istxlíistxli* 'gnats'

Our final example is the intriguing case of the horse and dog. Contemporary Sahaptin speakers, as well as those who served as Pandosy's informants (1862), call the dog *k'usí-k'usi,* literally 'little horse.' However, the horse is the more recent introduction (Haines 1938). Dogs are known from the Pacific Northwest archaeologically since 10,400 BP (Lawrence 1968), and thus must have been the original referent of *k'úsi.* Horses were likened to dogs presumably because of the role they came to play in human social economy as highly useful and esteemed (but inedible) pets. The horse's large size and rapid incorporation as an essential mode of transport and currency of social exchange apparently produced the semantic shift now evident:

(6) *k'úsi* 'horse'

└─────────────────────────── *k'usíkusi* 'dog'

A similar process occurred in Tzeltal with deer and sheep and peccaries and pigs (Berlin 1972: 82–83).

We have not counted here cases of reduplication used to name early growth stages of a plant or animal, such as *aluqátaluqat* 'recently emerged frog/toad,' from *aluqát* 'adult frog,' and *tap'áytap'ay* 'Ponderosa pine seedling,' from *táp'aš* 'Ponderosa pine.' We have not counted *lalíklalik* 'columbine' (*Aquilegia formosa* Fisch.), derived from *naník* 'seed of white-bark pine,' as the resemblance is drawn between the seeds of the respective plants only, a naming pattern like that of corn and tomato.

Implicit Recognition of Prototype/Satellite Structural Relations.—The coordinate relationship between a prototypical category and one or more satellite taxa—explicitly recognized in the above examples by reduplication or the suffix *-wáakuł* '-like'—is frequently implicit in Sahaptin. Such implicit relationships are manifested by consultants' statements that taxon *X* is similar or related to taxon *Y* or by patterns of identification errors (Hays 1976). In each of the following cases a heterogeneous basic level taxon has a closely associated satellite taxon which—if not named in its own right—would be subsumed by the heterogeneous category as within the "sphere of influence" of the prototype (cf. Bright and Bright 1965).

(1) *x̣átx̣at* 'duck in general with the mallard prototypical,' except for,

  └──────── *táštaš* 'common merganser

(2) *pyúš* 'snake in general with variable focus,' except for,

  └──────── *wáx̣puš* 'rattlesnake'

(3) *watik'ásas* 'lizard in general with *Sceloporus/Uta* apparently protypical,' except for,

  └──────── *t'uulnawałá* 'unidentified lizard'[5]

(4) *kliwisá* 'ant in general with *Formica* spp. prototypical,' except for,

  └──────── *támšuy* 'a species of small, non-biting, black ant'

(5) *wix̣alx̣alí* 'spider in general with no apparent prototype,' except for,

  ├──────── *tíšpun* 'black widow spider,' and

  └──────── *káatlam wux̣á* 'harvestman,' literally 'long-leg'

(6) *ttáx̣š* 'willow in general with no apparent prototype,' except for,

  └──────── *haháw* 'peachleaf willow'

The rattlesnake and black widow spider are significant dangers; the peachleaf willow, due to its atypical growth form, is of special utility; while the common merganser warned Columbia River villagers of the approach of Paiute Indian raiders. In these cases the special utility of the satellite taxon seems of paramount significance in motivating its special recognition. Morphological singularity seems the dominant factor in the cases of *t'uulnawałá* and the harvestman. Why *támšuy* is deemed worthy of special attention remains a mystery.

DISCUSSION

We have examined 21 legitimate cases (and a number of marginal ones) in which pairs of taxa conceived to be related are linked nomenclaturally. In all cases the pattern is similar: the prototypical taxon provides the nomenclatural base for naming the peripheral relative. This pattern is obvious in the cases of reduplication (N=6) and in the use of the suffix *-wáakuł* '-like' (N=9). It is somewhat less clear in the binomally labeled cases (N=6). However, at least in the case of the snowy owl, the binomial *qúyx miimánu* carries no implication of taxonomic subordination to the unmarked prototype, *miimánu* 'great horned owl.' Thus at least 16 of 21 (76%) of these cases of indirect naming involve conceptual *coordination* between basic level taxa, one focal, the other peripheral, rather than hierarchic *subordination* between taxa at higher and lower levels or ranks of a taxonomy .

Sahaptin also contrasts with other cases cited in the literature in terms of the extent to which indirect naming of any sort is used. The percentage of taxa named by reference to other taxa, either by reference to a superordinate taxon or a coordinate, prototypical taxon, is 5%, compared to ca. 35% *binomially* named taxa in Tzeltal (Berlin, Breedlove, and Raven 1974: 37; Hunn 1977: 79). Thus, not only do Sahaptin speakers avoid subordinating one taxon to another nomenclaturally, but they also are less given to naming one taxon in terms of another. A related observation is that Sahaptin consultants are skeptical of "names" which are transparently descriptive of either form or function. For example, thistles (*Cirsium* spp.) are always referred to as *qutqút*, literally 'thorny.' In the same breath, consultants aver that *qutqút* is not the plant's "real name." No consultant has been able to recall what the "real name" is, but all agree it is not *qutqút* and that a "real name" does in fact exist. Consultants react similarly to the label *tutanikpamá*, literally 'for the hair,' applied to a variety of plants used "medicinally" to make their hair grow long or to prevent graying. By contrast, Tzeltal speakers freely accept names of the form '*X*-medicine.' This Sahaptin naming style may reflect a belief in the essential power of names. Naming ceremonies and the inheritance of ancestral names is a focal point of Sahaptin ritual observance even today. However, it is not clear that Sahaptin speakers differ in their regard for the sacred power of names from speakers of languages which use indirect naming more freely. Such a connection should be investigated.

The Sahaptin nomenclatural pattern we have described may be interpreted in several ways. These interpretations might be of three types, the pattern being: (1) illusory, (2) stylistic, or (3) evolutionary. Those who argue for the pattern as illusion might

assert that the Sahaptin data are the result of a degenerative process due to acculturation. Perhaps the pre-contact Sahaptin system more closely resembled the Tzeltal,
Ndumba, Aguaruna, or Hanunóo systems in reliance on binomial naming. The
restricted Sahaptin ethnobiological inventory, i.e., 450 Sahaptin basic level taxa versus
571 in Ndumba, 813 in Tzeltal, 1000+ in Aguaruna, and 1000+ in Hanunóo, might
suggest that the presently accessible inventory is significantly less than it once was.
If acculturative losses disproportionately affect productive lexemes, we should expect
acculturated systems to exhibit a smaller percentage of binomial names than fully
viable systems.

We do not believe acculturative loss explains the Sahaptin data. First, though it
is likely the pre-contact system was larger, it is doubtful that it was ever as large as the
comparison systems for the basic reason that the ecosystems familiar to the Sahaptin
people are less rich in species than those of the Tzeltal, Ndumba, Aguaruna, or
Hanunóo, all in humid, tropical environments. Furthermore, there is continued nomenclatural recognition of some very similar and closely related species, as those of the
genus *Lomatium* (Hunn and French 1981). Although one might expect binomials to
be applied to such cases, they are not. We call attention also to the fact that in many
languages binomials are most frequently employed in naming species of high cultural
salience (Berlin, Breedlove, and Raven 1973: 216). Such names are likely to be disproportionately persistent under acculturation. Finally, we note that in several instances
binomials and other productive lexemes have recently replaced unanalyzable linguistic
expressions in Sahaptin nomenclature as in the examples cited of **qutqút patátwi**
'spruce' and **nč'í pyúš** 'gopher snake.' Thus indirect naming may be more frequent in
contemporary Sahaptin than it was pre-contact.

It may be argued that patterns of naming simply reflect styles peculiar to the
"genius" of one language or another. We may appreciate such variation as illustrating
the rich diversity of human cultures, but draw no more general conclusions. For
example, French (1960) has documented dramatic differences in naming responses
between samples of native speakers of Sahaptin, Upper Chinookan, and English to
standardized collections of plants. Sahaptin speakers much more frequently labeled
unfamiliar plants with nonce forms indicating perceived relationship or similarity, i.e.,
of the form *X-wáakuł* 'like-X,' while Upper Chinookan speakers simply said, "I don't
know."[8] English speakers were particularly inclined to invent names or to subsume
unfamiliar plants within known categories. However, if the predilection for the use of
binomial names were purely stylistic, Berlin's universals could not be relied upon
(1973). The consistency with which binomials are applied for example in Tzeltal,
Ndumba, Aguaruna, and Hanunóo, is strong contrary evidence. It is also noteworthy
that published excerpts from languages such as Eskimo (Irving 1953), Groote Eylandt
(Waddy 1982), Agta (Headland 1983), and Khoisan (Lee 1979: 464–478) suggest that
these languages might closely resemble Sahaptin in their disuse of binomials. It is at
least suggestive that the former set of languages are of subsistence farmers, the latter
of hunter-gatherers. This brings us to our third alternative type of explanation.

Evolutionary explanations of this nomenclatural pattern may be of three basic
types, reflecting the evolution of: (1) intellectual capacities, (2) social organization, or

(3) ecological and economic systems. There are respectable proponents of each of these evolutionary perspectives. For example, Berlin (1972) argues that folk biological classification systems evolve in two steps; the initial step is one of "horizontal" expansion of the set of basic folk taxa by an analogical process of "concrete transposition." What we have labeled *coordination* here is an example. The subsequent evolutionary step—which complements but does not supplant the first—is one of "vertical" expansion from the basic folk taxa by means of generalization to produce named lifeforms and, ultimately, the unique beginner, and of differentiation, to produce folk specific and varietal taxa. Binomial names are indicative of this latter process. From this perspective *subordination* is a superior mode of classification, being more "abstract" than coordination. We believe this assessment has no basis in fact, but rather represents the bias of speakers of a language, English, that has enshrined binomial nomenclature as the scientific ideal. To recognize that X is like Y requires abstraction fully as much as to recognize that X is a kind of Y.

Durkheim and Mauss argued in *Primitive Classification* (1963) that the conceptual recognition of hierarchy, as in a taxonomy, is a byproduct of the experience of social hierarchy. Thus one might argue that Sahaptin folk classification lacks hierarchical development comparable to that of the Tzeltal because the pre-contact Sahaptin speakers were egalitarian hunter-gatherers within an acephalous polity, while the Tzeltal Mayans had long known the reality of state and nation. This hypothesis is tempting in that Sahaptin social relations stress coordination and do not emphasize subordination. Though chiefs (**miyáwax̱**) were recognized, their power was limited. Much more salient were bilateral kin ties and dyadic trading partnerships between 'friends' (cf. Marshall 1977). There is a curious parallel between the Sahaptin stress on individual autonomy and their stress on the essential uniqueness of plant and animal names. However, it is patently false that Hanunóo—which surpasses Tzeltal in degree of taxonomic hierarchy in the folk biological domains as far as Tzeltal surpasses Sahaptin—have experienced extremes of social hierarchy. Furthermore, the Wasco/Wishram place considerably greater stress on social hierarchy than do their Columbia River Sahaptin neighbors, yet share their aversion to hierarchy in their folk biological classifications. It seems the apparent correlation of taxonomic hierarchy with social hierarchy may be an epiphenomenon of the underlying subsistence systems. This brings us to a consideration of the third evolutionary perspective, the ecological.

The pattern we have observed here suggests that folk biological classification systems have evolved from a single-tiered system of coordinate taxa among hunter-gatherers to a multi-tiered system (a taxonomic hierarchy proper) exhibiting a high incidence of basic level polytypy (Geoghegan 1976) among subsistence agriculturalists. A further stage of development (or of devolution, if you will) has been suggested (Dougherty 1978, Brown 1979) to account for the progressive increase in the number of highly inclusive morphologically based life-form categories and parallel reduction in numbers of basic level taxa. The initial phase of this evolutionary pattern might be explained by reference to the process of domestication. Diverse cultivars might reasonably have been the initial recipients of binomial names. They are very commonly applied in such instances. However, many wild plants and animals are also so named.

Therefore, we must assume a process of generalization whereby binomial naming was extended to wild relatives of cultivated plants and animals, then used to label any closely similar set of plants or animals, domesticated or wild. The fact that the degree of polytypy among Tzeltal zoological terms is virtually identical to that of Tzeltal botanical terms—despite the far greater role of domesticated plants than of animals in Mayan subsistence—indicates that this hypothetic process has run its course in Tzeltal.

This is a plausible account but an incomplete explanation. There remains to be explained the apparent correlation of the degree of polytypy and the size of the folk biological inventory (Table 1). Independent of the domestication of plants and animals, an elaboration of taxonomic hierarchy might serve as a more efficient means to mentally store a larger quantity of folk biological knowledge. It is presumably easier to learn and to remember a set of five terms—one naming a basic level taxon and the others naming binomially labeled subdivisions, such as pine, Ponderosa pine, white pine, lodgepole pine, and white-bark pine—than to learn the unrelated names of four genera—as in Sahaptin, *táp'aš* 'Ponderosa pine,' *pak'inákaas* 'white pine,'[9] *kalám-kalam* 'lodgepole pine,' and *naníkaaš* 'white-bark pine.' Thus we might expect the use of binomials to increase rapidly beyond a certain threshold of basic level name expansion, and to continue to increase in proportion to the size of the total inventory of basic level terms. Such as interpretation fits the data of Table 1. However, we have not explained the expansion of knowledge which, by this hypothesis, gives rise to the increase in binomial naming. In fact, we might have predicted quite the opposite, that is, that hunter-gatherers should have the largest folk biological inventories, subsistence agriculturalists the next largest, with modern urban dwellers having the smallest, in relation to the degree to which each system depends upon detailed, widely-shared knowledge of natural history. Thus binomial nomenclature, if functionally linked to the scope of a folk biological domain as hypothesized above, should be inversely correlated with this progression of modes of production. This seems not to be the case.

We would like to propose a possible resolution of this seeming contradiction. First, we believe it likely that hunter-gatherers will have smaller folk biological inventories than subsistence farmers in the same habitat. This accords with an otherwise curious fact that Kalahari San hunter-gatherers are *more selective* of the plants they use than nearby agricultural Bantu (Lee 1979: 180). They can afford to be more selective because of their low population densities and high mobility. Subsistence farmers are subject to periodic crop failures (Colson 1979), at which times they are forced to rely on wild foods the hunting-gathering San consider inedible. Their sheer numbers force them to recognize a wider range of species as of potential use than is true of the San. If this hypothesis is correct, the increased reliance on binomial naming by agriculturalists may be understood as a response to the need for an expanded ethnobiological repertoire. Brown (1985) has recently arrived at precisely this conclusion on the basis of an extensive series of cross-language comparisons.

Subsequent industrialization and urbanization reduces the need for detailed knowledge of natural species among the general population. As a consequence, the sweeping generality of life-form categories proves adequate in most circumstances. Binomial nomenclature, however, does not disappear, since the *cultivars* frequently so named remain important. Thus the elaborate taxonomic hierarchy proposed by Berlin as the ultimate expression of our evolving capacity to comprehend natural diversity is seen rather to result from a sequence of economic developments affecting our *need to know* aspects of that natural diversity (cf. Hunn 1982).

ACKNOWLEDGMENTS

E. Hunn's research has been supported by NSF Grant BNS7616914 and by grants from the Melville and Elizabeth Jacobs Research Fund. D. French's research has been supported in part by a PHS research grant, GM-11287, from the National Institute of General Medical Sciences. Student assistance was supported by grants to Reed College under the Shell Assists program and the National Science Foundation (GY-4746, GU-3364). French would like to thank the Wenner-Gren Foundation, Carl N. Reynolds, the Social Science Research Council, and the American Philosophical Society for earlier aid, and Nancy Fowler and Kathrine S. French for a critical reading of the manuscript. Terence E. Hays and Paul M. Taylor provided most helpful critical comments. This work would not have been possible without the generous instruction, advice, and encouragement of our Sahaptin-speaking consultants. We dedicate our efforts to honoring their cultural achievements.

LITERATURE CITED

Berlin, Brent. 1972. Speculations on the Growth of Ethnobotanical Nomenclature. Lang. and Soc. 1: 63–98.
———. 1973. Folk Systematics in Relation to Biological Classification and Nomenclature. Annu. Rev. Ecol. Syst. 4: 259–71.
———. 1976. The Concept of Rank in Ethnobiological Classification: Some Evidence from Aguaruna Folk Botany. Amer. Ethnol. 3: 381–99.
Berlin, Brent, Dennis E. Breedlove, and Peter H. Raven. 1973. General Principles of Classification and Nomenclature in Folk Biology. Amer. Anthro. 75: 214–42.
———. 1974. Principles of Tzeltal Plant Classification: An Introduction to the Botanical Ethnography of a Mayan-Speaking Community of Highland Chiapas. Academic Press, New York.
Bright, Jane O., and William Bright. 1965. Semantic Structures in Northwest California and the Sapir-Whorf Hypothesis. Amer. Anthro. 65(5), Part 2 (Special Publication): 249–58.
Brown, Cecil H. 1977. Folk Botanical Life Forms: Their University and Growth. Amer. Anthro. 79: 317–42.
———. 1979. Folk Zoological Life Forms: Their University and Growth. Amer. Anthro. 81: 791–817.
———. 1985. Mode of Subsistence and Folk Biological Taxonomy. Cur. Anthro. 26(1): 43–62.
Brown, Cecil H., John Kilar, Barbara J. Torrey, Tipawan Truong-Quang, and Phillip Volkman. 1976. Some General Principles of Biological and Non-Biological Folk Classification. Amer. Ethnol. 3: 73–85.
Brunel, Gilles. 1974. Variation in Quechua Folk Biology. Unpulb. Ph.D. dissert. (Anthrop.), Univ. California, Berkeley.

Bulmer, Ralph N. H. 1974. Folk Biology in the New Guinea Highlands. Soc. Sci. Inform. 13: 9–28.

Colson, Elizabeth. 1979. In Good Years and in Bad: Food Strategies of Self-Reliant Societies. J. Anthrop. Res. 35: 18–29.

Conklin, Harold C. 1954. The Relation of Hanunóo Culture to the Plant World. Unpubl. Ph.D. dissert. (Anthrop.), Yale Univ., New Haven, Conn.

———. 1962. Lexicographical Treatment of Folk Taxonomies. International J. of Amer. Ling. 28(2), Part 4: 119–41.

Curtis, Edward S. 1911. The North American Indian. Volume 7. The Plimpton Press, Norwood, Mass.

Dougherty, Janet W. D. 1978. Salience and Relativity in Classification. Amer. Ethnol. 5: 66–80.

Durkheim, Emile, and Marcel Mauss. 1963. Primitive Classification. Translated and edited by Rodney Needham. University of Chicago, Chicago. (Originally published 1903 in French.)

French, David H. 1957. An Exploration of Wasco Ethnoscience. Pp. 224–26 in Amer. Philosophical Society Year Book 1956.

———. 1960. Taxonomic and Other Conceptual Processes. Paper presented to the Amer. Anthrop. Soc. Ann. Meeting, Minneapolis, Minn. November 1960.

———. 1981. Neglected Aspects of North American Ethnobotany. Canad. J. Botany. 58: 2326–30.

Geoghegan, William H. 1976. Polytypy in Folk Biological Taxonomies. Amer. Ethnol. 3: 469–80.

Gunther, Erna. 1973. Ethnobotany of Western Washington. Revised edition. Univ. Washington Press, Seattle.

Haines, Francis. 1938. The Northward Spread of Horses among the Plains Indians. Amer. Anthro. 40: 429–37.

Hays, Terence E. 1974. Mauna: Explorations in Ndumba Ethnobotany. Unpubl. Ph.D. dissert. (Anthrop.), Univ. Washington, Seattle.

———. 1976. An Empirical Method for the Identification of Covert Categories in Ethnobiology. Amer. Ethnol. 3: 489–507.

———. 1977. Tzeltal Folk Zoology: The Classification of Discontinuities in Nature. Academic Press, New York.

———. 1979. Sahaptin Fish Classification. Northwest Anthrop. Res. Notes 14: 1–19.

———. 1980. Final Project Report to the National Science Foundation. Manuscript, Dept. Anthrop., Univ. of Washington, Seattle.

———. 1982. The Utilitarian Factor in Folk Biological Classification. Amer. Anthro. 84: 830–47.

Hunn, Eugene S., and David H. French. 1981. Lomatium: A Key Resource for Columbia Plateau Native Subsistence. Northwest Science 55: 87–94.

Irving, Laurence. 1953. The Naming of Birds by Nunamiut Eskimo. Arctic 6: 35–43.

Jacobs, Melville. 1931. A Sketch of Northern Sahaptin Grammar. Univ. Washington Publ. Anthrop. 4: 85–292.

Johnson-O'Malley, Consortium of Committees of Region IV. 1977. Yakima Language Practical Dictionary. Toppenish, Washington. Prototype.

Lancy, David and Andrew Strathern. 1981. "Making Twos": Pairing as an Alternative to the Taxonomic Mode of Representation. Amer. Anthro. 83: 773–95.

Lawrence, Barbara. 1968. Antiquity of Large Dogs in North America. Tebiwa 11: 43–49.

Lee, Richard B. 1979. The !Kung San: Men, Women, and Work in a Foraging Society. Cambridge University Press, London.

Lyons, John. 1977. Semantics. Two volumes. Cambridge University Press, London.
Marshall, Alan G. 1977. Nez Perce Social Groups: An Ecological Interpretation. Unpubl. Ph.D.
   dissert. (Anthrop.) Washington State Univ., Pullman.
Pandosy, M. C. 1862. Grammar and Dictionary of the Yakima Language. Translated by G.
   Gibbs and J. G. Shea. Cramoisy Press, New York.
Peattie, Donald Culross. 1950. A Natural History of Western Trees. Bonanza Books, New York.
Randall, Robert A. 1976. How Tall is a Taxonomic Tree? Some Evidence of Dwarfism. Amer.
   Ethnol. 3: 543–53.
Rigsby, Bruce J. n.d. Sahaptin Grammar. In Handbook of North American Indians: Language,
   edited by I. Goddard, Volume 16. Smithsonian Institution, Washington, D. C. In press.
Taylor, Paul. 1982. Plant and Animal Nomenclature in the Tobelorese Language. In Halmahera
   dan Raja Ampat sebagai Kesatuan Yang Majemuk, E. Masinambow, ed. Bulletin
   LEKNAS, Tahun II, No. 3 (Special Edition). Jakarta, Indonesia.
Waddy, Julie. 1982. Biological Classification from a Groote Eylandt Aborigine's Point of View.
   J. Ethnobiology 2: 63–77.

NOTES

1. Earlier versions of this paper were presented by Hunn to the 5th Annual Ethnobiology Conference in San Diego, California, April 1982, and by Hunn and French to the 17th International Conference on Salish and Neighboring Languages in Portland, Oregon, August 1982. The Sahaptin examples cited are primarily from Hunn's John Day and Umatilla data. French's Warm Springs Sahaptin data differ in detail but are supportive of all key conclusions.

2. Sahaptin words are written in a phonemic orthography adapted from Rigsby (n.d.) as follows: plain stops, and affricates are *p, t, c, λ, č, k, kʷ, q, qʷ;* glottalized stops and affricates are *p', t', c', ʌ', č', k', kʷ', q', qʷ';* spirants are *s, ł, š, x, xʷ, x̣, x̣ʷ;* sonorants are *m, n, l, w, y;* laryngeals are *h, ʔ;* and vowels are *i, ii, ɨ, u, uu, a, aa.*

3. For some consultants *wiwlúwiwlu* refers instead to a wild blueberry, *Vaccinium caespitosum* Michx.

4. In Northwest Sahaptin dialects *twiní* 'tail' replaces *wáł was.* Some speakers prefer *qúyx̣* 'white, animate' to *pláš* 'white, inanimate.'

5. Our consultants are unsure as to the characteristics of *t'uulnawałá* agreeing that it is a snake-like lizard that 'jumps.' Some informants may apply the term to alligator lizards (two species of *Gerrhonotus*); others may have in mind the rare and local western whiptail *(Cnemidophorus occidentalis).*

6. Contemporary consultants assert the *pápš* is equivalent to very large individuals of *Pseudotsuga* or *Abies,* while *patátwi* refers to all others of these genera. This seems unlikely to represent the original classificatory situation and contradicts some facts of the contemporary situation, most notably the fact that *patátwi* very clearly implies a prototype with the characteristics of *Abies,* to wit, highly aromatic foliage. This characteristic—and important uses contingent upon it—are not cited for *pápš.*

7. For some speakers the iris is *nunaswáakuł,* named after the mariposa lily *Calochortus macrocarpus* Dougl. The classificatory principle is the same, as *C. macrocarpus* is a valued winter emergency ration.

8. A form functionally parallel to Sahaptin *-wáakuł* '-like' is used by speakers of the Wasco dialect of Upper Chinookan, but only to *describe,* not to *name* categories.

9. This term was not cited in previous discussions of Sahaptin tree terms as it is apparently restricted today to the Northwest dialects.

Part Three

Foods and Medicines

Foods and Medicines

An Introduction

TIMOTHY JOHNS

The topic of foods and medicines differs from the others in this reader by referring to plants as a commodity of use, rather than as categories of classification within a process which can be ecological, cognitive or otherwise. In many ethnobotanical contexts usefulness is the sole reason for studying foods or medicines, although a utilitarian motive is increasingly called into question. The chapters in this section on foods and medicines still focus on processes and relationships and only begin to illustrate the kinds of ways in which human interrelationships with medicinal and edible plants can be understood. I invite readers to review recent issues of the Journal of Ethnobiology to expand their knowledge of the many uses of plants and animals for food and medicines. [Other overviews of this topic can be found in works such as Johns (1990, 1996) and Etkin (1994).]

Since J. W. Harshberger's (1896) first definition of ethnobotany as "the use of plants by aboriginal peoples," the utility of plants as food, medicines, and other items of material culture has been central to the discipline. Much of the emphasis on ethnoscience in this century has focused the mission of natural history and exploration as a search for plants with economic potential, especially for those that can be used as food and medicine. In a sense what distinguished Harshberger's definition of ethnobotany from other sciences already in practice was his drawing attention to the *use* of plants by aboriginal peoples. Such studies of foods have added to our knowledge of agricultural systems involving major foods crops, although rather than introduce many new species to the global food supply, the studies mostly expanded catalogues of more obscure edible plants.

Economic rewards from ethnobotanical undertakings are more typically associated with medicinal plants. While some historically well-known medicinals such as foxglove *(Digitalis purpurea)*, opium *(Papaver somniferum)*, and belladonna *(Atropha belladonna)* have provided the source of major pharmaceuticals such as digoxin, morphine, and atropine respectively, efforts in this century have led to the development of important drugs such as reserpine *(Rauvolfia serpentina)*, podophyllotoxin *(Podophyllum peltatum)* and vinblastine *(Catharanthus roseus)*.

In the public mind ethnobotany is often associated with such success stories. And in actuality emphasis on the compilation of the variety of uses of the diverse flora of the world persists among professional ethnobotanists and still represents the majority of ethnobotanical papers published in journals such as *Economic Botany, Ethnobotany, International Journal of Pharmacognosy,* and the *Journal of Ethnopharmacology.* Most of these data seldom describe new wonder drugs, but the papers are additional contributions to the growing catalogue of data on medicinal and food plants of indigenous peoples.

The ethnobotanical papers published in the *Journal of Ethnobiology* diverge somewhat from this pattern. While the authors of many of them, including those reproduced in this volume, use food and medicines as their raw material and even make lists of plant uses, their central purpose usually concerns some aspects of human interactions with plants. In this respect, the ideas presented in these papers are closer to the definitions of ethnobotany of Richard Ford or Volney Jones (Cotton 1996) which are concerned with both humans and plants. Emphasis on humans is consistent with the priorities of the social sciences; emphasis on plants is more consistent with those of biological sciences. Because ethnobotany bridges both of these perspectives, it always held out promise of a new synthetic discipline. A century after Harshberger, such a synthesis that extends ethnobotany beyond the emphasis on documentation and exploration is not only desirable as ever, but is rapidly becoming essential if the study of ethnobotany is to continue much beyond the beginning of the next century.

Investigations and publication of data on the uses of plants are becoming problematic, at the same time that these studies are increasingly promoted as holding great economic potential. The global destruction of plant biodiversity and the loss of traditional knowledge about the value of species has been lamented by ethnobotanists, conservationists, and public observers alike. However, it is not the loss of situations for research offering new drugs, foods, or other products that makes the road ahead uncertain; certainly where opportunities for discovery exist, the recording of such knowledge is deemed more imperative than ever. Rather, the potential for economic benefit makes access and control over traditional knowledge and resources increasingly contentious. Concerns for intellectual property rights (IPR) and traditional resource rights are recognition of the legitimate economic rights of indigenous peoples but also reflect the fact that as extant groups of indigenous peoples become more sophisticated, they are more able to raise their concerns about a range of issues involving their land, spirituality, economic development, self-sufficiency, health, and education. Within the global agenda on conservation, indigenous peoples have found allies and a voice. Whether ethnobotanists are sympathetic to the "rightness" of this or not, the reality is that the standard kinds of studies we have done since the time of Harshberger are not likely to continue as usual.

In the study of the uses of plants by aboriginal peoples, both plants and peoples' knowledge of them have been commodities for extraction. Undoubtedly, efforts to document uses of plants for foods and medicines will continue within participatory relationships between scientists and indigenous communities, although requirements for informed consent, research agreements, and royalties may reduce the motivation for many plant explorers. Some novel models for working in this new environment, represented by organizations such as Shaman Pharmaceuticals and Andes Pharmaceuticals, are emerging. But because they rely on access to capital, such undertakings seem to exclude academic research, thus making students of ethnobotany hard pressed to define ethnobotanical investigations in ways that are viable, ethical, and worthwhile.

Fortunately, once the perspective of looking at foods and medicines is broadened to encompass the interrelationships between humans and plants, the number of interesting questions that can be and are asked expands greatly. Within this context ethnobotany is much more than a technique directed toward a product. Rather, the application of knowledge about the use of plants for food and medicines is currently being defined less in utilitarian terms and more within terms of a conservation agenda which recognizes that such knowledge can play a potential role as a mediator between the needs of human communities and the maintenance of the integrity of their environments. It is important to know not only *what* plants people use and how they use them, but also *why*. What are the biological, cultural, and social roles of plants important in human adaptation in a particular environment in the past, present, and future? What is the cost in health and well-being if the plants are no longer available? How can traditional plant resources be used in a sustainable manner to better meet the needs of indigenous communities? In relation to conservation concerns, ethnobotany is subsumed under ethnoecology (Martin 1996) as one aspect of human interrelationships with the environment. It is only as these dynamics are understood that interventions to ensure protection of the essential components of the environment and of human lifestyle can be formulated. This goal is seemingly applied in current ethnobotanical studies, but as within any discipline, the complement of curiosity-driven and applied research is essential if complex phenomena are to be understood.

The chapters in this section approach the variety of ways in which human relationships with food and medicines can be considered, and there are number of points that they illustrate very well. First, it should be emphasized that ideas on the place of food and medicinal plants in human ecology are not new and that valuable models for this approach are found throughout ethnobotanical literature. The chapter by Robert Bye, while originally published in the first issue of the *Journal of Ethnobiology*, takes a very modern ethnoecological approach that is supported through ties to earlier literature. It also illustrates how the application of basic science encompassing both plant and human biology can help us to understand human-plant relationships. His discussion of domestication reflects a plant focus. Nutrition, a central component of human biology, is important in this chapter and it also takes a central place in the paper by Eugene Hunn. In the chapters by Bye and Paul Minnis, toxicity is brought forward as another biological issue.

These chapters also draw from other scientific disciplines and illustrate other aspects of scientific inquiry. Hunn's paper is a particularly good example of the use of data to test a hypothesis, in this case the relative importance of vegetable food in supplying the energy needs of hunter-gatherers of the Columbia Plateau. While each of the papers in this volume deals with specific case studies, one of the strengths of each is the insight the authors show in drawing general applicability from their observations. Bye's paper recognizes the parallels of the use of leafy vegetables in Mexico with reports from Africa, and since this study the general pattern of leafy vegetable use has become much more central to international concerns for food security and micronutrient deficiencies in tropical areas. Similarly, the paper by Hunn has applicability to larger debates on dietary subsistence patterns, that of Minnis to the phenomena of famine-food use in general, and those of Voeks, Bye, and Jan Timbrook to understanding principles of diffusion and plant use, the cultural transfusion of knowledge, and the dynamic evolutionary nature of human-plant relationships.

Timbrook and Voeks both draw particular attention to cultural concepts of plant use. In both the traditions among the Chumash that Timbrook describes and those among the Candomblé that Voeks describes, plants are considered in sacred terms first with lesser distinctions of their secular roles. Timbrook and Voeks describe folk concepts of disease and of medicinal-plant classification and the potential lack of correspondence between emic ("insider") and etic ("outsider") categories. Voeks illustrates well the validity of spiritual classification of plants as a classification in its own right and the importance of understanding this level of reality if one is truly to understand human relationships with plants.

Demonstrations that research in ethnobotany can proceed without being exploitative are encouraging. Both Minnis and Timbrook show that published historical data can be used for original interpretations, and Minnis connects these data with archaeological research. Hunn uses a well-documented situation in human biology as a focus for gathering supporting scientific data. Bye and Voeks rely to a significant degree on the compilation of new indigenous knowledge. In Bye's chapter the subject is vegetables of widespread distribution; knowledge of their use is not proprietary to a single cultural group and its publication is not contentious. Similarly, knowledge of sacred plants of the Candomblé is unlikely to be exploited for economic gain. Nonetheless such knowledge has great significance to the indigenous peoples to whom it belongs and its publication without their agreement would be just as much a violation of their rights as using their medicinal plants without their agreement.

The chapters in this section are all examples of types of ethnobotanical data that can be drawn upon in a contemporary context. At a time when the right of access to ethnobotanical data is questioned it is useful to consider the source of and nature of the information on food and medicinal plant use recorded in each paper. Because future ethical standards are likely to be more stringent, ethnobotanists will need to rely on a greater and more creative range of approaches to draw meaningful conclusions about human-plant interactions.

LITERATURE CITED

Cotton, C. M. 1996. Ethnobotany: Principles and Applications. John Wiley and Sons, Chichester, England.

Etkin, N. L., ed. 1994. Eating on the Wild Side: the Pharmacologic, Ecologic and Social Implications of Using Noncultigens. University of Arizona Press, Tucson.

Harshberger, J. W. 1896. The purposes of ethno-botany. American Antiquarian 17: 73–81.

Johns, T. 1990. With Bitter Herbs They Shall Eat It: Chemical Ecology and the Origin of Human Diet and Medicine. University of Arizona Press, Tucson.

———. 1996. Origins of Human Diet and Medicine: Chemical Ecological Approaches. University of Arizona Press, Tucson.

Martin, Gary M. 1995. Ethnobotany: a Methods Manual. Chapman and Hill, London.

FURTHER SUGGESTED READINGS

Arvigo, R. and M. Balick. 1993. Rainforest Remedies: One Hundred Healing Herbs of Belize. Lotus Press, Twin Lakes, Wisc.

Chadwick, D. J. and J. Marsh, eds. 1994. Ethnobotany and the Search for New Drugs. John Wiley and Sons, Chichester, England.

Posey, D. A. and G. Dutfield. 1996. Beyond Intellectual Property. International Development Research Centre, Ottawa.

CHAPTER SEVEN

Candomblé Ethnobotany
African Medicinal Plant Classification in Brazil

ROBERT A. VOEKS

INTRODUCTION

Brazil witnessed the forced immigration of over four million African souls during its colonial and imperial history, roughly eight fold the number that reached the United States (Rawley 1981). Uprooted principally from Yoruba-speaking areas of Nigeria and from Angola, they found themselves in a social and physical environment altogether alien. Forced to adapt to the rigors of slave existence and the lifeways of an evolving Portuguese civilization, African slaves lost much of what constituted their material culture. They succeeded, however, in introducing significant elements of their religious and ethnomedical systems. In the northeastern state of Bahia (Figure 1), Yoruba slaves and freedmen had successfully transplanted the seeds of their belief system by the early 19th century (Costa Lima 1977). Candomblé, as the religion came to be called, expanded geographically and numerically to the point that today it represents a powerful cultural influence in the region.

Although various factors contributed to the perseverance of Candomblé (Bastide 1978, Camara 1988, Voeks 1993), one of the most important is its preoccupation with achieving happiness and good health for adherents during this as opposed to the next life. Candomblé *pais* and *mães-de-santo* (priests and priestesses), serving as healers for the Afro-Brazilian community, divine the spiritual source of illness and prescribe culturally acceptable treatments. Purely physical problems, such as colds, headaches, and muscle pain, are treated with an array of drug plants. This portion of their plant pharmacopoeia, however, was largely assimilated from Amerindian and European sources, and has minor relevance to health and healing concepts held by the Candomblé community (Voeks 1999). It is when physical or emotional symptoms become chronic and recourse to medicinal plants and western medicine fails that imbalances with the spiritual realm are suspected. Illness is then viewed as a physical manifestation of forces outside the realm of secular comprehension. Priests seek out the other-world sources of such spiritual distress, and treat them with a plant pharmacopoeia that is systematically organized and ceremonially administered much as it was in West Africa.

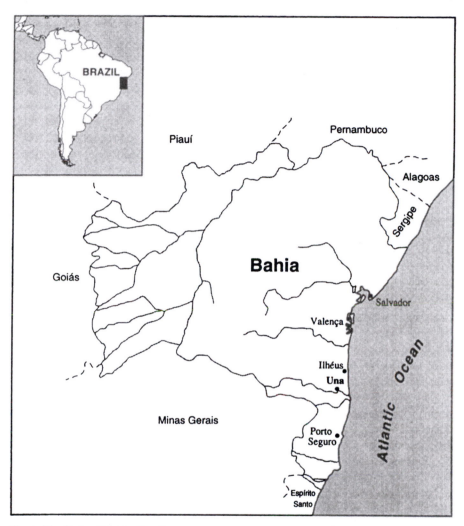

Fig. 1. The State of Bahia, Brazil.

   This paper examines the role of ritual plants in healing among Candomblé adherents and secular clients. I focus on the plant pharmacopoeia administered in spiritual healing ceremonies and the system of classification used to organize this ethnoflora. Field research was carried out in the cities of Salvador, Itabuna, and Ilhéus, Bahia between 1988 and 1992. I gathered data through interviews and participant observation with four *pais* and two *mães-de-santo* representing the four principal Candomblé traditions—Ketu, Ijexá, Jeje, and Candomblé de Angola.
   Ethnobotanical knowledge represents one of Candomblés closely guarded secrets. In the course of this study, *pais* and *mães-de-santo* seldom responded to direct questions regarding specific plant use and significance. Plant information was provided in

each case when the priest felt that I was knowledgeable enough to understand it and to respect it. Moreover, what was considered part of 'the secret' varied among temples. Some priests were thus willing to discuss one dimension of plant use, such as medicinal application, but not another, such as deity correspondence.

A total of 162 species employed in Candomblé spiritual healing ceremonies were discussed by informants or observed being used. Of these, I collected or otherwise identified 105 ritual species and determined their associated deities (Table 1). Plants were collected in various locations. Many of the cultivated species were gathered in temple gardens in the company of the *pai* or *mãe-de-santo*. Other plants were collected in disturbed areas, roadsides, pastures, second growth forests, or in old growth forest. I gathered the remaining species at Candomblé herb stands in Salvador. Collections and duplicates were vouchered and deposited in the herbarium at the Centro de Pesquisa do Cacau, Itabuna, Bahia.

RITUAL PLANT USES

The Candomblé ethnoflora is prepared in a myriad of ways for a multitude of disorders. Unlike plant prescriptions for illness perceived to be organically based, ritual species are seldom ingested and occasionally do not even come in contact with the body. Decorative plants are placed near the house or kept on the body to repel evil eye. Priests remove negative fluids from patients by brushing or whipping the body with a bundle of leaves. Adherents wear small cloth amulets around their necks containing leaves, magical phrases, and other sacred objects in order to avoid magical spells. Selected leaves are scattered on the floor and hung above entry ways before public ceremonies to neutralize negative energies that might enter with strangers. Aromatic leaves are burned as incense to cleanse the room and its inhabitants of negative spirits.

Among the African Yoruba and their Brazilian descendants several plant species are considered indispensable to primary initiation ceremonies. These include the seeds of **obí** (*Cola acuminata*) and **orobô** (*Garcinia kola*), species employed in West Africa and Brazil during divination and initiation (Verger 1981). Secret foliar concoctions are used to wash the sacred necklaces of adepts, and magical powder prepared from leaves, seeds, and chalk is painted on the shaved heads of initiates. During the early months of initiation, the novice spends his or her nights in a small room (**roncó**) sleeping on a bed of sacred leaves.

The **abô** (leaf bath) represents the most common plant prescription for novices and secular patients. Baths are employed for initiation, for financial improvement, and for purification (Williams 1979). Their most important role, however, is medicinal. **Abô** are taken for organically based medicinal problems, such as rheumatism, skin ailments, headaches, and the like. More commonly, the *pai* or *mãe-de-santo* prescribes baths for psychological disorders, such as anxiety and depression, particularly where these are viewed as spiritual in origin.

Leaf baths are prepared according to the individual needs of the patient. There is no predetermined set of foliar recipes. The priest or priestess determines the etiology

TABLE 1. Candomblé ritual species. Species and associated deities were provided by six informants. Vernacular names are listed in the order of their most frequent use in the *terreiro*. OW = Old World origin, NW = New World origin, Unkn. - unknown origin, Cosm. = cosmopolitan, Cult. - cultivated. Portuguese names are in italics. African names are in bold-face italic. Tupí names are italicized and underlined. Voucher specimens are housed at the herbarium, Centro do Pesquisas do Cacau, Bahia, Brazil.

Family Species/collection number [geographical origin-status]	Vernacular names	Associated Orixá(s) (number of informants)
Agavaceae		
Dracaena fragrans (L.) Ker Gawl./172 [OW-cosm. cult]	***peregun****/nativo*	Ogun (4), Oxóssi, Ossâim
Sansevieria cf. *aethiopica* Thunb./nc [OW-cosm. cult.]	*espada de Ogun/* ***ida orixá***	Ogun (4)
Sansevieria cf. *aethiopica* Thunb./nc [OW-cosm. cult]	*espada de Oxóssi*	Oxóssi (4)
Anacardiaceae		
Mangifera indica L./nc [OW-cosm. cult.]	*manga*	Ogun
Schinus terebinthifolus Raddi/191, 220 {NW-cosm. weed]	*aroeira/****perôko/ajobiewe***	Ogun, Iansã (2)
Tapirira guianensis Aubl./354, 389 [NW]	*pau pombo*	Oxalá (2)
Apocynaceae		
Catharanthus roseus (L.) G. Don/398 [NW-cosm. cult. & weed]	*bom dia*	Nanã
Catharanthus roseus var. *albus* Sweet/399 [NW-cosm. cult. & weed]	*boa noite*	Oxalá
Araceae		
Dieffenbachia maculata (Lodd.) G. Don/222 [NW-cosm. cult]	*comigo ninguem pode*	Ogun
Philodendron sp./260 [NW]	*sete chagas*	Omolu (2)
Arecaceae		
Elaeis guineensis Jacq./NC [OW-cosm. cult.]	***dendê/mariuô***	Exu, Ogun, all the orixás
Asteraceae		
Baccharis sp./151 [NW]	*abre caminho*	Ogun (3), Oxóssi
Bidens pilosa L./204 [NW-cosm. weed]	*carrapicho/picão/****ewe susu***	Exu (2)
Blanchetia heterotricha DC./154 [NW]	*selva de Ogun*	Ogun (2)

Family Species/collection number [geographical origin-status]	Vernacular names	Associated Orixá(s) (number of informants)
Conocliniopsis prasiifolium (DC.) K. & R./227 [NW]	*cama de coelho*	Oxóssi
Mikania glomerata Spreng./334 [NW]	*folha do ar*	Oxalá
Pluchea sagittalis (Lam.) Cabrera/286 [NW]	*assa peixe branco*	Ogun
Pluchea suaveolens (Vell.) Kuntze/213, 236 [Unkn.]	*quitoco*	Omolu, Ossâim
Rolandra fruticosa (L.) Kuntze/263 [NW]	*vence tudo*	Ogun (3), Oxóssi
Vernonia condensata Baker/177, 243 [NW]	<u>*alumã*</u>/**ewe auro**	Ogun, Omolu
Vernonia cf. cotoneaster Less./249 [NW]	*vence demanda*	Ogun
Vernonia schoenanthus L./190 [Unkn.]	<u>*alumã*</u>/**ewe auro**	Ogun, Omolu
Wedelia paludosa DC./383 [NW]	*mal-me-quer*/**bai joco**	Oxum (2), Omolu
Wulffia baceata (L. f.) Kuntze/265 [NW]	<u>*acoci*</u>	Oxum
Bignoniaceae *Newbouldia laevis* Seem./319 [OW-cult.]	**akokô**	Xangô
Boraginaceae *Cordia sp./352 [NW]	*baba de boi*	Oxalá
Caesalpiniaceae *Bauhinia ovata* Vog./373 [NW]	*unha da vaca/pata da vaca/**abafé**	Ogun, Yemanjá, Exu
Caesalpinia pulcherrima (L.) Sw. [NW-cosm. cult.]	*maravilha/barba de barata*	Oxum
Senna occidentalis (L.) Link/184 [NW-cosm. weed]	*fedegoso*	Iansã
Campanulaceae *Centropogon cornutus* (L.) Druce/158 [NW]	*bico de papagaio/ crista de peru/ **ewe akuku***	Xangô (2)
Caprifoliaceae *Sambucus australis* Cham. & Schlecht./254 [NW]	*sabugueiro*	Oxalá, Oxum
Caryophyllaceae *Drymaria cordata* (L.) Willd. ex. Roem. & Schult./160 [Unkn.-cosm. weed]	*vintém*	Oxum
Chenopodiaceae *Chenopodium ambrosioides* L./238, 244 [NW-cosm. weed]	*mastruz*	Xangô, Iansã

Family Species/collection number [geographical origin-status]	Vernacular names	Associated Orixá(s) (number of informants)
Clusiaceae		
Garcinia kola Heckel/300 [OW-cult.]	***orobô***	Xangô, all the orixás
Commelinaceae		
Commelina diffusa Burm. f./385 [NW-cosm. weed]	*marianinha/**opodo odo***	Yemanjá
Convolvulaceae		
Ipomoea pes-caprae (L.) Sweet/384 [Unkn.-cosm.]	*salsa da praia/* ***orobo aiba***	Nanã
Crassulaceae		
Kalanchoe pinnata (Lam.) Pers./175 [OW-cosm. cult. & weed]	*folha da fortuna/* *milagre de São* *Joaquim/saião/* ***oju oro***	Oxum (2), all orixás
Kalanchoe integra (Medic.) O. Ktz./169, 224 [NW-cosm. cult. & weed]	*folha da costa/* ***ewe dudu***	Oxalá, Yemanjá (3) all orixás
Cyperaceae		
Cyperus rotundus L./392 [OW-cosm. weed]	***dandá***	Oxalá, Ogun (2), Yemanjá
Fuirena umbellata Rottb. [Unkn.-cosm. weed]	<u>*tiririka*</u>/***labe labe***	Exu (2)
Euphorbiaceae		
Centratherum punctatum Cass. ssp. *punctatum*/250 [NW]	*balainho do velho*	Omolu
Cnidoscolus urens (L.) Arthur/170, 180 [NW]	*cansanção/**jojofa***	Exu (5)
Dalechampia ilheotica Wawra./281 [NW]	*urtiga/**esimsim***	Exu (4)
Jatropha curcas L./218 [NW]	*pinhão branco*	Oxalá
Jatropha gossypifolia L. [NW-cosm. cult. & weed]	*pinhão roxo*	Omolu
Pera cf. *glabrata* (Schott) Baill./257 [NW]	*açoita cavalo*	Exu
Ricinus communis L./NC [OW-cosm. cult. & weed]	*mamona/**ewe lara***	Yemanjá, Omolu/Abaluaiê
Fabaceae		
Erythrina poeppigiana (Walp.) O.F. Cook/310 [NW-cult.]	<u>*mulungú*</u>	Omolu, Exu
Machaerium angustifolium Vog./271 [NW]	*sete capote*	Exu
Zornia cf. *gemella* (Willd.) Vog. vel aff./256 [NW-cosm. weed]	*arrozinho*	Oxum

Family Species/collection number [geographical origin-status]	Vernacular names	Associated Orixá(s) (number of informants)
Flacourtiaceae		
Casearia sp./306 [Unkn.]	*São Gonçalinho*	Oxóssi, Xangô, Iroko
Gentianaceae		
Coutoubea spicata Aubl./253 [NW]	*papai nicolau*	Oxalá
Irlbachia purpurascens (Aubl.) Mass/264 [NW]	*corredeira*	Exu (3)
Lamiaceae		
Hyptis fruticosa Salzm ex. Benth./255 [NW]	*alecrim*	Oxalá, Oxum, Nanã, Yemanjá
Hyptis suaveolens (L) Poit./164 [NW-cosm. weed]	*neve cheiroso*	Nanã
Leonotis nepetifolia (L.) Alt. f./229 [OW-cosm. weed]	*cordão de São Francisco*	Ogun, Xangô
Mentha sp./205 [Unkn.]	*hortelã grosso*	Nanã
Mentha pulegium L./233 318 [OW-cosm. cult.]	*poejo*	Oxum (2), Yemanjá
Ocimum canum Sims/211 [OW-cosm. cult.]	*mangericão/ catinga da criola*	Oxóssi, Yemanjá (3)
Ocimum gratissimum L./ 219, 230, 247 [OW-cosm. cult. & weed]	**quiôiô**/*alfavaca cravo*	Xangô (2)
Plectranthus amboinicus Lour./152, 304 [OW-cosm. cult.]	*tapete da Oxalá*	Oxalá (3)
Pogostemon cf. *cablin* Benth./NC [OW-cosm. cult.]	*patchulí*	Oxum (2), Oxumarê, Nanã, Yemanjá, Iansã
Lythraceae		
Cuphea racemosa (L.f.) Spreng. [NW]	*barba de São Pedro*	Iansã
Malpighiaceae		
Byrsonima sericea DC/294, 349 [NW]	<u>*muricí*</u>	Ogun, Oxóssi, Xangô
Malvaceae		
Gossypium barbadense L./NC [NW-cosm. cult.]	*algodão/**ewe oxu***	Oxalá (2)
Sida linifolia Cav./258 [Unkn.-cosm. weed]	*lingua de teiú*	Oxóssi
Melastomataceae		
Clidemia hirta (L.) D. Don/159, 363 [NW]	*folha do fogo/**ewe aina***	Xangô, Exu (2)
Miconia hypoleuca (Benth.) Triana/356 [NW]	*candeia branca*	Oxalá, Omolu
Miconia sp./178, 276 [NW]	*canela de velho*	Omolu (3)
Tibouchina cf. *lhotzkyana* (Presl.) Cogn./279 [NW]	*folha do fogo de Iansã*	Iansã (2)

Family Species/collection number [geographical origin-status]	Vernacular names	Associated Orixá(s) (number of informants)
Mimosaceae		
Mimosa pudica L. [NW-cosm. weed]	*malissa*	Exu
Moraceae		
Cecropia pachystachya Trécul/355 [NW]	*embaúba*/**abao**	Omolu, Xangô
Ficus sp./NC [NW]	**iroko/loco/** *gameleira branca*	Iroko (6)
Myrtaceae		
Eugenia uniflora L./189 [NW-cosm. cult.]	*pitanga*	Katende/Iroko
Syzygium jambos (L.) Alston/394 [OW-cosm. cult.]	*jambo branco*	Oxalá
Passifloraceae		
Passiflora alata Dryand./NC [NW-cosm. cult.]	*maracujá*	Oxumarê
Phytolaccaceae		
Petiveria alliacea L./171, 295 [NW-cosm. cult. & weed]	*guiné/pipi/**ojusaju***	Ogun, Iansã (2)
Piperaceae		
Peperomia pellucida HBK./176 [NW-cosm. weed]	*alfavaquinha de cobra/**iriri/oriri***	Oxum, Oxalá
Piper aduncum L./210, 376 [NW]	*betis branco*	Xangô
Piper sp./283 [Unkn.]	*betis cheiroso*	Oxum, Oxumarê, Nanã, Iansã
Pothomorphe umbellata (L.) Mia./231 [NW-cosm. weed]	*capeba/**agogo iya***	Omolu/Abaluaiê
Plantaginaceae		
Plantago major L./208 [OW-cosm. cult. & weed]	*transagem*	Yemanjá
Plumbaginaceae		
Plumbago sp./165 [Unkn.]	*loquinho*	Iroko, Exu (2)
Poaceae		
Andropogon schoenanthus L./187 [OW-cosm. cult]	*capim santo*	Oxalá
Lasiacis ligulata Hitchc. & Chase/314 [NW]	*taquara*	Oxóssi
Zea mays var. *rugosa* Bonaf./NC [NW-cosm. cult]	*pipoca*	Oxóssi
Rubiaceae		
Borreria verticillata (L.) G. Mey./275, 296 [Unkn.-cosm. weed]	*caiçara*	Ogun (2), Oxóssi
Borreria sp./269 [Unkn.]	*corredeira*	Exu (3)

Family Species/collection number [geographical origin-status]	Vernacular names	Associated Orixá(s) (number of informants)
Rutaceae		
Citrus aurantium L./NC [OW-cosm. cult.]	*laranja da terra*	Oxum (2)
Murraya paniculata (L.) Jack [OW-cosm. cult.]	*murta da praia*	Nanã
Ruta graveolens L./201 202 [OW-cosm. cult.]	*arudda*	Oxóssi
Zanthoxylum sp./273 303 [Unkn.]	*tira teima*	Ogun, Oxóssi, Omolu
Schizaeaceae		
Lygodium volubile Sw./262 [NW]	*samambaia/ewe **amin***	Oxóssi
Scrophulariaceae		
Scoparia dulcis L./207 391 [NW-cosm. weed]	*vassourinha santa/ v. da Nossa Senhora*	Oxum
Solanaceae		
Brunfelsia uniflora (Pohl) D. Don./203, 317 [NW]	<u>*macaçá*</u>	Oxum (3), Oxumarê, Nanã (2), Yemanjá (4), Iansã
Nicotiana tabacum L./NC [NW-cosm. cult]	*fumo*	Ossâim (3)
Solanum americanum Mill./185, 215 [NW]	*maria preta/erva Santa Maria*	Iansã
Sterculiaceae		
Cola acuminata (Beauv.) Schott & Endl./307 [OW-cosm. cult.]	***obí**/noz de cola*	Ifá, all the orixás
Verbenaceae		
Lantana camara L./312 396 [NW-cosm. weed]	<u>*cambara branca*</u>	Oxalá
Lantana camara L./386 [NW-cosm. weed]	<u>*cambara amarella*</u>	Oxum
Vitex sp./232 [Unkn.]	*alfazema*	Oxum
Violaceae		
Hybanthus colceolaria (L.) Schulze-Menz [Unkn.]	*purga do campo*	Oxalá
Zingiberaceae		
Aframomum meleguetta K. Schum. [OW-cult.]	***atarê**/pimenta da costa*	Exu (3)
Alpinia zerumbet (Pers.) B. L. Burtt & R. M. Sm./192 [OW-cosm. cult.]	*leopoldina*	Oxalá, Oxum (2), Odudua
Hedychium coronarium J. König/305 [OW-cosm. weed]	*jasmin do brejo*	Oxum

and the prescriptive remedy during a divination ceremony using the *jogo de búzio,* or cowry toss (Braga 1988). Introduced along with other divination methods during the course of the slave trade, the *jogo de búzio* system allows the temple leader to consult directly with the deities. After rolling sixteen shells on a board, the *pai* or *mãe-de-santo* identifies the number of open and closed shells, that is, apertures facing up or down. The shell combination corresponds to one or several specific *odu,* or Yoruba myths, which suggests the cause of the problem and the appropriate course of action. When a bath enters into the prescribed remedy, the appropriate leaves are placed in a basin of cool water and slowly macerated with the hands. Physical manipulation of the leaves is essential, as this transfers *axé* (vital energy) from the priest to the developing bath. The resultant greenish concoction, charged with the innate power of the leaves and that of the priest of the *terreiro* (Candomblé temple), is placed inside a small altar dedicated to one or another of the African deities until the medicine has assimilated further *axé.* Finally, the patient pours the cool leaf bath over his or her body, usually starting at the shoulders, and allows it to dry before dressing.

GODS AND LEAVES

Candomblé revolves around propitiation of a pantheon of African deities, the *orixás.* Although their number in Africa may have been enormous (Bascom 1991), only a dozen or more *orixás* gained prominence in the newly constituted Brazilian *terreiros.* Devotees recognize the existence of a high god, Olórun, but he is perceived to be distant and unapproachable by humans. It is the *orixás,* serving as the earthly ambassadors of Olórun, who are directly linked to the health and happiness of mortals (Povoas 1989).

Each *orixá* is associated with a distinct realm of nature: earth, wind, water, and fire (Elbein dos Santos 1988). Ogun is the god of agriculture and iron, Xangô the god of lightning and thunder, Nanã the goddess of swamps, rain, and soil. Temperament and behavior further divide the deities; masculine *orixás* are generally hot tempered and unpredictable whereas feminine *orixás* are cool and balanced. Thus, Oxóssi is the volatile *orixá* of the hunt and of the forest. His personality as well as that of his mortal devotees is characterized by keen intelligence and curiosity. He is the itinerant seeker and explorer. Oxum, on the other hand, is the feminine deity of fresh water streams and rivers. Like the other water goddesses, Yemanjá and Nanã, her temperament reflects the perceived condition of her physical realm—cool and calm.

The *orixás* are also connected with specific symbols, preferences, and prohibitions (*euó*). These include color choices of clothing and sacred beads; offerings of food, drink, and sacrificial animals; food taboos, icons, and geographical locations. Oxalá, for example, the creator god of peace and love, prefers lofty locations. Avoiding the color black, he and his followers dress in white from head to foot. He is prohibited from consuming crabs, hot peppers, and salt.

Candomblé adherents are connected with one or two *orixás,* and they must strictly respect the preferences and prohibitions of their guardian deities. The perceived essence of the devotee's personality, in turn, corresponds to the recognized archetype of one or more of the *orixás* (Lepine 1981). Thus, a vivacious and impulsive follower will "belong" to Iansã, fiery goddess of storms; an inquisitive foreign researcher will belong to Oxóssi, restless god of the hunt. In order to avoid spiritual problems, adherents must remain within the cosmic equilibrium imposed by their particular *orixás.* These limits, in turn, correspond with the behavioral attributes of the deity. For example, a client who belongs to Oxum, female goddess of fresh waters, is preoccupied with personal appearance and material wealth. This is the natural state of Oxum and that of her devotees. However, when this otherwise normal behavior becomes compulsive, spending grocery money on perfume, for example, the limits of Oxum have been violated and disequilibrium with the spirit world has occurred. By trespassing his or her established limits, the adherent invites physical, material, and spiritual disaster. Overheated or overcooled, he or she must propitiate the appropriate deity promptly with material offerings, more diligent observance of taboos and, in most cases, take the prescribed leaf bath.

Ossâim, guardian of the sacred leaves and medicine, is the deity most directly involved in health and healing. His domain is the forest and the field, wherever curative plants grow spontaneously. Among the Yoruba and their New World diaspora, his image is one of extreme physical disability—one eye, one leg, one enormous ear, and a humorous high-pitched voice (Thompson 1975). As the dedicated but reticent steward of the vegetal realm, Ossâim's knowledge was coveted by other deities who sought to share in his secrets. The following legend, recorded in Africa (Verger 1981), Cuba (Cabrera 1971), as well as Brazil, describes how the *orixás* came to possess individualized plant pharmacopoeias:

There is a legend of rivalry between Ossâim, the *orixá* of medicine and leaves, and Iansã, the *orixá* of stars, winds, and storms. Everything began as a result of jealousy. Iansã went to visit Ossâim. Ossâim is very reserved, quiet, silent. Iansã wanted to know what he was doing. When Ossâim has the opportunity, he explains things. But Iansã is always rushed, she wants everything done immediately. She is always asking questions, and she needs to know everything that's going on. When Iansã arrived at the house of Ossâim, he was busy working with his leaves. It happens that there are certain types of work with leaves that you can't talk about, you need to remain silent. Iansã started asking, "What are you doing? Why are you doing this? Why are you doing that?" And Ossâim remained silent. "Alright, if you don't want to tell me what you're doing, then I'll make you talk." That's when Iansã began to shake her skirt and make the wind blow. The house of Ossâim is full of leaves, with all of their healing properties, and when the wind began to blow, it carried the leaves in every direction. Ossâim began to shout, **"Ewe O, Ewe O"** ['my leaves, my leaves']. Ossâim then asked the help of the *orixás* to collect the leaves, and the *orixás* went about gathering them. And it happens that every leaf that an *orixá* collected, every species, he or she became the owner of that leaf.

Scattered by the winds of Iansã, the sacred leaves became divided among the *orixás.* Whereas the mysterious power of the vegetal kingdom was retained by

Ossâim, each deity nevertheless came to be associated with his or her own personal pharmacopoeia. The following is a summary of the principal characteristics used to divide medicinal species among the deities. Only *orixás* with well developed plant correspondences are discussed.

MEDICINAL PLANT CLASSIFICATION

As the god of love and peace, Oxalá embodies the white dimension of nature. His color preference represents the major organizing force in his pharmacopoeia. The white infructescence of cultivated *algodão (Gossypium barbadense)* places this shrub within the domain of Oxalá, as do the aromatic white racemes of *sabugeiro (Sambucus australis)*. The pantropical herb *boa noite (Catharanthus roseus* var. *albus)* has both white flowers and latex. The weeds *candeia branca (Miconia hypoleuca), purga do campo (Hybanthus colceolaria),* and *cambara branca (Lantana camara* L.) have white flowers, and *jambo branco (Syzygium jambos),* a domesticate from Asia, produces pale colored fruit.

Unlike the other masculine deities, whose temperaments are hot and warlike, Oxalá is most intimately associated with the female entities, spiritual forces that serve to soothe and cool. One of his healing roles, as well as that of his associated flora, is to counteract illness associated with overheating, a condition that frequently troubles adherents and clients who are connected to the hot deities. Thick-leaved plants that exude liquid when crushed, such as *folha da costa (Kalanchoe integra),* are considered to have cooling properties, and are thus usually associated with the cool-tempered *orixás* like Oxalá (Figure 2). In addition to cooling foliar baths, this plant is also employed as a remedy for headache, a perceived hot symptom, by placing the leaf as a poultice on the patient's forehead. These characteristics, along with the belief that Oxalá controls illness associated with the head, places this species firmly within his domain (Sandoval 1979, Williams 1979). Another of his species, the medicinal grass *capim santo (Andropogon schoenanthus),* is prepared as an infusion to treat hypertension, another illness associated with heat. Other cooling, thick-leaved species dedicated to this pacifist god include *folha do ar (Mikania glomerata), alfavaquinha da cobra (Peperomia pellucida),* and *tapete da Oxalá (Plectranthus amboinicus),* the leaves of which are so densely pubescent as to appear white.

Oxum is the feminine *orixá* of running water. She is a voluptuous fertility figure who is anatomically associated with the female organs and the stomach. Vain and materialistic, Oxum adores gold, jewelry, and perfume. Reflective of her love of perfume, nearly all of her leaves and flowers are sweetly fragrant. These aromatic plants are added to baths for their soothing properties, underscoring the cooling influence of Oxum. The mint family, noted for its essential oils, is represented in her pharmacopoeia by *alecrim (Hyptis fruticosa), poejo (Mentha pulegium),* and *patchulí (Pogostemon* cf. *cablin).* Other aromatics associated with Oxum include *sabugueiro (Sambucus australis), macaça (Brunfelsia uniflora), jasmin do brejo (Hedychium coronarium),* and *beti cheiroso (Piper* sp.). *Laranja da terra (Citrus aurantium),* which has fragrant flowers and leaves, retains a cooling medicinal influence as a

Fig. 2. The herb *folha da costa* (*Kalanchoe integra* [Medic.] O. Ktz.) belongs to Oxalá. Its thick
leaves distinguish this as a cool plant.

sedative when taken as an infusion. Water retention is believed to be a hot ailment,
hence Oxum's ownership of *arrozinha* (*Zornia* cf. *gemella*), a plant employed medicinally as a diuretic. *Leopoldina* (*Alpinia zerumbet*) is particularly well suited to Oxum
(Figure 3). Its flowers are prepared into an infusion that is believed to have a tran-
quilizing effect, diminishing the heat associated with anxiety, whereas its scented
leaves are a frequent component of perfumed baths. The leaf extract of *vassourinha
santa* (*Scoparia dulcis*) is employed to reduce fever, an obvious hot symptom, hence
its possession by a cool deity.

Oxum's remaining flora reveals her obsession with wealth. Her love of gold is
symbolized by the bright yellow flowers of *arrozinha* (*Zornia* cf. *gemella*), *mal-me-
quer* (*Wedelia paludosa*), *maravilha* (*Caesalpinia pulcherrima*), *cambara amarella*
(*Lantana camara*), and *acocí* (*Wulffia baceata*). Oxum's material interests account

Fig. 3. The sweetly scented leaves of *leopoldina (Alpinia zerumbet)* pertain to Oxum. The leaves enter into aromatic baths whereas the flowers are brewed into an infusion for the treatment of anxiety.

for her association with *folha da fortuna (Kalanchoe pinnata)*, a fleshy-leaved garden cultivar with perceived cooling properties. It has the curious habit of sprouting roots and seedlings viviparously at its leaf margins, hence its perceived ability to create something from nothing. This 'leaf of fortune' has long been employed to attract money by attaching it to the doors of adherents homes (Voeks 1990). Another of Oxum's leaves, *vintém (Drymaria cordata)*, is used for similar material ends.

Yemanjá is another fertility figure whose aquatic home is the ocean. Her preferred geographical location is the shoreline. Warm, maternal, and stable, Yemanjá is the archetype mother image. Her favorite colors are transparent or crystal blue, symbolic of her watery domain. Many of her species are aromatics, including *alecrim (Hyptis fruticosa), macaçá (Brunfelsia uniflora), patchulí (Pogostemon* cf. *cablin), manjericão*

Fig. 4. *Unha da vaca (Bauhinia ovata)* represents one of Yemanjá's species. The characteristic hoof-shaped leaves of this genus, which occurs in the Old and New World, allowed early Candomblé healers to substitute a Brazilian species for the original African taxon. In some terreiros, this species is still known by its Yoruba name, *abafé.*

(Ocimum canum), and **dandá** *(Cyperus rotundus).* This latter Africa sedge often inhabits coastal wetlands, reflecting Yemanjá's physical domain. *Marianinha (Commelina diffusa)* has pale blue flowers, Yemanjá's color choice, and is employed to treat inflammation, a hot symptom.

Like Oxum, Yemanjá is connected with problems of the uterus and female organs. This may explain the inclusion of *transagem (Plantago major),* a medicinal herb that is prepared as an anti-inflammatory tea for uterine problems. The leaves of *unha da vaca (Bauhinia ovata)* are prepared as an infusion to treat diabetes, a hot disease, hence its association with this cool deity (Figure 4). Yemanjá's maternal image—she is popularly referred to as the "milk *orixá*"—is reflected in her association with *mamona (Ricinus communis).* The use of this weedy shrub to treat lactation problems is widespread in the Old and New Worlds (Ayensu 1978, Morton 1981). According to an elderly Candomblé *pai-de-santo,* African wet nurses in Brazil used to hang pieces of the stem of *mamona* around their necks in the belief that it relieved painful lactation. Derived from the verb *mamar,* to suckle, *mamona* in colloquial Portuguese refers to a female baby who nurses well, again suggesting this plant's connection with mother's milk and hence Yemanjá.

Nanã, the aged female goddess of rain, swamp, and soil, represents the grandmother of the **orixás.** Like the other cool deities, she is associated with regeneration.

Her colors are lavender or blue and white. Nanã's leaves are mostly aromatic, including *neve cheiroso (Hyptis suaveolens), hortelã (Mentha sp.), alecrim (Hyptis fruticosa), beti cheiroso (Piper* sp.*), patchulí (Pogostemon* cf. *cablin),* and *macaçá (Brunfelsia uniflora).* Two of her plants, *bom dia (Catharanthus roseus)* and *salsa da praia (Ipomoea pes-caprae),* display large lavender-colored flowers, representative of her color preference.

Iansã is the female deity of wind, storms, and stars. Unlike the cool female deities, Iansã can be either hot or cool, bellicose or compassionate, depending on her mood. The fiery side of her temperament is symbolized by her red color preference. The leaves of Iansã, like her archetype, vacillate between the extremes of hot and cool. Several are sweetly aromatic, such as *macaçá (Brunfelsia uniflora), beti cheiroso (Piper* sp.*),* and *patchulí (Pogostemon* cf. *cablin),* which she shares with the other water *orixás*—Nanã, Yemanjá, and Oxum. The majority of her leaves, however, symbolize her warlike qualities. Many have an acrid or foul smell as well as pointed apices, representing her sword. These species include *aroeira (Schinus terebinthifolius),* which has bright red, acrid berries; *fedegoso (Senna occidentalis),* which has strong smelling leaves shaped like daggers; and *mastruz (Chenopodium ambrosioides),* which also has pointed, rank smelling leaves. *Folha do fogo do Iansã (Tibouchina* cf. *Ihotzkyana),* literally 'Iansã's fire leaf,' has pointed leaves and is covered by a dense layer of reddish pubescence, representing her color choice. Iansã's nature is best elicited by *guiné (Petiveria alliacea).* Aside from acrid-smelling leaves, this herb is used medicinally as a tranquilizer and somniferant, hence its cooling dimension. If ingested for prolonged periods, however, the root extract of *guiné* is reported to produce anxiety, hallucinations, and even death (Cravo 1984). Thus, like Iansã herself, *guiné* swings unpredictably between the extremes of hot and cold.

Omolu is the dreaded god of smallpox and dermal ailments. Powerful and vengeful if ignored by his supplicants, Omolu is one of the most feared of the Yoruba deities. His image is ancient, bent, and arthritic, with skin so scarred by smallpox that he conceals himself in a suit of palm straw. His colors are white and black. Many of his leaves have rough and punctate surfaces, suggesting his own pockmarked skin. These include *balainho do velho (Centratherum punctatum* Cass. ssp. *punctatum), candeia branca (Miconia hypoleuca),* canela do velho *(Miconia sp.),* and capeba *(Pothomorphe umbellata).* One of Omolu's plants is *sete chagas (Philodendron* sp.*),* 'seven sores,' although this plant's connection with skin disease is unclear. *Quitoco (Pluchea suaveolens)* represents a medicinal treatment for rheumatism, one of Omolu's noted afflictions.

Popcorn is one of Omolu's principal offerings and bath ingredients. With its contorted shape, popcorn symbolizes the skin eruptions associated with smallpox. Its explosive kernels may also be seen to reflect Omolu's volatile temper. Fearing even to mention the name of this plant for fear of invoking Omolu's wrath, devotees refer to popcorn as '*a flor*' (flower) within the confines of the *terreiro. Mamona (Ricinus communis)* is another of his plants. The spiny red fruits of this species suggest Omolu's skin condition, as well perhaps as his piqued anger (Thompson 1983). The explosive nature of *mamona's* fruit, which can send its seeds flying several meters, is reflective of this god's violent temperament. *Pinhão roxo (Jatropha gossypifolia)*, which has reddish leaves and petioles, further suggests Omolu's fiery temper.

Xangô is the volatile god of thunder, lightning, and fire. He is geographically associated with high places, and his colors are red and white. Xangô's temper is reflected by the reddish-purple floral display of some of his species, including **akokô** *(Newbouldia laevis), bico de papagaio (Centropogon cornutus)*, and *cordão São Francisco (Leonotis nepetaefolia)*. The reddish pubsecence of *folha do fogo (Clidemia hirta)* further suggests his color preference. Xangô's flora is further characterized by a high representation of trees and shrubs. Sixty-four percent of his flora is arborescent, compared to less than 21% of the combined Candomblé pharmacopoeia. His tree flora includes *bico de papagaio, São Gonçalinho (Casearia* sp.*), muricí (Byrsonima sericea), embaúba (Cecropia pachystachya), betis branco (Piper aduncum)*, **akokô,** and **orobô** *(Garcinia kola)*. Xangô's link to arborescent as opposed to understory vegetation may stem from his preference for elevated locations. It may also follow, as one informant suggested, from the fact that trees are frequently struck by lightning, the source of **axé** for Xangô, and that this vital force is transferred from the skies via these conductors to the sacred foliage inhabiting the ground.

The masculine deities Oxóssi and Ogun are brothers according to legend. Oxóssi, who holds sway over the hunt and the forest, shoulders an iron bow and arrow. His colors are green and red. Ogun is the god of iron and war. Forever hammering out his iron implements at the forge, Ogun is by nature very hot. He is the consummate warrior figure, fending off evil, opening up passages, winning battles. His colors are green or blue.

The leaves of these brother deities, many of which they share, are characterized by long blades and pointed apices representing the spears and arrows of these two warrior gods. These species are typified by **peregun** *(Dracaena fragrans)* and the bowstring hemps *espada de Oxóssi* and *espada de Ogun (Sansevieria cf. aethiopica)*. The vernacular names of Ogun and Oxóssi's leaves evoke their aggressive archetypes, their ability to solve the problems of their followers. These species include *abre caminho (Baccharis* sp.*)* 'open the way,' *vence tudo (Rolandra fruticosa)* 'conquers everything,' *comigo ninguem pode (Dieffenbachia maculata)* 'no one overpowers me,' *tira teima (Zanthoxylum* sp.*)* 'take away stubbornness,' and *vence demanda (Vernonia cf. cotoneaster)* 'achieve objectives.' Ogun's association with **dandá** *(Cyperus rotundus)* reflects the perceived magical attributes of this plant, as both West Africans and Brazilians chew the rhizomes of **dandá** in order to influence the opinion of others (Dalziel 1948).

Exu is the deity of passageways and crossroads. Capricious and at times malicious, Exu serves as messenger to the **orixás,** the transporter of **axé.** Although he is a notorious troublemaker, and great effort is expended to placate him during Candomblé ceremonies, Exu is also the god of potentiality, the catalyst that make things happen. Properly propitiated, he clears obstructions to human wants and desires. Ignored, Exu brings calamity with a vengeance. Symbolic of his temperament, Exu's colors are red and black.

The leaves of Exu are as threatening as his personality. Many give off a burning sensation when touched, and most are employed for malevolent purposes—to destroy intimate relationships, to bring bad luck, and to create general chaos. Covered with spines and prickly pubescence, several are painful to the touch, including *urtiga (Dalechampia ilheotica), folha do fogo (Clidemia hirta), cansanção (Cnidoscolus urens),* the fronds of **dendê** *(Elaeis guineensis),* and the stems of *malissa (Mimosa pudica).* The razor sharp leaf margins of *tiririka (Fuirena umbellata)* readily cut the skin of those who choose to handle it. The prickly fruits of this weedy sedge, along with those of *carrapicho (Bidens pilosa),* cling to the legs of passersby, finding by this means transport to trails and roads, the preferred haunts of Exu.

Nearly all of Exu's leaves enter into black magic formulas. The red seeds of **atarê** *(Afromum meleguetta),* for example, an African domesticate imported since the 19th century, are ground into powder and scattered in the homes of victims in order to create disorder, a practice still carried out in Nigeria (Voeks 1990). The nearly black flowers of *corredeira (Irlbachia purpurascens* and *Borreria* sp.*),* symbolizing Exu's dark side, are ground into a powder in combination with grave dirt in black magic ceremonies.

HOT AND COLD IN CANDOMBLÉ

The hot-cold opposition that is symbolized by the archetypes of the Yoruba pantheon is one of the organizing principles in the Candomblé medicinal plant classification system. As the gods are seen to gravitate towards either one or the other perceived temperature states, so also do their associated illnesses and healing plants. Hot deities are prone to hot illness, physical and psychological, and their medicinal treatments are often drawn from the pharmacopoeias of the cool goddesses. The leaves of hot gods are, at least in principle, employed to heat the cool feminine deities.

From the perspective of a cohesive ethnomedical paradigm, however, the hot and cold syndrome suffers from noticeable irregularities. First, the characteristics of several Candomblé plants fail to conform to the behavioral attributes of their associated god. *Assa peixe branco (Pluchea sagittalis),* for example, is one of Ogun's leaves. However, this plant produces a white floral display, suggestive of Oxala's color preference, and is employed medicinally as a febrifuge, a hot symptom that should place this taxon within the purview of a water deity. Likewise, whereas *sabugueiro (Sambucus australis)* is shared by Oxalá and Oxum, both cool tempered deities, the medicinal use of this plant to treat skin problems suggests an association with Omolu, a hot god. These apparent inconsistencies, at least in some cases, reflect the range of properties that characterize individual taxa. For example, one informant connects the aromatic sedge **dandá** *(Cyperus rotundus)* with Yemanjá, suggesting the physical domain of this deity. Two other informants place **dandá** with Ogun, a god known for his ability to clear obstructions that serve to constrain his supplicants. This latter correspondence reflects the perceived magical properties of this species. Other apparent inconsistencies in god-plant associations, however, are not so readily explained.

The classification and treatment of hot and cold illness exhibits further problems. Although a host of hot medical problems are associated with masculine gods, and cooling prescriptions are associated with cool deities, the reverse situation is relatively rare. Few of the leaves used to treat cool illness are connected to the hot deities. This is not for lack of perceived cool medical problems, which include colds, flu, hypotension, and hypoglycemia, nor appropriate plant prescriptions to treat these ailments. Healers discussed the use of *mamão (Carica papaya), capim estrella (Rhynchospora nervosa), malva branca (Sida carpinifolia),* and other plants to treat colds, a cool illness, although none of these species correspond to a masculine deity. They are simply medicinal plants with no perceived spiritual significance. Avocado *(Persea americana)* is likewise not associated with a deity, although the leaves of this New World cultigen are prepared as a diuretic, a perceived heating property. For reasons that are unclear, the hot plant-cool illness concept is poorly developed within Candomblé.

The hot-cold syndrome is not unique to Brazilian Candomblé. This ancient concept is at the heart of early European and Asian health and healing theories, and is a dominant organizing principle in many Latin American and African American folk medical systems as well (Anderson 1987, Currier 1966, Laguerre 1987). Although the presence of a hot and cold etiology among Hispanic Americans can often be attributed to diffusion from Old World sources, the existence of this concept among Mesoamerica's pre-Hispanic civilizations, the Mayas, the Aztecs, and the Zapotecs, as well as among isolated indigenous South American societies, argues for the independent evolution of the hot-cold paradigm in the New World (Colson and de Armellada 1983, Messer 1987).

The origin of the hot-cold dichotomy within Candomblé ethnomedicine is problematic. Although hot and cool temperature states characterize the dispositions of the Yoruba deities, both in Africa and Brazil (Thompson 1983, Verger 1981), evidence that Candomblé's hot and cold etiology traces its roots to Africa is lacking. This binary system does not appear among the sacred oral texts of the Yoruba *babalaô* (Bascom 1991). Nor do the incantations recited by the *babalaô* to invoke the vital energy of the medicinal leaves allude to any hot and cold properties (Verger 1967). Yoruba herbalists, a separate class of healers who tend to organic rather than spiritual and magical illness, prescribe medicines that are bitter, sweet, sour, or peppery. But like their *babalaô* counterparts, they do not classify either illness or medicine along hot and cold lines (Buckley 1985).

There is no evidence one way or the other regarding the possible contribution of Amerindian health and healing concepts to Candomblé's hot and cold opposition. Motivated by practical concerns, particularly the virgin soil epidemics that decimated the indigenous population, sixteenth century Bahian planters and missionaries went to considerable efforts to document the local Tupinambá plant pharmacopoeia, which was extensive (Cardim 1939, Sousa 1971). Other contemporaries described how the indigenous shamans directed the women to sing and dance in a circle, after which they fell into trance and were "able to foretell future things," ceremonies that are highly reminiscent of those currently carried out in Candomblé (Staden 1928: 150, Lerivs 1625). Focused on what was considered useful or exotic, these early reports not surprisingly failed to explore the more theoretical dimensions of indigenous etiology and healing.

Among Brazilians of European descent, however, the concept of environmental control of illness, particularly the deleterious effects of heat and cold, has a long pedigree. In the early 1600s, Dutch physician Guilherme Piso counseled recent arrivals to Brazil against the overuse of hot and cold baths (Piso 1948: 10). During the colonial period, Brazil's excessive heat was blamed on a multitude of venerial and childhood disorders (Freyre 1986). Today a seemingly endless array of illness episodes, some life threatening, are attributed to the environmental effects of imbalanced temperature states. Activities such as drinking cold water on a hot day, taking a cool shower after a hot meal, or sitting in a recently vacated warm chair are all perceived as unnecessary health risks (Cascudo 1967).

Centuries of culture contact and miscegenation in the Northeast of Brazil has blurred the racial and cultural distinctions that separated Europeans and Africans. In the area of religion and magic, Africans borrowed liberally from their oppressors, particularly when these beliefs were found complementary to their own. Incorporating alien materials and beliefs represented both a survival mechanism—Catholicism was Brazil's only sanctioned religion—as well as actual changes in the convictions of adherents. This flexibility is characterized by the syncretism of African *orixás* and Catholic saints, a process that was well advanced in Bahia by the late 19th century (Rodrigues 1935). Such a fusion of spiritual images and meanings was facilitated by the nearly parallel roles played by the African pantheon and Catholic hagiology in the attainment of practical goals, for example, warding off disease, increasing fertility, and maintaining good health (Camara 1988). The malleability of African healing systems, the ability to change and adapt as social, economic, and biological conditions necessitate, is further underscored by the wholesale adoption of European and Amerindian medicinal and magical species by Afro-Brazilian healers (Voeks 1999).

This process of redefinition and assimilation may well have extended into the conceptual dimensions of ethnomedicine. Two components of the hot and cold system, division of the Yoruba deities into hot and cold categories and correspondence of deities with ritual and medicinal species, arrived with African priests and priestesses during and after the slave trade. Adherents who stray from the archetypal equilibrium imposed by their guardian deities become overheated or overcooled and, in so doing, open the door to spiritual retribution. This simple opposition was, in a sense, preadapted to the addition of and modification by complementary concepts. These would have included the belief that physical and emotional distress is at least partly mediated through relations with the spirit world, to which both belief systems already subscribed. It also could have facilitated the correspondence of hot and cold deities, an African concept, with the folk belief that many illnesses are the outcome of hot and cold imbalance, concepts that are in all likelihood of Portuguese origin.

CONCLUSIONS

In spite of seemingly insurmountable social, economic, and material obstacles, African slaves and their descendants introduced significant elements of their native ethnomedical systems to Brazil. One of the material dilemmas that confronted newly arrived priests was how to continue practicing a plant-based healing system in an alien floristic landscape. As slave laborers and later poor freedmen, Africans had limited opportunities to directly transplant their original *materia medica*. Two products of apparent intentional introduction are **akokô** *(Newbouldia laevis)* and **obí** *(Cola acuminata)*, both of which were brought to Brazil specifically to fulfill Candomblé ritual

(Voeks 1990). A few other taxa, such as *orobô (Garcinia kola)* and *atarê (Afromum meleguetta),* continue to be imported by Afro-Brazilians for ritual purposes, but have apparently failed to reproduce in Brazil. Although other useful African taxa were intentionally introduced as well, such as *dendé (Elaeis guineensis), peregun (Dracaena fragrans),* and *espada de Oxóssi (Sansevieria* cf. *aethiopica),* these most likely represented the commercial and decorative interests of Portuguese colonists rather than the demand of their captive laborers. Arriving Africans also encountered and incorporated a host of familiar herbaceous plants, such as *dandá (Cyperus rotundus), tiririka (Fuirena umbellata),* and *jasmin do brejo (Hedychium coronarium),* opportunistic Old World weeds that had successfully colonized the increasingly disturbed Brazilian landscape. Thus, by means of intentional and accidental plant introductions, Afro-Brazilian healers continued to employ at least a small percentage of their native African ethnoflora.

African immigrants must nevertheless have recognized early that the ability to practice magic and medicine in the Americas depended upon their capacity to adopt the flora immediately at hand. This ethnobotanical flexibility was provided, at least in part, by the Yoruba folk taxonomic system. In West Africa, ritual and medicinal species correspond with one or another of the ancient deities, a relationship mythically underpinned by the legend of Ossâim's leaves. The nature of these god-plant associations, which are encoded in the medicinal recipes and incantations of the *odu,* are maintained as oral text and recited during divination by *babalaô* priests, the most respected class of Yoruba healer (Bascom 1991). Although *babalaô* priests are known to have arrived in Brazil both during and after the slave trade, their highly complicated system of divination ultimately failed to survive (Carneiro 1967). Rather, in the newly constituted Candomblé *terreiros,* priests and priestesses continued to divine the source of problems, but now by means of the simpler *jogo de búzio* method (Braga 1988) and with reference to a much diminished and modified corpus of mythical text.

It is unlikely that many of the original Yoruba god-plant correspondences were maintained in Brazil. Among the various African *babalaô,* there is considerable variation in the verses of the *odu* (Bascom 1991), and it seems likely that such diversity of opinion extended to the area of god-plant associations as well. If this were the case, then obviously no single set of correspondences could have arrived in Brazil. Regardless, several introduced African taxa did retain a significant measure of their ritual and magical significance—*akokô (Newbouldia laevis), obí (Cola acuminata), orobô (Garcinia kola), atarê (Afromum meleguetta), dandé (Cyperus rotundus), peregun (Dracaena fragrans),* and *dendé (Elaeis guineensis).* More importantly, however, priests were able to incorporate hitherto unknown species into their pharmacopoeias based upon a broad suite of characteristics corresponding with the personalities, physical appearances, and preferences of each of the African *orixás.*

The Yoruba gods that survived in Brazil are divided between those perceived to be hot and cool, masculine and feminine. Hot *orixás* are associated with fiery personalities—aggressive, warlike, volatile—and many of the New World species that were assigned to these gods symbolically reflect these behavioral attributes. Leaves and stems are spiny or prickly. Flowers and fruits are red or black reflecting their hot temperaments. Leaves exhibit linear blades, acuminate tips, foul or acrid aromas, or rugose surfaces. The feminine deities, on the other hand, represent cooling and calming influences. They are maternal, sensuous, fertile, and materialistic. Their designated personal floras, in turn, are characterized by sweetly aromatic leaves and flowers with white, gold, blue, or lavender corollas. Leaves tend to be fleshy with abundant sap. Several species enter into medicinal prescriptions to cool down illness associated with the hot deities.

The resultant Candomblé spiritual pharmacopoeia is highly representative of Bahia's evolving floristic landscape. Of those species for which origins could be determined, over 70% are of New World origin. This figure represents endemic American species that were entirely new to Africans, as well as many New World taxa that had been transported to Africa during the course of European colonization, either as weeds or cultigens. South American *algodão (Gossypium barbadense)* and *fumo (Nicotiana tabacum)*, for example, which were introduced to West Africa during the colonial period, must have been familiar to most Africans prior to their enslavement and transport to Brazil (cf. Bosman 1705, Purseglove 1984). These species were incorporated into the corpus of medicinal knowledge retained in the Yoruba *odu* (Verger 1976– 1977), and were likely transported to Brazil in the memories of arriving priests and priestesses. This process of recognizing and adopting New World species that had been previously introduced to Africa may have been particularly common with weedy taxa, which constitute a significant proportion of the Candomblé ethnoflora. An array of weedy species diffused to Africa during the slave trade, and many assumed importance in Yoruba healing rituals. These included *alfavaquinha de cobra (Peperomia pellucida), folha da costa (Kalanchoe integra), malissa (Mimosa pudica),* and *vassourinha santa (Scoparia dulcis),* all of which enter into healing recipes employed by African Yoruba and their Brazilian descendants (Verger 1976–1977).

Candomblé medicinal folk taxonomy bears little resemblance to its western scientific counterpart. Floral structure is seldom considered in determination, and phylogenetic hierarchy plays no role whatsoever in classification. Salience is wholly defined by those features, tactile, olfactory, visual, geographical, or medicinal, that suggest association with the archetypes of one or another deity. Closely related taxa, for example *manjericão (Ocimum canum)* and *quiôiô (O. gratissimum),* pertain to different *orixás,* as do varieties of the same species, such as *bom dia (Catharanthus roseus)* and *boa noite (Catharanthus roseus* var. *albus).*

Candomblé *terreiros* function independently of each other, and competition rather than cooperation characterizes their relationship. There is limited exchange of information among *terreiros* and nothing approaching a Candomblé collective medicinal knowledge. Exposed to a diverse and largely unknown flora, early priests and priestesses determined independently which species belonged to which deity based on the legend of Ossâim's leaves as well as their own perceptions of the essence of each plant. These decisions were passed on to devotees, who founded their own temples and continued to assimilate additional taxa. This independence is evidenced by the Candomblé ritual floras which, although organized by means of the same conceptual framework, nevertheless exhibit limited floristic overlap from one priest to another and from one *terreiro* to another (Barros 1983, Fichte 1976, Williams 1979).

ACKNOWLEDGMENTS

Field work for this project was funded by grants from the National Geographic Society (#4247–90) and the Hughes Foundation, California State University, Fullerton. I thank Andre M. de Carvalho and Talmon Santos, of the CEPLAC herbarium, for species determinations, and Kelly Donovan for cartographic assistance. I also thank Ruy Póvoas and Pierre Verger for their insights into the meaning of the leaves.

LITERATURE CITED

Anderson, E. N. 1987. Why is humoral medicine so popular? Social Science and Medicine 25: 331–37.

Ayensu, Edward S. 1978. Medicinal Plants of West Africa. Reference Publications, Algonac, Mich.

Barros, Jose Flavio Pessoa de. 1983. Ewó o Osányín: sistema de classificação de vegetais nas casas de santo Jéjé-Nagô. Unpublished Ph.D. dissertation, University of São Paulo.

Bascom, William. 1991. Ifa Divination: Communication Between Gods and Men in West Africa. Indiana University Press, Bloomington.

Bastide, Roger. 1978. The African Religions of Brazil: Toward a Sociology of the Interpretation of Civilizations. Helen Sebba (translator). The Johns Hopkins University Press, Baltimore, Md.

Bosman, William. 1705. A new and accurate description of the coast of Guinea, divided into the Gold, the Slave, and the Ivory Coasts. Pp. 337–547 in A General Collection of the Best and Most Interesting Voyages and Travels in All Parts of the World. Edited by John Pinkerton. Longman, Hurst, Reis, Orme, and Brown, Paternoster-Row, London.

Braga, Julio. 1988. O Jogo de Búzios: Um Estudo da Adivinhação no Candomblé. Editora Brasiliense, São Paulo.

Brown, Karen McCarthy. 1989. Systematic remembering, systematic forgetting: Ogou in Haiti. Pp. 65–89 in Africa's Ogun: Old World and New. Indiana University Press, Bloomington.

Buckley, Anthony. 1985. Yoruba Medicine. Clarendon Press, Oxford.

Cabrera, Lydia. 1971. El Monte. Miami, np.

Camara, Evandro M. 1988. Afro-American religious syncretism in Brazil and the United States: A Weberian perspective. Sociological Analysis 48: 299–318.

Cardim, Fernao. 1939. Tratados da Terra e Gente do Brasil. São Paulo, NP.

Carneiro, Edison. 1967. Candomblés da Bahia. Editora Tecnoprint, Rio de Janeiro.

Cascudo, Luiz da Camara. 1967. Folclore do Brasil. Fundo de Cultura, Rio de Janeiro.

Colson, Audrey Butt and Cesareo de Armellada. 1983. An Amerindian derivation for Latin American Creole illnesses and their treatment. Social Science and Medicine 17: 1229–49.

Costa Lima, Vivaldo da. 1977. A família-de-santo nos Candombles Jéje-Nagôs da Bahia: um estudo de relações intra-grupais. Unpublished Master's Thesis, Federal University of Bahia, Salvador.

Cravo, Antonieta B. 1984. Frutas e Ervas que Curam. Hemus Editora, São Paulo.

Currier, Richard L. 1966. The hot-cold syndrome and symbolic balance in Mexican and Spanish-American folk medicine. Ethnology 5: 251–63.

Dalziel, J. M. 1948. Useful Plants of West Tropical Africa. Crown Agents, London.

Elbein Dos Santos, Juana. 1988. Os Nágó e a Morte. Vozes, Petrópolis.

Fichte, H. 1976. Xango: Die Afroamerikanischen Religionen. S. Fischer, Frankfurt.

Foster, George M. 1976. Disease etiologies in non-western medical systems. American Anthropologist 78: 773–82.

Freyre, Gilberto. 1986. The Masters and the Slaves: A Study in the Development of Brazilian Civilization. University of California Press, Berkeley.

Laguerre, Michel S. 1987. Afro-Caribbean Folk Medicine. Bergin & Garvey, South Hadley, Mass.

Lepine, Claude. 1981. Os estereôtipos da personalidade no Candomblé Nágó. Pp. 13–31 in Olóorisá: Escritos Sobre a Religão dos Orixás (Carlos Eugênio Marcondes de Moura, coordinator). Agora, São Paulo.

Lerivs, John. 1625. Extracts out of the Historie of John Lerivs, a Frenchman who lived in Brazil (1557 and 1558). Pp. 1333–46 in Purchas his Pilgrimes, Contayning a History of the World, in Sea Voyages & Lande-Travells, by Englishmen & Others. Samuel Purchas (editor). William Stansby, London.

Messer, Ellen. 1987. The hot and cold in Mesoamerican indigenous and hispanicized thought. Social Science and Medicine 25: 339–46.

Morton, Julia F. 1981. Atlas of Medicinal Plants of Middle America: Bahamas to Yucatan. Charles C. Thomas, Springfield, Ill.

Piso, Guilherme. 1948. Historia Natural do Brasil Ilustrada. A. Taunay (translator). Companhia Editora Nacional, São Paulo.

Povoas, Ruy do Carmo. 1989. A Linguagem do Candomblé: Níveis Sociolingüisticos de Integração Afro-Portuguesa. José Olympio, Rio de Janeiro.

Purseglove, J. W. 1984. Tropical Crops: Dicotyledons. Longman, Essex, England.

Rawley, James A. 1981. The Transatlantic Slave Trade: A History. Norton, New York.

Rodrigues, Nina. 1935. O Animismo Fetichista dos Negros Bahianos. Civilização Brasileira, Rio de Janeiro.

Sandoval, Mercedes C. 1979. Santeria as a mental health care system: an historical overview. Social Science and Medicine 13B: 137–51.

Sousa, Gabriel Soares de. 1971. Tratado Descritivo do Brasil em 1587. 4th Edition. Companhia Editora Nacional, São Paulo.

Staden, Hans. 1928. Hans Staden: The True History of his Captivity, 1557. Translated by Malcolm Letts. George Routledge and Sons, London.

Thompson, Robert Farris. 1975. Icons of the mind: Yoruba herbalism arts in Atlantic perspective. African Arts 8: 52–59, 89–90.

———. 1983. Flash of the Spirit: African and Afro-American Art and Philosophy. Random House, New York.

Verger, Pierre. 1976–77. Use of plants in traditional medicine and its linguistic approach. Pp. 242–97 in Seminar Series, Number 1, Part 1. University of Ife, Ife.

———. 1981. Bori, primeiro cerimônia de iniçiacão ao culto dos orisá na Bahia, Brasil. Pp. 35–55 in Olóorisá: Escritos Sobre a Religão dos Orixás. Carlos Eugênio Marcondes de Moura (coordinator). Agora, Sío Paulo.

———. 1981. Orixás. Corrupio, São Paulo.

Voeks, Robert. 1990. Sacred leaves of Brazilian Candomblé. Geographical Review 80: 118–31.

———. 1993. African medicine and magic in the Americas. Geographical Review 83: 67–83.

———. 1999. Roots of Candomblé healing. Pp. 113–25 in Proceedings of the Pacific Coast Council on Latin America Studies Vol. 17. Edited by Donald Castro. PCCLAS, Fullerton, Calif.

Williams, Paul V. A. 1979. Primitive Religion and Healing: A Study of Folk Medicine in North-East Brazil. Rowman and Littlefield, Totowa, N.J.

CHAPTER EIGHT

Virtuous Herbs

Plants in Chumash Medicine

JAN TIMBROOK

*We are constantly walking on herbs, the virtues of which no
one knows.*

—Chumash tradition (Hudson 1979: 56)

INTRODUCTION

At the time of initial European settlement in the late 18th century, the Chumash
Indians of southern California were a group of about 15,000 people. Their ancestors
had occupied the Santa Barbara Channel coast and offshore islands for 8,000 years or
more. By the late prehistoric era they had become a classic example of "affluent
foragers," with a complex, stratified society at the chiefdom level supported on a
hunting-gathering-fishing economic base.

Among the elite members of Chumash society were a variety of occupational
specialists who belonged to trade unions or guilds, the membership of which was
based partly on wealth and partly on supernatural sanction. Makers of stone bowls,
plank canoes, sinew-backed bows and certain other artifact classes each belonged to
the appropriate guild and received pay for their products (Hudson, Timbrook and
Rempe 1978: 153–154).

Religious specialists also had their own organization, an esoteric ritual cult called
the *'antap*. As in much of native America, the Chumash made little distinction between
religious and political spheres, or between sacred and secular aspects of life. Members
of the *'antap* group served as leaders of ceremonies, dancers, musicians, community
chiefs and their assistants, and shamans (Hudson and Underhay 1978).

There were many kinds of shamans—bear shamans, weather shamans, astrologers,
rattlesnake shamans and others—whose power was based partly on training but also
on a close relationship with one or more supernatural spirit guides, or "dream helpers,"
acquired through visions (Applegate 1978). The same was true of shamans who were
medical specialists, who used various pharmaceutical and therapeutic techniques to
cure illness. There were smoke or pipe doctors, sucking doctors, ant doctors, herb
doctors and others (Walker and Hudson 1993).

These specialists were understandably quite secretive about the exact nature of the remedies they used. Their medical knowledge was the basis of their livelihood and may sometimes have been passed down in families from father to son (Geiger and Meighan 1976: 73, 75).

Shaman doctors were probably not the only individuals who practiced medicine among the Chumash. Although there is little evidence to confirm it, a sort of folk medicine based on commonly known remedies, largely herbal, may have existed from the earliest times. The lack of information is not surprising, since explorers, missionaries and others who observed Chumash life in the early stages of European contact focused on what to them was strange and exotic behavior. The less spectacular, everyday practices were virtually ignored until John P. Harrington's work in the present century.

Most medical treatments, among both specialists and folk practitioners, made use of plants, the so-called "virtuous herbs." In this paper, I will describe a few of the most important plants the Chumash used in curing, and discuss changes that occurred in historic times. Sources consulted include explorers' journals, mission documents, late 19th century authors, John P. Harrington's extensive unpublished field notes and botanical collections, and more recent interviews.

PLANTS WITH LASTING IMPORTANCE

Yerba mansa (Anemopsis californica).—In the late 19th century, several authors in Santa Barbara and Ventura counties compiled information on medicinal herbs used by local Indian people and Spanish Californians. These early writers noted that a high value was placed on tea of yerba mansa root as a healing wash for cuts and ulcerated sores (Bard 1894: 7; Bingham 1890: 37; Birabent n.d.). Yerba mansa tea was also drunk for colds and as a blood purifier (Birabent n.d.; Benefield 1951:21).

Ethnographer-linguist John P. Harrington conducted interviews with Chumash people during the first half of this century, most actively from 1912 through the 1920s. Harrington's Chumash consultants called yerba mansa a "good medicine" (Maria Solares, Simplicio Pico, in Harrington 1986). The root tea was drunk for cough (Luisa Ygnacio, Simplicio Pico), applied to cuts and sores (Luisa Ygnacio), or used as a hot bath for rheumatism (Maria Solares, in Harrington 1986). Yerba mansa root was also chewed, drunk as tea, or inhaled to purify and strengthen a person who was to carry dangerous substances (Fernando Librado c. 1914, in Harrington 1986).

Yerba mansa is quite often mentioned by early writers and Harrington's consultants as an effective remedy for venereal disease (Bard 1894: 7; Fernando Librado c. 1914, in Harrington n.d.). After Spanish contact and colonization both syphilis and gonorrhea affected the Chumash, and these diseases devastated the mission populations. Yerba mansa, long used as a wash for sores, was logically applied to similar conditions. It was also taken internally in cases of venereal disease, probably being intended to aid by purifying the blood.

The Chumash believed that many diseases were really just one, blood trouble (Fernando Librado c.1914, in Harrington n.d.). "Freshening" or purifying the blood, thereby restoring balance and harmony in the patient's body, was the goal of a number of treatments. Many of these were herbal, such as yerba mansa; other treatments, such as seawater drinking, were considered effective as well.

Today, Chumash people still consider the yerba mansa plant to be good for "cualquier dolor." They take yerba mansa tea as a blood purifier, use it to soak or wash infected cuts, and drink it for relief from colds, asthma and kidney problems (Gardner 1965: 197; Weyrauch 1982: 22).

Because of yerba mansa's reputed medicinal value, the plant has been intentionally spread by humans, and large patches have become established in new localities such as the California islands (Smith 1976: 107). Yerba mansa is reportedly used all over Hispanic America as a liniment for skin problems and as a tea for blood disorders (Jepson 1914: 376; Ford 1975: 341–343). Its popularity seems not to be a post-contact phenomenon, however, since yerba mansa is valued medicinally by Native American people in whose territory it occurs, and names for it exist in several Indian languages. I think its use among the Chumash dates from prehistoric times, although it may have expanded somewhat under the influence of Mexican-American folk medicine.

Chuchupate (Lomatium californicum).—Mission-era writers noted the importance of chuchupate to the Chumash, both for its medicinal value and as a sort of talisman. The Chumash habitually carried or wore a piece of the root, and soldiers with the Longinos expedition in 1792 purchased bits of it "at a good price" from the Indians (Longinos 1792, in Simpson 1961: 46). What benefit the chuchupate was expected to confer to either Indians or soldiers was, unfortunately, not specified.

The Chumash practice of carrying chuchupate root on the person was observed in the following century as well. According to an author of the late 1800s, this was done in order to repel rattlesnakes (Bard 1894: 9).

In the early 20th century, Harrington's consultants were familiar with the use of chuchupate to control rattlesnakes. The root was thought to be capable of stupefying the snake or attracting it if one wanted to capture it (Fernando Librado c. 1914, in Harrington 1986); and a snake would rattle, but not bite, a person who carried a piece of chuchupate root in the clothing (Maria Solares 1918, in Harrington 1986).

Medicinal uses of chuchupate were recorded in early mission times. The aromatic root was chewed for headache, chewed and rubbed on the body for any sort of pain, and the scent inhaled for headache (Longinos 1792, in Simpson 1961: 45; Mission San Fernando 1814, in Geiger and Meighan 1976: 73).

A late 19th century physician said that chuchupate root was chewed as a tonic, and "was useful in flatulence, headache, and neuralgia" (Bard 1894: 6). For stomach trouble, it was taken as a decoction or soaked in a bottle of brandy and drunk (Birabent n.d.; Benefield 1951: 24).

In the early 20th century, Harrington's consultants mentioned most of these same uses for chuchupate. For pain relief, the root was chewed and rubbed on; it was applied the same way or drunk as a tea for rheumatism (Fernando Librado, Juan Justo, Luisa Ygnacio, Maria Solares, in Harrington 1986). It was also applied as a poultice to sores and used in a number of other ways; it was said to be very strong (Maria Solares, in Harrington 1986).

Among modern Chumash chuchupate is still important but restricted to medicinal applications. These medicinal uses seem to have expanded somewhat, possibly influenced by outsiders. The fresh or dried root is chewed or made into tea which is considered "good for everything from diarrhea to toothache," coughs, sore throat, nausea, upset stomach and constipation (Gardner 1965: 298; Weyrauch 1978: 25). One person is said to carry pieces of chuchupate root around in his pocket "for whenever he feels bad," but none of the people recently interviewed mentioned any connection with rattlesnakes.

In the Great Basin, Southwest and Mexico, *Ligusticum porteri* is known as chuchupate or oshá (Ford 1975: 182, 253–254; Bye and Linares 1986: 290). That species is not found in the Chumash region, but its uses are strikingly similar to those reported for *Lomatium californicum* among the Chumash. The evidence indicates that medical and magical uses of the plant *(L. californicum)* have a long tradition in this area and probably were not introduced by Mexican Indian or Hispanic people in historic times.

PLANTS FORMERLY IMPORTANT, BUT NO LONGER USED

Datura (Datura wrightii)—In the sense that Native American medicine is integrally involved with religious beliefs and practice, datura [usually called **toloache**] probably was the single most important medicinal plant of the Chumash. This was recognized by the early missionaries, one of whom stated in 1814: "With this they intoxicate themselves. They take it in order to become strong, in order not to fear anyone, to prevent snakes from biting them and that darts and arrows may not pierce their bodies, etc." (Geiger and Meighan 1976:48).

Datura is, of course, a hallucinogenic plant and was used by the Chumash for three principal purposes (Applegate 1975): first, establishing contact with a supernatural guardian to provide protection, special skill and a personal talisman; second, contacting the dead, finding lost objects, seeing the future, seeing the true nature of people; and third, curing the effects of injury, evil omens or breaches of taboo, and providing immunity from danger. For example, a person whose form was assumed by a coyote was in grave danger and should immediately take datura to prevent soul loss and death.

Datura's visionary applications did sometimes play a role in medicine but are too elaborate for discussion here. It was administered by a specialist when one was seeking visions, especially the first time, and there were always concomitant restrictions on diet and sexual behavior.

As a medicine, datura was prepared by a relative, usually the mother or grandmother of the patient. The leaves or roots were taken internally as a tea and/or applied as a poultice for broken bones and wounds. This was used as the treatment of last resort when other methods failed, and was also thought to cure the ill effects of a narrow escape from death. Datura and seawater were considered the best tonics for freshening the blood (Applegate 1975).

Harrington's consultants provided some additional data. The four most important Chumash remedies were said to be datura, seawater drinking, cauterizing, and big red ants (Fernando Librado c. 1914, María Solares 1918, in Harrington 1986). Datura was considered to be an effective remedy for tapeworm (Fernando Librado c.1914, in Harrington 1986). For broken bones, datura was taken internally (Fernando Librado, Simplicio Pico, María Solares, in Harrington 1986). It is unclear whether this was intended as an anesthetic for setting bones or as a way of restoring spiritual balance after injury.

It was believed that datura played a role in death from snakebite. According to Maria Solares, when a rattlesnake plans to bite a certain person, it sinks its fangs into a *toloache* root and sucks up the poison; the person it bites will die quickly (Applegate 1975: 11).

Today, the traditional use of datura to induce visions is barely remembered, and medicinal uses seem to be completely forgotten. "The present-day Chumash know that in the past people used *toloache* . . . It is said that it made one 'crazy'" (Gardner 1965: 294). Older people in the late 1950s were aware that their ancestors practiced sweating and vaguely associate datura drinking with the sweathouse. This is thought to have made the men feel well (Gardner 1965: 297). Actually, it was not datura but tobacco that was used in this way.

Datura was avoided by nearly all of the Santa Barbara area Indian and Hispanic people interviewed in the late 1970s. One unidentified informant spoke of inhaling the smoke from burning dried datura leaves as a treatment for asthma, although he had never used it for this himself. Most of the other people interviewed had no knowledge of datura use or said it was a dangerous drug; one said it was a form of liquor, a "bad medicine" (Weyrauch 1978: 33).

These statements from older Chumash people indicate to me that traditional knowledge of datura use has not been passed down to the present generation from their elders. The use of datura as a hallucinogen may be undergoing a revival among some younger Chumash descendants who are seeking to recapture their ethnic identity and follow ancestral traditions. It appears that current knowledge of datura use is based on personal experimentation and on information obtained from anthropological publications.

Tobacco (Nicotiana attenuata et al.).—Wild tobacco was formerly eaten not only as a recreational drug but also to promote good health. This practice made quite an impression on the Spanish explorers and missionaries; it is mentioned in several accounts and frequently likened to the alcoholic drinks with which Europeans were more familiar (e.g. Longinos 1792, in Simpson 1961: 55). Priests at missions in Chumash territory stated that the Chumash used a mixture of wild tobacco and lime as an intoxicant, either chewed or drunk in water (Geiger and Meighan 1976: 89).

According to Harrington's consultants, the wild tobacco was dried, ground and used plain or mixed with lime ash from burned shells. This mixture was called *pespibata.* Eating tobacco in the evenings after dinner, especially by gatherings of men, was a popular social recreation, "like people serve coffee or chocolate now." The resulting euphoria was generally accompanied by vomiting, which was considered a healthful practice (Fernando Librado, Simplicio Pico, Candelaria Valenzuela, Luisa Ygnacio, Maria Solares, Rosario Cooper, various dates in Harrington 1986).

One consultant told Harrington that when people were still living at the missions, "the priests objected to Indians eating *pespibata*. At Santa Ynez the alcaldes [Mission Indian constables] used to go around looking for *pespibata* indulgers and would bring them in and whip them" (Hudson 1979: 147–148).

Tobacco smoking was also practiced by the Chumash, but not in a recreational way. For example, in 1777 the explorer Fages witnessed tobacco smoke being blown over a corpse before burial (Priestley 1937: 33–34). This is consistent with later information provided by Harrington's consultants. Only rarely, they said, were cane tubes filled with pure tobacco and smoked for pleasure. Smoking of tobacco in stone pipes was done only by specialists and intended as a blessing, for purification or for curing (Fernando Librado c. 1914, María Solares 1918 in Harrington 1986).

The pipe doctor, an old man, was accompanied by two other old men, one a sort of messenger whose duty was to ascertain if anyone was sick and the other a singer. The pipe doctor blew tobacco smoke as an incense to treat the sick person. "A sick man would sometimes actually recover as a result of that treatment." There were special ways of handling the pipe, and the owner took an oath never to carry it around for fun or use it in play. He was paid for his services in chia, acorns, bead money, or whatever they had (Fernando Librado c. 1914, in Harrington 1986).

Tobacco had a number of other medicinal uses. In 1814, a mission priest noted that one of the best known curative methods was a fermented mixture of wild tobacco, lime and urine, drunk to relieve stomach pain and to heal wounds (Geiger and Meighan 1976: 73).[1] The same remedy was mentioned by Harrington's consultants: tobacco mixed with water was drunk to relieve pains in the stomach (Fernando Librado c. 1914, in Harrington 1986). Walker and Hudson (1993) speculate that Chumash medicine may have emphasized purgatives and emetics for relief from internal parasites acquired from eating undercooked fish and sea mammals.

Tobacco was used externally as well as internally. The dried leaves were chewed or moistened with water and then rubbed on the body for topical pain relief, as for muscle soreness or when one's ears were being pierced (Fernando Librado c. 1914, María Solares 1918, in Harrington 1986).

Neither medicinal nor ceremonial use of tobacco is mentioned in recent sources based on actual interviews (Gardner 1965, Weyrauch 1982). The medicinal uses of this plant which were formerly so important have been completely eclipsed by its use as a recreational drug. Many Chumash descendants do smoke tobacco nowadays. Some of them smoke wild tobacco, often mixed with other substances, and for these individuals it may be symbolic of Indian identity.

Poison Oak (Toxicodendron diversilobum).—Poison oak was formerly an important Chumash medicinal plant. Mission records from the early 19th century state that plasters of powdered poison oak were very effective in healing wounds and lacerations (Geiger and Meighan 1976: 75).[2] A hundred years later, poison oak juice was still being applied to staunch the flow of blood from a cut (Luisa Ygnacio c. 1914, in Harrington 1986).

According to Harrington's consultants in the early 20th century, the juice from stems and leaves freshly cut in early spring was considered to be the most effective remedy for warts, skin cancers and other persistent sores. It was dripped onto the area and after contact with the skin turned black on exposure to air. When the black surface healed and fell off, the cancer was cured. This method was also used for calluses and corns on the feet (Fernando Librado c. 1914, in Harrington 1986).

Poison oak was also taken internally as a remedy for dysentery or diarrhea. The root was boiled—taking care not to let the vapor get into the eyes lest blindness result—and the decoction drunk cold (Fernando Librado c. 1914, in Harrington 1986).

Apparently Indian peoples generally did not experience the severe contact dermatitis which affects many contemporary Anglo Americans following contact with poison oak leaves and stems. In northern California, for example, the Pomo used the stems in basketry, the juice or ashes from burned leaves in tattooing, the leaves to wrap acorn bread for cooking (Chesnut 1902: 364; Goodrich *et al.* 1980: 82).

Harrington's Chumash consultants commented on differences in poison oak susceptibility even among Indians; the Yokuts, a neighboring inland group, were said to be severely affected by it when they visited the coast, but the local Chumash were affected only a little or not at all (Juan Justo, Fernando Cardenas, in Harrington 1986). One woman said her mother used to work out in the field cutting poison oak and would "get it just a little on her arms" (Mary Yee c. 1955, in Harrington 1986).

Immunity seems to have diminished along with the proportion of Chumash ancestry in modern descendants. Remedies for poison oak rash have been known for some time, but have become much more important in recent decades. Harrington's consultants treated the rash by rubbing on dry ashes from burned tule *[Scirpus acutus]* or rush *[Juncus textilis]* (María Solares c. 1918, in Harrington 1986). Other remedies mentioned were bathing the area in lime water (used by the mission priests), mugwort tea *[Artemisia douglasiana]*, or nightshade leaves *[Solanum douglasii]* mixed with salt; or spitting on and rubbing the affected part (Fernando Cardenas, in Harrington 1986).

By the late 1950s, Chumash descendants no longer used poison oak medicinally but eagerly sought remedies for its effects. The rash is bathed in a tea made from mugwort leaves, coyote brush *[Baccharis pilularis]* or coffeeberry *[Rhamnus californica]* (Gardner 1965: 297–298). Currently, some believe that immunity can be obtained by spitting on the plant or by drinking a tea of boiled poison oak root (Weyrauch 1982: 14).

PLANTS WHOSE USES HAVE CHANGED HISTORICALLY

Mugwort (Artemisia douglasiana).—Chumash doctors cauterized wounds of their patients with small cones made from dried mugwort leaves, which were placed on the skin and ignited. The cones slowly burned down, becoming hot and painful (Walker and Hudson 1993: 83–84). This method, similar to the moxa of Asian medicine, was also used to treat skin cancers and rheumatism. Older people often had many scars from the treatment, especially on their legs. *'Apin*, as it was called, was considered by Harrington's consultants to be one of the most important Chumash remedies, along with seawater, datura, bloodletting and red ants (Fernando Librado c. 1914, María Solares 1918, in Harrington 1986).

The Chumash also practiced a variation on this technique, described by an early physician in Ventura (Bard 1894: 9). A stone tube or pipe, heated by burning dried leaves, was held over the diseased spot to induce a blister. Stone tubes and pipes were restricted paraphernalia used by the sucking doctor and smoke doctor, respectively. If cupping or cauterizing with mugwort was originally employed by these specialists, it may be fairly ancient in Chumash medicine.

Harrington's consultants mentioned other medicinal uses of mugwort, including plasters applied for a sore neck and lying on a bed of the leaves over hot coals for paralysis [pasmo] (Luisa Ygnacio, María Solares, in Harrington 1986). They also said it could be used as a remedy for headache and poison oak rash (various consultants, in Harrington 1986).

Today, the best known use of mugwort is as a remedy for rashes, particularly as a wash for poison oak and measles (Gardner 1965: 298; Weyrauch 1982: 8–9). A tea of the leaves is drunk for headache and asthma (Gardner 1965: 298), and also taken for severe fright (Juanita Centeno, pers. comm. 1978). The leaves are applied topically for headache (Gardner 1965: 298) and toothache (Weyrauch 1982: 9).

Among Chumash people interviewed in recent years, the cupping technique described by Bard (1894: 9) was barely remembered by one Santa Ynez Chumash woman (Jennie Guillen): "They blew smoke or air into the cup and applied it to the person's back to take away pain, I believe." She saw this done in the presence of her grandmother, who had been one of Harrington's consultants in the early 1900s (Weyrauch 1982: 2).

NATIVE PLANTS USED IN INTRODUCED DISEASES
OR DISEASE THEORIES

In some cases, new uses were introduced or developed for plants which had already been part of Chumash medicine. This has already been mentioned in the case of foreign diseases or conditions which were brought to the Chumash after contact with Europeans. Yerba mansa, it was noted, became a specific for venereal diseases, and mugwort has become a preferred treatment for poison oak. Many traditional cold remedies were probably applied when influenza and pneumonia struck mission Indian populations.

New theories about the causes of illness were also introduced. Most important of these was the idea of hot-cold balance which is so prevalent in Hispanic medicine throughout Latin America and the Southwest. This belief seems not to have been indigenous to the Chumash, and although they adopted some of its methods they apparently did not internalize the theory behind it.

For example, one syphilis remedy described by a Harrington consultant entailed drinking a concentrated mixture of sea water and chile peppers; this "hot" remedy for a "hot" disease would never be used by a Latin American folk healer (Walker and Hudson 1993: 117). On the other hand, cutting a newborn infant's umbilical cord with a carrizo cane knife was consistent with this theory; in some areas metal or stone knives are considered "cold" and therefore injurious (Walker and Hudson 1993: 107). However cane knives are sharp and the Chumash traditionally used them when skinning game animals and slicing deer meat (Maria Solares 1918, in Harrington 1986).

PLANTS INTRODUCED ALONG WITH THEIR USES

In mission times and afterward, many new plants were brought into the Chumash area, both deliberately as garden cultivars and accidentally as weeds. Some medicinal plants were very obviously introduced, often along with recipes for using them, by people from Mexico.

Rue (Ruta chalapensis).—Rue was brought in as a garden and medicinal plant. In the late 19th century it was drunk as a tea for nerves and heart palpitations, and also used for ear problems (Birabent n.d.).

Harrington consultants did not mention this plant at all, but it has become well known among Chumash descendants today. Its most important use is for earache, the leaves being inserted into the ear either alone or with warmed oil (Gardner 1965: 298; Weyrauch 1982: 17). This is now one of the most common herbal remedies in the area.

Ruta is used medicinally for earache and deafness throughout the Hispanic Southwest and northern Mexico; sometimes it is also taken for abdominal pain and nerves (Ford 1975: 293–294). These uses have been adopted by other California Indians (Bocek 1984: 252; Hinton 1975: 217).

Horehound (Marrubium vulgare).—Franciscan friars are said to have introduced this plant as a medicinal herb in the late 18th century (Jepson 1943: 397–398). By the late 19th century it was abundant on roadsides and waste places, and much used for coughs and lung diseases (Bingham 1890: 37). Harrington consultants said they sometimes made tea of horehound leaves, but did not consider it to be medicinal (Juan Justo c. 1925, in Harrington 1986).

About 1960, horehound tea was vaguely remembered by some Chumash people as an old-time way of inducing abortion, and no other uses were recorded at that time (Gardner 1965: 296-27). Currently it is most used as a cough medicine and for sore throats, colds and lung ailments, often mixed with honey (Weyrauch 1982: 10).

Horehound has a wide variety of medicinal uses throughout Mexico and the Southwest (Ford 1975: 237–238), but only the respiratory and throat remedies seem to have been adopted by Chumash descendants.

NEW PLANTS AS SUBSTITUTES FOR TRADITIONAL ONES

Introduced species which had their own distinctive uses are fairly easy to identify. It is more difficult to talk about new plants which may have replaced indigenous ones as remedies for particular ailments. Much depends on availability. The disruption of trade networks and restriction of access to private property have affected choices of medicinal materials. Mountain tea *[Ephedra viridis]*, valued for the blood and kidneys, grew in remote inland areas; horsetail *[Equisteum spp.]*, which also has green, cylindrical, jointed stems, was much more common along the coast. Notes with plant specimens collected by Harrington's consultants indicate that horsetail may have been used medicinally when *Ephedra,* the preferred form, was not available.

Investigators in the 1920s and 30s suggested that one particularly desirable remedy, *Adenostoma sparsifolium,* called ribbonwood or yerba del pasmo, was formerly found in the Santa Ynez range and offshore islands, but overzealous collecting by early-day Mexican Californians exterminated it from these localities (Barber correspondence on file at Santa Barbara Museum of Natural History). In the 1920s, Harrington's consultant Lucrecia Garcia labeled a specimen of a different plant, *Haplopappus arborescens,* as yerba del pasmo. *Haplopappus* and other genera of Asteraceae are known as yerba del pasmo in Mexico and the Southwest, but locally I think this is not a matter of mistaken identity. It may be that when "real" yerba del pasmo *(Adenostoma sparsifolium)* became unavailable, people began gathering a similar-appearing plant which they had always considered "another kind" of yerba del pasmo *(Haplopappus arborescens)* and adjusted the folk category accordingly.

CONCLUSION

Medical practices are dynamic by nature, and culture change did not begin with European contact in the 1500s. Many remedies were probably learned from other Indian peoples in prehistoric times. The Chumash have always been quite willing to experiment with new remedies, both on the basis of information received from others and by trying whatever is at hand (Gardner 1965: 297; Weyrauch 1982: 1).

Today it is difficult to separate elements of traditional Chumash medicine from the folk medicine of the Mexican-American community since each group has learned from the other. The Harrington materials from the first part of this century include information on 95 Chumash medicinal plants, only 9 of which were introduced species (Timbrook 1984: 144), and use of cultivated or store bought remedies has increased since then. Nearly half of the 49 medicinal plants which a recent study listed as used by Indians of Santa Barbara County are non-native species (Weyrauch 1982).

Many Chumash have expressed a general distrust of the competence and motives of Western physicians. One of Harrington's consultants said, "The doctors nowadays are more for getting money than they are for curing people. They do not have the power of curing people like the old Indians had" (Harrington n.d.). This belief remains widespread today.

Since the traditional specialists—pipe, sucking, and other doctors—died out shortly after mission times without passing on their technical knowledge, folk medicine practiced by non-specialist individuals has played an increasingly important role. But the Chumash today still feel the need to consult expert practitioners of traditional medicine. In the absence of curing specialists on the Santa Ynez Reservation in the late 1950s, some individuals occasionally went to Mexican healers and Chinese herbalists (Gardner 1965: 296).

> *My grandfather told me that it was good to learn about*
> *medical herbs, but that people will die just the same. It is*
> *merely a pastime.*
> —Fernando Librado (Hudson 1979: 56)

ACKNOWLEDGMENTS

This paper was presented in a shorter form at the Tenth Ethnobiology Conference, Florida State Museum, March 1987. I owe a debt of gratitude to the late Travis Hudson, though some of my interpretations differ from his earlier work on Chumash medicine. Thanks are also due to Margarita Kay and Willard Van Asdall for their encouragement and editorial skills.

LITERATURE CITED

Applegate, R. 1975. The datura cult among the Chumash. J. California Anthr. 2(1): 1–17.
Bard, C. L. 1894. A contribution to the history of medicine in southern California. Southern California Practitioner, August 1894, pp 3–29.
Benefield, H. S. 1951. For the Good of the Country: The Life Story of William Benjamin Foxen. Lorrin L. Morrison, Los Angeles.
Bingham, Mrs. R. F. 1890. Medicinal plants growing wild in Santa Barbara and vicinity. Santa Barbara Soc. Nat. Hist. Bull. 1(2): 34–37.
Birabent, F. L. n.d. Wild herbs used by the Indians and Spanish People in Santa Barbara County for medicinal purposes. Unpubl. manuscript on file, Santa Barbara Museum of Natural History.
Bocek, B. R. 1984. Ethnobotany of the Costanoan Indians, California, based on collections by John P. Harrington. Econ. Botany 38(2): 240–55.
Bye, R. A. and E. Linares. 1986. Ethnobotanical notes from the Valley of San Luis, Colorado. J. Ethnobiol. 6(2): 289–306.
Chesnut, V. K. 1902. Plants Used by the Indians of Mendocino County, California. Contributions of the U.S. National Herbarium 7: 295–422. Reprinted 1974, Mendocino County Historical Society, Fort Bragg, Calif.
Ford, K. C. 1975. Las Yerbas de la Gente: A Study of Hispano-American Medicinal Plants. Anthropological Papers No. 60. Museum of Anthropology, Univ. Michigan, Ann Arbor.
Gardner, L. 1965. The surviving Chumash. Archaeol. Survey Annu. Report 7:277–302. Univ. California, Los Angeles.
Geiger, Fr. M., O.F.M. and C. W. Meighan. 1976. As the Padres Saw Them: California Indian Life and Customs as Reported by the Franciscan Missionaries 1813–1815. Santa Barbara Mission Archive Library, Santa Barbara.
Goodrich, J., C. Lawson and V. P. Lawson. 1980. Kashaya Pomo Plants. American Indian Studies Center, Univ. California, Los Angeles.
Harrington, J. P. 1986. The Papers of John Peabody Harrington in the Smithsonian Institution 1907–1957, Vol. 3. Native American History, Language and Culture of Southern California/Basin, Reels 1–96. Edited by Elaine L. Mills and Ann J. Brickfield. International Publications, Millwood, N.J.
Hinton, L. 1975. Notes on La Huerta Diegueño ethnobotany. J. California Anthr. 2(2): 214–22.
Hudson, T., ed. 1979. Breath of the Sun: Life in Early California as Told by a Chumash Indian, Fernando Librado, to John P. Harrington. Malki Museum Press, Morongo Indian Reservation, Banning, Calif.
————, J. Timbrook and M. Rempe. 1978. Tomol: Chumash Watercraft as Described in the Ethnographic Notes of John P. Harrington. Ballena Press Anthropological Papers No. 9.

————, and E. G. Underhay. 1978. Crystals in the Sky: An Intellectual Odyssey Involving Chumash Astronomy, Cosmology, and Rock Art. Ballena Press Anthropological Papers No. 10.

Jepson, W. L. 1909–43. A Flora of California. Univ. California Press, Berkeley. 3 vols.

Priestley, H. I. 1937. A Historical, Political and Natural Description of California by Pedro Fages, Soldier of Spain. Univ. California Press, Berkeley.

Simpson, L. B., ed. 1961. The Journal of José Longinos Martinez: Notes and Observations of the Naturalist of the Botanical Expedition in Old and New California and the South Coast, 1791–1792. John Howell Books, San Francisco.

Smith, C. F. 1976. A Flora of the Santa Barbara Region, California. Santa Barbara Museum of Natural History, Santa Barbara.

Timbrook, J. 1984. Chumash ethnobotany: a preliminary report. J. Ethnobiol. 4(2): 141–69.

Walker, P. and T. Hudson. 1993. Chumash Healing: Changing Health and Medical Practices in an American Indian Society. Malki Museum Press, Banning.

Weyrauch, R. 1978. Herb and plant remedies used in the Santa Barbara area. Santa Barbara Urban Indian Health Project. Unpubl. manuscript on file, Santa Barbara Museum of Natural History.

————. 1982. Herbal Remedies. Solstice Journal 1(1). Santa Barbara Indian Center, Santa Barbara.

NOTES

1. These authors suggest "urine" may be a mistranslation of Spanish, and perhaps "water" is meant (Geiger and Meighan 1976: 158). But urine was commonly used in folk medicine, according to Margarita Kay (personal communication 1987).

2. Original document (Feb. 20, 1814): Los remedios que toman son de Plantas, Cortezas, Raizes, y ojas de Arvoles de los que no conozco ninguno sino es la Yedra con la que e visto hacer primores pues a un hombre hecho pedazos por un oso en brazos, piernas, costillas e spalda, con solo espolvonear la yerda [sic] sanó.

Although Geiger and Meighan (1976: 75) translated yedra as "ivy," to Harrington's consultants yedra meant poison oak. Bright also suggests this interpretation for the Luiseño term *hial,* called yedra in Spanish, translated by these authors as "ivy." The Luiseño drank the powdered root mixed with water as a purgative (Geiger and Meighan 1976: 157).

CHAPTER NINE

On the Relative Contribution of Men and Women to Subsistence Among Hunter-Gatherers of the Columbia Plateau:

A Comparison with *Ethnographic Atlas* Summaries

EUGENE S. HUNN

INTRODUCTION

Lee's data on the relative caloric contribution of the products of hunting and gathering among !Kung Bushmen (Lee 1968: 39) clearly demonstrate that the pervasive stereotype of men as providers, women as economically dependent childrearing specialists, does not apply to all foraging societies. In fact, comparable figures reported for other Bushman groups (Tanaka 1976) and for Australian Aborigines (Gould 1977) suggest that the female economic contribution as gatherer (measured as percent of caloric requirement provided) ranges between 60% and 80% generally among foragers in the arid tropics. Lee's cross-cultural sample drawn from the *Ethnographic Atlas* (Murdock 1967) indicates that only above ca. 40° latitude does the male economic contribution through fishing and hunting meet the bulk of subsistence requirements (Lee 1968: 43).

However, the case is apparently not yet considered conclusive. Ember has recently argued to the contrary that among the 181 *Atlas* hunter-gatherer societies—those rated zero on Murdock's "subsistence dependence" code for animal husbandry and agriculture—"men, not women, . . .typically contribute substantially more to primary subsistence" (1978: 441). If we accept the *Atlas* data at face value and sample as representative, Ember is correct, since 77% of the *Atlas* cases rate hunting and fishing (in which males are nearly always the primary producers) of greater value than gathering to subsistence. However, Ember chose to ignore the significance of the geographical bias in the *Atlas*. Fifty-seven percent of the hunter-gatherer cases in the *Atlas* are from at or above 42° latitude compared to only 17% of the total cases at or above that latitude. Eighty-four percent of the hunter-gatherer cases in the *Atlas* are from North America, while only 25% of the total cases are from that continent (see Table 1). The statistics from North America do not differ significantly from worldwide figures, however the correlation of latitude with the importance of gathering shows up clearly. Hunting and fishing are rated as exceeding the contribution of gathering among only 49% of societies below 42° but among 98% of those at or above that latitude.

Fig. 1. Map of the Columbia-Fraser Plateau Region of the Pacific Northwest indicating approximate locations of 13 *Ethnographic Atlas* societies.

There remains the questions of the face value of the *Atlas* subsistence ratings.
Ember equates Murdock's scale with percentage of caloric requirements met (1978:
441, 445). Murdock made no such claim. Rather, his 5 major subsistence factors—
gathering, hunting, fishing, animal husbandry, and agriculture—are rated 0 to 9 with
respect to "the relative dependence of the society" on the factor in question (Murdock
1967: 46). There is no mention of calories, nor is any operational definition of "subsistence dependence" offered. To interpret Murdock's subsistence scale in terms of calories is to impute a spurious objectivity to the *Atlas* data. I hope to show here that in at
least one major culture area, the Columbia-Fraser Plateau—which represents 13 of
the 181 hunter-gatherer cases in the *Atlas*—Murdock's subsistence codes are seriously

TABLE 1. The correlation of latitude and the importance of gathering to subsistence among, North American hunting-gathering societies (data from the *Ethnographic Atlas* [Murdock 1967]).

	Number of Societies with Gathering Rated ≥ r on Murdock's Subsistence Scale		/ Total number of Societies
SUBREGION	**≥ 42° N**	**≤ 42° N**	**Total**
Arctic/Subarctic	0/37	—	0/37
Northwest Coast	0/27	0/ 5	0/32
California	0/ 1	18/29	18/30
Plateau/Great Basin	2/20	9/13	11/33
Plains	0/11	0/ 5	0/16
Southwest	—	2/ 2	2/ 2
Northern Mexico	—	1/ 2	1/ 2
TOTAL: NORTH AMERICA	2/96	30/56	32/152
PERCENT WITH GATHERING ≥ 5	2.1	53.6	21.1
TOTAL: WORLDWIDE	2/103	40/78	42/181
PERCENT WITH GATHERING ≥ 5	1.9	51.3	23.2

•Murdock (1967) rates each society's subsistence economy on 5 major types of subsistence activity, gathering, hunting, fishing, animal husbandry, and agriculture, on the following scale: (0) zero to 5%, (1) 6% to 15%, (2) 16% to 25%, (3) 26% to 35%, (4) 36% to 45%, (5) 46% to 55%, (6) 56% to 65%, (7) 66% to 75%, (8) 76% to85%, (9) 86% to 100% dependence on the subsistence type in question. The factors must add to equal 10.

and systematically biased in favor of the hunting-fishing contribution if interpreted in caloric terms.

These 13 societies represent an area of 750,000 sq km drained by the Fraser and Columbia Rivers in what is now British Columbia, Washington, Idaho, and Oregon (see Fig. 1). The northern or British Columbia portion of the Plateau area is largely forested, while the southern portion is an arid sagebrush steppe and grassland surrounded by pine parkland and mountain forest. A diverse subsistence economy based on gathering, fishing, and hunting has supported continuous aboriginal populations for 10,000+ years (Cressman 1977). In no Plateau case does Murdock rate gathering as contributing more than 35% to "subsistence dependence."

DISCUSSION

The Data Base for Estimating Subsistence Contributions

Lee was able to measure actual consumption over a period of several months among a group of hunter-gatherers little affected by contact with modern civilization. The Columbia Fraser Plateau situation, however, is quite different. European influences date to ca. 1730 when horses reached the area indirectly from Spanish sources in the Southwest (Haines 1938). Epidemics of smallpox dating to before 1780 (Boyd MS*a*) spread from early coastal or Great Plains contacts. Fur traders, missionaries, settlers, treaties and consequent Indian wars followed close on the overland explorations of Mackenzie and Lewis and Clark, leading to the restriction of most of the native population to reservations by the end of the nineteenth century. Hydroelectric dam construction on the Columbia begun in 1931 has now all but eliminated any semblance of traditional subsistence fishing patterns (Pacific Northwest Regional Commission 1976). Thus estimates of the relative contribution of gathering, hunting, and fishing to the caloric requirements rest on limited ethnohistorical documentation by early explorers and missionaries and the statements of elderly informants recorded by twentieth century ethnographers. These ethnobiological data—often quite detailed and extensive as to species recognized and used and the time and place of harvest—must now be interpreted in the light of scientific knowledge of the natural history and biochemistry of resource species.

Previous attempts to characterize the ecological parameters of Plateau subsistence have focused almost exclusively on salmon (Hewes 1947, 1973; Kew MS; Palmer 1975a; Sneed 1971). No attempt has yet been made to quantify the vegetable input. This one-sided emphasis on the economic value of the native fisheries seems to reflect a misunderstanding of the potential nutritional contribution of native plant foods. For example, Hewes (1973: 134) assumed that "the satisfaction of this demand [for calories] must have been largely up to the fisheries. . . , since other natural foods available in the area in quantity are notoriously low in fuel value," among which he specifically includes bitterroot and camas (Ibid.: 151), Plateau staples. Hewes's estimation of the fuel values of native plants is simply wrong (e.g., for camas see Konlande and Robson 1972). Furthermore, recent ethnobiological and cultural ecological research in the area[1] clearly indicates a much more important role for vegetable products as sources of food energy than Hewes recognized.

For example, French and I have documented a folk classification system of extraordinary detail applied to a single taxonomically difficult genus, *Lomatium,* of the Umbelliferae. Fourteen basic folk taxa are named in Sahaptin, the language of the middle Columbia, at or below the scientific species level. Most of these species are important native foods including the staples, *Lomatium canbyi* Coult. & Rose and *L. cous* (S. Wats.) Coult. & Rose. These along with bitterroot (*Lewisia rediviva* Pursh), camas (*Camassia quamash* [Pursh] Greene), and huckleberries (especially *Vaccinium membranaceum* Dougl. ex Hook.) account for the bulk of vegetable foods gathered in the southern half of the Plateau region. Preliminary studies of densities and harvest rates of these species suggest the feasibility of reliance on vegetable resources in this area for the bulk of the calorie requirement (Hunn and French MS).

Estimates of Salmon Consumption

Hewes's estimates of salmon consumption are the most comprehensive attempted to date for the region. However, his interpretation of the nutritional factors is misleading.

He does not allow for the fact that the edible fraction of whole salmon is generally considered to be approximately 80% of the total weight (Martinsen, pers. comm.). Furthermore his caloric calculations are based on commercial samples. These are biased in two respects. They selectively represent the fattest species, chinook (*Oncorhynchus tschawytscha*) and sockeye (*O. nerka*), and they represent individuals taken at the beginning of the spawning migration. Yet Idler and Clemens (1959) have shown that migrating salmon (Fraser River sockeye) lose on average 75% of their caloric potential during this migration, as do Amur River Chum Salmon (*O. keta*) (Pentegov et al. 1928).

Table 2 cites salmon samples on which the present argument rests. The 20 samples represent 6 species (including steelhead trout, *Salmo gairdneri*) and average 170 kcal/100 g. Table 3 lists Hewes's salmon consumption estimates for the 13 *Atlas* societies of the Plateau with kcal/person/day equivalents based on 80% edibility and the present 170 kcal/100 g standard energy value. These equivalents are then reduced by a variable migration calorie loss factor, which for Fraser River groups is as calculated by Kew (MS).[2] For Columbia River groups I determine the calorie loss factor by taking the ratio of the total length of the river (1936 km) to the distance up the main stem of the Columbia to the mid-range of the group cited. For groups resident on tributary streams only, I calculated the ratio as that of the distance from the Columbia River mouth to the mid-range of the group to the total distance to the limit of salmon migration on that tributary.[3] This ratio is then multiplied by 0.75, the average caloric value lost by salmon in migration, and the result subtracted from one. I use Hewes's value of 2000 kcal/person/day as the minimal daily requirement (MDR), in the absence of reliable estimates of body weight or population structure for pre-contact populations of the region.

The tabulated calculations clearly show that estimates of salmon consumption fall consistently well short of the percentages of subsistence dependence cited by Murdock, with the exception of Thompson. The caloric contribution of salmon throughout the Plateau based on Hewes's consumption figures averages 26% compared to the 44% average dependence on fishing cited by the *Ethnographic Atlas*. While other fish contributed to the total dependence on fishing (Hunn 1979), waste, loss to scavengers, and the use of salmon as fuel (Thwaites 1959: 124) should tend to offset any increment from non-salmon fishing sources, except among groups such as the Flathead with restricted access to salmon.

The Contribution of Vegetable Staples

If no more than 30% of the calories come from fish, what might have supplied the rest? For the southern half of the Plateau there is solid evidence that the bulk of the remainder, and certainly in excess of 50% of the MDR, came from vegetable staples. The evidence is of 2 sorts. First, the following ethnohistorical and ethnographic observations may be used to estimate per capita consumption rates as they cite daily harvest rates, annual harvest totals, lengths of harvest season, and indicate elements of native procedure relevant to the estimation of harvest rates, such as the fact that roots are peeled before packaging.

TABLE 2. Salmon proximal analyses used, per 100 g.

	G WATER	G PROTEIN	G FAT	KCAL*
Rivera 1949: Canned				
11 samples, 6 species	66.95	22.17	8.61	172
Rivera, 1949 fresh				
2 samples, sockeye & steelhead	67.7	22.0	9.13	176
Watt and Merrill 1963: fresh				
1 sample, Chinook	64.2	19.1	15.6	222
1 sample, pink	76.0	20.0	3.7	119
Watt and Merrill 1963: Canned				
1 sample, Chinook	64.4	19.6	14.0	210
1 sample, chum	70.8	21.5	5.2	139
1 sample, Coho	69.3	20.8	7.1	153
1 sample, pink	70.8	20.5	5.9	141
1 sample, sockeye	67.2	20.3	9.3	171
AVERAGES	67.7	21.5	8.7	170

*kcal for fish is calculated on the basis ol 4.27 kcal/g of protein and 9.02 kcal/ g of fat (Watt and Merrill 1963).

TABLE 3. Estimates of salmon consumption (pounds/person/year), caloric yields (kcal/person/day), and percents of estimated MDR (2000 kcal/person/day).

SOCIETY	Annual Con-sumption	Gross Caloric Yield	Calorie Loss Factor	Net Caloric Yield	% of MDR	*Atlas* Rating	Percent Differ-ence
WISHRAM	400	676	.88	594	30	50	−20
TENINO	500	845	.87	735	37	50	−13
UMATILLA	500	845	.81	684	34	40	− 6
NEZ PERCE	300	507	.52	264	13	40	−27
	582	983	.52	511	26	40	−14
SINKAIETK	500	845	.67	566	28	40	−12
SANPOIL	500	845	.62	524	26	50	−24
COEUR D'ALENE	100	169	.25	42	2	30	−28
FLATHEAD	100	169	.25	42	2	40	−38
KUTENAI	300	507	.25	127	5	40	−35
CHILCOTIN	600	1014	.64	649	32	50	−18
SHUSWAP	500	845	.675	570	28	40	−12
LILLOOET	600	1014	.80	811	41	50	− 9
THOMPSON	900	1521	.81	1232	62	50	+12

Annual consumption figures are from Hewes (1973) except for the larger Nez Perce figure which is from Walker (1967). Calorie loss factors for the Fraser River groups, Chilcotin, Shuswap, Lillooet, and Thompson, are from Kew (MS).[2] Gross caloric yields are derived from annual consumption figures by converting to kg/day and multiplying by 0.8, the edible portion. The calorie loss factor is calculated as the distance fromthe mouth of the Columbia River to the center of the particular group's range divided by the length of the main stem of the Columbia or, if the group occupied a tributary, by the distance to the limit of salmon migration on that tributary.[3] The resultant ratio is multiplied by 0.75, the fraction of caloric value lost by salmon in migration, and subtracted from 1.0. The net caloric yield is simply the gross caloric yield times the caloric loss factor.

I saw a young woman at the Skitsoe village [Coeur D'Alene], who had collected and prepared sixty sacks of good Gamas *[Camassia quamash]*, each sack containing 1-1/5 bushel; she was spoken of in the best terms throughout the village (Geyer 1845–1846, quoted in Hart [1976: 16]).

The digging of Gamass takes place as soon as the lower half of the flowers on the raceme begin to fade, or better, when the time of flowering has already passed (Ibid.).

Gathering bitterroot was a tedious, although not difficult task. Women often worked three or four days to fill a fifty-pound sack. Each woman gathered at least two sacks, enough to sustain two people through the winter. A sack of bitterroot was worth . . . a horse, . . . (speaking of the Kutenai [Hart 1976: 49]).

The Sanpoil root digging grounds consisted of the entire portion of their territory lying south of the Columbia river, an area of over a million acres. . . . the entire Sanpoil population moved from its winter home on the river and set up temporary quarters at various spots on this prairie early in April of each year. Here they remained for thirty to forty days, during which time the entire energies of the women were devoted to digging roots, for in this short period it was necessary to accumulate a sufficient supply to last the entire year. . . . Each woman dug over about one-half acre in one day. . . . The several varieties of camas [local vernacular for *Lomatium* spp., as well as the true camas, which does not occur in the region under discussion] were gathered in greatest quantity: Bitter root was second in importance. . .A good day of camas digging often netted as high as a bushel of roots. . . The skins of roots. . . were slipped off as they were dug, or more commonly at camp in the evening (Ray 1933: 97–98).

May and early June is the main collection season, . . . This root *[Lomatium cous]*, along with camas, formed the bulk of the plant foods stored for winter use. A good digger gathered 50–75 pounds of /qamsit/ *[L. cous]* in a single day (speaking of the Nez Perce [Marshall 1977: 52]). These different locations had camas marshes which matured at different times; the lowest, warmest ones were exploited in early to mid-June; the highest, collest [sic.] could be worked until September. . . Harbinger (1966) said that a good digger could gather 80–90 pounds per day of hard labor, while less intensive work would yield 40–50 pounds easily. . . My informants estimate that women gathered camas for two to three weeks (speaking of the Nez Perce, Marshall 1977: 55, 57]).

People moving to the mountains for berries. They obtain at this season the large mountain huckleberry *[Vaccinium membranaceum]*. . .They are usually absent on these excursions [away form their village at the Dalles on the Columbia River], from four to six weeks; during which, each family lays in, for winter use, four or five pecks of nice dried berries (speaking of a Tenino-Wishram group, diary entry for August 19, 1843, of the missionary H. K. W. Perkins [Boyd MS*b*]).

The second source of consumption rates for vegetable staples is from my preliminary time-and-motion studies of contemporary Indian root-digging. One Umatilla woman, working at a normal pace and using the contemporary steel version of the traditional digging stick, dug 33 *L. cous* tubers/h, or 3.79 kg/h of peeled roots. I find that I can dig and "pocket" a *L. canbyi* tuber in 7 s. Allowing 3 s to find the next plant, we have 6/min or 360/h, which at 11.0 g/tuber (N=52) gives 3.96 kg/h. These estimates tend closely about a figure of 4 kg/h or a bushel (ca. 30 kg) in 7.5 h, not an unreasonable day's work. The close accord between the ethnohistorical/ethnographic estimates and my experimental figures is encouraging. These estimates are summarized in Table 4. The low value for the Kutenai bitterroot harvest cited is perhaps due to the fact that the Kutenai are on the northern fringe of that species' range (Daubenmire 1975), and the high value for the Flathead camas harvest is noted as a remarkable achievement (Geyer, in Hart 1976:16).

Per capita caloric consumption is based on a producer, consumer ratio of 1:4 with kcal/100 g standards as in Table 5. The harvest periods of tubers in spring, camas in summer, and huckleberries in fall were largely distinct. Thus we may add the estimates for spring tubers, camas, and the berry harvest to arrive at a rough but conservative annual per capita consumption figure:

SPRING (*Lomatium* spp. and bitterroot)	900 kcal
EARLY SUMMER (camas)	400 kcal
LATE SUMMER/FALL (huckleberries)	50 kcal
ESTIMATED ANNUAL PER CAPITA CONSUMPTION	1350 kcal

This figure is more than double the estimated contribution from salmon for this area and 67.5% of the estimated MDR. Compare this to the 30% "subsistence dependence" attributed by Murdock to the Wishram, Tenino, Umatilla, Nez Perce, Sinkaietk, Sanpoil, Coeur D'Alene, and Flathead, all known to have harvested several of these species in quantity.

It might be argued that harvests were not continuous during the periods of resource maturity. It is certainty true that women were called upon to preserve both fish and game harvested by the men. However, length of harvest figures cited in Table 4 are generally conservative.[4] Transport of the harvest to the winter villages might also pose problems, given the quantities involved, especially in prehorse times. However, spring roots and huckleberries were dried before transport reducing their weight by over 50%. In addition, there were many other fruits, berries, tubers, bulbs, and greens eaten on the spot which have not been included in this estimate. Thus 1350 kcal/person day from gathering seems reasonably applicable throughout the southern Plateau. The more northerly groups generally lacked these staples, relying instead on a variety of liliaceous bulbs other than camas, such as *Fritillaria* spp., *Erythronium grandiflorum* Pursh, and *Lilium columbianum* Hanson in Baker, and to a more considerable extent upon hunting (Palmer 1975a).

On Measuring Subsistence Dependence

The data compiled here do not demonstrate that the Atlas subsistence scale is incorrect, only that those scales cannot be reliably interpreted in caloric terms.

TABLE 4. Estimates of plant food harvest rates (kg/woman/day), total harvests (kg/women/year), and caloric yields (kcal/person/day).

SPECIES	Estimated Daily Harvest	Harvest Period/ Days	Total Annual Harvest	kcal Yield	Locale
SPRING:					
Lomatium canbyi	30	30–40	1050	800	Sanpoil[1]
Lomatium cous	22.7–34.1	ca. 40	1136	988	Nez Perce[2]
	33.3*	ca. 30	999	869	Umatilla[3]
Lewisia rediviva	30.3*	ca. 60	1818	1121	Umatilla[3]
	6.5	7	45	28	Kutenai[4]
EARLY SUMMER:					
Camassia quamash	36.4–40.9	14–21	677	524	Nez Perce[2]
	18.2–22.7	14–21	358	277	Nez Perce[2]
			2160	1672	Flathead[5]
LATE SUMMER/FALL:					
Vaccinium spp.		28–42	63.9–80.2	31	Tenino-Wishram[6]
			98	42	Umatilla[3]

Sources: (1) Ray 1933, (2) Marshall 1977, (3) Hunn and French MS, (4) hart 1976, (5) Geyer 1845–46, Boyd MS*b*.
Note: Ranges of values are averaged for subsequent calculations.
*Based on 8-hour days.

Murdock's figures are based on ethnographic reports that are almost without exception mere impressions. For example, his rating to the Sanpoil as "32500"(i.e., 26–35% gathering, 16–25% hunting, 46–55% fishing, 0–5% animal husbandry and agriculture) is clearly in accord with Verne Ray's characterization of Sanpoil subsistence emphases. Gathering, says Ray, the Sanpoil ethnographer of record, is but "a valuable supplement to the meat and fish that hold first place in the diet of the Sanpoil (1933: 97)." Ray devotes 20 pages each to fishing and hunting among the Sanpoil and but 9 to fruits and vegetable products. Yet Ray's own statements on the spring root harvest (quoted above) proves the contrary. Clearly the *Ethnographic Atlas* reflects both the bias of the ethnographer and of *his* informants for the less predictably available foods (cf. Lee 1968: 40, for a similar informant bias among the Bushmen), which seem most always to be the special task of men to pursue.

In the final analysis, subsistence dependence cannot be reduced to calories. Though calories are the body's first and largest requirement, survival obviously requires an adequate balance of nutrients over the long run. Salmon provided protein in more than adequate amounts, a nutrient the region's starchy staples largely lack. And salmon is rich in Vitamins, especially A and D (Rivera 1949). Game might be relied upon when other foods were in short supply. Fruits and berries, even lichens

(Turner 1977), contributed other vitamins and a variety of mineral nutrients, while "Indian celeries," eagerly sought in late winter and early spring after a winter on a diet of dried stores, are rich sources of Vitamin C.[5]

To single out one resource, one nutritional requirement, or one sex as the key to understanding the success of hunting-gathering adaptations is to miss the point entirely. Human foragers survived to colonize nearly the entire land surface of the earth by virtue of judicious selection of an ample and varied diet from an extensive, empirically sound folk biological inventory of the flora and fauna. To argue that either men or women were of paramount importance in the evolutionary history of the human species is to ignore the most human ecological characteristic, familial economic cooperation.

CONCLUSIONS

I have summarized evidence which demonstrates that the importance of vegetable resources gathered by women as sources of food energy is not confined to Bushmen or Australian Aborigines. Nor do plant foods play an insignificant role everywhere above 40° latitude. Murdock's *Ethnographic Atlas* "subsistence dependence" code summaries to the contrary, the food-collecting societies of the southern half of the Columbia-Fraser Plateau of northwestern North America (at ca. 45°–48° N latitude) obtained in the neighborhood of 70% of their food energy needs from plant foods harvested by women. The wide divergence between the *Atlas* summaries and comparable figures based on the best available evidence for this region, raise serious doubts about the general validity of the *Atlas* subsistence codes.

TABLE 5. Plant food proximal analysis used, per 100 g.

SPECIES	G Water	G Protein	G Fat	G Carbo-hydrate	kcal
Lomatium canbyi					
av. 6 dried root samples[1]	11.68	2.58	1.48	82.41	352
same, adjusted for water content	71.9	0.9	0.47	26.22	112
1 sample, fresh[2]	71.9	0.8	0.12	25.9	108
Lomatium cous					
1 sample, fresh[2]	67.9	1.0	0.4	30.0	127
Lewisia rediviva					
1 sample, fresh[2]	76.6	0.7	0.1	21.6	90
Camassia quamash					
1 sample, fresh[2]	70.0	0.7	0.23	27.1	113
Vaccinium sp.					
blueberries, raw[3]	83.2	0.7	0.5	15.3	62

Sources: (1) Washington MS, (2) Benson et al. 1973, (3) Watt and Merrill 1963.

ACKNOWLEDGMENTS

My research on Plateau ethnobiology has been supported by NSF grant BNS 76-16914 and by grants from the Melville and Elizabeth Jacobs Research Fund, Whatcom Museum Foundation, and the Graduate School, University of Washington. This work has also benefited from the collaboration and assistance of the Kamiakin Research Institute of the Yakima Indian Nation, and the Botany and Nutritional Sciences departments of the University of Washington.

LITERATURE CITED

Benson, D. M., J. M Peters, M. A. Edwards, and L. A. Hogan. 1973. Wild edible plants of the Pacific Northwest. J. Amer. Dietetic Assoc. 62: 143–47.

Boyd, R. 1990. Demographic History, 1774–1874. Pp. 135–48 in Handbook of North American Indians, William C. Sturtevant (general editor), Vol. 7, Northwest Coast, edited by Wayne Suttles. Smithsonian Institution, Washington, D.C.

———. 1996. People of the Dalles: The Indians of Wascopam Mission. University of Nebraska Press, Lincoln.

Cressman, L. S. 1977. Prehistory of the Far West: Homes of Vanished Peoples. Univ. Utah Press, Salt Lake City.

Daubenmire, R. 1975. An ecological life-history of Lewisia rediviva (Portulacaceae). Syesis 8: 9–23.

Ember, C. E. 1978. Myths about hunter-gatherers. Ethnology 17: 439–48.

Fagot, D. M. 1970. Recent Changes in the Numbers of Salmon (Oncorhynchus) and Steelhead (Salmo) that Return to their Producing Areas in the Columbia River Basin. Unpubl. M.S. Thesis, Univ. Washington, Seattle.

Geyer, C. A. 1845–46. Notes on the vegetation and general characteristics of the Missouri and Oregon Territories, during the years 1843 and 1844. London J. Botany 4:479–92, 653–62; 5: 22–41, 198–208, 285–310, 509–24.

Gould, R. A. 1977. Discovering the Australian Desert Culture. Pacific Discovery 30: 1–11.

Haines, F. 1938. The northward spread of horses among the Plains Indians. Amer. Anthro. 40: 429–37.

Harbinger, L. J. MS. The Importance of Food Plants in the Maintenance of Nez Perce Cultural Identity. Unpubl. M.A. Thesis, Washington State Univ., Pullman.

Hart, J. 1974. Plant Taxonomy of Salish and Kootenai Indians of Western Montana. Unpubl. M.A. Thesis, Univ. Montana, Missoula.

———. 1976. Montana—Native Plants and Early Peoples. Montana Hist. Soc., Helena, Montana.

Hewes, G. W. 1947. Aboriginal Use of Fishery Resources in Northwestern North America. Unpubl. Ph.D. dissert., Univ. California, Berkeley.

———. 1973. Indian fisheries productivity in pre-contact time in the Pacific Salmon area. Northwest Anthropol. Res. Notes 7: 133–55.

Hunn, E. 1979. Sahaptin fish classification. Northwest Anthropol. Res. Notes 13: 1–19.

———. and D. H. French. 1981. Lomatium: A Key Resource for Columbia Plateau Native Subsistence. Northwest Science 55: 87–94.

Idler, D. R., and W. A. Clemens. 1959. The energy expenditures of Fraser River Sockeye during the spawning migration. Internatl. Pacific Salmon Fisheries Commission, Progress Report No. 6. New Westminster, British Columbia.

Kew, M. MS. Salmon Abundance, Technology and Human Populations on the Fraser River Watershed. MS, Dept. Anthrop. and Sociol., Univ. British Columbia, Vancouver, April 23, 1976.

Konlande, J. E., and J. R. K. Robson. 1972. The nutritive value of cooked camas as consumed by Flathead Indians. Ecol. Food Nutr. 2: 193–95.

Lee, R. B. 1968. What Hunters Do for a Living, or, How to Make Out on Scarce Resources. Pp. 30–54, in Man the Hunter, edited by R. B. Lee and I. DeVore. Aldine, Chicago.

Marshall, A. G. 1977. Nez Perce Social Groups: An Ecological Interpretation. Unpubl. Ph.D. dissert., Washington State Univ., Pullman.

Martinsen, C. 1979. Personal communication. Univ. Washington, Seattle.

Murdock, G. P. 1967. Ethnographic Atlas. Univ. Pittsburgh Press, Pittsburgh.

Pacific Northwest Regional Commission. 1976. Columbia Basin Salmon and Steelhead Analysis. Pacific Northwest Regional Commission, Summary Report, September 1, 1976.

Palmer, G. 1975a. Cultural ecology in the Canadian Plateau: pre-contact to early contact period in the Territory of the Southern Shuswap Indians of British Columbia. Northwest Anthropol. Res. Notes 9: 199–245.

———. 1975b. Shuswap Indian Ethnobotany. Syesis 8: 29–81.

Pentegov, B. P., Y. N. Mentov, and E. F. Kuranaev. 1928. Physico-Chemical Characteristics of Breeding Migration Fast of Keta. Bull. Pacific Sci., Fisheries Res. Sta. (Vladivostok) 2 (Part 1).

Ray, V. 1933. The Sanpoil and Nespelem: Salishan Peoples of Northwestern Washington. Univ. Washington Publ. Anthrop. 5: 1–237.

Rivera, T. 1949. Diet of a Food-Gathering People, with Chemical Analysis of Salmon and Saskatoons. Pp. 19–36, in Indians of the Urban Northwest, edited by M. Smith. Columbia Univ. Press, New York.

Sneed, P. G. 1971. Of Salmon and Men: Investigation of Ecological Determinants and Aboriginal Man in the Canadian Plateau. Pp. 229–38, in Aboriginal Man and Environments on the Plateau of Northwestern America, edited by A. Stryd and R. Smith. Student Press, Calgary, Alberta.

Tanaka, J. 1976. Subsistence Ecology of Central Kalahari San. Pp. 98–119, in Kalahari Hunter-Gatherers, edited by R. B. Lee and I. DeVore. Harvard Univ., Cambridge, Mass.

Thwaites, R. G., ed. 1904–05. Original Journals of the Lewis and Clark Expedition, 1804–1806. Vol. 3. Reprinted 1959. Antiquarian Press, New York.

Turner, N. 1973. Plant Taxonomic Systems and Ethnobotany of Three Contemporary Indian Groups of the Pacific Northwest (Haida, Bella Coola, and Lillooet). Unpubl. Ph.D. dissert., Univ. British Columbia, Vancouver.

———. 1977. Economic importance of Black Tree Lichen (Bryoria fremontii) to the Indians of western North America. Econ. Botany 31: 461–70.

———, L. C. Thompson, M. T. Thompson, and A. Z. York. 1990. Thompson Ethnobotany: Knowledge and Usage of Plants by the Thompson Indians of British Colombia, Memoir No. 3. Royal British Columbia Museum, Victoria, British Columbia.

———. R. Bouchard, and D. I. D. Kennedy. 1980. Ethnobotany of the Okanagan-Colville Indians and of British Columbia and Washington. MS, British Columbia Provincial Mus. No. 21, Occ. Paper Ser., Victoria, British Columbia.

United States House of Representatives. 1952. The Columbia River and its Tributaries. 81st Congress, 2nd Session, House Document No. 531 (8 volumes).

Walker, D. E., Jr. 1967. Mutual Cross-Utilization of Economic Resources in the Plateau: An Example from Aboriginal Nez Perce Fishing Practice. Washington State Univ. Anthrop., Report Invest. No 41. Pullman, Wash.

Washington, N. MS. Tsukalotsa *(Lomatium canbyi)*—Key to Understanding Central Washington Nonriverine Archaeology. Paper presented to the 29th Annu. Northwest Anthropol. Conf., April 10, 1976, Ellensburg, Wash.

Watt, B. K., and A. L. Merrill. 1963. Composition of Foods. U.S. Dept. Agric., Agric. Handbook No. 8. Washington, D.C.

NOTES

1. These studies include research with Wishram and Tenino by D. and K. French, Umatilla and Yakima by E. Hunn, Nez Perce by A. Marshall, Wanapum and Sinkaietk by N. Washington, Thompson, Lillooet, and Okanagan Colville by N. Turner and the British Columbia Indian Language Project, Kutenai and Flathead by J. Hart, and Shuswap by G. Palmer (Hart 1974; Hunn and French MS, Marshall 1977; Palmer 1975a, 1975b; Turner 1973, MS; Turner, Bouchard, and Kennedy 1980; Washington MS).

2. Kew's caloric loss ratios are almost certainly overestimates since he states that, "Total caloric value of a sockeye measured at the river mouth will be reduced to nearly one half when it reaches the Upper Stuart spawning grounds . . ." (MS: 6). Idler and Clemens cite losses of 69.1% for males and 79.8% for females at the time of death on the Stuart Lake migration path (1959: 18).

3. For the groups cited here, the Wishram mid-range is taken as the Dalles (Columbia River mile 190), the Tenino at the Deschutes River mouth (Columbia River mile 202), the Umatilla at the mouth of the river of that name (Columbia River mile 300), the Nez Perce at the confluence of the Clearwater and the Snake Rivers (Columbia River mile 324 + Snake River mile 140), the Sinkaietk at the mouth of the Okanogan River (Columbia River mile 534), the Sanpoil at the Sanpoil River mouth (approximately Columbia River mile 615), the Coeur D'Alene at Spokane Falls, limit of salmon migration on the Spokane River, the Flathead at Metaline Falls, limit of salmon migration on the Clark Fork-Pend O'Reille River, and the Kutenai at the head of migration on either the Columbia River (Columbia Lake) or the Kootenai River (below Kootenay Lake). Limit of migration on the Snake River is at Upper Salmon Falls (approximate Snake River mile 400). Mileage figures abstracted from Fagot (1970: 111–24) and United States House of Representatives (1952).

4. In 1978 *L. canbyi* was exceptionally early and could have been harvested as early as February. In 1979 *L. canbyi* and *Lewisia rediviva* were commonly available up to ca. 600 m elevation by April 1. In 1977 *L. cous* and *Lewisia rediviva* were still being harvested by Umatilla Indians at 1400 m in the Blue Mountains of Oregon on June 22. Since camas may be harvested into September (Marshall 1977: 57), a root harvest period of 100+ days is possible.

5. Benson et al. cite 66 mg/100 g ascorbic acid for the young growth of *Lomatium nudicaule* (Pursh) Coult. & Rose (1973: 145), an important "Indian celery" of the region.

CHAPTER TEN

Quelites—Ethnoecology of Edible Greens—
Past, Present, and Future

ROBERT A. BYE, JR.

INTRODUCTION

Until recently, the significance of uncultivated edible greens in the traditional native American diet has not been appreciated. As the intensity and depth of botanical, ethnological, and archaeological investigations increase, practical and theoretical concepts are being applied to the elucidation of the principles of resource exploitation by man. The employment of undomesticated greens—referred to as "quelites" in Mexico—as food provides an opportunity to investigate the ethnoecology1 of this poorly understood food resource.

The ideas expressed and part of the data presented in this paper are based upon ongoing ethnoecological-ethnobotanical studies among the Tarahumara Indians (Bye 1976). This group of southern Uto-Aztecan speakers number about 50,000 and live in the sierras and barrancas of southwestern Chihuahua. They are considered subsistence agriculturalists (maize, bean, cucurbit, and chile) who supplement a significant portion of their diet with plants procured through hunting and gathering. The statements regarding the Tarahumara are restricted to data obtained in the pine oak forest of the sierras (2000–3000 msm) although general comments include observations in the sub-tropical barrancas (500–2000 msm) as well.

Uncultivated edible greens are generally herbaceous plants whose young leaves and tender tips are consumed. In some cases, especially in the barrancas, these "greens" may include underdeveloped inflorescences and tender, thickened stems. The Tarahumara refer to these greens as "guiribá" to which the Spanish term, "quelite," is generally applicable. These plants are usually immature when consumed and are eaten raw (in a few cases) or lightly cooked in warm water and are consumed fresh in season or dried for use during the dry season.

DISCUSSION

From the ethnoecological viewpoint, I would like to discuss 6 aspects which are being considered in formulating the general ecological principles of human

TABLE 1. Some common edible greens or quelites of the Tarahumara. All of these species are commonly found in and along cultivated fields.

Scientific Name (Arranged by Family)	Tarahumara Name Mexican Name	Season of Procurement
AMARANTHACEAE		
Amaranthus retroflexus L.	basorí, wasorí quelite del agua	spring/summer
CHENOPODIACEAE		
Chenopodium ambrosioides L.	chu'á´ epazote	summer/fall
Chenopodium berlandieri Moq.	chu'á quelite de cenizo	spring/summer
COMPOSITAE		
Bidens odorata Cav.	sepé	spring/summer
Cosmos paraviflorus (Jacq.) HBK.	hu've	spring/summer
CRUCIFERAE		
Brassica campestris L.	mekuásare coles	spring/summer fall-cultivated
Lepidium virginicum L.	rochíwari	winter/spring fall-cultivated
MALVACEAE		
Anoda cristata (L.) Schlecht.	rewé	spring/summer
PORTULACACEAE		
Portulaca oleracea L.	chamó verdulaga	summer/fall
URTICACEAE		
Urtica dioica L.	ra'urí, ra'oke	spring/summer

exploitation of vegetal resources. These points include: 1) diversity[2] of resources, 2) importance of human disturbances, 3) measurements of productivity, 4) ecological importance of plants in agricultural systems, 5) evolutionary significance in domestication process, and 6) the importance of these resources in the future.

Species Richness

Richness in the number of species and in the phenological types is an important parameter in evaluating the ecological potential of any resource system. The Tarahumara are known to employ over 120 species of quelites. Most of these plants are ingested in the form of immature leaves and stems of herbaceous dicots although a few plants have the edible portion represented by bulbous leaf bases (e.g., *Pitcarnia palmeri*), pseudobulbs (e.g., *Gongora* sp.), succulent stems (e.g., *Opuntia* spp.), and

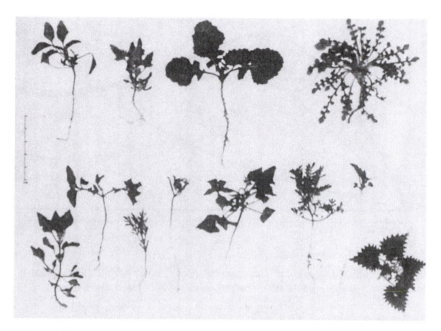

Fig. 1. Some edible weeds form an anthropogenic community (maize fields and margins; May 1978; Cusárare, Chihuahua). Top row (left to right): *Amaranthus retroflexus*, Chenopodium berlandieri*, Brassica campestris*, Lepidium virginicum**. Bottom row (left to right): *Galinsoga semicalva, Simsia eurylepis, Bidens ordorata*, Cosmos parviflorus*, Ipomoea hirsutula, Dalea* sp., *Anoda cristata, Urtica dioica*. An asterisk (*) denotes the preferred species. Scale equals 5 cm.

immature inflorescences (e.g., *Jacobinia candicans*). Of these 120 plus edible species, only 10 are consistently consumed today in the sierras (Table 1) and all are found in anthropogenic communities (Fig. 1).

These common species have been erroneously referred to as "wild greens" although a few researchers recognized their relationship to human disturbance (Messer 1972; Wilken 1970). Biologically, these plants are weeds which are evolutionary and ecological products adapted to survival in habitats disturbed by human activity. Without constant human interaction over thousands of years, these forms would not be present or in sufficient density to be an adequate food resource. These common quelites are annual and represent 3 major life forms which are important in the availability of culturally acceptable and seasonally distributed resources: 1) winter annuals (e.g., *Lepidium*), 2) spring-summer annuals (e.g., *Amaranthus, Bidens*), and 3) summer-fall annuals (e.g., *Portulaca*).

It should be noted that there are only a few perennials and that the ecologically wild species play a relatively minor role in the total diet. One notable exception to this statement would include certain species of prickly-pear cacti, *Opuntia* spp., found wild in the barrancas (although it is known to be a tolerated weed, encouraged weed, or even cultivated wild plant in some regions).

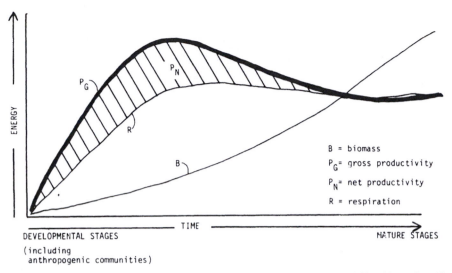

ENERGY

B = biomass
P_G= gross productivity
P_N= net productivity
R = respiration

TIME

DEVELOPMENTAL STAGES   MATURE STAGES
(including
anthropogenic communities)

Fig. 2. Generalized Ecosystem Development Model (after Odum 1969). Note that Net Productivity is available in the development stages and not in the mature stages.

Human Disturbance

Human disturbance is an important factor in determining the presence and density of these common edible weeds. They are members of various anthropogenic communities[3] which are maintained by the Tarahumara and include cultivated fields, field-fence margins, dwelling sites, corrals and trailsides. A general ethnoecological principle to be documented in the future states that the existence of large human populations depends on the net productivity of the ecosystem which is available only in the early developmental stages of succession. Based on Odum's (1969) Ecosystem Development Model (Fig. 2), net productivity[4] in an ecosystem is available for harvest, storage and consumption in the developmental stages but not in the mature stages or climax. Consequently, human activities tend to push succession back to the early stages and to maintain those stages. In these early stages, certain resources can be manipulated directly (e.g., cultivated fields) or indirectly (e.g., weed communities) so as to concentrate those exploitable resources in time and space. Recently, this principle has been illustrated in a restricted sense by the development of the "garden hunting" concept using a tropical ecosystem and animal resources (Linares 1976). The exploitation of quelites represents an analogous situation with plant resources. Interestingly, Bohrer's (1977) speculations on the food habits in hominid evolution suggest that plants of the early successional communities were exploited as food rather than members of the more mature communities.

Many of the characteristics of the developmental stages of Ecosystem Development (Odum 1969) are beneficial to human exploitation of concentrated resources. These characteristics include: 1) low species diversity, 2) low biomass, 3) linear food chains, 4) grazing food chains, and 5) short lived organisms with simple life cycles (e.g., annual plants). The attributes of low species diversity and low biomass may

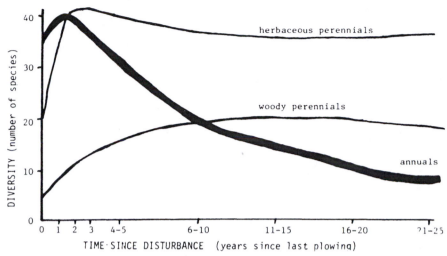

Fig. 3. Generalized model of relative change of annuals, herbaceous perennials and woody perennials in the early stages of succession in abandoned agricultural fields (after Beckwith 1954).

seem contradictory until one assesses the quality of the species and the biomass. In general, species richness and diversity increase with ecosystem development but the relative importance of herbs to woody plants is greater in the early stages (Fig. 3) (Beckwith 1954). The biomass is relatively low due to the nature of herbaceous annual plants which do not accumulate tissue as do inedible, woody perennials of later stages.

The presence and density of edible greens depend on several factors which are only poorly known today. Many weed seeds have evolved mechanisms for long distance dispersal (in order to colonize distant habitats when available) and for short distance dispersal (in order to increase the seed bank for maintenance of local population) (Baker 1974; Harper 1977). Disturbance (by digging, plowing, etc.) of the upper layer of the soil is critical to the germination of weed seeds so that seeds near the surface and light germinate and emerge faster than if they were deeper in the soil (Fig. 4) (e.g., Dawson and Burns 1962; Wiese and Davis 1967). The ecological importance of disturbance to light flash and seed germination has been discussed by Sauer and Struik (1964). Density of certain species in early stages of succession tends to be related to the surface area of the disturbance. Davis and Cantlon (1969) found that *Amaranthus retroflexus* tends to increase in density as the open area increases during the first year of experimental secondary successional studies in New Jersey. It is possible that agricultural practices originated, in part, in response to human preference for genetically altered plants in ecologically altered habitats. Partially domesticated plants (i.e., genetically altered from domesticated progenitors) may have been encouraged, sown and subsequently selected in the manipulated habitats which developed into agricultural and garden habitats rather than wild progenitors of domesticated plants transferred from refuse mounds to manipulated fields and subsequently selected.

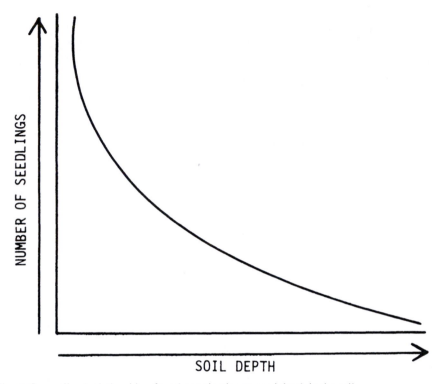

Fig. 4. Generalized relationship of seed germination to seed depth in the soil.

Productivity

Quelites are an important primary producer of the manipulated ecosystem exploited by the Tarahumara. The significance of this productivity to these subsistence agriculturists can be measured in several ways. A few considerations are outlined below.

Being subsistence agriculturists, the Tarahumara depend on an annual diet cycle based upon maize, bean, cucurbit and chile which are consumed from fresh plants in August through October and from stored, dried forms in October through May. Often times the stored cultivated food supplies are limiting from April through July. During this latter period, the diet is augmented by hunted and gathered resources such as fish, wild greens, roots, bulbs, and "hearts" of maguey (Agave spp.). It is during this period that quelites from the cultivated fields dominate the diet. May–June period also marks the end of the dry season and the beginning of the rainy period and the start of the annual growing season. The seeds of weeds as well as planted maize emerge in the fields in mid to late May in response to the increased temperature and moisture. The coincidence of the marked change to warm moist regime with the germination and emergence of edible weed seedlings with the depleted food reserves is critical to the survival of the Tarahumara populations in the sierras.

The weeds can also provide food after the initial growing period. July and August may be frequented by severe hail storms which destroy the young maize plants. Also, animal pests such as crows and insects can destroy portions of the maize crop at different stages. The tender apices of the older weed plants as well as the late emerging seedlings can be collected and consumed. The quelites represent a living emerging food reserve.

When considering primary productivity in ethnobotanical terms, one must account for not only quantity in time but also quality. Although studies are in progress, preliminary data indicate that in the sierran cultivated maize fields, 100 g of edible seedlings of *Amaranthus retroflexus* (Fig. 5) can be harvested in May and early June from a plot varying from 1–4 m². Regeneration of another 100 g of edible weed seedlings can occur during this period in about a week. A daily serving of *A. retroflexus* consists of about 100 g per adult individual and is prepared by slightly cooking it in warm water and rinsing it in cold water 2 or 3 times and then eating it with a little salt along with tortillas or pinole.

The quality of quelites can be measured in several ways. One system involves cultural preference based upon beliefs and cross-cultural comparisons. For example, some Mexicanized Tarahumara no longer eat certain quelites because the dominating Mexican culture looks down upon such practices. Older Tarahumara do not eat certain species because "only the Apaches" or "only the pigs" eat those particular weeds. Another system considers the biological components such as nutritive quality, toxicity, palatability, pharmacology and flavoring.

Fig. 5a. Tarahumara woman collecting *Amaranthus retroflexus* (Bye 8532; 30 May 1978; San Ignacio Arareco, Chihuahua).

Fig. 5b. Seedlings of A. retroflexus at the early developmental stage when they are consumed as quelites (Bye 8510; 28 May 1978; Cusarare, Chihuahua).

The nutritional requirements of the Tarahumara and the value of their present diets are not known at this time. A preliminary evaluation of the Tarahumara maize-bean-cucurbit diet indicates that the following items are deficient: protein, calcium, vitamin A, thiamine, riboflavin, and vitamin C. The first 3 components are only present at about a quarter of the minimum Recommended Dietary Allowance (RDA) for an adult (National Academy of Sciences 1974) while the latter 3 components are marginally deficient. An addition of 100 g of quelites (e.g., *Amaranthus, Brassica,* and *Chenopodium;* see Table 2) has only a slight impact on the protein yet provides sufficient calcium, vitamin A, thiamine, riboflavin and vitamin C to meet the RDA standard for the United States. It should be noted that nutritional loss by traditional Tarahumara preparation techniques using warm (not boiling) water is probably minimal based upon knowledge of loss of ascorbic acid through various cooking methods (Caldwell and Gim-Sai 1973). Other preparation techniques such as sun wilting and mineral additions may enrich the value of quelites as well.

Toxic materials may be removed from food plants through selective breeding and genetic manipulation of domesticated plants or through gathering and preparation techniques applied to non-domesticated plants. The Tarahumara collect only the young, tender leaves which have low amounts of the nitrates and tannins that tend to accumulate in the older, senescent leaves. Aqueous cooking and leaching (rinsing) practices can also reduce these substances. Palatability is another factor which affects

TABLE 2. Nutritional value of some weedy greens (per 100 g edible portion) (Leung 1961).

Plants	Ca (mg)	Vit. A (IU)	Thiamine (mg)	Riboflavin (mg)	Ascorbic Acid (mg)
Amaranthus spp.	313	1600	0.05	0.24	65
Brassica campestris	252	1335	0.12	0.29	118
Chenopodium berlandieri	156	2765	0.17	0.47	109
Average	240	1907	0.11	0.33	97

the edibility of quelites. In general, only the young leaves and stem tips are consumed. These tender structures are relatively unlignified compared to mature tissue.

Chemical constituents of certain edible weeds may provide additional values due to flavoring and pharmacological activity. *Chenopodium ambrosioides,* a common weed along margins of fields and fences, is often added to beans and meat dishes. It imparts a distinctive flavor to the food. Also, the leaves contain ascoridole as part of the Oil of Chenopodium which is known to be an effective anthelminthic medicine (Guenther 1948–1952; Santos 1925).

The Tarahumara often collect edible weed seedlings from week 2 to week 6 after germination. After this time the plants are often too large and lignified for consumption (although the stem apices and terminal leaves can be consumed in times of emergency or famine). A recent study on the nutritional value of leaf protein in Africa included species of *Amaranthus, Solanum,* and groundnuts (Oke 1973). The extractable protein nitrogen, a measure of leaf protein, was found to peak during week 5 to 6 and was followed by rapid decline in nutritional value in later weeks (Fig. 6). It

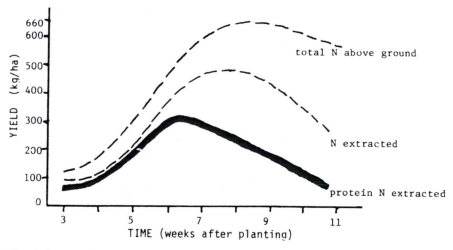

Fig. 6. Change of nitrogen and protein content in leaves over time (based upon harvested groundnut leaves; from Oke 1973).

appears that the Tarahumara gathering of palatable leaves occurs when the potential extractable nutrient value reaches its peak.

Ecological Benefits

Although the Tarahumara practice of leaving the weeds in the field for extended periods (Fig. 7) may appear uneconomical, this strategy may be ecologically sound. Unconscious dispersal of weed seeds by Tarahumara movements while harvesting maize during the previous year and turning over the soil for planting enables the weed seed bank to build up in the soil and to be closer to the surface to insure high rate of germination. When the weeds emerge, they are not weeded out until 6–8 weeks later. Subsequent weeding of cultivated fields at similar intervals allows for the establishment of new weed populations which provide emergency food reserves. This system allows weeds to be the first crop with the second crop, maize, being available later. This double crop system allows for the harvest of reliable yields of one type of net productivity in an environment where maximum yields of one crop systems are not possible due to poor soil fertility, limited moisture and unpredictable pests and weather.

Only recently have the practical aspects of multiple cropping systems been considered in applied techniques and theoretical terms (Papendick et al. 1976). The essence of the multiple cropping is the complementary use of growth resources by

Fig. 7. A field consisting of two crops: 1) edible weeds (*Amaranthus, Chenopodium, Bidens* and *Cosmos*) and 2) maize. (June 1973; San Ignacio Arareco, Chihuahua).

different components of the system. The rate of exploitation of each resource by each component is separated by space and/or in time. Hence, the shallow rooted amaranth weeds should be extracting water and nutrients in the upper soil surface above the deeper planted maize seeds. After a certain period of growth the roots of both species would be competing for the same resources in the same space and time, to the detriment of each species. Future research will investigate the hypothesis that the Tarahumara remove weeds when they begin to compete with maize for the same resources. Before that time (6–8 weeks) the weeds do not compete with maize and therefore should not negatively affect the maize yield. Net productivity of reliable yield therefore has 2 temporal peaks—early in the growing season with weed seedlings or quelites and late in the growing season with the harvested maize.

Tentative support for this reasoning can be seen in experimental work carried out at Chapingo, Mexico (Alcalde Blanco and Hernandez X. 1972). Plots of maize were treated with different weeding practices. It was found that the weeds left in the fields for days 1 to 30 and for days 1 to 62 after planting had no effect on the maize yield compared to the control (weed-free plots). Maize yield decreased if weeds were left in the fields after these periods (Fig. 8). The 2 weeds used in this experiment were *Amaranthus* and *Simsia*, 2 Tarahumara quelites.

The Tarahumara concept of multiple, reliable yields appears to illustrate multiple cropping ecological theory. Weeds may also provide other ecological benefits such as soil protectors, dispersion of food resources for various predators, and other factors which merit further investigation.

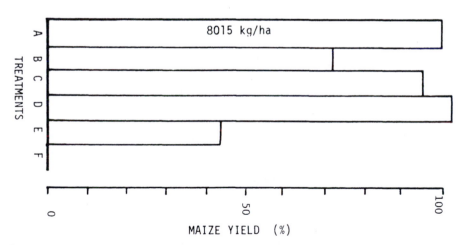

Fig. 8. Competition study of maize and weeds (*Amaranthus* and *Simsia*) (based upon data from Blanco and Hernandez X. 1972). A, maize free from weeds at all times (control); B, maize free from weeds days 1–30 (after planting); C, maize free from weeds days 31–62; D, maize free from weeds days 63–94; E, maize and weeds together during total growing season; F, weeds alone.

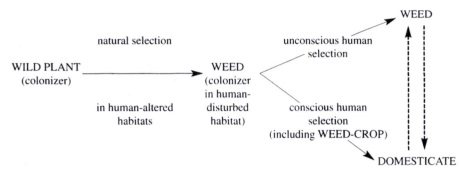

Fig. 9. A generalized pathway of domestication involving weeds and domesticates.

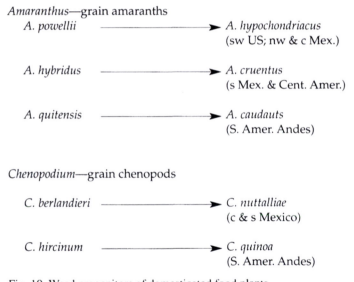

Fig. 10. Weed progenitors of domesticated food plants.

Domestication

The exploitation of weeds may represent one pathway to domestication and subsequent agriculture. Weeds and domesticates represent end products of genetic and ecological alterations mediated by human activities (Fig. 9). Domesticates appear to be the result of human directed evolutionary changes in plants in order to increase and stabilize genetically the valued plant parts. These plants produce valued yields in a manipulated environment. Weeds, on the other hand, are not directed by conscious human selection but are evolutionary responses to human disturbed habitats which vary in time and space. As we know more about domestication, the more important weeds become in understanding this evolutionary process (De Wet and Harlan 1975).

This domestication process recognizes weeds as one type of progenitor which was suggested by Vavilov (1951) with respect to secondary centers of origin of crop plants (e.g., rye, originally a weed in wheat fields, became the domesticated grain when wheat did poorly in cultivation in northern Europe). People's response to edible resources found in human disturbed environments could trigger conscious sowing and selection of weed seeds. Domesticated amaranths and chenopods are derived from weed progenitors (Fig. 10) (Sauer 1967; Wilson and Heiser 1979) in both the northern and southern continents of the Western Hemisphere. This North-South pattern may also be present with peppergrass, *Lepidium*. Cultivated *Lepidium meyenii* is a restricted domesticate of high altitudes of South American Bolivia and Peru (Gade 1976; Leon 1964). Although no native *Lepidium* is known to be domesticated in North America, the Tarahumara plant seeds of *Lepidium virginicum* as a weed-crop in cultivated fields (Fig. 11). Perhaps the domestication of *Lepidium* in the northern latitudes is proceeding slower. An "experiment" to examine this domestication hypothesis started nearly 300 years ago and is still in progress. *Brassica campestris,* a weedy mustard introduced by the Spaniards, has been considered a potential candidate for domestication in South America although there has been no conscious sowing and selection of this weed (Gade 1972). In North America, the Tarahumara presently have *Brassica* as a weed-crop (Bye 1979).

Future Resources

As we begin to understand the evolution, ecology and nutritional values of edible weeds, these plants can become more beneficial in the future. Strategies of germplasm conservation of economically important plants should incorporate sampling surveys of weedy relatives as well as wild progenitors. Domesticates, weeds progenitors and weed byproducts result from ongoing plant-man interactions and represent a process and not an event. These interactions involve degrees of symbiosis as well as synergism between plants and man with changes in response to various biological, ecological and cultural factors.

For our agroeconomic societies, quelites should provide new stimuli for evaluating productivity, cultural perception and value systems. A few grams of certain edible weedy greens grown in low energy input ecosystems may be more nutritious and cheaper than cultivated vegetables from high energy input industrialized ecosystems. Despite negative cultural pressure, some edible weeds (e.g., *Portulaca, Chenopodium*) are still available in Mexican open air markets and supermarkets (Fig. 12). Perhaps our young, modern civilization has a lot to learn about subsistence and productivity from older civilizations which have survived thousands of years by eating weeds as one component of their subsistence.

CONCLUSIONS

Survival of the agricultural Tarahumara populations is dependent upon edible weedy greens from cultivated fields. The diversity of plants and the ecological and

Fig. 11a. Cultivated plot of *Lepidium virginicum*, a weed-crop.

Fig. 11b. Plants of cultivated weed-crop, *L. virginicum*, from plot in Fig. 11a. (Bye 7040; 7119; 10, 15 Oct. 1975; east of Cusarare, Chihuahua).

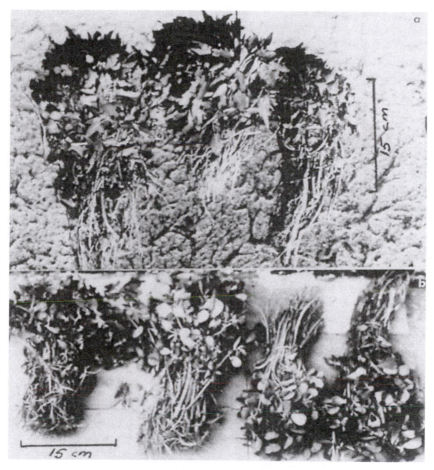

Fig. 12a and b. Weeds sold as quelites in Chihuahua market. a, *Chenopodium berlandieri* (Bye 9322; 30 March 1979); b, *Portulaca oleracea* (Bye 9100, 9101, 9102; 2 September 1978).

evolutionary bases of their exploitation of quelites suggest that certain generalities could be drawn and applied to the development of ethnoecological principles. One principle appears to be that disturbance of the ecosystem in order to push the ecosystem back to the early developmental stages and to maintain the communities at these stages is important to the biological existence of human populations. Net productivity is available for exploitation in the early stages of succession and is subjected to variation in quantity and quality depending on human activities.

We are able to study the processes of plant-man interactions today in order to elucidate ethnoecological principles. Edible weeds are consumed by the Tarahumara. This plant-man interaction appears to be based upon biological and ecological theory. The principle of this resource exploitation should apply to other present-day cultures as well. Because these processes are evolutionary in nature, we should expect evidence of weed food resource exploitation from archaeological studies in the forms of phytoliths and epidermal tissues from coprolites, field soils, and preparation implements. This principle should also apply to the future. Once it is understood and applied, we should expect a more realistic basis for developing relationships between human populations and their ambient vegetal environment.

ACKNOWLEDGMENTS

I wish to express my sincere appreciation to the Tarahumara Indians for their cooperation and assistance. Enthusiastic encouragement from C.W. Pennington, L.J. Verplancken (S.J.), J. Candler, J. Bock and R. Shuster is greatly appreciated. Financial support covering travel in Mexico during which certain data were obtained was extended by the Botanical Museum and Department of Biology of Harvard University; Department of Environmental, Population and Organismic Biology, University Museum, and Council on Research and Creative Work of the University of Colorado; National Geographic Society; and National Science Foundation (GB-35047). Although not cited, voucher specimens for the Tarahumara work are deposited at ECON, CHAPA, COLO, GH, and MEXU (abbreviations in accordance with *Index Herbariorum*). The plants were collected with the permission of the Tarahumara Indians, Secretaria de Agricultura y Ganaderia de Mexico (Departamento de Forestales), Consejo Nacional de Ciencia y Tecnologia de Mexico, and Universidad Nacional Autonoma de Mexico (Instituto de Biologia).

LITERATURE CITED

Alcalde Blanco, S., and E. Hernandez X. 1972. Estudio preliminar sobre la competencia nutrimental entre arvenses y el maiz, y sus efectos sobre el rendimiento del cultivo., pp. 94–96, *Resumes,* I Congreso Latinoamericano, Sociedad Botanical de Mexico, S.C.

Baker, H. G. 1974. The evolution of weeds. Annu. Rev. Ecol. Syst. 5: 1–24.

Beckwith, S. L. 1954. Ecological succession on abandoned farm lands and its relationship to wildlife management. Ecolog. Monogr. 24: 349–76.

Bohrer, V. L. 1977. West African dietary elements as relicts of hominid evolution. J. Anthropol. Res. 33: 121–32.

Bye, R. A. 1976. Ethnoecology of the Tarahumara of Chihuahua, Mexico. Unpubl. Ph.D. dissert. (Biol.), Harvard Univ.

————. 1979. Incipient domestication of mustards in northwestern Mexico. Kiva 44:237–56.

Caldwell, M., and Y. Gim-Sai. 1973. The effect of cooking method and storage on the ascorbic acid content of Malaysian leaf vegetables. Ecol. Food Nutr. 2: 35–38.

Davis, R. M., and J. E. Cantlon. 1969. Effect of size of area open to colonization on species composition in early old-field succession. Bull. Torrey Bot. Club 96: 660–73.

Dawson, J. H., and V. F. Burns. 1962. Emergence of barnyardgrass, green foxtail and yellow foxtail seedlings from various soil depths. Weeds 10: 136–39.

De Wet, J. J. M., and J. R. Harlan. 1975. Weeds and domesticates: evolution in the man-made habitat. Econ. Botany 29: 99–107.

Gade, D. W. 1972. Setting the stage for domestication: *Brassica* weeds in Andean peasant ecology. Proc. Assoc. Amer. Geogr. 4: 38–40.

———. 1976. Personal communication, 18 March 1976.

Guenther, E. 1948–52. The Essential Oils. Van Nostrand, New York.

Harper, J. L. 1977. Population Biology of Plants. Academic Press, New York.

Leon, J. 1964. The "maca" *(Lepidium meyenii),* a little known food plant of Peru. Econ. Botany 18:122–27.

Leung, W-T. W. 1961. Food Composition Table for Use in Latin America. Institute of Nutrition of Central America and Panama (Guatemala) and Interdepartmental Committee on Nutrition for National Defense (U.S.A.) Natl. Inst. Health, Bethesda, Md.

Linares, O. F. 1976. "Garden hunting" in the American tropics. Human Ecol. 4: 331–49.

Messer, E. 1972. Patterns of "wild" plant consumption in Oaxaca, Mexico. Ecol. Food Nutr. 1: 325–32.

National Academy of Sciences. 1974. Recommended Dietary Allowances, Washington, D.C.

Odum, E. P. 1969. The strategy of ecosystem development. Science 164: 262–70.

Oke, O. L. 1973. Leaf protein research in Nigeria: a review. Tropical Sci. 15: 139–55.

Papendick, R. I., P. A. Sanchez, and G. B. Triplett. 1976. Multiple Cropping. Amer. Soc. Agr. Spec. Publ. No. 27. Madison, Wis.

Santos, J. K. 1925. A pharmacological study of *Chenopodium ambrosioides* L. from the Philippines. Philippine J. Sci. 28: 529–47.

Sauer, J. D. 1967. The grain amaranths and their relatives: a revised taxonomic and geographic survey. Ann. Missouri Bot. Garden 54: 103–37.

Sauer, J. and G. Struik. 1964. A possible ecological relation between soil disturbance, light-flash and seed germination. Ecology 45: 884–86.

Vavilov, N. I. 1951. The origin, variation, immunity and breeding of cultivated plants. Chronica Botanica, vol. 13.

Wiese, A. F. and R. G. Davis. 1967. Weed emergence from two soils at various moistures, temperatures and depths. Weeds 15: 118–21.

Wilken, G. C. 1970. The ecology of gathering in a Mexican farming region. Econ. Botany 24(3): 286–95.

Wilson, H. D., and C. B. Heiser. 1979. The origin and evolutionary relationships of 'huauzontle' *(Chenopodium nuttalliae* Safford), domesticated chenopod of Mexico. Amer. J. Botany 66: 198–206.

NOTES

1. Ethnoecology is the area of study which examines the ecological bases of human interactions with and relationships to the ambient environment.

2. Ecological diversity is generally considered to consist of 2 components: richness and evenness. For the purpose of this paper, the emphasis is upon richness, which can be defined as the variety of species present in a given community.

3. Anthropogenic community is a plant community initiated and maintained by human activities and represents an early secondary successional community.

4. Net productivity represents the amount of energy which accumulates in the ecosystem over a period of time (usually on an annual basis). It can be defined by the difference between Gross Productivity and Respiration in a given community or ecosystem.

CHAPTER ELEVEN

Famine Foods of the North American Desert Borderlands in Historical Context

PAUL E. MINNIS

*Through want and hard hunger they gnaw at the dry and
desolate ground, they pick mallow and the leaves of bushes.*
—Job 30:3

INTRODUCTION

Not all foods are equal. Some are relished, others only tolerated, and still others are loathed, being eaten only when necessary. On occasion the Trobriand Islanders, for example, "have to fall back on the despised fruit of the *noku* tree, which is hardly edible but hardly ever fails" (Malinowski 1935: 16). As should be the case, greatest scientific attention concentrates on the most common foods. Yet this emphasis should not blind us to the value of studying less desirable foods, often called "famine foods," "starvation foods," "emergency foods," or "queer foods" as so quaintly termed by Kagwa (1934).

Here, I briefly examine the ethnobotanical literature on famine food use by indigenous groups of the Desert Borderlands, emphasizing agriculturalists but also including information on other groups in the southwestern United States and northernmost Mexico. After reviewing general characteristics and importance of famine foods, specific examples from the Desert Borderlands are enumerated. Then I outline a historical process of change in food preference patterns under changing socio-political contexts and suggest that famine food use has changed dramatically through time since European contact. This illustrates that food preference patterns are clearly embedded within their social, economic, historical, and political contexts and are not simply a function of the biological character of these plants.

Characteristics of famine foods.—Famine foods must meet two minimal characteristics. First, they have to be edible, and second, they must be available even when more frequently consumed rations cannot be acquired. Famine foods can often barely claim the first and may require substantial processing to make them edible or to reduce their toxic constituents. The second characteristic is particularly interesting, because we might be able to predict what classes of resources will be famine foods based on their biological character and ecological requirements. Some of the most important famine foods should be those plants that are especially resistant to the factors which reduce yields of more preferred foods. When droughts are the primary factor reducing food procurement, then drought resistant plants should be important famine foods. Most likely these will be xerophytic plants, such as cacti, perennials, or plants growing in environments not affected by precipitation deficits. When predation is a primary limiting factor, plants with particularly effective biochemical or structural defenses against predation should be major famine foods.

Just as food shortages range from "hunger seasons" (e.g., Richards 1939; Annegers 1973; Ogbu 1973; Colson 1980) to massive famines, so too there are various types of low preference foods. First are foodstuffs consumed only during severe food shortages. In addition, traditional populations often endure seasonal periods of low food availability, and there are "seasonal hunger" foodstuffs eaten at these times. Another category of low preference foods are those that are normally consumed and whose use is intensified during periods when other foods are unavailable. An example of the latter group is mesquite fruits *(Prosopis glandulosa)* which are staples for some groups of the Desert Borderlands. During times when crops fail, the collection of these plants simply may be increased. Century plant (mescal, *Agave*) and various cacti are other examples of widely and frequently consumed native food resources in the Desert Borderlands which also provide an unusually stable resource during food shortages. The Seri on the coast of Sonora, Mexico, present an example:

> During extended droughts ephemerals fail to appear, substantially fewer century plants are edible because they do not become reproductive, and many other major perennials have reduced production. Nevertheless, it appears that most Seri were able to locate edible plants at any time of the year. During extended drought on San Esteban Island, however, the only plant available was *Agave cerulata,* which is rich in carbohydrates but low in protein and lipids. (Felger and Moser 1985: 95)

The status of a particular plant as a famine food is dependent upon many factors including its biological and biochemical constitution. Some low preference foods have toxic constituents which cause discomfort after eating, yield products of low nutritional value, are foul-tasting, or their consumption requires substantial processing to render them edible. Alamgir (1980: 121) reports from Bangladesh that "starvation and the use of alternative 'famine foods' led to epidemics of diarrheal diseases in many areas " Similarly, Irvin (1952) mentions several examples of the deleterious effects due to the consumption of famine foods in the Sudan and other areas of Africa. Other biological factors determine whether a foodstuff might be used only as famine food. These can include low population densities, irregular production, or availability at the wrong time of the year.

Variables other than resource biology are important in understanding famine foods; cultural factors are, likewise, critical. Some low preference foods are tabooed to all or a portion of a population. Ritually tabooed foods, however, are known to be consumed during periods of starvation (e.g., Honigman 1954; Cerulli 1964), and it is quite likely that this practice is more frequent than reported. Seed stock saved for future planting is clearly a famine food of last resort for farmers because of the long-term consequences of this action. Plantain saplings, for example, are a famine food in parts of Bangladesh (Alamgir 1980) as were maize seed among the Hopi (Beaglehole 1937). Agricultural by-products also can be consumed. Of the six major classes of famine foods mentioned for one Bangladesh community, two are agricultural by-products, rice hulls and rice water, not normally eaten by humans (Alamgir 1980). Yue (1985: 80–81) illustrates well the use of what would otherwise be crop by-products during a Chinese famine in 1959:

> The sent-down cadres organized a group to investigate other ways of obtaining nourishment, by crushing corncobs into powder, for example, and mixing this with a little corn flour to make buns . . . An even cruder kind of bun was made by mixing crushed rice husks and corncobs together with a small amount of ground corn. We also gathered apricot leaves, dried them in the sun, and ground them into flour, sometimes mixing this with powdered elm tree bark to make a porridge. It was a desperate time.

Some resources could be available in the territory of hostile groups, and thus the social cost of use may be quite high. Castetter et al. (1938), as an example, mention that in the past some Pima of the Sonoran desert would not collect the century plant in certain areas because of possible attacks by Apache. Another cultural factor is processing technology. Foods requiring unfamiliar preparation may be less preferred. Various relief rations to Ethiopia were at first not well-integrated into the local cuisine, because these foods were unfamiliar (Mason et al. 1974). Likewise, Woodham-Smith (1962) discusses how the importation of maize in the 1840s during the Irish Potato Famine created confusion, because it was a food unfamiliar to both peasants and administrators.

Finally and perhaps most importantly, the characterization of a food as low preference is, of course, logically dependent upon the availability of more preferred foods. Changes in the foods available, therefore, should change preference patterns. This factor is one overlooked in discussion of famine foods because such studies have tended to be ahistorical. With the introduction of new crops and edible wild foods between areas, the role of native foods can change. I attempt to demonstrate that such a change occurred in the Desert Borderlands during the past four centuries, since Spanish contact and conquest followed by governmental administration by Mexico and then the United States.

Famine foods: importance and frequency.—The study of low preference foods has theoretical and practical value. The use of famine foods seems to be a universal strategy for coping with severe food shortages; it is impossible to estimate how many lives have been spared by the use of these foods. Not only does the study of famine foods document a little known set of foods, but they have characteristics that might be exploitable. These plants survive and can produce food, however tenuous the claim of edibility may be, under extremely unfavorable conditions, and this characteristic may be manipulated in the development of new crops and economic products. It is quite likely that some of these plants could become cultigens if bred to reduce undesirable biochemical properties and other factors limiting use.

Because of infrequent use and lowest status, low preference foods seem to be underrecorded in ethnobotanical literature, even though many such foods surely exist. The use of famine foods is one of the most commonly recorded actions taken by peoples throughout the world to cope with food shortages, based on a cursory survey of the Human Relations Area File. Unfortunately, most of the examples are simply superficial and anecdotal references that rarely identify the famine foods adequately. One example from ancient China does, however, clearly demonstrate the extensive use of famine foods, and I believe accurately reflects the diversity of famine foods. The *Chiu-Huang Pen-ts'ao* published in 1559 describes 414 plant famine foods used in Hunan province alone (Read 1946). Such a large number of famine foods from only one small region suggests that the number of famine foods throughout the world could be truly staggering. A large corpus of folk information on famine foods must reflect their critical importance to humanity. As Scudder (1962: 211) states in regard to the Gwembe Tonga of central Africa:

> . . . while I believe that a number of these reports are overly optimistic about the ability of wild produce alone to support an agricultural population for extended periods of time without widespread malnutrition and starvation, it cannot be denied that time and again crop failure has led to intensive exploitation of the rich flora of the Valley.

There may be many reasons why the use of starvation foods seems to be reported so infrequently in ethnobotanical literature. Practices of traditional rural peoples who often form the lowest stratum of nation-states are frequently viewed negatively. And most likely the use of famine foods, which are barely edible, might be considered especially "primitive" and suffer a harsh judgement. Consequently, the use of these resources would not be widely acknowledged. Furthermore, with the increasing incorporation of traditional peoples into industrial, national, and international economies, the use of local famine foods surely has decreased as other strategies for coping with food shortages, such movement to urban areas or increasing use of international relief supplies, have gained importance. Combined with increased urbanization, these factors can lead to the substantial loss of information about foods useful during famines. The lack of this knowledge was so acute during severe food shortages in World War II that the Dutch government felt compelled to issue a publication describing emergency food plants locally available and methods for preparing them (Den Hartog 1981).

THE DESERT BORDERLANDS

Environments of the Desert Borderlands vary from the desert coasts, rich with marine resources, through the inland Mohave, Great Basin, Chihuahuan, and Sonoran deserts to the rugged mountains and plateaus of the major continental mountain masses of the Sierra Occidental in Mexico and the Rocky Mountains in the United States (Fig. 1). Deserts basins are low, from less than 305 m in elevation for the Sonoran Desert up to 1,525 m for the Chihuahuan, Great Basin, and Mohave deserts. Precipitation in the deserts is sparse, approximately 200–300 mm per year. Grasslands and desert scrub communities dominate the deserts with relatively lush riparian vegetation along the larger drainages. Low deserts have cool winters, whereas the upland deserts experience cold winters. Major mountain ranges rise up to 4,200 m with precipitation ranging from 305 mm to over 1,020 mm annually. Mountain vegetation is composed largely of conifer woodlands with oaks and coniferous forests at higher elevations. Within these major zones is a great diversity of biological communities that have been most recently described by Brown (1982).

The present natural environments of the Desert Borderlands have undergone significant changes even within the past several hundred years (e.g., Brown 1982; Hastings and Turner 1965; Wauer and Riskind 1977). Many of these changes can be attributed to anthropogenic factors. Severe grazing pressure, hydrological modification, urban development, industrial farming, use of water far beyond recharge rates and suppression of natural fires, among other factors, have altered the environment, including the former distribution of native food plants. Bohrer (1975), for example, discusses the recent widespread reduction of cool-season grasses, whose seeds were once important foods for indigenous peoples.

The cultural environment of this region is, likewise, complex and ever changing; native populations have developed a rich suite of adaptations to the environmental and cultural conditions in the Desert Borderlands. Some groups have been mobile hunters and gatherers, whereas for at least 2000 years, others have been farmers, and more recently some have raised livestock.

The ethnographic present for groups considered here dates from the last century for most cultures to the present for others, such as the Seri. Famine foods have been recorded for the largely agricultural Puebloan groups of the Colorado Plateau and Rio Grande valley (Hopi, Zuni, Acoma, Laguna, San Felipe, San Juan, and Keresans). Agriculturalists of the Sonoran desert or Colorado River are also included (Pima, Mohave, Yuma), as are the Papago, a Sonoran desert group combining more hunting and gathering with agriculture. The Navajo and Ramah Navajo of the Colorado Plateau focus on herding and agriculture, whereas the Seri are hunter-gatherers of the desert coasts of Sonora, Mexico.

The political and economic impacts on native populations by Spanish, Mexican, and North American occupations have been profound and have not been the same for all populations in the Desert Borderlands. While many groups became extinct following European domination of the region, others partially maintained their cultural integrity to varying degrees. Even for those groups that have been marginally integrated into national economies, many changes have affected them. Traditional areas of economic exploitation have been significantly reduced, and new economic pursuits, such as animal husbandry, use of new crops, and sale of crafts, have been added to their economies. The Hopi, often cited as one of the more traditional cultures of the Desert Borderlands, now have a diet composed largely of nonlocal foods with little use of traditional resources (Kuhnlein and Calloway 1977).

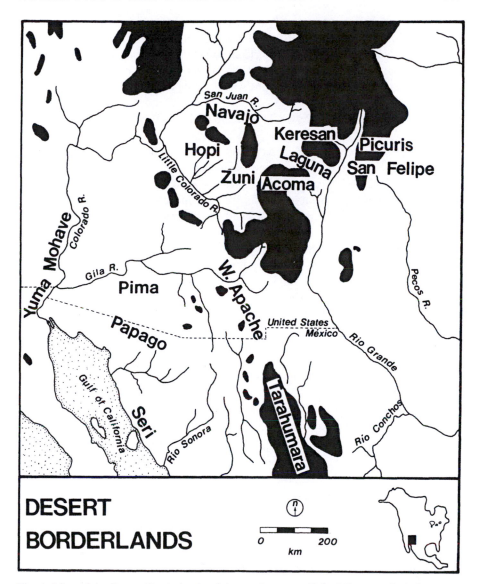

Fig. 1. Map of the Desert Borderlands of the southwestern United States and northernmost Mexico showing the location of indigenous groups mentioned. The dark areas are major mountains, including the Rocky Mountains in the north, the Sierra Madre Occidental to the south, and the Mogollon highlands in the center of the map.

Many environmental (e.g., fire, flood, pest infestation) and cultural factors (e.g., conflict, change in economic relationships) can reduce food availability. I believe, however, that one of the primary causes of food shortages in the Desert Borderlands has been unusually low precipitation. Paleoclimatic and historic records demonstrate periods of sustained and widespread droughts, both during prehistoric and historic times (e.g., Tuan et al. 1973; Sellers and Hill 1974; Dean and Robinson 1978; Euler et al. 1979; Dean et al. 1985; Hall 1985; Minnis 1985). Consequently, native populations in the Desert Borderlands have been familiar with food shortages for thousands of years and have developed a repertoire of strategies to cope with these threatening circumstances.

FAMINE FOODS OF THE DESERT BORDERLANDS

Although most references to Desert Borderlands ethnobotany and socio-ecology emphasize only the most commonly used plants, the voluminous ethnobotanical literature does provide mention of some famine foods, even though important characteristics of famine food are now unavailable. We have inadequate understanding of the chemical composition of these resources, methods of preparation, who collects them, and precisely when and how these plants are used.

Table 1 lists probable famine foods recorded for the Desert Borderlands groups considered here. Not all plants listed are famine foods in the most restricted sense; also included are hunger season foods and those foods whose harvest is simply intensified under these conditions. The use of low preference foods is dynamic, yet few references provide sufficient documentation of their use. Therefore, the choice was made to include the widest number of possible famine foods in Table 1.

For sake of discussion, I divide Desert Borderlands starvation foods into seven categories, inner bark, cacti, agave and agave-like plants, other perennials, underground structures, annuals, and other. These categories mirror no indigenous folk classification, but plants within each category share some similarities. Resources availability in the first five groups should be quite stable; their availability is least affected by common environmental fluctuations in the Desert Borderlands. Abundance of food stuffs derived from plants in the sixth category, annuals, in contrast, may well be less stable, and they are, therefore, especially interesting.

TABLE 1. Famine foods of the desert borderlands.

Plant (common name)	Part Consumed	Group— Comments	Reference
Inner Bark			
Juniperus monosperma (Engelm.) Sarg. (one-seeded juniper)	inner bark	Navajo & others Navajo	Castetter 1935 Elmore 1944
Pinus edulis Engelm. (pinyon)	inner bark	Ramah Navajo	Vestal 1952
Pinus ponderosa Laws. var. *scopulorum* Engelm. (*Pinus scopulorum*) (western yellow pine)	inner bark	Zuni Pueblo & others	Castetter 1935
Populus tremuloides Michx. (aspen)	inner bark	Ramah Navajo	Vestal 1952

TABLE 1. Famine foods of the desert borderlands. (continued)

Plant (common name)	Part Consumed	Group—Comments	Reference
Cacti			
Carnegiea gigantea (Engelm.) Britt. & Rose (saguaro)	fruit	Papago	Castetter & Bell 1942
		Seri—possible famine food	Felger & Moser 1974, 1985
Ferocactus wislizensi (Engelm.) Britt. & Rose (barrel cactus)	stem pulp	Seri	Felger & Moser 1976, 1985
Opuntia sp.	stem	Hopi Pueblos	Hough 1897
Opuntia clavata Engelm. (cholla)	stem (?)	Laguna & Acoma Pueblos	Swank 1932
Opuntia imbricata Haw. *O. arborescence*) (cane cactus)	stem	Laguna & Acoma Pueblos	Swank 1932
Opuntia polyacantha Haw. (prickly pear)	stem	Hopi Pueblos	Whiting 1939
Opuntia whipplei Engelm. & Bigel. (whipple cholla)	fruit	Hopi Pueblos	Whiting 1939
Pachycereus pringlei (S. Wats. Britt. & Horak (*cardón*)	fruit	Seri—possible famine food	Felger & Moser 1974, 1985
Stenocereus alomoensis (Coult.) Gibs. & Horak (*pitaya agria*)	fruit	Seri—possible famine food	Felger & Moser 1974, 1985
Stenocereus thurberi (Engelm.) Buxb. (organ pipe cactus, *pitaya dulce*)	fruit	Seri—possible famine food	Felger & Moser 1974, 1985
Century Plant and Related Plants			
Agave sp. (century plants)	heart of plant (?)	Mohave & Yuma	Castetter et al. 1938
Agave cerulata spp. *dentiens* (Terl.) Gentry (century plant)	liquid from charred leaves	Seri	Felger & Moser 1970, 1985
Agave parryi Engelm. (century plant)	heart of plant	Pima	Castetter 1935
Dasylirion wheeleri Wats. (sotol)	heart of plant	—	Castetter 1935
Yucca spp.	heart of plant	"Pueblo Indians of New Mexico"	Castetter 1935
Yucca glauca Nutt. (yucca)	heart of plant	Laguan & Acoma Pueblos	Swank 1932

TABLE 1. Famine foods of the desert borderlands. (continued)

Plant (common name)	Part Consumed	Group—Comments	Reference
Other Perennials			
Acacia pennatula (*palo garabo*)	fruit and seeds	"Mexico"	Altschul 1973
Amaranthus sp. (pigweed)	—	Ramah Navajo—used ceremonially and during food shortages	Vestal 1952
Apondanthera undulata Gray	fruit	Pima Bajo	Pennington 1980
Atriplex lentiformis (Torr.) Wats. (quail bush)	seeds	Pima	Curtin 1949
Atriplex polycarpa (Torr.) Wats. (all scale)	seed	Pima	Curtin 1949
Baccharis salicifolia (R&P) Pers. (*Baccharis glutinosa* Pers.) (seepwillow)	greens	Mohave & Yumans	Castetter & Bell 1951
Juniperus monosperma (Englem.) Sarg. (one-seeded juniper)	fruit	Hopi Pueblos Laguna & Acoma Pueblo	Whiting 1939 Swank 1982
Lycium pallidum Miers. (wolfberry	fruit	Hopi Pueblos	Whiting 1939
Oryzopsis hymenoides (R&S) Ricker (*Eriocoma cuspidata*) (Indian ricegrass)	grains	Hopi Pueblos	Castetter 1935
Phoradendron juniperinum Engelm. (mistletoe)	fruit	Laguna & Acoma Pueblos	Swank 1932
Prosopis glandulosa Torr. (mesquite)	fruit and seed	Pima Hopi Pueblos (?) Yuma	Bell & Castetter 1937 Bell & Castetter 1937 Bell & Castetter 1937
Prosopis glandulosa Torr. var. *torreyana* (L. Bens.) M.C. Johnst. (western honey mesquite)	fruit	Seri—possible famine food	Felger & Moser 1971, 1985
Prosopis pubescens Benth. (screwbean)	fruit	Pima & Papago (?) Yuma Seri	Bell & Castetter 1937 Bell & Castetter 1937 Felger & Moser 1971, 1985
Quercus grisea Liebm. (gray oak)	fruit	Ramah Navajo—"not good food"	Vestal 1952
Quercus undulata Torr. (wavyleaf oak)	fruit	Ramah Navajo—"not good food"	Vestal 1952
Rhizophora mangle L. (mangrove)	fruit	Seri	Felger & Moser 1976, 1985
Ribes inebrians Lindl. (squaw currant)	fruit	Hopi Pueblos	Whiting 1939

TABLE 1. Famine foods of the desert borderlands. (continued)

Plant (common name)	Part Consumed	Group—Comments	Reference
Rosa arizonica Rydb. (rose)	fruit	Hopi Pueblos	Whiting 1939
Simmondsia chinensis (Link) Schneid. (jojoba)	nut	Seri	Felger & Moser 1976, 1985
Underground Structures			
Dichelostemma pulchellum (Salisb.) Heller var. *pauci-florum* (Torr.) Hoover (*Brodiaea capitata* var. *pauciflora*) (bluedick, incorrectly cited as "Papago blue bells")	tuber	Papago	Castetter & Bell 1942 Castetter & Underhill 1935
Habenaria sparsiflora Wats. (bog orchid)	bulb	San Felipe Pueblo	Castetter 1935
Solanum fendleri Cav. (nightshade)	tuber	Keresan Pueblos—raw/boiled with clay	White 1944
Solanum jamesii Torr. (wild potato)	tuber	Keresan pueblos—same as for *S. fendleri*	White 1944
Sphaeralcea coccinea Pursh. (globemallow)	root	Navajo	Elmore 1944
Annuals			
Acanthochiton wrightii Torr.	greens	Hopi Pueblos	Hough 1897; Castetter 1935; Whiting 1939
Aster spinosus Benth. (spiny aster)	greens	Mohave & Yumans	Castetter & Bell 1951
Chamaesaracha coronopus (Dunal) Gray (small groundcherry)	fruit	Hopi Pueblos	Whiting 1939
Chenopodium sp. (goosefoot)	seed	Ramah Navajo—used ceremonially and during food shortages	Vestal 1952
Cleome serrulata Pursh. (Rocky Mountain beeweed)	greens	Ramah Navajo—used ceremonially and during food shortages	Vestal 1952
	greens seeds	Picuris Pueblo (?) New Mexican Hispanics	Krenetsky 1964 Curtin 1965
Dicoria brandegei Gray	flower/fruit	Hopi Pueblos	Whiting 1939
Mentzelia pumila (Nutt.) T&G (blazing star)	seed	Hopi Pueblos	Whiting 1939
Mentzelia multiflora (Nutt.) Gray (blazing star)	seed	Hopi Pueblos	Whiting 1939

TABLE 1. Famine foods of the desert borderlands. (continued)

Plant (common name)	Part Consumed	Group— Comments	Reference
Physalis hederaeofolia (Gray) var. *cordifolia* (Gray) (*Physalis fendleri* Gray) (groundcherry)	fruit	Hopi Pueblos	Whiting 1939
Solanum triflorum Nutt. (nightshade)	fruit	Acoma & Laguna Pueblos	Castetter 1935
Sonchus asper L. (spiny sow thistle)	greens	Mohave & Yumans	Castetter & Bell 1951
Sysymbrium irio L. (London rocket)	greens	Mohave & Yumans	Castetter & Bell 1951
Thelypodium integrifolium (Nutt.) Endl. (*Thelypodium liliacinum* Green)	greens	Mohave & Yumans	Castetter & Bell 1951
Other			
Washingtonia filifera Wendl. (desert palm)	stem pith	—	Cornett 1987
Zostera marina L. (eelgrass)	seed	Seri	Felger & Moser 1973, 1976, 1985
"grasses/pigweed/goose-foot" (see *Amaranthus* & *Chenopodium*)	seed	Ramah Navajo—used ceremonially and during food shortages	Vestal 1952
cactus/wild potato/grass	?	Hopi Pueblos	Beaglehole 1937

Nomenclature follows Benson 1969; Felger and Moser 1985; Gentry 1982; Lehr 1978; Martin and Hutchins 1980. Non-technical terms are used to describe for plant anatomy (for example, an achene is termed a "seed"). Scientific names in parenthesis are those used in the original citation. Plants listed here include food used only during food shortages, foods used during seasonal shortages, as well as those normally consumed and whose use is simply intensified with low food availability. In the absence of detailed descriptions of the use of possible Desert Borderland famine foods, I decided to include the widest possible range of these resources.

Inner bark.—A widely recorded category of starvation food in the Desert Borderlands is the inner bark (cambium and associated tissue) of various trees; inner bark is not recorded as a "normal" ration (e.g., Swetnam 1984). There is ethnographic documentation of inner bark use of the pinyon pine *(Pinus edulis)*, one-seeded juniper *(Juniperus monosperma)*, western yellow pine *(Pinus ponderosa* var. *scopulorum)*, and aspen *(Populus tremuloides)*. This mucilaginous food is widely available and is abundant throughout the forests of the Desert Borderlands. More importantly, it is a very stable resource. Environmental variation which reduces the availability of edible flowers, fruits, and seeds would be less likely to affect adversely the abundance of viable inner bark. Perhaps the factor limiting normal use of this resource is its probable low nutritional value and the considerable effort required to harvest sufficient quantities. Furthermore, sustained harvest of inner bark might seriously reduce tree populations.

Why is the inner bark of only certain plants utilized as famine food? Hundreds of different woody plants are present in the Desert Borderlands, yet the ethnobotanical record lists very few plants with edible inner bark. Many of the plants recorded to have edible inner bark are conifers which have easily removable bark. This alone cannot explain the pattern of use, however, because there are numerous conifers not cited as yielding edible inner bark.

Cacti.—Native peoples throughout the Desert Borderlands have long used cactus fruits as food. Saguaro fruits *(Carnegiea gigantea)* have been a major food for groups living within its range. The Seri use the fruits of several columnar cacti. The stems, joints, and pads of cacti, such as *Opuntia* (prickly pears and cholla), have been widely used by some groups throughout the Desert Borderlands.

The use of cacti as a famine food is well documented for indigenous peoples in the Desert Borderlands. By their nature, cacti are well adapted for survival and reproduction during periods of severe drought, a primary cause of crop failure. According to Felger and Moser (1974, 1985), the exploitation of various cacti, such as saguaro, *cardón (Pachycereus pringlei), pitaya agria (Stenocereus alomoensis),* and *pitaya dulce* or organ pipe cactus *(Stenocereus thurberi),* is increased during droughts, and the Seri also use the pulpy "stem" of the barrel cactus *(Ferocactus wislizeni)* as a famine food. Other cacti are also recorded as famine foods. The Pueblo Indians of Acoma, Laguna, and Hopi use various species of *Opuntia,* both cholla and prickly pear, during food shortages.

Century plant and related plants.—The century plant *(Agave)* and agave-like plants *(Yucca, Nolina,* and *Dasylirion)* are important foods for many groups in the Desert Borderlands and seem to have been prominent famine foods. These plants are perennial, can store enormous amounts of tissue, and can survive severe droughts. As cited earlier, at least one group of Seri rely on *Agave cerulata* when other foods are unavailable. The Pima, Mohave, and Yuma are recorded to have used the century plant (including *A. parryi*) as a starvation food. The stem of *Yucca glauca* is reported as a famine food at Acoma and Laguna. Sotol *(Dasylirion wheeleri)* is a famine food, although the group using sotol in this manner is not specified.

Other perennials.—We would expect many famine foods would be the reproductive structures of perennials, because some of them would be especially resistant to the effects of low moisture periods. The fruits of the one-seeded juniper *(Juniperus monosperma)* are a famine food for the Hopi, Laguna, and Acoma Indians. The bitter fruit of coyote melon *(Apodanthera undulata)* is a famine food among the Pima Bajo of central Sonora. The fleshy berries of the wolfberry *(Lycium pallidum),* squaw currant *(Ribes inebrians),* and the dry fruits of a native rose *(Rosa arizonica)* are Hopi famine foods. Fruits of a mistletoe *(Phoradendron juniperum),* a parasite on conifers, are a famine food for the Puebloans of Acoma and Laguna. Mesquite *(Prosopis glandulosa)* and screwbean *(Prosopis pubescens)* are recorded as a possible famine food for the Pima, Papago, Yuma, Seri, and Hopi. Mesquite and screwbean seeds are often used as famine foods, whereas the mesocarp of the pods is the preferred food. Acorns *(Quercus grisea, Q. undulata)* may have been famine foods for the Ramah Navajo, a group living east of Zuni Pueblo. A note on a herbarium specimen from Mexico collected by H.S. Gentry noted that the fruits (with enclosed seeds) of *Acacia pennatula* were used as a famine food in Mexico. Mangrove *(Rhizophora mangle)* and jojoba *(Simmondsia chinensis)* fruits are consumed by the Seri when more preferred foods are unavailable. The seeds of several saltbushes *(Atriplex lentiformis* and *A. polycarpa)* are recorded as famine foods among the Pima.

Many grasses are present in the Desert Borderlands, and they are important foods. Yet there are only a few references to unspecified grasses as famine foods, and only one specific grass, Indian ricegrass *(Oryzopsis hymenoides),* is listed as a famine food. This perennial has several characteristics that make it a particularly valuable food for humans. It was once present in dense stands, it matures early, has a relatively high protein content, and the seeds tend to remain on the plant longer than in many grasses. Its use as a famine food is enhanced by notable drought tolerance (Hanson 1972; Quinones 1981).

"Greens" (probably leaves or young stems) of only one perennial tree or shrub, seepwillow *(Baccharis salicifolia),* is recorded as a famine food for the Desert Borderlands. This is of interest in light of the numerous foodstuffs in other areas of the world which are derived from tree or shrub leaves. As a comparison, over half of the foods listed in the *Chiu Huang Pen-ts'ao* are leaves, and many are from woody plants (Read 1946).

Underground structures.—Another category of unusually stable resources used as famine foods is "tubers" and roots. The availability of these resources should be quite stable. Wild potato *(Solanum jamesii, S. fedleri)* tubers are famine foods for Puebloan groups of New Mexico. To counteract their naturally bitter taste, salty clay is added to the mashed tubers. People of San Felipe Pueblo are documented to have used the "bulb" of *Habenaria sparsiflora* as a famine food. Globemallow *(Sphaeralcea coccinea)* roots are a Navajo famine food. Bluedick bulbs *(Dichelostemma pulchellum* var. *pauciflorum),* incorrectly identified by Castetter and Bell (1942) as Papago blue bells, are a famine food for the Papago.

Annuals.—The sixth group of famine foods, annuals, is especially interesting because foodstuffs derived from these plants should be more susceptible to drought conditions, a primary cause of food shortages in the region. Many annuals simply fail to germinate during low moisture conditions. Consequently, we could expect them to be relatively unimportant famine foods. However, numerous annuals are listed as famine foods. The Hopi are reported to use immature *Acanthochiton wrightii* as greens, and Rocky Mountain beeweed *(Cleome serrulata)* is consumed in a similar manner by the Ramah Navajo. Greens of other plants *(Aster spinosus, Sonchus asper, Sysymbrium irio,* and *Thelypodium integrifolium)* are famine foods among the Mohave and Yuman groups, although the middle two are Euro-Asian weeds introduced in the region since European contact. Hispanics of northern New Mexico use Rocky Mountain beeweed seeds as a famine food. Hopi famine foods also include the fruits of the groundcherry *(Physalis hederaeofolia* var. *cordifolia)* and small groundcherry *(Chamaesartha coronopus).* The fruits of a nightshade *(Solanum trifolium)* are a famine food at Acoma and Laguna. The small dry "seeds" of pigweed *(Amaranthus),* goosefoot *(Chenopodium),* and blazing star *(Mentzelia pumila, M. multiflora)* are eaten by the Hopi when other foods are unavailable. The seeds and flowers of another annual, *Dicoria brandegei,* are famine foods for the Hopi.

As will be discussed later in more detail, the greater than expected number of annuals listed as famine foods might be due to a historical change in famine food classification, where plants once used as hunger season foods became today's famine foods.

Others.—Two plants recorded as famine foods do not neatly fit into the above categories. Eelgrass *(Zostera marina),* a marine plant, is extensively used by the Seri and may have been a famine food. Needless to say, this aquatic plant is not as affected by low precipitation as are terrestrial plants. The pith of the desert fan palm *(Washingtonia filifera)* is used as a famine food. In many ways, this resource is analogous to the hearts of the century plant, although its nutritional composition may be quite different.

DISCUSSION

The use of famine foods is a complex phenomenon involving a multitude of both biological and cultural factors. Simple enumeration of available famine foods, a worthy goal itself, does not, however, allow us to appreciate the dynamic nature of their use. Here I will discuss various aspects critical for an understanding of famine food use. First discussed is the historical change in famine food use, and I will argue that food preference patterns may actually encapsulate the history of changing diet. Therefore, patterns of famine food usage makes little sense without a historical perspective. Second is a consideration of how human populations transmit knowledge of famine foods to a new generation. How is knowledge of infrequently used resources maintained in a community, especially if use of famine foods occurs less than once per generation? I suggest that ritual and myth are unusually important in maintaining knowledge famine foods within a community. Thirdly, it is suggested that use of famine foods may be an indicator of the severity of food shortages. Finally, the value of a cross-cultural and comparative perspective on famine foods is briefly considered.

Historic change in famine food use.—In light of the hundreds of useful plants recorded in the ethnobotanical literature of the Desert Borderlands, relatively few famine foods are discussed. Undoubtedly, there are many unreported resources which have been used as famine foods by the indigenous populations in the region, and it is quite likely that much of the inventory of traditional famine foods has been lost since European contact and before intensive ethnographic documentation began around 100 years ago.

I suspect an additional dimension is also an important reason for the few famine foods recorded. By the time ethnographers recorded the ethnobotany of most native peoples in the area, many of these peoples had dramatically altered their subsistence base. Such changes included the introduction of new crops, new agricultural technology, animal husbandry, increased sedentism, and substantial involvement in market economies. I argue that traditionally important foods had been relegated to less frequent use. Some of these plants then became potential famine foods. In short, the introduction of a new set of resources caused a resorting of general food preference patterns with some newly acquired plants replacing some former foods and these in turn becoming less commonly used. Previous famine foods were then replaced by what were once more common foods. And the knowledge of the "original" famine foods may have been completely lost. Specifically, many of the famine foods recorded for modern groups in the Desert Borderlands may well have been seasonal hunger foods.

If this scenario is correct, then it provides an explanation for the unexpectedly large number of annuals now considered famine foods. If periods of low precipitation were the major cause of food shortages, as I believe, then one needs to understand why so many annuals are now viewed as famine foods. After all, annuals presumably would be one of the first groups of plants adversely affected by insufficient moisture. Drought resistance, however, would not necessarily be a characteristic important for hunger season plants. A shift of hunger season plants to famine foods could account for a large number of annuals being considered famine foods.

Prehistoric diet provides a needed comparative baseline to document change in famine food use through time, because it can be difficult to estimate how frequently these current famine foods were used by the prehistoric peoples of the Desert Borderlands. Many of the plants listed ethnographically as famine food seem to have been more common food plants before European contact. Grass (e.g., *Oryzopsis hymenoides*), pigweed (*Amaranthus* spp.), and goosefoot (*Chenopodium* spp.) seeds, for example, are now considered famine foods and are common prehistoric food remains found in archaeological sites in the Desert Border lands (e.g., Adams 1980; Minnis 1985; Wetterstrom 1986).

Perhaps the best paleodietary data to evaluate a model of changing food preference come from prehistoric feces, because these data are the direct remains of consumed food. The most extensive coprolite data come from cliff dwellings in a northern portion of the region, the Four Corners area of the United States. These dessicated fecal remains are from the prehistoric Anasazi tradition, one of many prehistoric populations ancestral to modern Puebloan groups. The fecal content information can be used as a controlled comparison between ethnographically documented famine food use by the Hopi, a modern Pueblo group in the Four Corners area, and an ancestral prehistoric Puebloan diet in the same region.

A recent summary of paleofeces shows that many plants now recorded as famine foods are some of the most frequent native plants found in these coprolites (Minnis 1989). Of particular interest for the purposes of this study are 139 paleofeces from the latest prehistoric time period, Pueblo III, A.D. 1100–1300, the time just before European contact and with the best paleodietary data. Coprolites considered here were recovered from three sites in or near Mesa Verde, southwestern Colorado, (Step House, n = 17; Lion House, n = 4; Hoy Elouse, n = 56), Glen Canyon, southeastern Utah, (n = 24), and two sites in northeastern Arizona (Inscription House, n = 16; Antelope House, n = 22). Macroscopic plant remains, mostly seeds and fruit fragments but also some tissue, were identified in the feces. Most of the analyses summarized in the study simply noted presence/absence of a taxon in each specimen and did not attempt to quantify the amount of each resource in each coprolite.

Cultivated plants, especially maize and squash, were the most commonly consumed foodstuffs, being found in the vast majority of the coprolites studied (Table 2). Of the natural flora, the most common remains from these feces are, in descending frequency: prickly pear, goosefoot, groundcherry, purslane (*Portulaca* sp.), pigweed, ricegrass, grass seeds, cactus, peppergrass (*Lepidium* sp.), pinyon, and Rocky Mountain beeweed. Other plants were identified as very infrequent constituents in these feces, often being found in only a single coprolite.

There is a surprisingly close correspondence between important native foods consumed by the prehistoric peoples of the northern part of the Desert Borderlands and foods ethnographically classified as famine foods within the past century, especially among the Hopi. Whiting (1939: 20–22) lists Hopi famine foods: wolfberry *(Lycium pallidum)*, cholla *(Opuntia whipplei)*, prickly pear *(O. polyacantha)*, squaw current *(Ribes inebrians)*, wild rose *(Rosa arizonica)*, groundcherry *(Physalis fendleri)*, Indian ricegrass *(Oryzopsis hymenoides)*, and blazing star *(Mentzelia pumila, M. multiflora)*. Prickly pear, goosefoot, groundcherry, pigweed, ricegrass, grass seeds, and the general category "cactus" are all documented in Table 1 as famine foods and are common prehistoric dietary items (Table 2).

The fact that many of the most frequently consumed prehistoric foods are now classified as famine foods can be explained in one of two ways. First, it can be argued that remains in these coprolites reflect the use of prehistoric famine foods. That is, the paleofeces document serious food provisioning problems. There are two reasons why I believe that this explanation is faulty. First and most importantly, maize is by far the most abundant foodstuff in these coprolites. Maize was found in nearly 90% of the coprolites, and where data are available it often comprises the bulk of feces (Minnis 1989). In contrast, the most common native plant (prickly pear) was noted in approximately 30% of the paleofeces. Maize cultivation, and ultimately yield, are more sensitive to drought than many native foods. Consequently, we would expect some reduction in maize consumption under drought conditions. It is unlikely that maize would be as common as it is in the feces if they are a record of famine food use. Second, the coprolite assemblages represent a time of expanding prehistoric populations and substantial construction of villages in the Four Corners area. If food shortages were so frequent, then it would be unlikely that the prehistoric cultures would have been as expansive.

The second possible explanation is, to my mind, more likely. Many of these resources, which are now famine foods, were basic constituents of the prehistoric diet in the area. Viewed in this light, there seems to have been a shift of resource use along a scale of preference. Robbins et al. (1916: 76), for example, obliquely narrate this shift for the Tewa of San Juan Pueblo:

TABLE 2. Plants from prehistoric Four Corners coprolites[1]

Plant[2]	Rank	Percentage of Coprolites containing Plant
Zea mays	1	87.8
Opuntia (prickly pear)	2	28.1
Cucurbita	3	25.9
Chenopodium	4	19.5
Gossypium hirsutum	5.5	16.6
Physalis	5.5	16.6
Portulaca	7	14.4
Phaseolus	8	13.7
Amaranthus	9	12.3
Oryzopsis hymenoides	10	11.5
Gramineae	11	10.8
Cactaceae	12.5	10.1
Lepidium	12.5	10.0
Pinus edulis	14	9.9
Cleome serrulata	15	7.9

[1] The data base is 139 paleofeces from six sites dating to the Pueblo III period, A.D. 1100–1300. For an in-depth discussion of this study, consult Minnis (1989).

[2] These are the most frequently encountered plant taxa. Less commonly recovered types are: buffaloberry *(Shepardia argentea)*, bugseed *(Corispermum)*, bulrush *(Scirpus)*, chokecherry *(Prunus virginiana)*, sunflower family (Compositae), dropseed *(Sporobolus)*, *Cryptantha* sp., hackberry *(Celtis occidentalis)*, horsetail *(Equisetum)*, juniper *(Juniperis osteosperma)*, knotweed *(Polygonum)*, bean family (Leguminosae), Mormon tea *(Ephedra)*, panicgrass *(Panicum)*, sagebrush *(Artemesia tridentata)*, saltbrush *(Atriplex canescens)*, skunkbush *(Rhus trilobata)*, sunflower *(Helianthus)*, and wild buckwheat *(Erigonum)*.

But nowadays, although wild berries and nuts are still gathered in autumn and green weeds are eagerly sought and eaten in the spring, there is a very general and increasing neglect of all but *the most common and best-liked.* Formerly it was a matter of necessity that the housewife should know them and store them; for although in normal years they were merely a pleasant addition to the diet, yet in drought, flood, fire, or a hostile raid might destroy the crops at any time, thus making the wild products an indispensable resource (emphasis added).

It is quite possible that the knowledge of foods traditionally used only during severe famines has been lost and that foods now recorded as famine foods are those that were consumed during periods of seasonal hunger, usually the late winter and early spring when stores are depleted early in the new growing season (Richard I. Ford, personal communication, 1988). Since hunger seasons are quite common, use of these less preferred foods should be known by many individuals. Therefore, knowledge of these foods would have been less likely to have been lost than knowledge of foods used during infrequent severe shortages.

If plants that were frequently consumed become famine foods and knowledge of previous famine foods is lost, then the stability of starvation foods may also have changed. There is no reason to assume a priori that a new set of famine foods will be as resistant to the factors which reduce food availability as the previous famine foods. Thus, stability of the food supply in the face of environmental perturbations may have been reduced. I doubt that is a problem for the perennials such as inner bark, cholla, prickly pear, mesquite, and century plant. This cannot be said for the many annuals listed in Table 1, including plants such as pigweed, goosefoot, groundcherry, blazing star, and various grasses. It may well be that the presumed change in famine foods of the Desert Borderlands has resulted in a less secure strategy should the circumstances necessitate the use of least preferred foods.

Native populations in the United States and Mexico are now relatively well buffered against famine by their participation in national economies with various economic security programs. Populations in other areas may have lost the knowledge of traditional famine foods during colonial disruption of their lifestyles. In other areas of the world which have experienced substantial changes in their native subsistence practices and with less well-developed economic security programs, groups could face specially severe problems with modern food shortages after losing the knowledge of traditional famine foods.

Unfortunately, we do not have as excellent a data base as the Anasazi paleofecal inventory to assess the extent of change in famine foods for other areas of the Desert Borderlands. While it has been cogently argued that maize was the focal foodstuff for many prehistoric groups in other areas of the Desert Borderlands, the biotic communities are much different from the Four Corners. To the south, there was a great diversity and abundance of high quality foods, including various leguminous trees (e.g., mesquite, ironwood, and palo verdes), many cacti, and a wide range of agavaceous and agave-like resources (e.g., century plant, sotol, yucca, and beargrass) (Gasser 1981). In addition, recent research has identified a suite of crops present in the low deserts not documented or uncommon in the northern portions of the Desert Borderlands. Minimally, these include a barley, *Hordeum pusillum* Nutt. (Adams 1986); century plant, *Agave murpheyi* F. Gibson or *A. parryi* Engelm. (Fish et al. 1985); tepary bean, *Phaseolus acutifolius* Gray var. *latifolius* Freem. (Nabhan and Felger 1984); scarlet runner bean, *Phaseolus coccineus* L. (Ford 1981; Huckell 1986); panic grass, *Panicum sonorum* Beal. (Nabhan and de Wet 1984); and devil's claw, *Proboscidea parviflora* (Woot.) Woot. & Standl. spp. *parviflora* var. *hohokamiana* Bretting (Nabhan et al. 1981; Bretting 1982). Therefore, the example of changes in diet as discussed for the Four Corners cannot be directly extrapolated to other regions. While the individual resources may be different, the process of change, that of the replacement of an assemblage of famine food by once more common resources, may well have occurred.

Learning famine food use.—The transmittal of famine food use between generations may provide a further understanding of how this shift occurred. Not only does this topic address ethnobotanical information transfer, but it may help explain how this information is lost. Desert Borderlands data are largely silent on this issue, but research from other areas provides some illumination. Presumably, children learn food availability, distribution, collection, and processing by watching and participating in normal adult activities. Beaglehole (1937) describes one informant's recollection of the actions taken by the Hopi in response to a famine which occurred during his childhood. The simple observation of behavior is effective for learning about common foods, including foods used during yearly hunger seasons, but could well be ineffective for the use of infrequently used foods, if these severe shortages are less frequent than once per generation. If so, then other mechanisms of learning may be particularly important for famine food use.

As many have pointed out, myths, legend, rituals, and stories about previous food shortages are critical for transmitting knowledge of famine food use (e.g., Roys 1967; Reining 1970; Cove 1978; Galt and Galt 1978; Colson 1980; Marcus 1982). Thus oral tradition may be especially important in perpetuating knowledge of famine food use. Special attention should focus on women's knowledge, because they seem to have the greatest familiarity with famine foods (Ali 1984). Yet, the role of male secular and ritual knowledge of plant foods cannot be ignored as will be seen in the forthcoming Zuni example.

Several Desert Borderland examples do illustrate the perpetuation of native plant food use through ritual. Vestal (1952) mentions that several Ramah Navajo famine foods are also used ritually, although he does not provide specific information. Two examples from Zuni, however, do mention famine foods in myths or in a ritual context. Bunzel (1932: 714) provides a translation of "Sayataca's night chant." In this prayer, a range of edible plants is enumerated after mention of cultigens:

> . . . and then the seeds of the pinon tree, the seeds of the juniper tree, the seeds of the oak tree, the seeds of the peach tree, the seeds of the black wood shrub, the seeds of the first flowering shrub, the seeds of the *kapuli* shrub, the seeds of the large yucca, the seeds of the branched yucca, the seeds of the brown cactus, the seeds of the small cactus, and then also the seeds of the wild grasses—the evil smelling weeds, the little grass, *tecukta, kucutsi, o'co, apitalu, sutoka, mololoka, piculiya,* small *piculiya, hamato, mitaliko,* and then also the seeds of those that stand in their doorways, namely the cat-tail, the tall flags, the water weeds, the water cress, the round-leafed weed . . .

Richard Ford (personal communication, 1988), who conducts ethnobotanical research with the Zuni, points out that seeds of these native edible plants are a part of some Zuni ritual paraphernalia. Thus these plants must be collected each year, and this maintains the knowledge of the use of native plants and collection location of various foodstuffs which might otherwise be ignored. Cushing (1920: 76) provides another example, the narration of a Zuni tale which mentions a time of famine and the collection of famine foods:

> At last despair filled the hearts of the people of Ha'-wi-k'uh. They went forth on the mesas to gather cactus fruit but even this was scarce. When winter came the

cloud swallower had gone. The god of the ice caves breathed over the whole country, and even in the Valley of the Hot Water great banks of snow fell, such as the oldest men had never seen. At last the corn was all gone. The people were pitiably poor. They were so weak that they could not hunt through the snow, therefore a great famine spread through the village. At last the people were compelled to gather old bones and grind them for meal, and for meat they toasted the rawhide soles of their moccasins.

Once a group's oral traditions are disrupted, it is very unlikely that future generations will retain knowledge of low preference foods. This problem is especially acute if famine food use is so infrequent that normal participant observation in food use is ineffective in passing this information on to future generations. If so, then plants used during hunger seasons might indeed become the only category of famine food knowledge passed on to future generations as alternative foods. An understanding of the dynamic nature of uses of plants mentioned in oral tradition is especially critical.

Famine food use as a monitor of shortage severity.—Use of famine foods may be a sensitive measure of the severity of food shortages. There are many actions people take when faced with food shortages. Such coping strategies include selling valuables, migration, stealing, change in agricultural strategies, cannibalism, raiding, and reduced or expanded cooperation within and between groups. Elsewhere I have argued that people faced with food provisioning problems choose strategies in a predictable sequence (Minnis 1985). Specifically, the least costly coping strategies tend to be used first (defining cost in cultural and social as well as economic terms). With increasing severity, more costly options will then be used. In other words, there is a "calculus" of human social and economic responses to food shortages. If so, the use of famine foods, as one such strategy, could be used to determine the severity of the shortage. Others have also suggested that the use of alternative foods, such as famine foods, may be a marker that a population is experiencing problems in food acquisition, even though signs of starvation and malnutrition may yet be lacking (e.g., Rahamani 1981; Curry 1984).

Cross-cultural study of famine foods.—The cross-cultural study of famine foods also provides a more subtle understanding of the intricate relationships between people and plants, interconnections which are not necessarily obvious from the ethnobotanical study of only one region or one population. The comparative study of famine foods has a simpler purpose and one with much practical value. Plants can be identified that are not recognized as edible within a single region, which, therefore, expands an area's practical ethnobotany.

A southwestern example includes two particularly loathsome plants. Goat's head or puncturevine (*Tribulus terrestris* L.) and burgrass (*Cenchrus* spp.) are thoroughly obnoxious weeds distributed throughout the Desert Borderlands and whose mature fruits have sharp spines which cause much discomfort to humans and other animals; "home owners and their dogs probably dislike puncturevine more than any other

weed" (Parker 1972: 198). Few native or non-native inhabitants of the Desert
Borderlands would recognize any value for these two taxa. Yet, these plants are
described as important famine food worldwide. According to Bhandari (1974: 75–77),
both are important famine foods in the Rajasthan desert of India; goat's head is the
"chief food of the people during the Madras Famine," and burgrass is "regarded as
the most nutritious of famine foods." The Yoruba of West Africa also use goat's head
as a famine food (Irvin 1952), and this plant, *chi li tzu,* is listed as a Chinese starvation food (Read 1946).

CONCLUSION

Famine foods have received little attention from ethnobotanists, relief workers,
and others despite their importance throughout human history and the potential they
may have for the future. Most records of their use are anecdotal and lack the detail
necessary to understand their use. For example, describing the methods for the
removal of toxic compounds from some famine foods is particularly important if these
plants are to be used more widely, either as famine foods or in agriculture.

There are many types of famine foods, including agricultural byproducts not
normally consumed, seed stock, and resources used only when more preferred foods
are unavailable, either as seasonal hunger plants or used only during famines. The status
of a resource as a famine food is not based solely on its biology and biochemical profile
but rather also involves a range of social, cultural, political, and economic factors.

Documentation of Desert Borderlands famine foods is not as extensive as one
could hope for. Yet several major categories do exist. The inner bark of some trees,
such as pinyon pine, ponderosa pine, aspen, and one-seed juniper, is a major famine
food, as are cacti, such as prickly pear and cholla. In addition, a number of other plants
are recorded to have been used as starvation foods. These include pigweed, goosefoot, grass seeds, wild potato, globemallow, century plant, yucca, saltbushes, seepwillow, groundcherry, Rocky Mountain beeweed, bluedick, blazing star, Indian
ricegrass, mistletoe, mesquite, screwbean, mangrove, rose, oak, jojoba, squaw currant,
juniper, London rocket, eelgrass, nightshade, sow thistle, and others.

Many of the famine foods recorded for the Desert Borderlands are resources that
we would expect to be used during food shortages. That is, most are very stable; they
are perennials with an unusually effective ability to tolerate periods of low moisture,
they have underground storage tissue, or they inhabit environments which are not
affected by the common factors reducing resource abundance. The unexpectedly large
number of annuals may reflect the historic change of hunger season plants becoming
considered famine foods as a result of cultural transformations since European contact.

The brief consideration of famine foods from the Desert Borderlands of North
America shows that patterns of the use of these foodstuffs changed through time and
can be an indicator of the history of changing diet. Specifically, once common aboriginal foods have become less preferred foods after domination by outside groups and
with the subsequent introduction of Euro-Asian crops, new technologies, markets, and
constraints on traditional catchments. It seems that these once common foods now

have become famine foods for the ethnographically documented native populations of the Desert Borderlands.

Knowledge of traditional famine foods seems to be one of the first categories of native ethnobotanical information lost. Not only is this information easily lost, but it seems to be particularly difficult data to secure in the first place, perhaps partly due to the low status afforded those who must rely on such plants. Yet these plants have been critical to human survival and constitute an additional set of edible resources not normally recorded. And some of these plants may, in fact, have an as yet unrecognized economic potential. Therefore, loss of this particularly vulnerable information should concern us. The efforts to save traditional crop genotypes, knowledge of agricultural strategies and technology, and ethnobotanical information on common plant uses should also include the study of the least esteemed foods, those which have saved countless individuals and populations from starvation throughout human history.

ACKNOWLEDGMENTS

Special thanks are extended to Barbara King and Leslie Raymer for their diligent work as Research Assistants as the University of Oklahoma. Karen R. Adams, Henry Dobyns, Richard I. Ford, Patricia A. Gilman, Scott M. Kwiatkowski, Joseph E. Laferrière, Gary P. Nabhan, and Deborah M. Pearsall provided valuable comments. Support for this research was provided by the National Science Foundation (BNS–80–08665) and the School of American Research.

LITERATURE CITED

Adams, Karen R. 1980. Pollen, parched seeds, and prehistory: A pilot study of prehistoric plant remains from Salmon Ruin, a Chacoan pueblo in northwestern New Mexico. Eastern New Mexico University, Contributions in Anthropology No. 9.

———. 1986. A model to assess New World *Hordeum pusillum* (barley) characteristics in natural and human habitats. Paper presented at the Ninth Annual Ethnobiological Conference, Albuquerque, N. Mex.

Alamgir, Mohiuddin. 1980. Famine in South Asia: Political Economy of Mass Starvation. Oelgeschlager, Gunn, and Hann, Cambridge, Mass.

Ali, Mehtabunsia. 1984. Women in famine: The paradox of status in India. Pp. 113–133 *in* Famine as a Geographic Phenomenon. Edited by B. Curry and G. Hugo. D. Reidel, Dordrecht, Germany.

Altschul, Siri Von Reis. 1973. Drugs and Foods from Little-Known Notes in Harvard University Herbaria. Harvard University Press, Cambridge, Mass.

Annegers, John F. 1973. Seasonal food shortages in Africa. Ecology of Food and Nutrition 2: 251–57.

Beaglehole, E. 1937. Notes on Hopi economic life. Yale University, Publications in Anthropology No. 15.

Bell, Willis H. and Edward F. Castetter. 1937. The utilization of mesquite and screwbean by aborigines in the American Southwest. University of New Mexico, Bulletin No. 314.

Benson, Lyman. 1969. The Cacti of Arizona. University of Arizona Press, Tucson.

Bhandari, M. M. 1974. Famine foods in the Rajasthan desert. Economic Botany 28: 73–81.

Bohrer, Vorsila L. 1975. The prehistoric and historic role of the cool-season grasses in the Southwest. Economic Botany 29: 199–207.

Bretting, Peter. 1982. Morphological differentiation of *Proboscidea parviflora* subsp. *parviflora* (Martynaceae) under domestication. American Journal of Botany 69: 1531–37.

Brown, David E. 1982. Biotic communities of the American Southwest-United States and Mexico. Desert Plants Vol. 4.

Bunzel, Ruth L. 1932. Zuni ritual poetry. Pp. 611–863 *in* Annual Report of the Bureau of American Ethnology: 1929–30, Vol. 47.

Castetter, Edward F. 1935. Uncultivated native plants used as sources of food. University of New Mexico, Bulletin No. 266.

———— and Willis H. Bell. 1942. Pima and Papago Indian Agriculture. University of New Mexico Press, Albuquerque.

————. 1951. Yuman Indian Agriculture. University of New Mexico Press, Albuquerque.

———— and Alvin R. Grove. 1938. The early utilization and distribution of *Agave* in the American Southwest. University of New Mexico, Bulletin No. 335.

Castetter, Edward and Ruth M. Underhill. 1935. The ethnobiology of the Papago Indians. University of Arizona, Agricultural Experiment Station, Bulletin No. 125.

Cerulli, Enrico. 1964. Nuove noti Sull' Islam. Ministero Degli Affari Esteri, Somalia, Scritti Vari ed Inediti (Rome) 3: 153–77.

Colson, Elizabeth. 1980. In good years and in bad: Food strategies of self-reliant societies. Journal of Anthropological Research 35: 18–29.

Cornett, James W. 1987. Indians and the desert fan palm. Masterkey 60(4): 12–17.

Cove, John N. 1978. Survival or extinction: Reflections on the problem of famine in Tsimshian and Kaguru mythology. Pp. 231–44 *in* Extinction and Survival in Human Populations. Edited by C. Laughlin and I. Brady. Columbia University Press, New York.

Curry, Bruce. 1984. Coping with complexity in food crisis management. Pp. 183–202 *in* Famines as a Geographical Phenomenon. Edited by B. Curry and G. Hugo. D. Reidel, Dordrecht, Germany.

Curtin, L. S. M. 1949. By the Prophet of the Earth: Ethnobotany of the Pima. San Vincente Foundation, Santa Fe.

————. 1965. Healing Herbs of the Upper Rio Grande. Southwest Museum, Los Angeles.

Cushing, Frank H. 1920. Zuni breadstuff. Heye Foundation Indian Notes and Monographs Vol. 8.

Dean, Jeffrey S., Robert C. Euler, George J. Gumerman, Fred Plog, Richard Hevly, and Thor N. V. Karlstrom. 1985. Human behavior, demography, and paleoenvironment on the Colorado Plateaus. American Antiquity 50: 537–54.

Dean, Jeffrey S. and William Robinson. 1978. Expanded tree-ring chronology for the southwestern United States. University of Arizona, Laboratory of Tree-Ring Research Chronology Series No. 3, Tucson.

Den Hartog, Adel P. 1981. Adjustments of food behavior during famine. Pp. 125–62 *in* Famine: Its Causes, Effects, and Management. Edited by J. Robson. Gordon and Breach, New York.

Elmore, Francis H. 1944. Ethnobotany of the Navajo. University of New Mexico, Bulletin No. 392.

Euler, Robert C., George J. Gumerman, Thor N. V. Karlstrom, Jeffrey S. Dean, and Richard H. Hevly. 1979. The Colorado Plateaus: Cultural dynamics and paleoenvironment. Science 205: 1089–1101.

Felger, Richard S. and Mary B. Moser. 1970. Seri use of *Agave* (century plant) The Kiva 35: 159–67.

————. 1971. Seri use of mesquite *(Prospois glandulosa* var. *torreyana).* The Kiva 37: 53–70.

————. 1973. Eelgrass *(Zostera marina* L.) in the Gulf of California: Discovery of its nutritional value by the Seri Indians Science 181: 355–56.

————. 1974. Columnar cacti in Seri Indian culture. The Kiva 39: 257–75.

————. Seri Indian food plants: Desert subsistence without agriculture. Ecology of Food and Nutrition 5: 13–27.

————. 1985. People of the Desert and Sea: Ethnobotany of the Seri. University of Arizona Press, Tucson.

Fish, Suzanne K., Paul K. Fish, Charles Miksicek, and John Madsen. 1985. Prehistoric *Agave* cultivation in southern Arizona. Desert Plants 7: 107–13.

Ford, Richard I. 1981. Gardening and farming before A.D. 1000: Patterns of prehistoric plant cultivation north of Mexico. Journal of Ethnobiology 1: 6–27.

Galt, Anthony H. and Janice W. Galt. 1978. Peasant use of some wild plants on the island of Pantelleria, Sicily, Economic Botany 32: 20–26.

Gasser, Robert E. 1981. Hohokam use of desert food plants. Desert Plants 3: 216–34.

Gentry, Howard Scott. 1982. Agaves of Continental Northern America. University of Arizona Press, Tucson.

Hall, Stephen S. 1985. Quaternary pollen analysis and vegetational history of the Southwest. Pp. 95–123 *in* Pollen Record of Late Quaternary North American Sediments. Edited by V. Bryant and R. Holloway. American Association of Stratigraphic Palynologists, Dallas.

Hanson, A. A. 1972. Grass varieties in the United States. United States Department of Agriculture, Agriculture Handbook No. 170.

Hastings, James R. and Raymond M. Turner. 1965. The Changing Mile: An Ecological Study of Vegetational Change with Time in the Lower Mile of an Arid and Semiarid Region. University of Arizona Press, Tucson.

Honigman, John J. 1954. The Kaska Indians: An Ethnographic Reconstruction. Yale University Press, New Haven.

Hough, Walter. 1987. The Hopi in relation to their plant environment. American Anthropologist 10: 33–44.

Huckell, Lisa W. 1986. Botanical remains. Pp. 241–269 *in* The 1985 Excavations at the Hodge Site, Pima County, Arizona. Edited by R. Layhe. Arizona State Museum Archaeological Series No. 170.

Irvin, R. A. 1952. Supplementary and emergency food plants of West Africa. Economic Botany 6: 23–40.

Kagwa, Apolo. 1934. The Customs of the Baganda. Columbia University Press, New York.

Krenetsky, John C. 1964. Phytosociogical study of the Picuris grant and ethnobotanical study of the Picuris Indians. Unpublished Masters thesis, Biology, University of New Mexico, Albuquerque.

Kuhnlein, H. V. and D. H. Calloway. 1977. Contemporary Hopi food intake patterns. Ecology of Food and Nutrition 6: 159–73.

Lehr, J. Harry. 1978. A Catalogue of the Flora of Arizona. Desert Botanical Gardens, Phoenix.

Malinowski, Bronislaw. 1935. Coral Gardens and Their Magic. American Book, New York.

Marcus, Joyce. 1982. The plant world of the sixteenth- and seventeenth-century lowland Maya. Pp. 239–273 *in* Maya Subsistence: Studies in Memory of Dennis E. Puleston. Edited by K. Flannery. Academic Press, New York.

Martin, William C. and Charles R. Hutchins. 1980. A Flora of New Mexico. J. Cramer, Vanduz, Germany.

Mason, J. D., R. W. Hays, J. Holt, J. Seaman, and M. R. Bwoden. 1974. Nutritional lessons from the Ethiopian drought. Nature 248: 646–50.

Minnis, Paul E. 1985. Social Adaptation to Food Stress: A Prehistoric Southwestern Example. University of Chicago Press, Chicago.

————. 1989. Prehistoric diet in the northern Southwest: Macroplant remains from Four-Corners feces. American Antiquity 54: 543–63.

Nabhan, Gary P. and Richard S. Felger. 1984. Teparies in southwestern North America: A biogeographical and ethnohistorical study of *Phaseolus acutifolius*. Economic Botany 32: 1–19.

———— and J. M. J. De Wet. 1984. *Panicum sonorum* in Sonoran desert agriculture. Economic Botany 38: 65–68.

————, Alfred Whiting, Henry Dobyns, Richard Hevly, and Robert Euler. 1981. Devil's claw domestication: Evidence from southwestern Indian fields. Journal of Ethnobiology 1: 135–64.

Ogbu, John. 1973. Seasonal hunger in tropical Africa as a cultural phenomenon: The Onicha Ibo of Nigeria and the Chakka Poka of Malwi examples. Africa 43: 317–32.

Parker, Kittie F. 1972. An Illustrated Guide to Arizona Weeds. University of Arizona Press, Tucson.

Pennington, Campbell W. 1980. The Pima Bajo of Central Sonora, Vol. 1: The Material Culture. University of Utah Press, Salt Lake City.

Quinones, Ferdinand A. 1981. Indian ricegrass, evaluation and breeding. New Mexico State University, Agricultural Experiment Station, Bulletin No. 681.

Rahamani, M. Mujibur. 1981. The causes and effects of famine in the rural population: A report from Bangladesh. Pp. 135–138 *in* Famine: Its Causes, Effects, and Management. J. Robson (editor). Gordon and Breach, New York.

Richards, Audrey. 1939. Land, Labour, and Diet in Northern Rhodesia: An Economic Study of the Bemba Tribe. Oxford University Press, London

Read, Bernard E. 1946. Famine Foods Listed in the Chui Huang Pen Ts'ao. Reprinted in 1977 by Southern Materials Center, Taipei.

Reining, Conrad C. 1970. Zande subsistence and food production. Pp. 125–164 *in* African Food Production Systems: Cases and Theory. Edited by P. McLoughlin. Johns Hopkins University Press, Baltimore.

Robbins, Wilfred W., John P. Harrington, and Barbara Freiremarreco. 1916. Ethnobotany of the Tewa Indians. Smithsonian Institution, Bureau of American Ethnology, Bulletin No. 55.

Roys, Ralph L. 1967. The Book of Chilam Balam of Chuymayel. University of Oklahoma Press, Norman.

Scudder, Thayer. 1962. The Ecology of the Gwembe Tonga. Manchester University Press, Manchester, England.

Sellers, William D. and Richard A. Hill. 1974. Arizona Climate: 1931–1972. University of Arizona Press, Tucson.

Swank, George R. 1932. The Ethnobotany of the Acoma and Laguna Indians. Unpublished Master's thesis, Department of Biology, University of New Mexico, Albuquerque.

Swetnam, Thomas W. 1984. Peeled ponderosa pine trees: A record of inner bark utilization by Native Americans. Journal of Ethnobiology 4: 177–90.

Tuan, Yi-Fu, Cyril E. Everard, Jerold G. Widdison, and Iven Bennett. 1973. The Climate of New Mexico. New Mexico State Planning Office, Santa Fe.

Vestal, Paul A. 1952. Ethnobotany of the Ramah Navajo. Papers of the Peabody Museum of American Archaeology and Ethnology, Vol. 40, No. 4.

Wauer, Roland H. and David H. Riskind. 1977. Transactions of the symposium on the biological resources of the Chihuahuan Desert region, United States and Mexico. National Park Service, Transactions and Proceedings Series No. 3.

Wetterstrom, Wilma. 1986. Food, Diet, and Population at Prehistoric Arroyo Hondo Pueblo, New Mexico. School of American Research Press, Santa Fe.

White, Leslie A. 1944. Notes on the ethnobotany of the Keres. Papers of the Michigan Academy of Science, Arts, and Letters Vol. 30.

Whiting, Alfred F. 1939. Ethnobotany of the Hopi. Museum of Northern Arizona, Bulletin No. 15.

Woodham-Smith, Cecil. 1962. The Great Hunger: Ireland 1845–1849. Harper and Row, New York.

Yue, Daiyun (with Carolyn Wakeman). 1985. To the Storm: The Odyssey of a Revolutionary Chinese Woman. University of California Press, Berkeley.

Part Four

Agriculture

Agriculture

An Introduction

RICHARD I. FORD

From the inception of the term *ethnobotany*, apparently coined by the prominent University of Pennsylvania professor of botany John Harshberger (Ford 1994), under-standing agriculture in prehistoric and modern ethnographic terms has been one of the discipline's objectives (Anonymous 1895). Agriculture represents one end of a continuum of plant manipulations by humans that is usually acknowledged as cultur-ally influenced human selection of plants that have the specific genetic characteristics desired to create domesticated plants, commonly called crops. But *agriculture* is used to describe the technological methods by which these crops are raised and maintained.

Ethnobotany has made two distinct contributions to our understanding of agri-culture. First by revealing ways to create genetically altered plants for human purposes. Second by describing and explaining the many different ways the same crop can be raised—some of which are guided by a desire for greater income, others for sustained yield, and still others for culturally specific purposes. Harshberger anticipated the first contribution but not the second. However, subsequent ethnobotanical studies have become sufficiently universal to permit a comparative base in which to analyze the genetic, economic, and cultural reasons underlying agriculture.

Many practitioners of Harshberger's style of ethnobotany deliberately sought only "primitive" societies to study. Since his time the idea that ethnobotany is "the study of plants used by primitive man" has evolved, and we now recognize that knowledge about human transactions with plants can be appreciated by studying the folk practices of the inhabitants of modern western cultures and not just those in marginal societies or "backward" ethnic enclaves. George Estabrook's paper about agriculture in Portugal, reproduced in this volume, is exemplary for the important kinds of new information that can still be learned about agricultural practices in socially and polit-ically complex countries.

A delineation of domesticated plants has received worldwide attention from ethnobotanists and those who identify archaeological plant remains, so-called paleo-ethnobotanists. The corpus of such information is ever-growing (cf. Cowan and Watson 1992; Smith 1998). At one time attention was devoted to the domestication of food plants based on the mistaken notion that since these plants are so critical for explaining the rise of civilizations, they must have had priority in an evolutionary scale. But this idea has been challenged by archaeological evidence that suggests that plants used for tools and implements may have had a critical role in prehistoric hunter and gatherer societies. Indeed, the bottle gourd *(Lagenaria siceraria)* with its light, durably hard useful shell but bitter-tasting seeds, is a baseline domesticate, or one of the first known domesticated plants, in parts of the New World and Asia (Heiser 1990). Furthermore, its domestication has not ceased. There continue to be processes that people practice today to select plants for phenotypic traits that they find beneficial for food, flowers, or useful objects. Professional horticulturalists are the modern-day descendants of people who have modified plants for their special ends for over ten thousand years.

A detailed examination of the processes of potential plant domestication can be found in the Greater Southwest by studying the devil's claw *(Proboscidea parviflora).* In their impeccably argued paper reproduced here, Gary Nabhan and others test the proposition that the longest, dark-epidermal fiber splints teased from the fruits of some devil's claw were from a domesticated variety. Their task was complicated by the fact that some of these plants produce white seeds—a trait suggesting a deliberately selected domesticate for food purposes—while others have black seeds, which are normally associated with wild fruited plants. The solution to their problem hangs on the very concept of domestication itself.

The authors diligently walk the reader through a logical progression of arguments starting with characteristics of domestication of the devil's claw and then follow with an examination of each trait in light of the morphological evidence of the plants themselves. First, they demonstrate that the phenotypic variation evidenced in Indian gardens and fields belongs to the same species and not with other members of the Martyniaceae. Next they use field studies to sort the effects of local habitats and ecology on genetic expression. The researchers had to show that some fibers are actually longer than others and are consistently so, and that the formations are not some ecologically opportunistic sport. Finally, they address the question of white seeds to demonstrate that these seeds were neither larger than the black seeds or nutritionally better. The presence of white seeds still had to be explained, and that problem brings the reader back to the original question: what is domestication and how has it changed? The authors conclude in convincing fashion that the long-fiber fruits are selected for their usefulness and white seeds are a by-product of the process of selecting enlarged claws to decorate baskets. And they show that this domestication may be recent, at least in historic time, reflecting the post-Hispanic demand for Indian baskets.

Nabhan's splendid paper is actually one of several examples of plant modifications by aboriginal people in the Sonoran Desert area. Robert Bye (1981) examined the vegetative transformation of weedy plants, including introduced mustard plants *(Brassica campestris),* into selected if not new domesticated plants by the Tarahumara of northern Mexico. Nabhan and Paul Mirocha (1985) described the complex human-plant interactions, including some additional local domesticated plants, in the same region.

Even when a culture's dependence upon domesticated plants is unquestioned, the plants may be genetically complex—as recognized by varieties and native nomenclature. The issue of why great variation exists and how it can be sustained in the face of economic and cultural changes is a world-recognized problem that ethnobotanists must address. Stephen Brush, in a seminal paper reproduced here, provides a detailed analysis of such a situation in the Andean highlands of Peru. In this region the Indians have grown diverse varieties of potatoes (*Solanum* spp.) since precontact times. Brush examines the native nomenclature and the agricultural procedures that sustain interspecific diversity. He established a comparative base between two valleys in which the inhabitants had contrasting adaptations to contemporary social conditions. The conclusions of his study are compelling: people maintain this particular agricultural diversity because different potatoes taste better than modern, economically enhanced varieties and the preferred potatoes are culturally salient, that is, they serve important functions as gifts in societies straining to maintain cultural identity.

Ethnobotanists have used the term *ethnoecology* (see Fowler's Introduction in this volume) to understand the agriculture and cultural persistence of other crops as well. Brush *et al.* (1988) did this for maize in Mexico, and Virginia Navarea-Sandoval (1995) has explored the same problem with sweet potato diversity in the Philippines. Nabhan (1989) provides a very readable account of ethnobotanists tackling traditional agricultural methods and preserving genetic diversity.

Too frequently, however, genetic diversity and traditional agricultural techniques are threatened by development before they have even been studied. George Estabrook faced this situation in Portugal where farmers in mountainous areas who eke a living from nutrient-deficient soils employ what he demonstrates to be ecologically sensible methods to grow their crops. There perennial plants growing in a vegetation type called *mato* are cut and spread in animal pens as bedding and absorbents before being buried in terrace soil where they provide badly needed nitrogen and phosphorous. And one woody plant, *Erica arborea,* an ecologically dominant component, is cut in the fall to burn as a special fuel to distill grape sludge to make the beverage *bagaco.* By these means the floral diversity of the mato is maintained, the fields receive a mineral supplement, the crops flourish, and the land can be used for multiple purposes. When this process is viewed systematically as Estabrook does, there are many mutual benefits in this agricultural technique. It is a system supported by cultural tradition that is ecologically wise, cost effective, and supportive of a complex agricultural economy. Destroying the mato, discouraging the production of bagaco, or ending herding could threaten this successful agricultural way of life that ethnobotanists are only now beginning to understand.

The ethnobotanical study of agriculture often yields unexpected surprises. Ethnobotanists enter a field situation with an ethnoscience methodology, sometimes called ethnoecology, that allows them to view the interactions of plants and humans differently than from the perspectives of other disciplines. The papers in this reader are complementary examples of research that explores and highlights the unique understanding ethnobotanists bring to field situations, and they reinforce the reason why ethnobotany continues to be a field-based science, as new information about agriculture is constantly revealed.

LITERATURE CITED

Anonymous. 1895. Some New Ideas in the Philadelphia Evening Telegraph, p. 2. Frontispiece *in* An Ethnobiology Source Book, edited by Richard I. Ford. Garland Publishing, Inc., New York.

Brush, Stephen B., Mauricio Beflon, and Ella Schmidt. 1988. Agricultural development and maize diversity in Mexico. Human Ecology 16: 307–28.

Bye, Robert A., Jr. 1981. Quelites-ethnoecology of edible greens- past, present, and future. Journal of Ethnobiology l(l): 109–23.

Cowan, C. Wesley and Patty Jo Watson, eds. 1992. The Origins of Agriculture. Smithsonian Institution Press, Washington, D.C. Ford, Richard I. 1994. Ethnobotany: historical diversity and synthesis. Pp. 33–50 *in* The Nature and Status of Ethnobotany, edited by Richard I. Ford. University of Michigan Museum of Anthropology Anthropological Papers 67, Ann Arbor.

Heiser, Charles B., Jr. 1990. Seed to Civilization. Harvard University Press, Cambridge.

Nabhan, Gary Paul. 1989. Enduring Seeds, Native American Agriculture and Wild Plant Conservation. North Point Press, San Francisco.

Nabhan, Gary Paul and Paul Mirocha. 1985. Gathering the Desert. University of Arizona Press, Tucson.

Nazarea-Sandoval, Virginia D. 1995. Local Knowledge and Agricultural Decision Making in the Philippines. Cornell University Press, Ithaca.

Smith, Bruce. 1998. The Emergence of Agriculture. Scientific American Library, New York.

CHAPTER TWELVE

Devil's Claw Domestication:

Evidence from Southwestern Indian Fields

GARY NABHAN, ALFRED WHITING, HENRY DOBYNS,
RICHARD HEVLY, ROBERT EULER

INTRODUCTION

To *domesticate* a plant literally means to bring it into the human household. The process of domestication involves cultural selection for economic characters, as well as natural selection in the man-altered environment where the plants are grown. The intensity of these selective pressures is not constant through time nor through space. It varies with the demand for the economic product, the kind of horticulture or agriculture practiced by the people involved, and the degree of geographical or phenological isolation between the cultivated plants and their wild relatives.

Often, an incipient domesticate has not been recognized as such. This is because the cultivated plant may still have the appearance of its wild relatives. Additionally, the early stages of cultural adoption may not involve formal husbandry so much as simple seed selection, sowing and protection in an otherwise unmanaged environment, which looks "wild" to observers from another culture.

Given these conditions, it is not surprising that it took Europeans more than 2 centuries in southwestern North America before they questioned whether certain plants the Indians utilized were more than merely wild crops. In the case of devil's claw *(Proboscidea)*, the use of the plant for food and fiber was recognized decades before its outright cultivation was noted (Fig. 1). Additional time passed before scientists first suggested the plant as a possible domesticate.

Early researchers suggested the presence of "introduced" kinds of devil's claw among the Indians. However, Castetter and Bell (1942: 113, 202) were the first to realize that one kind was almost completely dependent upon cultivation. They noted that a second kind of annual devil's claw among the Pima and Papago (O'odham)[1] was different from the wild kind in Arizona in respect to several characteristics. They claimed that this longer clawed, white seeded kind was found *only* under intentional cultivation or as a volunteer in agricultural fields.

Hevly has indicated (in Correll and Johnston 1970: 1448) that strains of *Proboscidea parviflora* (Woot.) Woot. and Standl. semi-cultivated by Southwestern aboriginal groups are anomalous for *Proboscidea* in that they have white seeds.

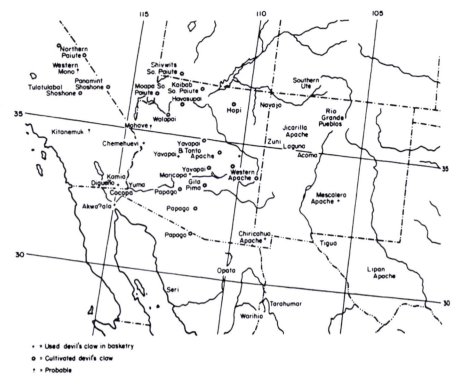

Fig. 1. Locations of tribes growing or using devil's claw (cartography by Alison Habel).

Recently, Yarnell (1977), without further data or analysis, concluded that *Proboscidea parviflora* was one of only 3 species definitely domesticated north of Mexico.

If one goes to the reservations of the Papago and Pima Indians today, one finds a somewhat more complicated situation than that described by Castetter and Bell (1942). Both black and white seeded devil's claw are cultivated in fields and gardens; additionally white seeded devil's claw can be found on roadsides and in arroyos within Papago *rancherias,* growing nearby the more common black seeded *Proboscidea parviflora* (Nabhan and Fritz 1977). Given this information alone, we feel that the data in Castetter and Bell's work do not place devil's claw in enough of a cultural and botanical context to convince the scientific community that domestication has actually occurred.

The proposed status of domesticate for *Proboscidea parviflora* has thus been largely unrecognized and untested. We will use the devil's claw example as a case study in how anthropologists and botanists methodologically determine when a plant has undergone cultural selection and domestication, over and above mere cultivation. Additionally, we discuss problems in the interpretation of historic specimens and ethnographic data, and suggest some testable indicators of domestication.

In presenting hypotheses regarding how and where the domestication process might have occurred for *Proboscidea,* we wish to emphasize how much has yet to be learned. We hope to encourage further research of devil's claw as well as of other little-known crops. Such research is urgently needed, since many minor crops have been abandoned within this century as modern monocultural agriculture has usurped the land and water formerly allotted to smaller scale mixed crops.

Devil's claw cultivation is a case in point. Today it is practiced in only a few "islands" within its former range. Due to the demise of traditional basketry and agriculture among several Southwestern cultures, considerable native knowledge and *Proboscidea* germ plasm have eroded within the last half century.

DISCUSSION

Botanical Background and Historical Recognition

Within the New World family Martyniaceae, the genus *Proboscidea* is divided into 2 subgenera: *Dissolphia,* including 3 yellow-flowered perennial species; and *Proboscidea,* including 10 species, most of which are annual, with flowers of cream, pink or purplish hues (Van Eseltine 1929; Hevly in Correll and Johnston 1970; Hevly 1969a; 1970). We will be concerned with 3 annual species of the southwestern United States and adjacent Mexico: *Proboscidea fragrans* (Lindl.) Decne.; *P. louisianica* Miller (Thell.), and *P. parviflora* (Woot.) Woot. and Standl.

Partially overlapping in range, (eg., in Texas), these species are nevertheless phenetically distinct and macroscopically distinguishable (Table 1). However, the 3 species have been found to be experimentally cross-compatible. First generation (F[1]) flowering and fruiting hybrids can easily be obtained, although F[1] fruits contain few seed (Anderson 1922: 141; Perry 1942; Hevly, unpubl. data). A more thorough treatment of the genetic and biogeographic relationships of these species is currently being prepared by Peter Bretting at Indiana University, in a taxonomic revision of the genus *Proboscidea.*

In the 1870s, Dr. Edward Palmer published 2 of the first specific notes on the use of Southwestern devil 's claw. Palmer (1871: 422) noted that the Apache Indians cooked the immature fruit of *Martynia violacea* for food, and utilized part of the ripened fruit as ornamentation in basketry. Additionally, Palmer (1875: 112) described the preparation of fruit of *Martenia proboscides* as a black basketry ornamentation, as it is used "by all the tribes of Arizona." At the time that Palmer made these comments, only 2 annual species of devil's claw were recognized in North America, both with large calyces; *M. fragrans,* for which *M. violacea* is a synonym—with purple flowers; and *M. louisianica,* for which *Martenia proboscides* is a misspelled synonym—with white to pink flowers.

Neither article acknowledges if Palmer collected voucher specimens to substantiate these identifications; thus there is no way of checking the suggestion that 2 species were then utilized. The paucity of voucher specimens, as we shall see, has persisted into recent decades; it is still not clear if more than one devil's claw species has been utilized in Southwestern basketry.

During the decades that followed Palmer's articles, it became apparent that the most common kind of devil's claw in Arizona, New Mexico and adjacent Mexico is

TABLE 1. Comparison of Proboscidea in the Southwest.

CHARACTER	(SUGGESTED DOMESTICATE) WHITE-SEEDED RACE	UNDER CULTIVATION: P. PARVIFLORA	IN THE WILD P. PARVIFLORA	P. LOUISIANICA	P. FRAGRAMS
Geographic distribution	Southern Nevada, southern Utah, southeast California, Arizona, & northeast Sonora	Arizona (a few tribes) & experimentally in Arizona & New Mexico	Arizona, south and west New Mexico, & Trans-Pecos Texas. North Mexico west of Sierra Madre. Rare in Californias; extremely rare in Nevada	Southern U.S. to Colorado, eastern New Mexico & central Texas. Adventive in California; elsewhere.	Tran-Pecos Texas & north-eastern Mexico east of the Sierra Madre.
Plant size	To 1.4m tall & 3m wide	To .9m tall x 1.8m wide	To .5m tall x 1.5m wide	To 17m tall x 1.2m wide	To .6m tall x 2m wide
Leaves	Sub-orbicular-ovate, sometimes deltoid-ovate; entire to 3–10 lobed; sinuses obtuse, denticulate; width up to 35cm; cordate to inequilateral at base.	Sub-orbicular-ovate to deltoid-ovate to deltoid-ovate; entire to 3–10 lobed; sinuses obtuse, denticulate; width up to 25 cm; cordate to inequilateral at base.	Bus-orbicular-ovate to deltoid-ovate; entire to 3–7 lobed; sinuses obtuse, denticulate; width up to 25cm; cordate to inequilateral at base.	Orbicular-reniform to broadly ovate; entire to sinuate; width up to 30 cm; cordate at base.	Deltoid to broadly ovate; nearly entire to 5–7 lobed; sinuses acute; width up to 25cm; cordate to equalateral at base
Inflorescence	Surpassed by, or rarely equalling the foliage	Equalling or surpassed by the foliage	Equalling or surpassed by the foliage	Surpassing the foliage.	Surpassing the foliage.
FLOWERS: Calyx length Corolla length Corolla color	15–27mm; bracts 8–17mm 34–54mm Dull white to pink; rarely reddish purple; limb often with faint purple blotches on upper lobes.	13–20mm; bracts 4–11mm 34–44mm Reddish-purple, pink to nearly white; limb often with purple on upper lobes	10–15mm; bracts 5–8mm 25–40mm Reddish-purple, pink to nearly white; limb often with purple on upper lobes	15–20Mm; bracts 7–10mm 35–55mm Dull white to somewhat pinkish purple; purple blotches absent or blotches on upper lobes	25mm; bracts 12mm 35–65mm Violet purple to reddish purple, rarely white; limb often with purple blotches
Corolla internal ornamentation	Bright yellow guidelines, & small red dots associated with them in lower half of tube; dark blotches absent	Bright yellow guidelines; & small red dots associated with them in lower tube; blotches usually lacking	Bright yellow guidelines; & small red dots associated with them in lower tube; blotches usually lacking	Yellow-orange guidelines, violet blotches, orange or red-purple dots around the entire tube.	Bright yellow guidelines; violet botches & dark red-purple dots the entire tube length.

Filament Pubescens	Glandular at or below their point of attachment but glabrous above the arcuately curved portion.	Glandular at or below their point of attachment but glabrous above the arcuately curved portion.	Glandular at or below their point of attachment but glabrous above the arcuately curved portion.	Glabrous, sparsely villous or tomentose below attachment point, glandular on arcuately curved portion.	Glabrous, sparsely villous or romentose below attachment point, glandular on arcuately curved portion
FRUIT:					
Number per plant	75–200	60–100	40–80	40–80	40–80
Claw/body ratio	2.5–3	2–2.5	2–2.5	1.5–3	ca. 1.6
Claw length	25.3±4.3cm	17.0±2.7cm	15.7±4.8cm	9–30cm	to 20cm
Pliability	Soft-pliable	Hard-brittle	Hard-brittle	Hard-brittle	Hard-brittle
Color	Darker black	Brown-black	Brown-black	Brown-black	Brown-black
SEED:					
Number per fruit	49.5±12	53.2±9	40–55?	15–67	
Size	.953-.039x516.040mm	.984-.070x.527.055mm	8–10X4.5–6mm	7–10x5–6mm	6.5–8x5.5cm
Color	White-gray	Black-gray	Black-gray	Black-brown	Black-brown
Germination	More immediate, even	Delayed, uneven	Delay, uneven	Delayed, uneven	Delayed, uneven
Per cent oil	39.2–40.3%	35–38.3%	35–40%	35–43.5%	39%
Per cent protein	23.9–25.5%	20–25%	20–30%	20–25%	
Pollination:	Crossing by bees	Crossing by bees	Crossing by bees	Crossing by bees	Crossing by bees
(& compatibility)	(Some selfing)	(Selfing 15% effective)	(Selfing?)	(Selfing rare or ineffective)	
Insect visitors (*pollinator)	Perdita hurdi, Bombus sonorus, Apis Melifera, Xenoglossa angustior, Melissodes so.*, Xylocopa brasilionorum, Xylocopa brasilionorum, Xylocopa orpifex androlenca	Xylocopa orpifex androlenca		Melissodes communis*, Anthophora occidentalis*, Augochlorella striata*, Bombus fervidus*, Lasioglassum spp., bombus americanorum*, Melissodes obliqua*, (Phillippii, personal communication 1976)	Xylocopa spp., Bombus sonorus

distinct from the above 2 species due to its smaller calyces, and differently colored flowers. This species was named *Martynia parviflora* Wooton in 1898, but was transferred along with *M. louisianica* and *M. frangrans* to the genus *Proboscidea* because their flower and fruit characteristics were incompatible with *Martynia* (Hevly 1969b).

Over the hundred years since Palmer's introductory notes, the use of devil's claw has been recorded for more than 30 native culture groups in southwestern North America (Table 2). In addition to basketmakers' use of fiber splints from the dried fruit, devil's claw fruit and seed have been eaten, and used medicinally; the fruit have been made into tools and ornaments, and have been given supernatural significance. Again, because written references have seldom been accompanied by voucher specimens, and because obsolete nomenclature has often been utilized, we can only guess which devil's claw species various ethnographers have seen.

After the turn of the century, ethnographers began to comment on the planting and protection of devil's claw (Table 3). Russell (1908: 133), Spier (1928: 134), and Roberts (1929: 141) imply that cultivation or lack of it was directly related to the abundance of wild devil's claw in their area at the time. It is usually stated that devil's claw is grown for its fiber used in basketry, although in certain cultures (e.g. the Papago), seeds were no doubt eaten also.

Although split devil's claw fiber splints have been found in cave deposits dating roughly A.D. 1150 in Arizona (Exhausted Cave - Hevly and Hudgens, MS) and New Mexico Tularosa Cave - Kaplan 1963), the antiquity of devil's claw cultivation is an open question: Did cultivation for basketry fiber occur in previous centuries, unrecognized or ignored by chroniclers, or did it begin this last century to keep pace with basketry sales?

Beginning with Spier (1928: 134–35), there are statements that a longer clawed cultivated variety is introduced rather than being indigenous to the localities where it is grown. Kissell (1916: 202) implies that the wild devil's claw in Papago country is seeded in their fields, and that cultivation produces longer clawed fruit with better qualities for basketry.

From the 1930s onward, specimens accompanied by limited ethnographic data were deposited in museums and herbaria (Table 4). Associated field notes are often unfortunately ambiguous. For instance, Percy Train's note that at Moapa, Nevada, devil's claw is "In Indian field," does not clarify whether or not he collected an intentionally planted crop, a self-seeded feral plant, or a wild "weedy" volunteer. Particularly in terms of fruit size, we don't know if collectors chose an atypically large fruit, a representative individual, or a conveniently small fruit that could be "pressed and mounted" easily. Botanists continued to label their specimens with obsolete nomenclature, and of course anthropologists were no more aware that finer taxonomic distinctions were possible. Fig. 2 maps the sites of cultivation.

Castetter and colleagues, during studies of Pima and Papago (O'odham) ethnobotany, amassed considerable information regarding devil's claw cultivation. Yet even their information is ambiguous on some major points, and at times it is contradictory. Castetter and Underhill (1935: 57) note that *Martynia fragrans* grows wild in Papago country (sic), but long ago, women began to protect fertile patches of it; later they

TABLE 2. Devil's claw use in southwestern North America: Early ethnographic references.

Culture Group	Basketry Use	Other Use	Early References	Early Identification	Other References
Santa Clara Pueblo		X	Robbins et al, 1916:57	*Martynia*	
Jemez Pueblo		X	Castetter, 1939:notes	*Martynia*	
Cochiti Pueblo		X	Lange, 1959:150		
Zuni Pueblo		X	Stevenson, 1909:46	*M. Louisiana*	this report
Hopi Pueblo	X	X	Hough, 1897:33–44	*M. Louisiana*	Whiting, 1939:92
Hano Pueblo			Robbins, et al, 1916:57	*Martynia*	
Apache (general)	X	X	Palmer, 1871:422	*M. Violacea*	Palmer, 1875:112
Warm Springs Apache	X		Gifford, 1940:45	*Martynia*	
Mescalero Apache	X		Gifford, 1940:45	*Martynia*	
Chiricahua Apache		X	Gifford, 1940:45	*M. Louisiana*	Castetter and Opler, 1936:45
Huachuca Apache	X		Gifford, 1940:45	*Martynia*	
			Gifford, 1940:45	*Martynia*	
Cibeque Western Apache	X		Gifford, 1940:45	*Martynia*	Buskird, 1949:164
White Mountain Western Apache	X		Mason, 1904:512	*M. Louisiana*	Rea, 1977:notes
San Carlos Western Apache	X		Hrdlicka, 1905:404	cat's claw	Roberts, 1929:141
Western Yavapai	X	X	Corbusier, 1886:324	cat's claw	Gifford, 1936:281
Northeastern Yavapai	X	X	Gifford, 1936:281	*Martynia*	
Walapai	X		Mason, 1904:517	*Martynia*	McKennan, 1935:80
Havasupai	X		Voth, 1890s:11	*M. Louisiana*	Spier, 1928:134
Southern Paiute (general)	X	X	Palmer, 1870s, noted in Bye 1972:98		
Virgin River and Moapa S. Paiute	X	X	this report		
Shivwits So. Paiute	X		Stewart, 1942:340	*M. proboscidea*	Drucker, 1941:110
Kaibab So. Paiute	X		Stewart, 1942:340	*M. proboscidea*	Kelly, 1964:78, 80
Chemehuevi	X		Mason, 1904:519	*Martynia*	Stoffle and Evans, 1976:4
Kawaiisu	X		Merrill, 1923:7	*M. proboscidea*	Zigmond, 1978:202
Panamint Shoshone (Koso)	X		Coville, 1892:358	*M. proboscidea*	Merriam 1903:826
Death Valley Shoshone	X		Steward, 1941:338	*M. proboscidea*	Jaeger, 1941:248
Northern Paiute	X		Steward, 1941:338	*M. proboscidea*	
Western Mono	X		Merrill, 1923:7	*M. proboscidea*	
Kern River Tubatulabal	X		Merrill, 1923:7	*M. proboscidea*	Voegelin, 1938:30
Kitanemuk	X		Merrill, 1923:7	*M. proboscidea*	
Akwa?ala (Pai Pai)	X?		Drucker, 1941:110	*Martynia*	
Maricopa	X	X	Forde, 1931:124	*Martynia*	Spier, 1946:129
Gila Pima & Papago	X	X	Mason, 1904:519	*Martynia*	Russell, 1908:133
Yaqui		X	Watson, 1898:66	*M. palmeri*	
Seri		X	Felger & Moser, 1976:23	*P. altheaefolia*	
Warihio		X	Gentry, 1963:92	*M. annua, M. fragrans*	
Pima Bajo (Lowland) (Onovas)		X	Pennington, 1980	*P. arenaria* *P. sinaloensis*	Rea, 1978:notes

began to sow its seeds. Castetter and Bell (1942: 113) identify as *M. louisianica* both the wild black seeded variety, and the white seeded, longer clawed kind that "never grew wild," but is propagated by planting in holes. They doubted that Pimans who asserted that devil's claw has been cultivated for a long time, and suggested that only wild *Martynia* was utilized before a commercial stimulus increased basketry production.

TABLE 3. Ethnographic references to devil's claw cultivation.

Culture Group	Citation	Quotation
Pima	Hrdlicka 1906:43	The cat's claw is cultivated by the Pima in their melon patches.
Pima	Russell 1908:133	The pods of the devil's claw, *Martynia frgrans* Lindl., furnish the third material necessary for the ordinary basket. The supply of wild plants is not large enough, and a few martynia seeds are planted each year by the basket-makers.
Papago & Pima	Kissell 1916:202	Although martynia grows wild, most of the Indians seed it in their fields, since they find the cultivated plant yields pods with hooks of greater length, finer grain and a better black.
Pima	Breaseale 1923:42	The martynia, or devil's claw grows wild . . . but I have never seen it growing out upon the desert away from any cultivated field or wash. The Indians often plant a few stalks around their houses, as the wild varieties often have horns not suitable for basketry.
Papago	Castetter & Underhill 1935:57	The black was ihu'k, the unicorn plant or devil's claw (*Martynia frgrans*) . . . Now many sow the seed and raise a regular crop.
Pima & Papago	Castetter & Bell 1942:202	Only the white seeded form was grown, as its pods had longer, finer grained and deeper black strips of epidermal tissue, and therefore more suitable for use in basketry. They were planted in hills . . .
Pima	Curtin 1949:107	Ihuk is cultivated by the Pima for use in basket-making, although it grows wild on plains and mesas.
Papago	Dobyns 1952:211	Papagos domesticated *eohuk* (*Martynia louisiana*), the pod bark being their black material for basket designs.
Havasupai	Spier 1928:134–135	The second variety, with hooks 25 to 30 cm long, was introduced by pagad-jahuda, a Walapai. Although the wild plants are also used, it is customary to plant martynia at the same time as corn.
Havasupai	Whiting 1942:378	[Pagadjahuda planted a whole field of the introduced variety, selling a superior product. Another Havasupai woman, however, claimed she had herself introduced the plant from the Mohaves. Another thought the seeds had been obtained from the Hopi long ago, while still another suggested the Yavapai as a source.]
Havasupai	McKee, McKee & Herold 1975:13	. . . and an introduced variety with hooks about four inches longer is commonly cultivated. The latter yields adequate crops of the black claws for local use, so few basketmakers gather the smaller wild form.
Apache	Roberts 1929:141	. . . the San Carlos do not cultivate the plant as do some other tribes, for it is plentiful in their country in its wild state.
Tubatulabal Shoshone	Voegelin 1938:30	Coiled basketed decorated in . . . black material from . . . antennae of pods of devil's horn, *Martynia proboscidea* Glox . . . which is classified as weed, grown occasionally in gardens now, pods sometimes saved.
Shoshone & Northern Paiute	Steward 1941:338	NP-Fsp [Northern Paiute, Fish Springs, California, near Bishop]: procured it from Saline V., through TS said his father had planted it at Fish Springs . . . S-Lida [Shonshoni of Lida, Nevada, north of Death Valley]: planted devil's claw in gardens.
Shoshone	Jaeger 1941:248	. . . *M. Parviflora* . . . was introduced into Death Valley eighty years ago by a brother of Hungry Bill, a Shoshone Indian, who visited Fort Mohave and found the Indians there making black patterns in their baskets from fiber of the fruits. He procured seeds and planted them in Johnson Canyon; the plant still flourishes there.
Shivwits & Kaibab Southern Paiute	Steward 1942:340	Devil's claw (*Martynia proboscidea*) SK [Southern Paiute, Kaibab]: Use learned from SS [Southern Paiute, Shivwits] and material still purchased from them. (Kelly, ms, states seeds have been planted near Mocassin, Arizona).
Kaibab Southern Paiute	Kelly 1964:80	With the development of decorated ware, seeds of *Martynia* (tuusupi *Martynia proboscidea*) obtained from St. George, Utah, planted locally.
Panamint-Death Valley Shoshone now near Bishop	Smith and Simpson 1964:46	Mamie Button's basket is woven of willow, Joshua tree roots and fibers from the fruit of devil's claw . . . The dark brown designs are woven of Martynia parviflora which Mamie called devil's claw. The Hunters and Buttons cultivate this black-seeded annual in their garden for use in basket-making.

Castetter and Bell's conclusions were based primarily upon several interviews between 1938–40; we have not come across any voucher specimens collected by them, or notes on the plants themselves. In the interviews, only the white seeded variety is noted as being cultivated, and only the black seeded variety is mentioned as growing away from fields. For one interview, notes imply that a Pima farmer responded negatively to the question of whether his people cultivated wild plants, but later acknowledged that devil's claw is cultivated (Castetter 1939: 44). Dobyns (1952: 211) concluded that the Papago had domesticated devil's claw based on similar (unpublished) observations.

Yarnell (1977) has concluded that the distinctive characteristics of the cultivated form described by Castetter and Bell—white vs. black seeds, longer "pods," plus finer grained and deeper black pod-epidermis—justify its status as a cultigen. He suggests that several centuries of artificial selection is a reasonable estimate for the duration of the domestication process in devil's claw. Yarnell also hypothesizes that the original motivation for cultivation was possibly the food-value of the pods and seeds, and that more recently, cultivation has emphasized basketry material production. He does not mention the presence of the domesticate in groups other than the Pima-Papago.

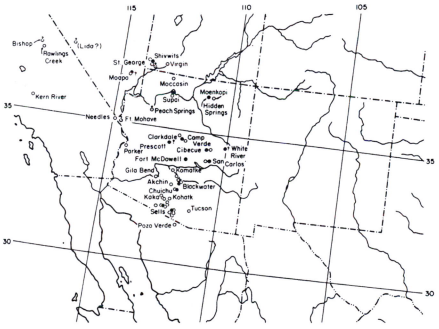

o = White seeded race in cultivation (specimen)
● = Black seeded _P. parviflora_ in cultivation (specimen)
♂ = Ethnographic record of cultivation (no specimen)

Fig. 2. Locations of devil's claw cultivation by Native Americans (cartography by Alison Habel).

TABLE 4a. Possible records of the suggested domesticate (not recognized as *P. parviflora* var. *hohokamiana*) in museums and herbaria.

Original ID	Locality	Culture	Collector & #	Date	Museum or Herbaria	Suggestive Characteristics
M. pobosidea	Weldon, Kern Co., Calif.	Tubatulabal Shoshone	E.W. Voegelin #13	7/7/32	UC	"Used for black basketry material . . ." (no notes on specimen, but Zigmond (1978) suggests it was introduced from Needles, with claw length of 20 cm)
M. louisianica?	Monolith, Paiute Mts. Kern Co., Calif.	Kawaiisu	Zigmond 5772	7/22/37	F	
P. louisianica?	Keene, Kern Co., Calif.	Shoshone?	J.D. Woolsey	9/04	UC	"Escaped" (No other notes: inference same as above)
M. louisianica	Moapa Indian Reservation, Clark Co., Nevada	Moapa Southern Paiute	Percy Train #1917	6/6/38	NY, ARIZ	"In Indian field." (Light flower color. Leaves surpassing inflorescence. Rare in wild in Nevada)
M. louisianica	Moapa Indian Agency, Clark Co., Nevada	Moapa Southern Paiute	Eva Murphey #675	9/27/37	RENO, UC	"Garden . . . Rich soil." (Claws 21 & 24.3 cm; white seed; leaves surpassing inflorescence)
M. louisianica	Virgin, Washington Co., Utah	Virgin River Southern Paiute?	Marcus Jones #6086	9/27/1894	UC, NY, US, MBG	(Rare in Utah. Claws 28, 27, 26, 22.2cm; leaves large, up to 19 x 17 cm)
M. proboscidea	Havasupai Canyon, Coconino Co., Ariz.	Havasupai	Elzada Clover #5179	7/17/40	ARIZ	"In fields. Used by Indians in basket weaving." (Fruit immature; possibly the wild race, but too young to tell).
P. parviflora	Havasu Canyon, Coconino Co., Ariz.	Havasupai	A.F. Whiting #1047/B4504	10/18–25/40	MNA	Long claw (32.3 cm); white seed. Planted in fields. *halaa' kakivula* (hooked long). Used in basketry
P. parviflora?	Havasupai Canyon, near Navajo Falls, Coconino Co., Ariz.	Havasupai	C.F. Deaver #4454	10/3/53	NAU	White seed, claws up to 17 cm on immature fruit. Not clear if in fields or beyond.
M. parviflora	Wilkerson Ranch, Rawson Creek, 6 mi so. of bishop, Inyo Co., Calif.	Panamint Death Valley, Shonshone	R. Enfield for G. Smith	3/14/64	San Bernardino Co. Museum	White seed, claws 25.5 cm. "The Hunters & Buttons cultivated this black-seeded (sic) annual in their gardens."
P. parviflora	Seed from Kitt Peak, Papago Indian Reservation, Pima Co., Ariz.	Papago	Vorsila Bohrer #1257, 1258	10/27/67	ARIZ	"White seed; flowers white with purple spot." (Claws 15.5–25.5 cm).
Proboscidea	Little Tucson, Papago Indian Reservation, Pima Co., Ariz.	Papago E-74	Wetmore Dodge	to 12.38	ASM	"Cultivated e'hook. The soft variety is white. A white seed is called s-moik . . ." (claw 27 cm; white seeds).
P. parviflora	Fresnal, Papago Indian Reservation, Pima Co., Ariz.	Papago #7916	R.H. Peebles		ARIZ	"Flowers light purple . . . Papago name 'Ee' kuk.' Used in basketry." (White seed, claw 21 cm).
Proboscidea	Pozo Verde, Sonora, Mexico	Papago	Edmund Faubert #54–30, 31	11/19–28/74	CRN, INAH	(White seed, claw 18 cm.)

?=Some doubt as to identification due to lack of field notes, or poor quality of specimen.

TABLE 4b. Our collections of culturally utilized devil's claw in herbaria.

Proposed Status	Locality	Culture	Collector & #	Date	Herb	Suggestive Characteristics
Wild	Oraibi, Navajo Co., Ariz. 5,675 ft.	Hopi	Whiting 854.B2851	9/14/37	MNA	Immature. Roadside. Tolerated weed when in fields. Used in Kachinas, for awls; associated with lightning and rain bringing. *tumo ala.*
Domesticate	Supai Village, Coconino Co., Ariz. 5,600 ft.	Havasupai	Whiting 1047/B4505	10/18–25/40	MNA	Long claws, white seed. Planted in fields. halaa kakiyula-(hooked long). Used in basketry.
Wild	Supai Village, Coconino Co., Ariz. 5,600 ft.	Havasupai	Whiting 1047/B4504	10/18–25/40	MNA	Short claw, black seed. Wild in fields and waste places near the village. Tolerated when self-seeded in fields. Used in basketry.
Domesticate	Clarksdale, Yavapai Co., Ariz. 3,400 ft. Seed grown in Cornville	Apache	Whiting 3099/B24, 344 and 3099/B24, 311	6/19/76, 6/21/76	MNA	Seedlings cultivated from white-gray seed. Cultivated in Clarkdale for basketry fiber.
Domesticate	Supai Village, Coconino Co., Ariz. 5,600 ft. Seed grown in Cornville	Havasupai	Whiting 3099/B24, 343 from R.E. Euler	7/23/76	MNA	White seed, low claws. Cultivated in Supai for basketry fiber.
Domesticate	Topowa, Pima Co., Ariz. 2,474 ft.	Papago	Bretting and Nabhan x465	8/14/76	ARIZ	Volunteer in garden with squash, being watered to produce fiber for basketry. Pale flower. Large leaves.
Domesticate	Anegam, Pima Co., Ariz. 2,400–3,000 ft.	Papago	Bretting and Nebhan x467	8/14/76	ARIZ	White seed, long claws, pale flowers. Planted and irrigated in dooryard garden; also volunteers watered and tolerated in watermelon patch. Grown to sell to basketmakers.
Domesticate	Chiawuli Tak, Pima Co., Ariz. ca 2,500 ft.	Papago	Nabhan x526B	10/1/76	ARIZ	Cultivated annual up to .8 cm tall x 1.5 m diam. White seeds, claws 24 cm. Corolla color variable in population. Grown in 15 x 15 m patches in rainwater-fed field. *I-hug.*
Domesticate	Coolidge-Gila River Reservation area, Pinal Co., Ariz. Seed grown in Tucson	Pima	Nabhan 585	7/26/76	ARIZ	Corolla white, with purple on lobes, seed white, leaf 22 x 16 cm. Cultivated for basketry fiber by Gila Pima.
Domesticate	Komatke, Maricopa Co., Ariz. 1,040 ft. Seed grown in Tucson	Pima	Nibhan 584	8/1/76	ARIZ	Corolla white, with purple on lobes, claws 24 cm, seed white, leaf 16 x 16cm. Cultivar grown for basketry in "old fields."
Domesticate & cultivated wild	San Simon, near Tracy, Pima Co., Ariz.	Papago	Nibhan x534	10/76	ARIZ	Both long clawed (18 cm) white seeded race and black seeded "wild type" (13.5) cultivated in garden behind house. Irrigated. Grown to sell as basketry fiber.
Wild	Santa Rosa, Pima Co., Ariz.	Papago	Nabhan x535	10/76	ARIZ	Wild plant .4 m tall, claws 14 cm avg., black seed. In Santa Rosa wash.
Feral Domesticate?	Santa Rosa, Pima Co., Ariz.	Papago	Nabhan x569	10/76	ARIZ	White and gray seed in claws 12.5 cm avg. On semi-erect plant in roadside disturbance area with *Cucurbitas* and *Amaranthus*. Presumed to be feral or genetically influenced by domesticates grown nearby.

TABLE 4b. Our collections of culturally utilized devil's claw in herbaria. (continued)

Proposed Status	Locality	Culture	Collector & #	Date	Herb	Suggestive Characteristics
Wild	Santa Rosa, Pima Co., Ariz.	Papago	Nabhan x570	11/76	ARIZ	Dark seed, claws 27 cm avg., wild plant 100 m from closest houseyard (where domesticate is grown). In depression on side of dirt road.
Wild	Supai Village, Coconino Co., Ariz., 5,600 ft. Seed grown in Tucson	Havasupai	Nabhan 584-II from R.C. Euler	8/1/76	ARIZ	Corolla white, claw 17 cm., black seed. Wild around village.
Domesticate	Ak-chin near Maricopa, Pinal Co., Ariz. Seed grown in Tucson	Papago	Nabhan 662 from Fritz & Nabhan 617a	8/5/77	ARIZ	Corolla, pale cream; infl. surpassed to equalling foliage, white seed. Grown in backyard, with watering, for basketry fiber. *E hook.*
Wild?	Blackwater area, Pinal Co., Ariz. 1,400 ft. Seed grown in Tucson	Papago?	Nabhan 663 from 610d	8/5/77	ARIZ	Black seed, 4 carpelled fruit, claws short. Leaves smaller than domesticate, flowers pale, infl. equalling or surpassed by foliage. Produces fruit with 2, 3, and 4 carpels.
Domesticate	Chuichu, Pinal Co., Ariz. 1,400–1,500 ft.	Papago	Nabhan 664 from 568h	8/5/77	ARIZ	Corollas pale cream, infl. surpassed by or equalling foliage, white seed. Grown in yard for basketry fiber. *E hook.*
Black seeded incipient domesticate	Cibecue, Navajo Co., Ariz. 4,940 ft.	Cibecue Apache Apache	Nabhan 665	8/9/77	ARIZ	Corollas pale, claws extremely long, seeds black. Apaches report white seeds in population too. Apparently some grown, some weeds. In field with maize, beans, sunflowers. Used in basketry.
Wild	Below Old Oraibi, Navajo Co., Ariz. 5,400 ft.	Hopi	Nabhan 1035	8/15/78	ARIZ	Apparent agrestal volunteer in sandy plowed field of cucurbits, below mesa. Short claws, black seeds.
Wild?	5 mi. east of Cibecue, Navajo Co., Ariz. 6,600 ft.	Apache	Nabhan 1032	8/12/78	ARIZ	Apparent volunteer in dry farmed cornfield; not seen in surrounding wild lands. Immature seedlings; synaptospermous from old fruit.
Domesticate	San Carlos, Gila Co., Ariz. 5,300 ft.	Papago	Nabhan 1031, 1007 / Nabhan 1007	8/12/78; 7/16/78 / 7/16/78	ARIZ / ARIZ	Dooryard garden, intentionally cultivated. Plants .7 m tall, large leaves, pale flowers, prolific. Used in basketry.
Domesticate	Little Tucson, Pima Co., Ariz. 2,400 ft.	Papago	Nabhan 863b	8/4/78	ARIZ	Dooryard garden. Pale flowers, large fruit. Plants .5 m tall. *I-hug.*
Wild	Whiteriver, Navajo Co., Ariz. 5,300 ft.	Apache	Nabhan 1013	7/17/78	ARIZ	Apparent volunteers in maize and beanfield, 312 plants in 50 m. Black seeds, short claws. Harvested for fiber.
Wild	San Carlos, Gila Co., Ariz. 5,300 ft.	Apache	Nabhan 1005	7/16/78	ARIZ	Roadside by field, volunteer weed. 30 cm tall, 1.3 m across. 1mm fruit, pale flowers.
Wild	San Carlos, Gila Co. Ariz. 5,300 ft.	Apache	Nabhan 1006	7/16/78	ARIZ	Volunteer, thick, weedy patch in maize field. Pale flowers, black seed.
Wild	Fresnal Village (Chiwuli Tak) Pima Co., Ariz. 2,500 ft.	Papago	Nabhan 705	9/11/78	ARIZ	Volunteer in fallow field. Red-purple to cream flowers, black seeds. 15–45 cm tall.

Category	Location	Collection	People	Date	Herbarium	Notes
Domesticate	Supai Village, Coconino Co., Ariz. 5,600 ft.	Nabhan 899	Havasupai	8/22/78	ARIZ	In plowed field. Flowers unusually pale. Fruit immature. Used in basketry. Plant 1.5 m tall x 2 m across *Halak(a)*
Wild	Supai Village, Coconino Co., Ariz. 5,600 ft.	Nabhan 889	Havasupai	8/19/78	ARIZ	Diversion-irrigated field. Plants 1 m tall, black seeds, smaller fruit than domesticate in mixed patch of both races.
Domesticate	Supai Village, Coconino Co., Ariz. 5,600 ft.	Nebhan 890	Havasupai	8/19/78	ARIZ	Diversion-irrigated field. Plants 1–1.5 m tall, white seeds, claws as much as 30 cm. In mixed patch of both races.
Wild?	Supai Village, Coconino Co., Ariz. 5,600 ft.	Nabhan 900	Havasupai	8/20/78	ARIZ	In plowed field. White corolla with purple and yellow. Fruit immature. Plant 1.5 m tall x 2 m across. Apparently feral and protected. Used in basketry. *Halak(a)*
Feral Domesticate?	Peach Springs, Mohave Co., 4,800 ft.	Nabhan 904	Havasupai, Walapai	8/21/78	ARIZ	Immature seedling feral in yard of Sarah Cook, Havasupai basketmaster among the Walapai. Probably volunteer from fruit brought up from Supai.
Feral Domesticate?	Lower Moenkopi, Coconino Co., Ariz. 4,777 ft.	Nabhan 884	Hopi	8/15/78	ARIZ	River diversion bean and melon field. Agrestal or protected plant, apparently not intentionally sown. Plants 1.5 m across, large fruit, white seeds, leaves 25 x 23 cm. Used by Hopi woman making Paiute baskets. *Tumoala.*
Feral Domesticate?	Lower Moenkopi, Navajo Co., Ariz. 4,777 ft.	Nabhan 1102	Hopi	8/23/79	ARIZ	Not intentionally planted. Scattered in tepary plot. Plants 4 m tall, 1.7 m across. White seed.; claw 36 cm, body 11 cm.
Feral Domesticate	Kaibab, Mohave Co., Ariz. ca. 4,600 ft.	Nabhan 1106	Kaibab So. Paiute	8/24/79	ARIZ	Volunteering plants in partially cultivated, irrigated field. Plants .35 m tall. White seed, claw 20.8 cm, body 9.9 cm.
Feral Domesticate or wild?	Shivwits to Irving Rd., Washington Co., Utah, ca. 4,000 ft.	Nabhan 1113	Paiute? or none	8/25/79	ARIZ	Volunteering plants in meadow/field, scattered. Plants 1 m tall. 2.2 m across. White seed, claw 36 cm long.
Wild under Cultivation	Shivwits, Washington Co. Utah ca. 4,000 ft.	Nabhan 1114	Shivwits So. Paiute	8/25/79	ARIZ	Apparently intentionally cultivated. Plants up to .7 m tall. Black seed, claw 18 cm long.
Domesticate	Shivwits, Washington Co., Utah ca. 4,000 ft.	Nebhan 1115	Shivwits So. Paiute	8/25/79	ARIZ	Cultivated and tended, in tomato field. Plants .5 m tall, 2 m across. White seed, claw 23 cm long.
Wild	Fort McDowell, Maricopa Co., Ariz. 1,400 ft.	Nabhan 1021	Yavapai (& Apache?)	7/24/78	ARIZ	Roadside near field. Black seeds, claw 20 cm. Plants 30 cm tall. *Helagah.*
Wild	2 mi west of Casa Blanca, Pinal Co., Ariz. ca. 1,200 ft.	Nabhan 1018	Pima	7/24/78	ARIZ	Ruderal weed between road and cottonfield. Plants .5 m tall, 1 m across. Black seeds.
Wild	Middle Verde, Yavapai Co., Ariz., ca. 3,200 ft.	Nabhan 1025	Yavapai-Apache	7/25/78	ARIZ	Tolerated agrestal weed in irrigated, mixed crop field. Flowers dark pink and purple. Fruit moderately long with black seeds.
Domesticate	Queen's Well, Pima Co., Ariz. ca. 2,500 ft.	Nabhan 1029	Papago	8/1/79	ARIZ	Hand irrigated dooryard garden. Pale flowers, immature plants. White seed obtained from owners. Fruit used as basketry fiber. *I-hug.*

We feel that with the limited data which Yarnell had available, it would be difficult to refute 2 arguments against his conclusion: 1) How do we know that the white
seeded variety is not another "wild" species of devil's claw imported into the area,
which is cultivated while the other indigenous species are not? 2) How do we know that
cultivation practices alone do not result in the longer, finer claws? Could the white seed
color be due to the early harvesting of cultivated fruits, which would keep the seed
from ripening to a black color? Thus, is it the treatment of the plants rather than distinct
genetic material due to domestication which account for the apparent differences?

Additionally, we have discovered that Castetter and Bell's "clean" correlation
of white seeds with agricultural fields, and black seeds with "wild" environments
does not hold true in Pima-Papago country (Table 5). We have located several fields
and gardens where Indians are propagating black seeds, and have also found white
seeded fruit on plants growing away from fields, although always within Papago
rancherias.

We therefore doubt that Yarnell's inductive reasoning that *Proboscidea parviflora* must be domesticated has really settled the matter. His contribution is, on the
other hand, that he has brought the suggestion of domestication of a native arid land
plant to the attention of a wider audience. We would like to answer his challenge, by
providing a methodology for evaluating whether devil's claw, or any other plant, has
been domesticated.

TABLE 5. A comparison of relative association with man-made habitats of two races of
Proboscidea parviflora.

Habitat	Wild Race Black Seeds	Domesticates White Seeds
A. Undisturbed or protected range	N=23	N=18
B. Minimally-managed & grazed range or desens	+	
C. Overgrazed & manipulated range	+	
D. Floodplains	13%	+
E. Riverbeds & arroyo channels	17.3%	5.5%
F. Managed meadows & corrals	4.3%	
G. Roadsides, paths & cleared areas	30.1%	11%
H. Abandoned fields	4.3%	5.5%
I. Dumps, houseyards (uncultivated) & plant-processing areas	4.3%	11%
J. Cultivated *temporal* (runoff) fields	13%	5.5%
K. Cultivaled irrigated fields	+	5.5%
L. Cultivaled (kitchen) gardens	13%	55%

(Documentation from specimens collected in Pimeria Alta: southern Arizona and northern
Sonora. Method based on index for comparing weediness in related plant taxa (Hart 1976).
"+" indicates lack of specimen, but valid observation.)

Domestication: Definitions and Testable Principles

In using the term *cultivated plant,* people often confuse the process of cultivation (i.e., planting, and tending plants and their environment) with the status of the plant itself. By the plant's status, we mean whether or not its genotype is different from the genotype of plants growing in the wild. A propagated plant may have the same genotype as untended plants in the wild, even though the conditions in a garden environment may influence its phenotype so that it appears different. When the genotype is different due to direct human influences, the plant is often termed a cultivated (or better), domesticated plant.

In order for us to consider the status of devil's claw, it is necessary to be more specific about our use of the term *domesticate.* Indeed, there are numerous definitions and descriptions of what a domesticated plant is (Table 6). Utilizing different definitions, one might actually come to conflicting conclusions regarding which of the world's plants are domesticated.

As a foundation for our study, we will use the explanation offered by Harlan (1975: 63–61): "In the case of domesticated plants and animals, we mean that they have been altered genetically from their wild state and have come to be at home with man. Since domestication is an evolutionary process, there will be found all degrees of plant and animal association with man and a range of morphological differentiation from forms identical to wild races to fully domesticated races. A fully domesticated plant or animal is completely dependent upon man for survival. Therefore, domestication implies a change in ecological adaptation, and this is usually associated with morphological differentiation."

To this basic explanation, it must be added that the intended human influences such as selection of desirable characteristics are joined by "accidental" or indirect selective pressures (Baker 1972: 32). The most significant indirect human influence is the modification of environments, particularly the maintenance of agricultural environments, where plants then undergo "natural" selection.

This process of natural selection in and adaptation to agricultural environments may begin before the plants are actually cultivated. Whitaker and Bemis (1975: 367–368) point out that plants adapted to disturbed soils may rapidly increase their geographic ranges by following man and his edaphic disturbance; this in turn affects their genetic variabilities. They hypothesize that certain cultigens evolved a high degree of dependence upon manmade conditions, as well as numerous potentially useful characteristics, before humans began to cultivate and directly select these characteristics.

Because so many economic characteristics of domesticated plants can develop without direct human selection, and are in fact common in agricultural weeds, we must be cautious in utilizing these characteristics as indicators of domestication. Thus the presence of any subset of indicative features in a plant cannot "prove" in itself that domestication had occurred. The data must be viewed within the context of plant's natural history and use, known instances of selection, and other factors. Otherwise, we may be contrasting a weedy race of a species with a less opportunistic race in a manner in which the weedy race appears to be a domesticate.

TABLE 6. Domestication: Alternative definitions and explanations.

Quotation	Citation
"domestication . . . complete and regular reproduction of the species through more or less controlled and selective breeding in the company of man.	Meggitt 1965:23
. . . the crucial feature of domestication is man's control over the breeding of his domesticates. He improves his crops by sowing only selected seeds . . .	Watson and Watson 1971:5
Domestication implies that the plants or animals have been manipulated to such an extent that genetic changes have occurred resulting in new races of species . . . Cultivation, with the attendant element of human selectivity, conscious or unconscious, frequently results in genetic changes. Even so, there will be an intermediate stage where plants are sown and harvested but show no morphological changes. Helbaek . . . has therefore distinguished between 'cultivated' plants that have been sown and harvested but show no morphological alternations, and 'domesticated' plants where morphological change has occurred.	Bender 1975:1.52
. . . domesticates show both intended and accidental results from human actions, including selection.	Baker 1972:32
The stages of domestication are as follows: a) loose contacts, with free breeding. b) confinement to human environment, with breeding in captivity. c) selective breeding organized by man, to obtain certain characteristics, and occasional crossing with wild forms. d) economic considerations of man leading to the planned 'development' of breeds with certain desirable properties. e) wild ancestors persecuted or exterminated.	Zeuner 1963:63
The cultivated plant never originates directly from the wild species, in perfect form, but evolves step by step over a long period of time. The farther it has come along, that is, the earlier it was taken under cultivation or the more intensely bred and selected, the fewer wild characters will be found in it . . . Their occurrence [wild-plant characters] in cultivated plants must thus be taken as a sign that a plant has not yet completed its evolution from a wild species to a cultivated plant.	Schwanitz 1966:63
The most immediately apparent change under domestication is in morphological characters such as size, shape and color, particularly of the part of the plant used by man . . . Up until now, crop plants have not evolved by any processes different from those operating in wild plants. The ultimate source of variability is mutation . . . The new forms produced are then subject to selection, but in crop plants new variants have to pass the test of human selection as well as, or sometimes instead of, natural selection.	Pickersgill and Heiser 1976:55

Nevertheless, we have gleaned from the literature a number of morphological and ecological characteristics which commonly change through the process of domesticating a plant (Table 7). Hypothesizing that these changes would occur in any *Proboscidea* if domesticated, we can use these indicators to examine the "real life situation." Individual characteristics which may be found in any useful plant, wild or cultivated, or in weeds, will be interpreted in light of these other possibilities.

We have made 2 major assumptions in applying these indicators to the problem of possible *Proboscidea* domestication. We have assumed that if devil's claw has been domesticated, the process increased the quantity or quality of the products which have been most pervasively and intensively utilized—the fiber in the dried fruit, and the seed. Thus we hypothesize that devil's claw was domesticated either for basketry material, for a food product, or for both, and not for other reasons: its value as an ornamental or religious item, the use of the young fruit as a vegetable, etc.

Secondly, we have decided to compare the white seeded, supposedly longer clawed devil's claw cultivated by Southwest Indians with the 3 most common annual *Proboscidea* in the Southwest. In particular, most of our quantitative comparisons are with wild *Probosicidea parviflora,* as it occurs in Arizona spontaneously, and when brought into cultivation.

In doing so, we have ruled out that the annual white seeded devil's claw 1) belongs in another genus; 2) is more closely related to *Proboscidea* perennials in either subgenus; 3) is more closely related to other annual *Proboscidea* in the Southwest, or elsewhere.

Our emphasis on comparison with Arizona populations of *Proboscidea parviflora* is in part due to logistics, since that material is more readily available to us. However, Table 1 makes evident that the white seeded devil's claw is more phenetically similar to wild *P. parviflora* than to *P. fragrans* or *P. louisianica,* as we understand these taxa today. Further more, Yarnell's suggestion that the white seeded devil's claw is a *Proboscidea parviflora* cultigen warrants our most critical attention. We will nevertheless note similarities to *P. louisianica* and *P. fragrans* whenever possible, and allow as an alternative hypothesis the development of the white seeded devil's claw from interspecific hybridization or introgression (Fig. 3).

Finally, following Harlan and DeWet (1971: 509–517), we will avoid using the terms variety, cultivar, line, strain, type, or kind for the rest of the discussion, due to their indiscriminate use in the past. The "white seeded race" of *Proboscidea* is now referred to as *P. parviflora* var. *hohokamiana.* Also, for the purposes of brevity, we will refer to all black seeded *P. parviflora* as the *P. parviflora* spontaneous race, even though there may conceivably be domesticated or weedy black seeded races which we are ignorantly lumping into this one category. We will also refer to the spontaneous race as wild or typical black seeded *P. parviflora* var. *parviflora.*

Skewed Distributional Range

The geographic range and ecological niche which the white seeded race occupy should be regarded in light of the distribution of wild *Proboscidea* in general. Yet it

TABLE 7. General trends in plant domestication, in reference to devil's claw.

Feature	Apparent difference in white seeded race	Should change if domesticated for seed for fiber	Change possibly due to deliberate human selection	Change possibly to selective pressures associated with harvest	Change possibly due to selective pressures in cultivated environment	General trend in domestication process discussed in
Disproportionate enlargement of desired plant produce	X	?	X		X	Schwanitz 1966:30; Baker 1972:32; Harlan 1975:137
Increase in leaf size	X	X			X	Schwanitz 1966:14, 21
Increase in size of other parts	X	X			X	Schwanitz 1966:14, 28
More determinate growth habit		X	X	X	X	Harlan 1975:137; Baker 1972:33
Change in color of product	X	X	X			Harlan 1975:138; Yarnell 1977
Change in texture of product	X		X			Harlan 1975:138
Change in protein/carbohydrate ratio (usually a decrease)	?	X	X		X	Harlan 1975:127, 131
Reduced toxicity of edible parts						Baker 1972:33; Schwanitz 1966:28–42
Loss of differential dormancy (or of germination-delaying mechanisms)	X	X	X		X	Baker 1972:34; Harlan 1975:132; Schwanitz 1966:43
More uniform maturation, more simultaneity in ripening						Schwanitz 1966:44; Harlan 1975:127
Difference in life span	?			X	X	Schwanitz 1966:44–44
Greater yield of desired produce	X	X	X		X	Schwanitz 1966:29; Baker 1972:34
Loss of natural seed dispersal mechanisms, or of synaptospermy		X	X	X	X	Schwanitz 1966:32; Baker 1972:34; Pickersgill and Heiser 1976:60
Greater frequency of unusual variants surviving	?	X	X		X	Harlan 1975:138; Pickersgill and Heiser 1976:60
"Bottleneck effect" in overall genetic variability	X	X	X		X	Pickersgill and Heiser 1976:60–61

is somewhat difficult to determine the "natural" distributional range of annual *Proboscidea* spp. in the Southwest. Whereas there are "core geographical areas" where each species is commonly found (Table 1), the intrinsic dispersibility of their fruit has allowed them to be transported by animals (including man) to many isolated localities far away from these cores.

Large native herbivores undoubtedly participated in the long distance dispersal of devil's claw to disjunct localities even before man and his domesticated animals became involved in this process. Natural historians have described the shape of devil's claw fruit as one ideally adapted to catching and persisting in the fetlocks of ungulates. They have hypothesized that this mechanism was responsible for the dispersal of *P. louisianica* to South Africa, and to a locality in Great Britain (Bancroft 1932: 62–64).

The habitats which annual devil's claw frequent are often corridors which allow further geographical extension of their range by animal, water or wind transport The habitat preferences of the 3 species of annual *Proboscidea* indicate adaptation to sporadically disturbed soils, particularly the sandy loams of floodplains and gravels of roadsides. Historic human modification of Southwestern floodplain environments, particularly through agriculture and road-building may have dramatically altered distributions from prehistoric times. Additionally, such modification maintains niches with disturbed soil where deliberately transported plants such as *P. louisianica* in the Palm Springs area, can establish themselves after escaping from cultivation (Robbins 1940: 86).

Although the distribution of the *P. fragrans, P. louisianica* and *P. parviflora* remain problematic, the range of the white seeded race is nevertheless peculiarly skewed in relation to them: 1) it is highly specific to the *rancherias* of native peoples of the Southwest's true deserts and nearby uplands. 2) It appears to extend northwest beyond where annual *Proboscidea* is commonly found in the wild in northern Arizona, southeastern California, and southern Nevada. 3) Its range overlaps to the greatest extent with the range of *P. parviflora*.

Today, the black seeded annual *Proboscidea* are strongly associated with man-disturbed environments, yet the degree of association is even higher for the white seeded race. A survey of annual *Proboscidea* specimens collected in one particular area—the aboriginal territory of Northern Piman groups in Arizona and Sonora—illustrates this point (Table 5). All available seed or herbaria specimens with detailed habitat notes were utilized to compare the location of the white seeded race and spontaneous *P. parviflora*, regardless of whether or not they were cultivated in those locations.

Although the presence of *P. parviflora* in fields and on pathways around human settlements indicates weediness and dependence on human disturbance, it ranges beyond these habitats to a greater extent that the white seeded race does. Beyond culti-vated fields and yards, the white seeded race has only been collected within distur-bance habitats in *rancherias*.

Although it is not possible to prove that all these plants are recent "escapes" from cultivation, subjective information suggests that the plants are feral cultivates. Papago informants have volunteered that white seeded plants growing in their yards "planted themselves" from seed that blew over from nearby devil's claw processing areas (see

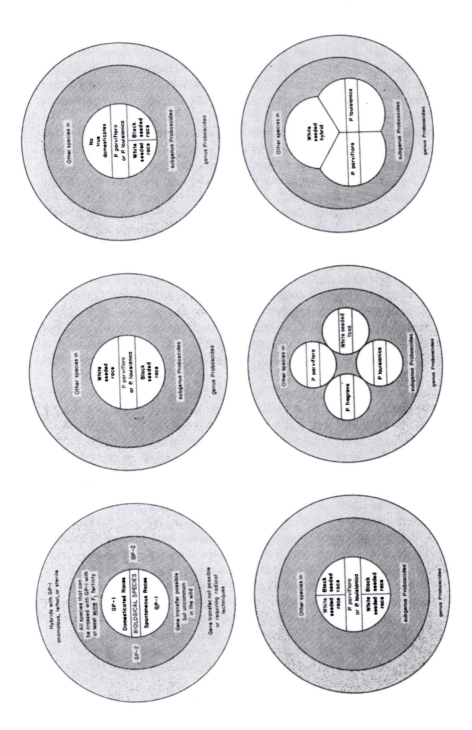

Fig. 3. Alternative hypotheses for gene pool relationships to the domesticate. Legend in upper left follows Harlan (1975).

Table 8, for processing site explanations). In both cases, large stands of the white seeded race were cultivated within the rancheria.

If the white seeded race were domesticated from *P. parviflora*, it is possible that the status of black seeded races as agricultural weeds played an intermediate role in this process. Since black seeded *P. parviflora* is considered a tolerated weed in fields beyond the range of devil's claw cultivation today—among the Hopi and Apache in Arizona (Whiting 1939: 92 and Anonymous 1976), and among mestizos in eastern Sonora—it is doubtful that in this case a weed race evolved as a result of introgression between domesticated and spontaneous races (see Harlan 1965: 173–176).

Finally, the white seeded race, because it can grow without intentional planting by man, is not an obligatory cultivate or cultigen. According to Harlan's definition, it cannot be a fully domesticated plant in the strict sense, since it can survive to some extent without direct dependence on man.

Seed Characteristics

If domesticated for the food value of its seed, devil's claw should have undergone changes in several of a number of characteristics, including a) number of seed per fruit; b) seed size; c) change in the nutritive value of the seed; d) change in seed coat color or texture; e) change in seed dispersal pattern; and f) loss of germination-delaying mechanisms. Several of these characteristics might also be affected if devil's claw was domesticated for the fiber in its fruit, particularly c, e and f.

We compared the number of seed per fruit in the white seeded race (n=69, from 4 populations), with the number in black seeded *P. parviflora* (n=50, from 3 populations), there is no statistical difference at the .05 level for the 53.0 + 9.8 seed per fruit of the white seeded race, and the 53.9 + 8.3 seed per fruit of the black seeded race.

These sample sizes are relatively small, and the populations analyzed do not allow considerations of variation within the region. From these data alone, however, it is apparent that there are no major differences in the seed number of the 2 kinds of fruit. We will therefore assume that the number of seed per fruit in the white seeded race has probably not been determined by deliberate human selection, or modified by selective pressures associated with cultivation and harvest.

In terms of seed size, the 3 annual species of *Proboscidea* with which we are concerned, all fall within the general range of 7–11 mm long x 4–6 mm wide x 2–4 mm thick. Size of a particular seed is affected by its place in the ovary, as well as by maturity of the fruit and other factors. Size variation within a fruit is considerable.

We measured seed sizes of all seed in only 2 average-sized fruit of the white seed race, and 2 averaged sized fruit of black seeded *P. parviflora*, grown in the same irrigated field. Mean sizes and ranges at one standard deviation are given in Table 1. These data suggest a slightly greater volume of the white seeds, but without a substantial sample, we will refrain from further speculation. A severalfold difference in seed volume, such as that between domesticated beans and their wild progenitors, is nevertheless not evident with these devil's claw.

TABLE 8. Behavioral chain for Pima and Papago use of devil's claw.

Purpose	Activities	Materials Correlates	Time/Frequency	Location	Wastes
To insure supply of fruit for processing	Broadcast or plant seed in holes 5 cm; clear weeds in 2 m circle around hole	Hoe or dibble stick; brush	May or later	Floodplain or garden	Weeds
	Find wild population nearby on floodplain & protect		Before first frost	In field or in wild	Unusable fruit (too small or deformed)
To acquire fruit when still pliant & prior to weathering	Harvest green fruit when claw tips become sharp				
To keep fruit pliant	Pile green fruit in sun, cover with ash, let dry (Papago); Soak in pottery bowl (Pima)	Ashes, or water and containers	Usually fall, for a week	Fieldside or by house	Ashes
To straighten & keep usable fruit for future use	Husk fruit of remnant epidermis; hook dried fruit into hoop		After drying	Same	Husked epidermis & broken fruit
To preserve for later use	Hang or cover hoop	Twine or cover	Fall & after	Under ramada	
To soften & ready dried fruit for splint-making	Unhook small number of claws; bury in sand & drench; Unhook desired number of claws; soak in bowl	Bowl or bucker; water	As needed, overnight or 2 days	Near house	
To strip splints of fibers from fruit	Slit claw tip with awl, & run awl under fiber. Peel 2 fiber splints off with teeth, from tip to claw/body transition	Awl or knife, teeth	After soaking	Ramada work area	Imperfect, torn splints
To store splints for future use	Bind splints into a bundle	Twine	While stripping	Same	Splinted, deseeded fruit
To thresh seeds from splinted fruit	Beat with stick & pry open	Stick fingers	Anytime	Near house	Seedcoats
To eat seeds (snack)	Crack seedcoat	Teeth	Anytime	Same	
To ready splints for immediate use	Scrape with knife and/or rock tool; soak in bowl	Bowl & water	As needed	House or ramada	Splint scrapings, rock tool
To tape splint for use	Pull splint through hole in can (after 1918)	Tin can or rock, & knife	Just prior to use in basket	House or ramada work area	Snipped splint remains
To work splints into basket design	Cross under previous splint, wrap around rod, snip off or tuck under where design ends	Awl, pick or knife	As needed	Same	

In terms of nutritive value, *Proboscidea* seed are non-toxic with high oil and protein content. Because of interest in the 1950s in developing devil's claw into a commercial oil seed, numerous chemurgic analyses of Southwestern *Proboscidea* were undertaken. After compiling protein and oil values in the literature (Earle and Jones 1962: 245; Ghosh and Beal 1979: 748), we see that the seed of Southwest annuals normally range between 35–43% oil, and 20–35% protein.

Two acquisitions of the white seeded race and one of the black seeded *P. parviflora*, grown in the same irrigated field in 1976, have been analyzed by nutritional biochemist Dr. James Berry. The white seeds cultivated by the Pima contained 40.3% oil and 25.5% protein, values remarkably high for *Proboscidea*. The white seeded race cultivated by the Havasupai, and the black seeded race originally growing wild in their area yielded 39.2% and 38.3% oil, plus 23.9% and 23.2% protein respectively (Barry et al. in press). Thus the white seeds apparently have a slightly higher nutritional content that black seeded *P. parviflora*, or at least they are at the high end of the range for *Proboscidea*. It is possible that selective pressures in the cultivated environment, or deliberate human selection for the fruit or seed have resulted in relatively more energy being funnelled into these reproductive parts of the plant.

We mentioned earlier that the white-gray seed coat of the commonly cultivated race is atypical for the genus *Proboscidea*. In analogy, Yarnell (1977) has pointed out that lighter colored seed distinguishes domesticated *Amaranthus* from its wild progenitors. In devil's claw, it can either be hypothesized that 1) natives found this character in the wild, and brought it into cultivation; 2) it was expressed after selective pressures associated with harvesting were initiated, or 3) it is a function of the greater frequency of variants, including recessives, which survive in cultivated environments.

It is probable that the lighter color is determined by one or a few major genes, i.e., it is a quantitative character. A crossing program to determine the inheritance of characters such as this is now in progress (Peter Bretting, personal communication). Seed coat morphology study by electron microscope has not yet identified any differences between races.

In terms of seed dispersal, Sappenfield (1954: 1) has calculated that approximately 10% of wild *Proboscidea* seed "shatter," or drop as the fruit dry and the claws split and curl. From our simple observations, we estimate that roughly 4–12% of the fruit's total seed are released as the white seeded fruit begins to dehisce. In spite of these crude estimates, we doubt that there are major differences in the seed dispersal of the various races and species. Certainly, there is not a dramatic difference in fruit dehiscence as there is between wild and domesticated legumes (Harlan 1975: 138–139).

Germination delaying mechanisms in wild *Proboscidea* include 1) germination inhibitors of the seed and 2) the leathery-textured ovary walls behind which the seed are trapped unless the fruit is physically torn apart. Through differential dormacy wild *Proboscidea* spp. avoid "putting all their eggs in one basket"; the proverbial basket here being the unpredictable moisture conditions of the Southwest.

Anderson (1968: 171) has determined that the germination inhibitors in wild *Proboscidea* include a) seed coat thickness; b) a water soluble chemical inhibitor in the seed coat; and c) a dark requirement, or light sensitivity factor in the embryo. Because of these inhibitors, agronomists have had difficulties getting good field germination with wild *Proboscidea* brought into cultivation (Quinones, personal communication).

Our attempts at utilizing a standard laboratory test to determine possible differences in rate and per cent of germination were somewhat unsatisfactory. At 85° and then at 90°F, we obtained 40% germination in one sample of the white seeded race, but there was no germination of one other sample of white seeds, and 2 samples of black seeded *P. parviflora* (n-25, at each temperature).

Our field plot observations indicate some difference in per cent emergence under irrigated conditions. In 1977, one month after an April 21 planting, 65% of the white seed had emerged (n=55, from 9 acquisitions) and 16% of the black seed of 2 P. parviflora had emerged (N#25, from 4 acquisitions).

We suspect that the white-seeded race may have lost at least one of its germination inhibitors, possibly due to long term selective pressures associated with planting seed, and utilizing seed from plants in surviving cultivated populations. Further paired tests are needed to determine a) if field emergence differences are significant for larger sample sizes and b) if an inhibitor which the black seeds have that is possibly absent in the white seeds can be isolated. We doubt whether other germination delaying mechanisms, such as the persistance of seed behind the placentae walls, are different for the white seeded race.

Floral Morphology and Ecology

Flower size, shape and color are characters which are sometimes altered indirectly through human selection for the economic products of a plant. If a plant, through domestication, comes to produce fruit much larger than that of its wild progenitors, the calyx size may be increased too in order to accommodate the fruit. Or often, linkages affect several characters at once, so that a flower color may increase in frequency in a population, due to its genic association with a selected character. On the other hand, overall floral design is fairly conservative, and within a species is little affected by short term selective pressures.

In addition, floral ecology is certainly affected by cultivation and domestication. For instance, in South America, where wild and domesticated tomatoes originate, they are predominately cross-pollinated by insects; when taken beyond the range of their pollination agents, they have evolved into a self pollinating plant (Rick 1976).

Such ecological factors may eventually work as selective pressures influencing floral characters. A species variable for flower color, dependent upon cross pollination by bees, may swamp bee populations in number when cultivated in large stands. Particularly bright flowers might have a selective advantage over less intense flowers by attracting a greater percentage of the available bees. Depending on the inheritance of flower color, this may influence the frequency of alleles affecting color over time.

In terms of flower size, our data indicate that while cultivation increases the lengths of the corolla, calyx and bracts of black seeded *P. parviflora,* these characters are still considerably longer in the white seeded race. In fact, the white seeded race overlaps in these characters as much or more with *P. fragrans* and *P. louisianica* as with *P. Parviflora.*

Several hypotheses can be proposed to explain this situation: 1) In the white seeded race, floral part sizes reflect a closer affinity with *P. louisianica* or *P. fragrans.* 2) A larger flower size has developed in the white seeded race while being domesticated from *P. parviflora;* the larger size accommodates the larger fruit. 3) It reflects introgression between 2 of the species.

Flower shape in the white seeded race is generally the same as that in *P. parviflora.* Among the largest flowers of the white seeded race, there is a tendency to be slightly more ventricose, though not as much as typical *P. louisianica* and *P. fragrans.* It is noteworthy that a wild, long clawed (32 cm), black seeded specimen collected on the Gila River Indian Reservation at the Pima village of Sacaton had a similar ventricose flower shape (Peebles, Kearney and Harrison #75, ARIZ). In addition, its flowers were mostly purple; because of these characters, Kearney and Peebles (1960: 795) suggested its affinity with *P. fragrans* even though that species is nowhere else in Arizona. Again, does this reflect hybridization between different races or species, or simple introduction? Abberrant flower shapes, including ones with an extra lobe and a wider tube, have been found in low frequencies on plants within cultivated plots of the white seeded race.

Flower color determination in wild annual *Proboscidea* is not well understood. Perry (1942: 43–47) reported that reciprocal crosses between *P. fragrans* and *P. louisianica,* and subsequent backcrosses, indicate that purple flower color dominates white flower color. Perry suggested that color inheritance was due to a single gene.

However, reciprocal crosses between 4 annual *Proboscidea* by Hevly (unpubl. notes) do not substantiate that purple flower color is dominate over white, since F^1 plants were intermediate. F^2 plants tended to have darker flower colors, but the F^2 population size was not large enough to suggest genotypic frequencies.

Most flowers of the white seeded race have similar color patterning and internal ornamentation as wild *P. parviflora;* however, all colors are usually less intense. Often, corolla color is pale cream or white, but we have also seen pink and reddish-purple flowers on white seeded plants on the Papago Reservation. However, these darker flowers were in a population within 50 m of where black seeded *P. parviflora* is cultivated. Does the variability in flower color in this white seeded population reflect the introgression of typical *P. parviflora* in the white seeded race?

We should note that white or pale cream flower color is not specific to the white seeded race; it also occurs in *P. louisianica,* and infrequently in wild *P. parviflora.* It has been suggested that different fruit types—of distinct lengths and shapes—are associated with different flower color types in *P. parviflora* (Paur 1952: 1), but we have noticed no such clear cut relationships. Finally, it is noteworthy that in other floral characters (e.g. corolla ornamentation, filament pubescens, and inflorescence position) the white seeded race is most similar to *P. parviflora.*

The pollination ecology of devil's claw has received an increasing amount of attention in recent years, but the picture is far from complete. Hurd and Linsley (1963: 249–250) reported the apparent cross-pollination of perrenial *Proboscidea altheifolia* by the corolla-cutting bee *Perdita hurdi*. However, their repeated examinations of wild *P. parviflora* flowers failed to show bee visitation for pollen, or a relationship with this bee. Dr. P.H. Timberlake (personal communication) has subsequently become aware of one example of *Perdita hurdi* visitation to annual *Proboscidea* in Mexico. To our knowledge, there are yet no reports of this bee pollinating wild *P. parviflora* in the United States.

Thieret (1976: 175–176) reports the insect visitors, including pollinators, to *P. louisianica* flowers on wild plants in Oklahoma and in his garden in Utah (see Table 1) Preliminary experiments with pollinator exlusion, plus self and cross-pollination, suggest that *P. louisianica* fruits do not develop if pollinators are excluded of if artificially selfed (Thieret 1976: 177). However, other investigators report that hand pollination of *P. louisianica* yields about 50% fruit set regardless of whether plants are self- or cross-pollinated (Moegenson, personal communication; Phillippii, personal communication).

Self-pollination, though still probably not the key pattern in wild populations, may also be effective in black seeded *P. parviflora*. In an experimental cultivated plot in New Mexico, of *P. parviflora* (and other species?), 15% of the 500 inflorescences bagged for self-pollination produced some seed (Anonymous 1953: 16).

Dr. Floyd Werner has identified for us a few of the fairly frequent bee visitors to cultivated plots of the white seeded race (Table 1), but we do not have concrete confirmation of actual pollination by any of these hymenopterids. Most noteworthy is our discovery of *Perdita hurdi* in the flowers of a large, annually planted houseyard plot of the white seeded race at the Papago village of Santa Rosa.

Exclusion experiments and detailed field observations on both Indian-cultivated plots of the white seeded race and black seeded *P. parviflora*, and in spontaneously occurring stands of *P. parviflora*, are needed to determine: 1) Will selfing occur in these populations, and have the selective pressures of cultivation in large stands increased the frequency of selfing in the white seeded race? 2) Is the frequency of visitations by various bee species different in cultivated plots as opposed to spontaneously occurring populations? 3) If *P. hurdi* is in fact pollinating the cultivated white seeded race, but not small stands of *P. parviflora* in the wild, is this due to greater reliability or abundance of reward for the bee, akin to that provided by perennial *Proboscidea*?

Fruit Size and Morphology

Among the features which might be modified, if *Proboscidea* were domesticated for their fruit's fiber, are: a) a disproportionate increase in the fibrous "claw" part of the fruit; b) changes in texture, color and quality of the fiber; c) a greater yield of fruit per plant d) an altered frequency of unusual fruit shapes surviving. If large seed were selected in the domestication process, changes might include a) a disproportionate increase in the seed-holding "body" part of the fruit, where the ovaries are; b) reduction in fruit dehiscence (see seed dispersal discussion); and possibly c and d as above. Additionally, because mean fruit lengths of populations vary within wild *Proboscidea* species ranges, a bottleneck effect might occur, where the wild populations would be more variable than the domesticated populations. The "bottleneck" in variability would be the original selection of germ plasm undergoing domestication from only a small portion of the "available" genetic variability within compatible races of species.

Table 9 indicates that there is significant differences in the claw/body ratios of the fruit of the white seeded race, and typical *P. parviflora,* in the wild and under cultivation. We defined the "claw" and "body" of the fruit in a somewhat arbitrary way, but were consistent in how these features were measured. The claw, as we defined it, is the appendage of the dried fruit from which the Indians derive their fiber splints (Fig. 4).

The 2.5+ claw/body ratio of the white seeded race may not necessarily indicate that a disproportionate increase in the usable part has occurred via domestication. Hevly has noted that in *P. louisianica* fruit, the ratio may vary from 1.5–3 (in Correll and Johnston 1969: 1449), and it is possible that populations of *P. parviflora* and *P. fragrans* unavailable to us may have fruit which have a ratio greater than 2.5. The white-seeded race could have simply been chosen from such wild material, without selective pressures for longer claws being active within the cultivated environment. It is noteworthy that Gila River Pima remember wild populations of *P. parviflora* with exceptionally long claws that are located as much as 150 km away from their present homes. If the white seeded race has had part of its fruit disproportionately enlarged via cultural selection, it appears that selection was for fiber and not for seed-holding capacity.

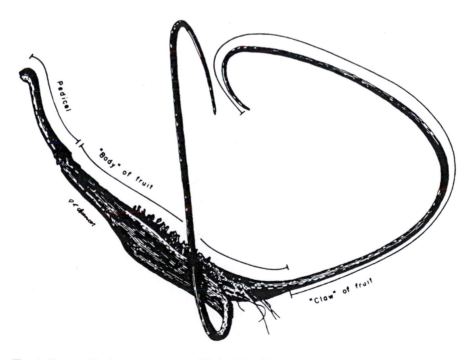

Fig. 4. Claw and body measurements of fruit of devil's claw (drawing by Judy Spencer).

TABLE 9. Claw/Body ratios for the white seeded race and the black seeded P. parviflora.

Seed Source	Locallily Crown	X claw/X body	Sample
White seeded race, cultivated (P. parviflora var. hohokamiana):			
Havasupai Indian	Cornvill	2.99	36
Apache Indian	Cornville	2.59	37
Pima Indian	Tucson	2.59	28
Papago Indian	Topowa	2.84	35
Black seeded race, cultivated by Indians (P. parviflora var. parviflora):			
Papago Indian	Chiawulí Tak	2.32	31
Black seeded race, wild*; or cultivated# (P. parviflora var. parviflora):			
Navajo Indian*	Wupatki	2.34	10
Havasupai Indian#	Tucson	2.21	21
Mestizo, for Papago*	Nogales	2.29	26
Botanists*	Tecoripa	2.21	15

We have measured the claw lengths of populations of the white seeded race, as well as those of typical *P. parviflora*, when a) harvested from the wild and b) grown in irrigated and *temporal* fields (Table 10). Statistical analyses of our data are summarized in Table 11. In the analysis of variance in and between populations of localities with 5 or more fruit of the cultivated white seeded race and wild and culti-vated black seeded *P. parviflora* var. *parviflora*, one or more populations are distinct at the .01 level of significance. Utilizing all localities with one or more fruit, including those of presumably "feral" white seeds, the distinction between popula-tions is still significant. This is due primarily to the extremely high values for the white seeded race under cultivation.

The greatest apparent difference in claw lengths is between the white seeded race when under cultivation, and all the other material measured, cultivated or unculti-vated. The cultivated white seed claws measure 25.3 cm ± 4.3 cm, whereas all other means fall below 20 cm, and the ranges at one standard deviation do not extend above 23 cm.

To better illustrate the relationships between different germ plasm under different treatments, pooled variances were utilized to contrast combinations of these popula-tions. When considered together, the white seeded race is significantly different from each of the black seeded *P. parviflora* treatments at the .01 level of confidence.

The comparison of spontaneously-growing black seeded *P. parviflora* with the black seeds in cultivated treatments is most revealing. The pooled variance analysis shows no significant difference between the uncultivated and cultivated *P. parviflora*. One variable interpretation of this analysis is that cultivation does not dramatically affect claw length of *P. Parviflora*.

TABLE 10. Samples of claw length listed by source and locality.

Locality and Source		Mean (X)	Range (G)	Population (n)
A-	White seeded race cultivated and/or irrigated	25.3 cm	±4.3 cm	249
A-1	Cataract Ganyon #(Havasupai)	26.1	3.9	62
A-2	Cataract Canyon (Havasupai)	25.0	0.7	2
A-3	Cataract Canyon *(Havasupai)	34.0	0.0	1
A-4	Camp Verde *(Apache)	26.9	4.1	36
A-5	Moapa, Nevada (Southern Paiute)	24.3	0.0	1
A-6	Kern Co., California (Tubatulabal)	32.7	0.0	1
A-7	Komatke #(Gila River Pima)	23.2	3.3	52
A-8	Casa Blanca #(Gila River Pima)	22.6	1.6	8
A-9	Blackwater (Gila River Pima)	22.6	2.9	17
A-10	Chuichu (Papago)	25.8	1.8	2
A-11	Santa Rosa (Papago)	22.5	3.7	3
A-12	Covered Wells (Papago)	25.8	0.0	1
A-13	Kitt Peak (Papago)	20.5	3.0	10
A-14	Ali Chukson (Papago)	27.0	0.0	1
A-15	San Simon (Papago)	25.6	3.8	7
A-16	Chiawuli Tak (Papago)	21.0	0.0	1
A-17	Topowa (Papago)	28.2	4.7	40
A-18	Ahegam (Papago)	23.2	0.0	1
A-19	Sells (Papago)	24.1	5.5	3
B-	White seeded race cultivated (feral?)	18.5	3.9	6
B-1	Kaka (Papago)	12.4	0.0	1
B-2	Santa Rosa (Papago)	20.0	1.2	2
B-3	Covered Wells (Papago)	19.4	3.9	3
C-	Black seeded P. parviflora. spontaneous	15.7	4.8	127
C-1	Cataract Canyon (Havasupti)	25.5	0.0	1
C-2	Wupatki (Navajo)	17.4	2.1	10
C-3	Sacaton	32.0	0.0	1
C-4	Sacaton	27.5	0 0	1
C-5	Ventana	14.5	3 3	37
C-6	Ventana	9 0	1.5	7
C-7	Wilcox	18.5	0.0	1
C-8	Rosemont	11.7	4.6	15
C-9	Hereford	13.5	1.6	12
C-10	Agua Prieta, Sonora	17.4	0.0	1
C-11	Nogales (Mestizo for Papago)	20.2	3.3	26
C-12	Tecoripa, Sonora	15.7	3.0	15
D-	Blackseed, cultivated by Indians	19.6	3.1	31
D-1	Chiawuli Tak (Papago)	19.6	3.1	31
E-	Black seed cultivated and/or irrigated	16.5	2.6	148
E-1	Cornville*	17.1	1.6	19
E-2	Sacaton	22.8	1.0	2
E-3	Cataract.Canyon #	15.8	2.5	78
E-4	Tucson #	15.1	1.5	16
E-5	Tucson #	18.3	2.8	17
E-6	Southern Arizona #	17.9	2.6	16

*grown in 1976 in Cornville. Arizona. #grown in 1976 in Tucson, Arizona.

TABLE 11. Statistical evaluation of claw measurements (see Table 10 for identifications of populations A-E).

1. Analysis of variance within and between populations for localities with 5 or more measurements (B is exluded): observed $F_{3,17} = 25.25$; greater than tabular $F_{3,17} = 5.18$. Therefore at least one population is significantly different at the .01 level of confidence.
2. Analysis of variance within and between populations for all localities (B is included): observed $F_{4,36} = 30.12$; greater than tabular $F_{4,36} = 3.58$. Therefore at least one population is different at the .01 level of confidence.
3. Contrast of pooled variance of combined populations via contrast coefficient matrix:
$$(A + B) \text{ vs } (D + E) \text{ - Pooled variance T value} = -1.195$$
Therefore pooled populations not significantly distinct at .01 level of confidence.
4. Contrast of Indian cultivated (d) black seed vs experimentally cultivated (e) black seeded *P. parviflora* (see conclusions . . .):
$$D = 19.55 \pm 1.14 \text{ (SE x T) vs } E = 516.49 \pm 0.41 \text{ (SE x T)}$$
Therefore populations significantly distinct at .05 level of confidence.

In general, these data suggest that claw lengths are more genetically than environmentally determined. The noticeable exception to this general rule is the small size of feral white seeded claws. Yet because of our extremely limited sample of uncultivated white seeded fruit, we hesitate in considering this a major contradiction of the general trend. Until additional data indicate otherwise, we conclude that the white seeded race is genetically different from *P. parviflora* in this economic characteristic, even if there is still gene flow between these taxa.

Table 1 indicates that there are some relative differences in the color, texture and quality of the claws and their fiber. These differences have been pointed out to us by native basketmakers, and will be discussed later. It is possible that these presumably quantitative characters have been gradually modified through cultural selection.

Our data on fruit yield are relatively subjective: we do not yet have good records for all taxa grown under the same conditions. However, we have counted at least 150 ripening fruit on a single plant in a Papago garden at Sells, and project that its yield could easily surpass 200 fruit over the entire growing season. None of the wild seed which we have brought into cultivation have approached this productivity, although several of our white seeded plants yielded at least 80–120 fruit.

There are also little data on the frequency of fruit variants, or mutants, surviving in wild and cultivated populations of *Proboscidea*. However, 3- and 4-clawed fruit are a curiosity readily collected by Pima and Papago basketmakers. They have provided us with a multiple clawed fruit with white seeds, and 2 informants have recalled 3-clawed germ plasm that was supposedly maintained for several generations. We have only come across one 3-clawed black seeded fruit, brought into a Backwater, Arizona trading post by an Indian. Because of the difference in the relative number of cultivated versus wild fruit we have examined, we cannot yet hypothesize whether the statistical frequency of surviving variants is actually higher among cultivated white seeded fruit.

Finally, it is notable that a number of Papago basketmakers volunteer that they "plant only the seeds of the longest ones, because when the plants come up, they make more big devil's claw." In other words, conscious selection for long claws is continuing. The majority of the Papago and Pima who note this selection also associate white seeds with intrinsically larger fruit.

CONCLUSIONS

In evaluating the available biological data in light of the alternative hypotheses presented (Fig 3), we will attempt to answer the following questions: With which established *Proboscidea* taxa does the white seeded race show the greatest affinity? How does it differ from this taxa? Are the differences similar to those between wild species, are they the effects of cultivation, or do they indicate true domestication? If so, what drove the domestication process: selective pressures for food or fiber?

Although the white seeded race has a geographic range which does not fall completely within the range of any of the recognized annual species, it has a great deal of overlap with *P. parviflora*, and little with *P. louisianica* or *P. fragrans*. The area where it may extend beyond the range of the recognized wild annual *Proboscidea* is in Nevada, where but one truly wild *P. parviflora* occurrence has been recorded (Dr. Wesley Niles, personal communication) and parts of eastern California. However, given the ease of dispersibility of devil's claw, we conclude that geographic range is in itself a poor indicator of affinities within the *Probosicidea* genus.

There is little doubt, however, that in regard to floral morphology, color and ornamentation, the white seeded devil's claw is most similar to *P. parviflora*, rather than *P. fragrans* or *P. louisianica*. Additionally, the feature of the foliage surpassing the inflorescence is shared with *P. parviflora* but not with *P. louisianica* or *P. fragrans*.

These features are not always clear on pressed herbaria specimens, so that collections noting white flower color, with relatively large flowers, have often been referred to as *P. louisianica* on these latter features alone. We are confident, however, that the flowers of the white seeded devil's claw show much more affinity with *P. parviflora* than with typical *P. louisianica*, except in terms of flower size, a trait easily influenced by both cultivation and selection.

Other diagnostic characters, such as leaf shape and filament pubescens bear out an affinity with *P. parviflora*. Less diagnostic features such as seed size and number of seed per fruit, oil and protein content also illustrate that the white seeded race and black seeded *P. parviflora* are within the same general range.

The characteristics in which the white seeded race diverges the most from typical *P. parviflora* are *not* those which distinguish wild species from one another, but those most commonly influenced by domestication. These include disproportionate enlargement of an economic product (the claw), increase in quality of the product (darker and more pliable), seed color change, and loss of delayed germination.

Other slight differences in characters, such as yield, leaf size, calyx and corolla size, and oil content are in features easily accounted for by indirect cultural selection. We conclude that the white seeded race does appear to have been domesticated from wild *P. parviflora,* since the spontaneous race of *P. parviflora* does not "take on" these characteristics when simply brought into cultivation.

Because the claw has been enlarged to a greater extent than the seed-holding body of the fruit, we feel that selection for fiber rather than food has been the driving force of domestication. Fiber quality has been considerably modified, whereas seed characteristics such as size, number per fruit, dispersibility, and protein have remained relatively the same. These characteristics are usually altered significantly when a plant is domesticated for the food value of its seed. The seed features, e.g.s., loss of delayed germination, white seed color, which have developed in the domesticate could evolve under pressures from cultivation and deliberate human selection for fiber as easily for food.

Thus we recognize numerous features which suggest disruptive selection of *P. parviflora* in cultivated environments and deliberate human selection, resulting in the evolution of a distinct white seeded race. This process is continuing, but to our knowledge has not yet developed a fully domesticated, obligatory cultigen. The presence of presumably feral white seeded devil's claw in Papago *rancherias* indicates that the domesticate is highly associated but not entirely dependent on humans and their intentional planting of seeds. It is possible, however, that in the Kern County, California and southern Nevada, beyond the range where wild annual *Proboscidea* are commonly found, that the survival of the white seeded race was more dependent on cultivation than it is in the Papago *rancherias.*

Finally, it is worth emphasizing that the situation is much more complex than simply having wild black seed and domesticated white seed. Characteristics such as slightly smaller floral parts, and more grayish hues in the white seeds suggest that "the domesticated qualities" of Camp Verde Apache devil's claw are not as pronounced as those of the Papago and Havasupai. The black seed which the Papago cultivate have claws 19.6 ± 3.1 cm, significantly longer than the black seeded claws which we brought into cultivation (Tables 10 and 11). Does this indicate incipient domestication, or merely that the Papago selected seed from longer claws in the wild to begin with? The frequent association of wild devil's claw with the gardens of Apache basketmakers on the Fort Apache Indian Reservation (Anonymous 1976), may well illustrate the "self-domestication" process discussed by Whitaker and Bemis (1975: 325–368).

Bretting (personal communication) has undertaken a systematic crossing program of various acquisitions of white seeded and black seeded *P. parviflora,* including some of our collections. Presently, variation within the white seeded domesticate's gene pool, as well as within *P. parviflora* in general, is poorly understood. We encourage others to investigate this variation, eliciting information from native basketmakers on less obvious characters that they recognize. To clarify the selective pressures driving devil's claw domestication, we urge scientists to actively work in the settings where this process took place - the agricultural fields and gardens of Southwestern *rancheria* people.

LITERATURE CITED

Anderson, Flora. 1922. The Development of the flower and embryogeny of *Martynia louisiana.* Torrey Bot. Club Bull. 49(5): 141–57.

Anderson, Loran C. 1968. Effects of Gibberellic Acid on Germination and Continued Growth of *Proboscidea louisianica.* Phytomorph. 18(1): 166–73.

Anonymous. 1953. Improvement of Native New Mexico. Agric. Sta. Annu. Report 64: 26.

Anonymous. 1876. Women Preserve Basket Art. Fort Apache Scout, May: 7.

Baker, Herbert G. 1972. Human influence on plant evolution. Econ. Botany 26(1): 42–46.

Bancroft, Helen. 1932. A puzzling discovery of a capsule of *Martynia louisiana.* Torrezia 32(3): 59–64.

Bender, Barbara. 1975. Farming in Prehistory - From Hunter-Gatherer to Food Producer. John Baker, London.

Berry, James, Peter Bretting, Gary Nabhan, and Charles Weber. In Press. Domesticated *Proboscidea parviflora:* a potential oilseed crop for arid lands. J. Arid. Environments.

Breazeale, James Frank. 1923. The Pima and His Basket. Arizona Archaeol. Hist. Soc., Tucson.

Buskirk, Wilfred. 1949. Western Apache Subsistence Economy. Unpubl. Ph.D. dissert., Univ. New Mexico, Albuquerque.

Bye, Robert A., Jr. 1972. Ethnobotany of the Southern Paiute Indians in the 1870's: with a Note on the Early Ethnobotanical Contributions of Dr. Edward Palmer. Pp. 87–104, *in* Great Basin Cultural Ecology, a Symposium. Edited by D. D. Fowler. Desert Res. Inst. Publ. Soc. Sci. 8.

Castetter, Edward F. 1939. Notes from Jemez Pueblo. *In* ethnobotany file for Southwest, Ethnobot. Lab., Mus. Anthrop., Univ. Michigan, Ann Arbor.

————. 1939. Interview with Manuel Lowe, Pima Farmer in Sacaton, Arizona, November 11, 1939, Field Notes on Papago Botany and Agriculture (1938–1939). Arizona State Mus. Archives, Tucson. 3–107.

————, and Willis H. Bell. 1942. Pima and Papago Indian Agriculture. Univ. New Mexico Press, Albuquerque.

————, and M. E. Opler, 1936. The Ethnobiology of the Chiricahua and Mescalero Apache. Ethnobiol. Stud. Amer. Southwest 3. Univ. New Mexico Bull. 297, Biol. Ser. 4(5): 3–63.

————, and Ruth M. Underhill. 1935. The Ethnobiology of the Papago Indians. Ethnobiol. Stud. Amer. Southwest 2. Univ. New Mexico Bull. 275, Biol. Ser. 4(3): 3–84.

Corbusier, William F. 1886. The Apache-Yuma and Apache-Mohaves. Amer. Antiquarian 8(6): 325–39.

Correll, Donovan Stewart and March Conring Johnston. 1970. Manual of the Vascular Plants of Texas. Texas Res. Found., Renner.

Coville, Frederick Vernon. 1982. The Panamint Indians of California. Amer. Anthro. 5: 351–59.

Curtin, Lenora Scott Muse. 1949. By the Prophet of the Earth. San Vincente Foundation, Santa Fe.

Dobyns, Henry F. 1952. Experiment in Conservation. Erosion Control and Forage Production on the Papago Indian Reservations in Arizona. *In* Human Problems in Technological Change—A Casebook. Edited by Edward H. Spicer. Russell Sage Found., New York.

Drucker, Philip. 1941. Culture Element Distribution: XVII: Yuman-Piman. Univ. California Anthropol. Records 6(3): 1–230.

Earle, F. R. and Quentin Jones. 1962. Analysis of seed samples from 113 plant families. Econ. Botany 16(4): 221–50.

Felger, Richard S. and Mary Beck Moser. 1976. Seri Indian food plants: desert subsistence without agriculture. Ecol. Food Nutr. 5: 13–27.

Forde, C. Daryll. 1931. Ethnography of the Yuma Indians. Univ. California Publ. Amer. Arch. Ethn. 28(4): 83–278.

Gentry, Howard Scott. 1963. The Warihio Indians of Sonora-Chihuahua: An Ethnographic Survey. Bur. Amer. Ethn. Bull. 186: 61–144.

Ghosh, Amitabha and Jack L. Beal. 1979. Seed lipid constituents of three species of *Proboscidea*. J. Nat. Products 42(3): 278–92.

Gifford, E. W. 1936. Northeastern and Western Yavapai. Univ. California Publ. Amer. Arch. Ethn. 34: 247–354.

————. 1940. Culture Element Distributions: XII. Apache-Pueblo. Univ. California Anthropol. Records 4: 1–207.

Harlan, J. R. 1965. The possible role of weed races in evolution of cultivated plants. Euphytica 14: 173–76.

————. 1975. Crops and Man. Foundations for Modern Crop Science Series. Amer. Soc. Agr. Crop Sci. Soc. Madison.

————, and J. M. J. DeWet. 1971. Toward a rational classification of cultivated plants. Taxon 20(4): 509–17.

Hart, Robin. 1976. An index for comparing weediness in plants. Taxon (2)3: 245–47.

Hevly, Richard H. 1969a. A new species of Proboscidea (Martyniaceae) from Mexico. Brittonia 21: 311–13.

————. 1969b. Nomenclature history and typification of *Martynia* and *Proboscidea* (Martyniaceae) . Taxon 18(5): 527–34.

————. 1970. A new species of *Proboscidea* (Martyniaceae) from Baja California, Mexico. Madrono 20(8): 393–94.

————, and B. Hudgens, MS. Archaeobiology and Paleoecology of Exhausted Cave, Yavapai County, Arizona.

Hough, Walter. 1987. The Hopi in relation to their plant environment. Amer. Anthro. 10(2): 33–44.

Hrdlicka, Ales. 1905. Notes on the San Carlos Apache. Amer. Anthro. 7(3): 480–95.

————. 1906. Notes on the Pima of Arizona. Amer. Anthro. 8(1):39–46.

Hurd, Paul D., Jr. and E. Gordon Linsley. 1963. Pollination of the Unicorn Plant (Martyniaceae) by an ologolectic, corrolla-cutting bee (Hymenopetra: Apoidea). J. Kansas Entomol. Soc. 36(4): 348–52.

Jaeger, Edmund C. 1941. Desert Wild Flowers, Stanford Univ. Press, Stanford (Third Ed., 1968).

Kaplan, L. 1963. Archaeoethnobotany of Cordova Cave, Mexico, Econ. Botany 17(4): 350–59.

Kearney, Thomas H. and R. H. Peebles. 1960. Arizona Flora, 2nd edition with supplement by John Thomas Howell, Elizabeth McClintock et al., Univ. California Press, Berkeley.

Kelly, Isabel. 1964. Southern Paiute Ethnography. Univ. Utah Anthropol. Papers 69.

Kissell, Mary Lois. 1916. Basketry of the Papago and Pima. Amer. Mus. Nat. Hist. Anthropol. Papers 17(4): 1–294.

Lange, Charles H. 1959. Cochiti: A New Mexico Pueblo, Past and Present. Univ. Texas Press, Austin.

Mason, Otis Tufton. 1904. Aboriginal American Basketry. Smithsonian Inst. Annu. Report for 1902: 173–548 & plates. (Rereleased in 1976 by Peregrine Smith, Inc., Santa Barbara).

McKee, Barbara, Edwin McKee and Joyce Herold. 1975. Havasupai Baskets and Their Makers: 1930–1940. Northland Press, Flagstaff.

McKennan, R. 1935. Basketry. Pp. 1–293, in Walapai Ethnography. Edited by A. L. Kroeber. Amer. Anthropol. Assoc. Mem. 42.

Meggitt, M. J. 1965. The Association Between Australian Aborigines and Dingoes. *In* Man, Culture and Animals. Edited by Anthony Leeds and Andrew P. Vayda. Amer. Assoc. Advan. Sci., Washington, D.C.

Merriam, C. Hart. 1903. Some Little Known Basket Materials. Science 17(438): 826.

Merrill, Ruth Earl. 1923. Plants Used in Basketry by the California Indians. Univ. California Publ. Amer. Arch. Ethn. 20. (Rereleased in 1970 by Acoma Books, Ramona).

Nabhan, Gary P. and Gordon L. Fritz. 1977. Devil's claw (Proboscidea): cash crop in the Papago basketry industry. (Abstract). J. Arizona Acad. Sci. 12: 4–5.

Palmer, Edward, 1871. Food Products of the North American Indians. U.S. Dept. Agric., Report of the Commissioner of Agric. for the year 1870. U.S. Government Printing Office, Washington, D.C. 404–428.

Paur, Sherman. 1952. Four native New Mexico plants of promise as oilseed crops. New Mexico Agric. Exp. Sta. Press. Bull. 1064. New Mexico College Agric. Mech. Arts State College.

Pennington, Campbell. 1980. The Pima Bajo of Central Sonora, Mexico: The Material Culture. Univ. Utah Press, Salt Lake.

Perry, Bruce Allen. 1942. Genetic and Ctyological Studies on the Euphorbiaceae, Martyniaceae and Malvaceae. Virginia Univ. Abstracts Dissert. 1942: 43–47.

Pickersgill, Barbara and C. B. Heiser, Jr. 1976. Cytogenetics and Evolutionary Change Under Domestication. Philosoph. Trans. Rev. Soc. London 275: 55–67.

Rick, Charles M. 1976. Tomato. Pp. 268–72, in Evolution of Crop Plants. Edited by N. W. Simmonds. Longman, New York.

Robbins, W. W. 1940. Alien plants growing without cultivation in California. Univ. California Agric. Exp. Sta. Bull. 637: 1–128.

Roberts, Helen H. 1929. Basketry of the San Carlos Apache. Amer. Mus. Nat. Hist. Anthropol. Papers 31(2): 1–218.

Robbins, Wilfred W., John Peabody Harrington and Barbara Freire-Marreco. 1916. Ethnobotany of the Tewa Indians. Bur. Amer. Ethn. Bull. 55.

Russell, Frank. 1908. The Pima Indians. Bur. Amer. Ethn. Annu. Report 26 (rereleased in 1975 by Univ. Arizona Press, Tucson).

Sappenfield, William P. 1954. January 29 letter to Ruth Branch of the National Farm Chemurgic Council, Inc., New York regarding devil's claw research at State College, New Mexico 1–2.

Schwanitz, Franz. 1966. The Origin of the Cultivated Plant. Harvard Univ. Press, Cambridge.

Smith, Gerald, Arthur and Ruth DeEtte Simpson. 1964. Basket makers of San Bernadino County. San Bernadino Co. Mus., Bloomington.

Spier, Leslie. 1928. Havasupai Ethnography. Amer. Mus. Nat. Hist. Anthropol. Papers 29(3): 1–392.

———. 1933. Yuman Tribes of the Gila River. Univ. Chicago Press, Chicago.

———. 1946. Comparative vocabularies and parallel texts in o Yuman languages of Arizona. Univ. New Mexico Publ. Anthrop. 2: 1–150.

Stevenson, Matilda Coxe. 1909. Ethnobotany of the Zuni Indians. Bur. Amer. Ethn. Annu. Reports 13: 31–102.

Steward, Julian. 1941. Culture Element Distribution XII: Nevada Shoshoni. Univ. California Anthropol. Records 4(2).

Stewart, Omer C. 1942. Culture Element Distributions: XVIII: Ute-Southern Paiute. Univ. California Anthropol. Records 6(4).

Stoffle, Richard W. and Michael J. Evans. 1976. Resource competition and population change: a Kaibab Paiute ethnohistoric case. Ethnohistory 23(2): 1–25.

Thieret, John W. 1976. Floral biology of Proboscidea louisianica (Martyniaceae). Rhodora 78(814): 169–79.

Van Eseltine, G. P. 1929. A preliminary study of the Unicorn Plants (Martyniaceae). New York State Agric. Exp. Sta. Tech. Bull. 149: 1–41.

Voegelin, Ermine W. 1938. Tubatulabal Ethnography. Univ. California Anthropol. Records 2(1): 1–90.

Voth, H. R. 1890S. Plants of the Hopis-Medicinal, Economic, and Ceremonial. Unpubl. MS, library of Field Mus. Nat. Hist., Chicago.

Watson, Richard A. and Patty Jo Watson. 1971. The Domesticator or Plants and Animals. *In* Prehistoric Agriculture. Edited by Stuart Streuver. Nat. Hist. Press, Garden City.

Watson, S. 1898. *Martynia Palmeri*. Proc. Amer. Acad. 24: 66.

Whitaker, Thomas W. and W. P. Bemis. 1975. Origin and evolution of the cultivated cucurbita. Bull. Torrey Bot. Club 102(106): 362–68.

Whiting, Alfred E. 1939. Ethnobotany of the Hopi. Mus. N. Arizona Bull. 15.

———. 1942. Havasupai habitat. Unpubl. MS library of the Mus. N. Arizona.

Yarnell, Richard A. 1977. Native Plant Husbandry North of Mexico. *In* The Origins of Agriculture. Edited by Charles Reed. Mouton, The Hague.

Zeuner, Frederick E. 1963. A History of Domesticated Animals. Harper and Row, New York.

Zigmond, Maurice. 1978. Kawaiisu Basketry. J. California Anthrop. 5(2): 199–215.

NOTE

1. Since the original publication of this article some group names have changed. For example, the Papago now prefer "O'odham."

CHAPTER THIRTEEN

Ethnoecology, Biodiversity, and Modernization in Andean Potato Agriculture

STEPHEN B. BRUSH

Profusion of crop diversity has long been a puzzle, and in recent times it has become a conservation issue. De Candolle (1882) and subsequently Vavilov (1926) noted that interspecific and infraspecific variation of crop species is not evenly distributed, that hyperdiversity in the form of numerous locally named varieties or landraces occurs in certain areas, and that these areas are the most likely centers of crop domestication. Vavilov emphasized the importance of centers of diversity as pools of genetic resources for crop improvement. Many agricultural scientists who are familiar with centers of crop diversity argue that the great profusion of species and genotypes is endangered by technical progress, social change, and environmental factors (Hawkes 1983). Yet, we have only a rudimentary understanding of how specific cultural traditions maintain and influence crop populations in centers of crop origin and evolution. Poor understanding of the ecology of crop diversity weakens our ability to assess the danger of genetic erosion and to plan effective conservation programs.

This paper questions whether the loss of biodiversity under conditions of agricultural modernization is as likely or widespread as purported. It examines the case of potatoes (*Solanum* spp.) in the Andes of Peru, the cradle of potato domestication and evolution. The paper begins with a general review of the ethnoecology of Andean potato agriculture. It then presents data on two Andean valleys that have different histories of agricultural modernization. It argues that diversity persists in peasant agriculture even after intensification and commercialization. While ecological and utilitarian factors are often cited as paramount in the maintenance of diversity (e.g., Clawson 1985), this paper concludes that these factors can only partially explain the practice of Andean farmers to conserve high levels of potato diversity.

One obstacle to understanding crop diversity has been that variation is at the infraspecific level. Burtt's advice on treating infraspecific variation is stark: "the best thing to do with a muck-heap is to leave it undisturbed so that it quietly rots down. In course of time the *Code of Nomenclature* will no doubt accept it as disposable refuse" (Burtt 1970: 238). Bulmer (1970) notes that a similar aversion seems to prevail among ethnobiologists. Nevertheless, there are several good reasons for grappling with the ethnobiological treatment of plant varieties, especially of crops. The infraspecific level is common to many ethnobotanical systems (Atran 1987; Berlin 1976; Dougherty 1978), and elaborate varietal classification is conspicuous in some folk systems. Variety identification becomes more significant with industrialization and implementation of intellectual property rights. Perhaps most importantly, the variety level is a primary unit in the management of agricultural ecosystems by farmers around the world. Several case studies reveal the merits of drawing a more explicit connection between ethnobiology and farmer decision making in agriculture (e.g., Johnson 1974; Richards 1985). These studies reflect Bulmer's (1974) point that one of ethnobiology's principal goals is to understand how the determination of biological species relates humans to the biological dimension, a point that has been reiterated in the recent emphasis on "indigenous knowledge systems" (Brokensha et al. 1980).

INTRODUCTION: ETHNOECOLOGY OF ANDEAN POTATOES

Bertonio's (1612) dictionary of the Aymara language mentions some of the many names applied to the vast diversity of potatoes found in the central Andes. Contemporary Andean farmers still use some of the same terms. While it is unlikely that the varieties currently grown are biologically the same as those grown 400 years ago, there is continuity in Andean ethnobiology. Many ethnobiologists and geneticists have come to believe that the biological diversity of Andean farming systems is endangered by contemporary trends, particularly the diffusion of new potato varieties (Ochoa 1975). The loss of biodiversity threatens the continuity of Andean agriculture that has withstood the upheaval of European conquest and colonization.

Two dominant approaches stand out for understanding cultural adaptation by Andean people to their high mountain environment. One focuses on the indigenous knowledge of Andean people, especially the identification and use of local plants, animals, and production zones, emphasizing the diversity of biological resources that are used (Franquemont et al. 1990; Gade 1975; Tapia Núñez and Flores Ochoa 1984). The other approach, referred to here as the cultural ecology model, focuses on the social mechanisms that determine the management of a heterogeneous landscape and provision social units from the household to the state (Murra 1975). The cultural ecology model emphasizes complementarity as one of the organizing principles of Andean society. The complementarity principle refers to the control and use of ecologically distinct, spatially separated production zones by single ethnic groups. This idea was originally articulated by Murra (1975) as "verticality." Thomas's (1973) work on energy flow showed that multiple zones were better able to provide sufficient energy than single zones, and Golte's (1980) research suggests that multiple zone use smooths out labor demand, thus making labor more efficient and productive than is possible within a single zone.

A prerequisite of complementary land use is an inventory of crops that are suited to the different physical conditions of the land: soils, temperatures, moisture, and evapotranspiration regimes. Describing the Vilcanota Valley of Peru, Gade (1975) found 36 species of Andean domesticates. The single most important Andean cultigen is the potato, and diversity within this crop in the Andes is greater than for any other crop grown there. Originally domesticated from tuber-bearing members of the Solanaceae family by Andean pastoralists, the potato has coevolved in the Andean environment for at least 6,000 years (Pickersgill and Heiser 1978). Potatoes are grown throughout most of the crop zones of the Andes, but they predominate in the upper zones, between 3,000 m and 4,000 m above sea level, and in some areas they provide up to 70% of the calories (Ferroni 1979). Eight different species and subspecies among four polyploid groups (diploid 2n = 24 to pentaploid 5n = 60) are cultivated. Some of these species (e.g., tetraploid, *Solanum tuberosum* subsp. *andigena*) are cosmopolitan, while others (e.g., S. *ajanhuiri*) are very localized in their distribution. Some 5,000 morphologically distinct varieties have been identified by the International Potato Center, out of more than 13,000 Andean accessions (Huamán 1986). Over 100 varieties may be found in a single valley and a dozen or more distinct varieties are kept by a typical farming household.

Indigenous knowledge and diversity.—Andean potato nomenclature was first described by LaBarre (1947) for the Aymara of Bolivia, and folk taxonomies have since been described for Quechua and Spanish speaking peasants of Peru (Brunel 1975; Brush et al. 1981; Zimmerer 1991a). Following LaBarre, recent descriptions of Andean folk classification find three or four taxonomic levels for potatoes: genus, species, variety, and subvariety. Four criteria are important in potato classification: ecology (cultivated/wild/weedy; production zone), use (edible; for boiling; for freeze drying), plant and tuber phenotype, and degree of polytypy (number of subclasses). The similarities of potato nomenclature across languages and types of production systems are notable. Both terms and taxonomy found in contemporary nomenclature are also evident in Bertonio's (1612) Aymara dictionary. In both the seventeenth and twentieth centuries, Andean potato farmers distinguish potatoes by tuber phenotype, ecology, and use.

Table 1 presents a schematic diagram of a folk taxonomy of potatoes from the central and southern highlands of Peru. At the genus level, the *Solanum* tuber group *(papa)* is distinguished from other Andean tubers such as *Oxalis tuberosa* and *Tropaeolum tuberosum*. At the species level, domesticated, wild, and weedy types are demarcated *(mikhuna papa, atoq papa, araq papa)*, and frost resistant, high altitude, bitter types *(haya papa)* with high glycoalkaloid content are differentiated from mid-altitude types without bitter compounds *(miski papa)*. Table 2 compares the different folk species according to the four criteria mentioned above.

Table 1. Schematic diagram of Andean taxonomy of potatoes (Cusco Quechua).

Taxonomic Level			Term(s)					
Genus				*Papa*				
Species	*atoq*	*araq*			*mikhuna*	*haya*		
	papa	*papa*			*papa*	*papa*		
Variety			*qompis*		*runtus*	*ruk'i*	*waña*	
Subvariety		*alqa*		*yuraq*			*yuraq*	*yana*
		qompis		*qompis*			*waña*	*waña*

Varieties are primarily distinguished according to tuber characteristics, such as tuber shape (oval, spherical, flat, long), the configuration of the tuber's "eyes" (depth, number, location, color), skin color and pattern (white to deep purple, solid color, multi-colored), and flesh color and color pattern (solid, ringed, white to deep purple). In rare cases, nontuber characteristics such as stem or flower color distinguish varieties. Tuber characteristics are highly subject to somatic variation and to environmental influences. The relationship between tuber characteristics and plant genotype is not well understood.

The final level of Andean potato taxonomy is the subvariety, where the only contrast is between tuber colors. Black (*yana*) and white (*yuraq*) subvarieties are frequent, and variegated skin color is labeled *alga.* Skin coloration varies continuously and is transitory in some varieties, and the subvariety label is often understood to be unstable. In other cases, however, subvarieties are stable and biologically distinct. *Yuraq waña* and *yana waña* are the two stable variants of a single species, *S.* x *curtilobum.*

Potatoes in two lowest taxonomic levels are grouped into named categories that constitute intermediate ranking rather than separate taxa. Table 3 presents a description of six intermediate ranks that are common in the central Andes. These intermediate ranks are labeled and usually group several varieties and subvarieties by a single criterion, such as use or ecology. One grouping distinguishes potatoes with a high water content (*uno papa* or *kal'wi papa*) that are suitable for soups or frying from varieties with high dry matter (*haku papa*) that are preferred for boiling or steaming. Farmers also contrast modern potato varieties that have been introduced since 1950

TABLE 2. Characteristics of folk species of Andean potatoes (Cusco Quechua).

Folk Species	Ecology	Use	Phenotype	Polytypy
mikhuna papa	broad adaptability; mid-altitudes, 2,500–3,700	boiling; soups; frying	nonbitter tubers; highly variable	very high
haya papa	frost resistant; high altitude, 3,700–4,100	processing by freeze-drying; *chuño*	bitter tubers	low
araq papa	weedy species; low medium altitudes, 2,500–3,200	boiling; soups	nonbitter	low
atoq papa	wild species; all altitudes	not used	small tubers	none

TABLE 3. Intermediate folk categories at variety level in Andean potato classification (Cusco Quechua).

Category	Distinguishing Criteria	Description	Contrast
wayk'u papa	use	dry/mealy potatoes for boiling or roasting	to unu papa
unu papa	use	watery potatoes for frying and soups	to wayk´u papa
k'usi papa	use	nonbitter tubers for freeze-drying (chuño)	to wayk´u papa
miska papa	ecology	fast growing; for short season (maway tarpuy)	to unnamed category for long season (hatun tarpuy)
chaqro/chalo	phenotype	mixed colors and shapes	to unnamed category for modern varieties (white potatoes)

with local or "native" varieties. Modern varieties (Spanish: *papa mejorada*) are light skinned, white fleshed, smooth, and generally larger than local varieties that are described as **chalo. Chalo** is used by both Quechua and Aymara speakers to describe mixed collections of potatoes with many colors and shapes. The word appears in Bertonio's (1612) Aymara dictionary *(cchalu),* suggesting that Andean farmers distinguished mixed collections long before the appearance of modern varieties.

The rich Andean nomenclature for potatoes is *prima facie* evidence for great diversity, and diversity at the species and infraspecific levels has been well documented for the Andes (e.g., Hawkes and Hjerting 1989). However, very little is known about the actual distribution of diversity either within or between regions or how diversity is affected by changes in agriculture. The measurement of genetic diversity and its distribution in Andean potato agriculture is confounded by the complexity within the group of cultivated *Solanums* and by the great number of phenntypes and genotypes at the variety level. Somatic variation, introgression between cultivated and wild species, and hybridization within cultivated species also pose problems for measuring diversity. Geneticists who work with the crop have preferred to work at the ploidy or species levels rather than at the variety level (Hawkes and Hjerting 1989). However, recent advances in biochemical characterization of potatoes (Quiros et al. 1990) may help overcome some of the obstacles to biological assessment of diversity. These measures rely on isozymes, and they focus on characteristics that are far less variable or environmentally determined than plant descriptors such as tuber shape.

While varietal naming is a centerpiece of the Andean folk classification of potatoes geneticists have long believed that this system is not a reliable gauge of diversity
for two reasons. First, the folk system is based on tuber characteristics that are only
partially relevant to the biological systematics of the crop. Second, Andean farmers are
believed to overclassify diversity (Hawkes 1947), a practice that is exemplified by the
use of several names in a single community for a single type of potato and by the habit
of changing names for such purposes as marketing. There is no evidence of a single,
master list of names that farmers know or agree on, although they are aware of
synonymy.

The individualistic, localized, and transitory nature of potato names would thus
seem to limit them as a general tool for measuring diversity. Nevertheless, Quiros et
al. (1990) found that there is a high degree of correspondence between farmer segre-
gation and identification of tubers and biochemical (isozyme) profiles of tubers that
reflect genotype differences. The isozyme analysis is particularly relevant here, since
one would not expect any degree of correspondence between a folk taxonomy largely
based on one criterion (tuber characteristics) and biochemical identity based on characters that are invisible to Andean farmers. Households are the primary management
unit of selection of potato varieties and the primary unit for maintaining diversity.
Assessment of the amount of diversity kept by different households is therefor essential to an oveall understanding of diversity in the agricultural system, and this assessment can rely on farmer identification. Thus, research on diversity can draw directly
on folk classification, as long as the unit of analysis is the household.

Cultural ecology of potato agriculture.—Isbell (1978) reports that households in
Ayacucho, Peru, initially receive gifts of seed potatoes from the couple's parents, but
afterwards they are generally on their own in selecting and maintaining varieties. This
pattern pertains both north and south of the Ayacucho area. Additional varieties are
acquired through trade, purchase, gifts, and wages in kind. Women play an especially
important role in the identification and selection of varieties, and women are involved
in every stage of potato production: seed selection, production, harvest, storage,
processing, and cooking. The key role of women has been described in Ecuador
(Weismantel 1988), Peru (Allen 1988), and Bolivia (Johnsson 1986). Men acknowledge women's superiority in plant knowledge and defer to them when questions arise
about potato identification.

The Andean potato crop, both within villages and across regions, includes a few
cosmopolitan varieties that are cultivated by virtually every household and many varieties that are cultivated by only a few households. Cosmopolitan varieties include
huayro in central and southern Peru, **qompis** in southern Peru, and **imilla** in southern
Peru and Bolivia. Approximately half of the total varieties in a household's inventory
are these common varieties, but only a small percentage of a region's varieties are
common (Zimmerer 1988). Common varieties include both native and modern ones
that are kept for different purposes; the native ones because of their culinary and
commercial value and the modern ones because of their yield and acceptance in the
market. Improved and native commercial varieties are often grown as monocrops in

single fields or blocks within fields, and they may account for 70–90% of the area planted in potatoes in many places (Mayer 1979). The prevalence of certain native and improved varieties means that most of the diversity can be kept in only a small portion of the farm, where modern and selected varieties are not grown. This pattern is facilitated by the fragmentation of Andean landscapes, by complementary land use by single households and villages, and by the practice of cultivating numerous fields in the same year.

The ethnographic literature provides strong evidence that consumption is critically important in maintaining diversity. Virtually every study of potato selection refers to the importance of subtle yet elaborate contrast in taste, color, and texture of Andean tubers (Johns 1990; Johnsson 1986). Carter and Mamani (1982) note that certain varieties are prized for special meals, the most favored also being the most delicate and least productive. Brush (1977) describes certain varieties that are saved for gifts. Johnsson's (1986) study in Bolivia discusses the importance of potatoes and potato diversity to the cultural identity of the Aymara. His emphasis reflects Carter and Mamani's (1982: 98) account of the Mauca family's pride and prestige in possessing seed of many rare potato varieties. The contribution of potato diversity to Andean identity and prestige is echoed by Weismantel's (1988) study of Zumbagua, Ecuador. Potatoes are not a primary staple for most Zumbaguan families, but they retain prestige. Serving meals without European introductions such as barley and fava beans is a privilege of more affluent families. This contradicts the popular and Eurocentric notion that potatoes are always judged to be inferior food to cereals.

Intuitive logic asserts that diversity also exists because it is adaptive, leading to more stable production in the face of great environmental heterogeneity and abundant pests and pathogens. Brush (1977) and Carter and Mamani (1982) report that farmers recognize specific agronomic characteristics in certain varieties, such as resistance to disease or insects. While diversity may endow an adaptive or ecological advantage to subsistence farmers without other means to control disease or limit the effects of poor weather, this advantage is not particularly evident in potato names at the variety level. One exception occurs within the bitter species *(haya papa)* where more frost resistant varieties *(ruki, Solanum juzepczuki)* are contrasted with less frost resistant varieties *(waña, S. x curtilobum)*. However, within the nonbitter folk species *(miski papa)*, where diversity is greatest, there are exceptionally few widely shared names that refer to tubers with special resistance to insects, disease, or poor weather.

It is possible that a more diverse collection of potatoes performs better than a less diverse one as it is moved over the heterogeneous landscape. However, this superior performance must ultimately be traced to the performance of specific varieties at certain places and under particular conditions. We might expect diversity to be retained because certain varieties perform best at certain locations that vary by soils, water availability, temperature, and so forth.

One-to-one relationships between particular varieties and environmental conditions, such as soils, insect predation, or disease, have rarely been reported or evaluated (Hawkes and Hjerting 1989). Strong resistance to disease, insects, and drought is rare in domesticated potatoes, although some resistance is found within the predominant subspecies of the Andean region *(Solanum tuberosum* subsp. *andigena)* (Hawkes and Hjerting 1989). While the ethnobiology of insects and crop diseases of the Andes has not been specifically studied, the observations of agronomists indicate that a folk classification of six insect species that attack potatoes exists (Universidad Nacional San Cristohal de Huamanga 1983). Plant disease taxonomy is the least developed of the folk systems. Andean farmers gloss several diseases under the Spanish term *rancha* (late blight), but they do not recognize several major pathogens, such as nematodes and viruses. Knowledge of soils has been documented (McCamant 1986), bul no single matrix seems to exist that maps potato varieties onto soil types.

The widely practiced sectoral rotation of fields (Orlove and Godoy 1986) is especially problematic to an ecological interpretation of diversity. This practice results in the yearly movement of the potato crop between fields in different parts of the community's territory. If ecological advantage of potato diversity results from fitting genotype to location, then this advantage would seem to be eliminated by the practices of frequent field rotation and the practice of growing diverse collections of potatoes together, instead of placing each variety in its special niche and keeping it there. Andean farmers do not emphasize site-specific adaptation in their nomenclature or management of potatoes, and agronomic trials suggest that most individual potato varieties perform equally well over a broad range of altitudes (Zimmerer 1991b). While the contrast at the folk species level between nonbitter, mid-altitude types *(miska papa)* and bitter, high altitude, types *(haya papa)* is salient on several axes (production zone, relative hardiness, processing, and consumption), the contrast between varieties is based primarily on tuber phenotype. Potato farmers report that the most diverse, native varieties are also the least resistant to disease, insects, and the effects of poor weather.

Diversity may have a very long-term advantage that is not specifically recognized in Andean folk biology or immediately apparent in the short-term. Long-term stability of potato production may be enhanced by having a large repertoire of genotypes, some of which have particular advantage as environmental conditions, pests, and pathogens change over time. Under different conditions, varieties that are now rare may become advantageous, and thus prevalent. A large repertoire may seem superfluous in the short run, but it allows farmers to adjust to new conditions, including market demand.

Loss of diversity.—Andean agriculture has never been a static system, and cultivators have long been able to accommodate new technology such as European crops and animals. However, the pace of change appears to have accelerated during this century. Market penetration, migration, population growth, political reform, and new technology are now ubiquitous. Integration of local communities into larger political and economic systems has been present since pre-Hispanic times, but this integration has changed both qualitatively and quantitatively in the twentieth century, with the spread of capitalism, through increased population, and the expansion of state power, roads, and mass communication. The Peruvian population almost tripled between 1950 and 1990, from 7.6 million to 21.9 million (Urban and Trueblood 1990). Rural areas have experienced far less growth because of emigration to urban areas, but demographic pressures are felt everywhere, as market systems have expanded and rural hinterlands have been more closely incorporated into national economics. The presence of central-ized state power has increased through means such as agrarian reform, education, and regional development. Andean production is now characterized as much by commodi-tization and the acquisition of new technology as by complementarity and commu-nity regulation. Virtually every household now uses not only some Old World crops and animals but also agricultural chemicals and improved Andean crop varieties.

Modern potato varieties were first released in Peru in the early 1950s, and they are now found in virtually every village in the highlands. These varieties were specif-ically bred to be higher yielding, better able to utilize fertilizer, and resistant to specific stresses such as disease or drought. Their adoption is directly encouraged by agricul-tural extension and credit policies of the government and indirectly by such factors as population increase or a farmer's wish to produce a larger surplus for the market. Two impacts of the diffusion of modern crop varieties in the Andes have been reported: increased productivity (Horton 1984) and loss of potato diversity (Ochoa 1975).

The concept of genetic erosion in farming systems is based on somewhat simplistic biogeography. Adopting modern crop varieties decreases the area that is planted to the traditional and more diverse varieties. Shrinking the area devoted to native crops should logically reduce diversity, just as the size of islands is directly related to biological diversity (McArthur and Wilson 1967). The basic flaw with this logic is that it assumes that farmer behavior towards traditional crops remains unchanged as improved crops are adopted. The biogeographic view of genetic erosion does not account for cultural, economic, and environmental buffers in agricultural systems that might protect diversity. Environmental heterogeneity, agronomic risk limit, market factors, and cultural factors are likely to limit the substitution of one or two varieties for the dozens that have evolved locally. The remainder of this paper will examine whether this conservation has occurred in Andean potato agriculture in two highland valleys of Peru.

METHODS

The impact on traditional crop diversity of the adoption of new varieties and agricultural intensification should ideally be studied in a historic framework by following the fate of diverse native crops as these changes occur over time. By all accounts, modern potatoes spread rapidly throughout the highlands after 1950. Unfortunately, we have neither biological nor socioeconomic benchmarks from a period before the diffusion of these varieties. The oldest systematic and preserved collections of native potatoes date only to the early 1970s, and our information on agricultural practices before 1950 is scanty and superficial. Without these historic benchmarks, comparison among regions, villages, and households is a valuable way to estimate the impact on diversity of such factors as commercialization of agricul-ture or the adoption of modern potato varieties. With this comparison in mind, research was undertaken in two valleys in eastern Peru. These valleys were chosen both because of their similarities and differences.

Study sites.—Reconnaissance in 1978 indicated that studying valleys in Peru's central and southern highlands would provide contrasting records of agricultural moderniza-tion and commercialization. Peasant villages in the central high!ands were known to have a longer record of the adoption of modern technology and greater integration into regional and national commercial networks. Reconnaissance in 1978 and 1984 suggested that the Tulumayo Valley, 50 km east of Huancayo in central Peru, was representative of areas with records of great potato diversity that had undergone exten-sive modernization and commercialization. Paucartambo Valley, 50 km east of Cusco in southern Peru, was representative of diverse farming systems that had experienced less modernization and commercialization. The Tulumayo and Paucartambo valleys are like many others along the eastern Andean escarpment. They share the traditions of complementary land use and community control mentioned above. Rolling upland pastures descend into steep and narrow valleys where crops are produced on slopes that have been landscaped into terrace-like fields by generations of farmers. In each valley, "peasant communities," or corporate villages, control agro-pastoral produc-tion over a large altitude range with different production zones. Each valley has some communities that existed independently and others that were part of *haciendas* before the agrarian reform of 1969-1970. The community provides the modern framework of complementary land use, but households make most of the in-field decisions, such as which crop and variety to plant. Production is destined both for home consump-tion and for the market, and each valley is located four hours by all weather road from a major urban center, Huancayo or Cusco.

The Tulumayo and Paucartambo valleys are also alike in their emphasis on potato production and in the organization of potato production. Potatoes are the predominant crop, accounting for 54% of the cultivated land in Tulumayo and 47% in Paucartambo. In both valleys, households cultivate numerous small plots across production zones that are differentiated according to altitude, crops, agricultural calendar, intensity of land use, and degree of community control. Each valley produces both bitter and nonbitter varieties; each divides mid-altitude production into a lower, short cycle *(maway tarpuy)* and a higher, long cycle *(hatun tarpuy);* each relies on sectoral fallow and the simultaneous cultivation of different plots by the same household. Finally, both the Tulumayo and the Paucartambo valleys share regional fame as places where particularly high levels of diversity are found. These two valleys show a pattern that is familiar to agricultural systems in cradle areas of crop evolution and diversity. Small islands of traditional agriculture remain in a sea of more uniform, commercial agri-culture based on the use of modern crop varieties and high energy inputs.

The major differences between the two valleys have to do with ethnicity, degree of commercialization of potato agriculture, and the history of adoption of modern potato varieties. A generation ago, the people of the Tulumayo were Quechua speakers, but today Spanish is the most widely spoken language. Labor migration from this valley to the mining industry in central Peru has been a significant force in shaping local cultural identity during this century (Long and Roberts 1984; Mallon 1983). Tulumayo people identify themselves as *mestizos,* and they are explicit about the cultural differences between themselves and Quechua speaking people who live south of the Mantaro Valley. Quechua is the predominant language of Paucartambo, where ethnic identity is Indian (Allen 1988). Paucartambo has not experienced such a singular integrating force as massive labor migration to mines. Its integration into the regional economy of southern Peru has been through the *hacienda* system and through periodic migration to Cusco and to commercial farms in the lowlands. This integration has not produced the fundamental shift in ethnic identity experienced in the central highlands. Differences in potato agriculture between the two valleys can be seen by comparing three types of potatoes: improved varieties, native commercial varieties, and mixed native varieties. These types are salient to the farmers in the study in terms of classification and management.

Sample and survey strategies.—The object of studying the Tulumayo and Paucartambo valleys was to model the impact on traditional potato diversity of the adoption of improved potato varieties by comparing households and valleys. The Tulumayo and Paucartambo valleys are each heterogeneous in similar ways. Different production systems are distributed according to altitude, and these vary by agricultural intensity, community control, crop, and crop variety. Different areas in each valley are more readily accessible to the principal town, the local nexus between peasant communities and regional market and administrative systems. We assumed that better access to the principal town lowered transportation costs and made more available modern technological inputs, including information and new potato varieties. The complexity of potato agriculture in the Andes, heterogeneity within each valley, and differences between valleys were issues in determining a research design. These issues were addressed by surveying in several villages within each valley, by sampling a reasonably large number of households, and by focusing on three categories of potato varieties: improved, native commercial, and mixed native.

The first step in surveying was to select villages for sampling, and this was done by reconnaissance in November 1984. Potato producing villages were selected using two criteria: altitude and distance (travel time) to each valley's administrative center. Villages were chosen in each valley at three altitudes: high (village at > 3,500 m), middle (village at 3,000–3,500 m), and low (village at < 3,000 m). The distances from the administrative center varied by the existence and quality of roads. In the Tulumayo Valley, 14 villages were surveyed. The closest of these to Comas, the economic and administrative center of the Tulumayo Valley, was 30 minutes by car, and the most distant was three hours over a road that had opened in 1984, the year our fieldwork began. In Paucartambo, 10 villages were surveyed. The closest to the town of Paucartambo was 30 minutes by car, and the most distant was four hours by foot.

The researchers contacted the elected officials of each village or peasant community to explain the research, obtain permission, and select the sample. Peasant communities in Peru keep membership lists of their inhabitants. A short questionnaire was prepared to gather information from the elected officials about the village inhabitants, using the membership list as the base. The village officials were asked to estimate age of the household head, marital status, family size, educational background, extent of land holdings, off farm employment, and socio-economic status of each member of the community. This information was then used to select a sample of households for the main survey. The objective was to include households of different socio-economic status in a survey of between 15 and 20 households in each village. A total of 154 surveys were conducted in the Tulumayo Valley and 204 in Paucartambo.

The main survey instrument was applied between January and July, 1985, in the Tulumayo Valley and between January and September, 1986, in the Paucartambo Valley. The survey instrument included questions on household characteristics and farming practices and the use of the production from each cultivated parcel. Questions about fallow land were also asked. We gathered information about each of the three general types of potatoes, improved, native commercial, and mixed native, such as how seed was acquired and how often, and advantages and disadvantages of the types. Finally, an inventory of varieties was made by drawing a random lot of 100 tubers from the potatoes stored in the farmer's house. These tubers were then sorted by the farmer into varieties that he recognized, and three to six tubers of each variety were requested for analysis and conservation in the collections of the International Potato Center and the University of Cusco. In the early stages of interviewing, it became apparent that we would not be able to conduct an inventory of the entire sample of households that were being surveyed, because of difficulties of logistics and gaining access to the farm's store of potatoes. Our solution was to revisit a smaller number of households that were chosen randomly from the larger sample after completion of the survey. In the Tulumayo Valley we obtained inventories from 87 households, and in Paucartambu we completed 85 inventories.

The survey took approximately one and a half hours to complete. A survey team of five interviewers was employed in each valley. One surveyor worked in both valleys. The surveyors had university training in anthropology, economics, and agronomy. More than half of each team had previous fieldwork and survey experience. Team members lived in villages for one to three months while conducting the survey. Besides the survey on potato varieties and farming practices, the surveyors made ethnographic notes on each of the households that they surveyed. In addition to the variety survey, the research team also produced a land use map of each valley and completed a detailed study of the economics of peasant potato agriculture (Mayer and Glave 1990).

A principal object of the survey on potato varieties was to compare the extent and treatment of three different types of potatoes, improved, native commercial, and mixed native. Improved potatoes are bred for their adaptability to a wide range of Andean environments. They are planted in both of the production zones for nonbitter potatoes, although they are more common in the lower one (*maway tarpuy*). They are usually smooth and white skinned and somewhat higher in water content than native potatoes. Improved varieties are especially important for commercial production, and they represent a large proportion of all potatoes sold (78% in Tulumayo and 62% in Paucartambo). The native commercial varieties are local varieties that have been intensively selected and are grown in monocultures for the market. They are regarded as excellent eating potatoes by farmers and urban consumers alike. They have moderately deep eyes, colored skin, and cream colored flesh with a high percentage dry matter. These are varieties that are grown by virtually every household. They are well known

TABLE 4. Potato distribution in the Tulumayo and Paucartambo valleys. Values are percentages of potato types by zone.

	Tulumayo Valley (n = 154)			Paucartambo Valley (n = 204)		
	Improved	Native Commer.	Native Mixed	Improved	Native Commer.	Native Mixed
Hatun Tarpuy (Long Season Zone)	23	75	89	28	10	98
Maway Tarpuy (Short Season Zones)........	77	25	11	72	90	2
Total	100	100	100	100	100	100

to merchants and urban consumers, and commercial demand has led farmers to plant them in uniform fields that are managed much like fields of improved varieties. Mixed native varieties are the prime source of diversity in Andean potatoes. Their tubers are usually small and come in many shapes and colors, inside and out, a characteristic that is captured in the label *chalo.* These mixed native varieties have tubers with many different degrees of dryness and different flavors. They are planted as random collections in the high zone *(hatun tarpuy).* Production from mixed native collections is sold, but they are not subject to the same selection pressures as the specifically commercial varieties. These collections are planted by almost every household in the two valleys but in only a small portion of the total land of Tulumayo farms.

RESULTS AND DISCUSSION

Comparison between the two valleys and among the three types of potatoes reveals a number of predictable contrasts but some intriguing surprises. Table 4 shows the distribution of different potato types according to the weight of seed reported by farmers in the survey. The important contrast here is between improved and mixed types in the two production zones. Predictably, improved varieties are grown primarily in the lower zones that are farmed more intensively throughout the central Andes for commercial purposes (e.g., Mayer and Fonseca 1979). Native types, especially mixed varieties, are concentrated in the high zone where agriculture is less intensive and community control more direct. Another striking contrast between the two valleys is the location of native commercial varieties. In the Tulumayo Valley, these are primarily grown in the high zone *(hatun tarpuy)* while in Paucartambo, they are grown mostly in the lower zone *(maway tarpuy).* In both valleys, the lower zone is dedicated to commercial production of the high-yielding improved and high-value native commercial varieties, to take advantage of high off-season prices. The difference in location of native commercial varieties reflects the fact that Paucartambo farmers plant another

TABLE 5. Potato farming systems in Tulumayo and Paucartambo valleys. Values are percentages of potato types.

| | Tulumayo Valley (n = 154) | | | | Paucartambo Valley (n = 204) | | | |
	Improved	Native Commer.	Native Mixed	Total	Improved	Native Commer.	Native Mixed	Total
Area in potatoes	59	30	11	100	31	8	61	100
Percentage of potatoes sold	78	20	2	100	62	7	31	100
Percentage of potatoes consumed	41	37	22	100	30	8	62	100

commercial crop, barley, in the upper zone. Native commercial types are less important in Paucartambo than in Tulumayo.

Table 5 presents data on the percentage of potato area planted in the three types and the use of the entire potato crop for sale and consumption for each valley. These figures refer to the total seed planted and harvest weight of potatoes as estimated by farmers. Eighty-nine percent of the Tulumayo Valley's potato area is planted to the more commercial types, in comparison to only 39% of the Paucartambo Valley. This contrast suggests that potato production in the Tulumayo Valley is more commercially specialized. Improved types comprise the bulk of potatoes that are sold in each valley. In Paucartambo the consumption of mixed native potatoes is considerably higher, reflecting their greater area there than in Tulumayo.

Table 6 presents data on potato use (sale, consumed, saved for seed) of each of the three types of potatoes. The data in Table 6 show that improved potatoes are

TABLE 6. Potato use by type in Tulumayo and Paucartambo valleys. Values are percentages of potato types.

| | Tulumayo Valley (n = 154) | | | Paucartambo Valley (n = 204) | | |
	Improved	Native Commer.	Native Mixed	Improved	Native Commer.	Native Mixed
Percentage sold	80	62	45	64	50	25
Percentage consumed	9	26	43	20	39	55
Percentage saved for seed	11	12	12	16	11	20
Total	100	100	100	100	100	100

primarily grown for sale in both valleys, but the data also reveal that relatively high percentages of the mixed native varieties are also sold. The data presented in Tables 4–6 suggest that variation in use is continuous rather than discrete. Farmers in both valleys grow different varieties and mixes of varieties in separate fields, but the production from all fields is used for both consumption and sale. Comparing Tables 5 and 6 indicates that no simple division can be made between production for sale of improved potatoes versus production for use of mixed native potatoes. The consumption of native potatoes is higher in Paucartambo, but so is their sale, since modern potatoes represent a smaller proportion of all potatoes produced.

The variation of diversity, management level, and commercialization between fields of different varieties and combinations of varieties is continuous. Tulumayo and Paucartambo farmers do not create, conceive of, or manage fields according to a matrix of discrete types: low input or high input, commercial or subsistence. The continuous gradation of management, selection, and use allows ample opportunity for different mixes of local and outside inputs, enabling the conservation of traditional varieties and production technology throughout the system.

Keeping diversity.—The social framework of Andean agriculture is experiencing fundamental changes: incorporation of local communities into larger regional systems (especially markets), demographic growth, development of economic and technological infrastructure, and political and social restructuring of Andean society through land reform. It has been common to assume that such changes will bring about the rapid decline of diversity, as "traditional" agriculture is replaced by a "modern" system (Hawkes 1983).

Improved potatoes came into the Tulumayo Valley almost as soon as they were released in 1950, but they did not appear in Paucartambo until 1960. Tulumayo farmers average almost twice as many years as their Paucartambo counterparts in producing these varieties (Table 7), and this longer period of adoption is reflected in the higher percentage of potato area in the Tulumayo Valley that is planted with improved varieties. Tulumayo suggests a glimpse of the path of agricultural change that Paucartambo may follow, as measured by agricultural intensification, commercialization, and adoption of new technology. If we accept the model that the diversity of traditional crops will be adversely affected by the increased use of modern technology—in particular, seed varieties and increased integration into the market—then a comparison between the two valleys may give us some idea about the fate of native potatoes.

On a biogeographical basis, we may expect crop diversity to decrease as commercial and more intensive agriculture relying on modern potato varieties takes hold over a larger and larger portion of the two valleys. Table 5 showed that fields of mixed native varieties represented only 11% of the Tulumayo's potato area. These fields are small islands of diversity, surrounded by biologically more uniform fields. The size of these islands of traditional, mixed potatoes is critical to conserving diversity. In Paucartambo, mixed native fields comprise 61% of the potato area. Biogeographically, we should thus expect Tulumayo to have much less diversity than the southern valley.

TABLE 7. Technology adoption and potato diversity.

	Tulumayo Valley	Paucartambo Valley
Average number years using improved varieties[1]	13.9	7.8
Year of first introduction of improved varieties[1]	1950	1960
Percentage of farmers who have ever planted improved varieties[2]	95.8	79.0
Cumulative number of improved varietieci planted since introduction[2]	16	7
Percentage of farms using purchased fertilizer[2]	97.9	85.8
Percentage of farms using pesticides[2]	95.7	77.2
Average number of native varieties per farm[1]	12.8	9.6

[1] n = 87 for Tulumayo and 85 for Paucartambo
[2] n = 154 for Tulmayo and 204 for Paucartambo

In fact, the average number of varieties per household in the Tulumayo Valley is 12.8, compared to 9.6 varieties per household in Paucartambo. Table 7 sets this comparison in the context of adoption of improved varieties, illustrating the idea that the farmers of Paucartambo are at an earlier stage in the adoption process of improved potato varieties. It also suggests that diversity of native potatoes remains, even after adoption becomes virtually complete, as long as some area is planted to native potatoes.

Tulumayo's higher average number of potato varieties per household may result from its history of having greater diversity than Paucartambo before the introduction of modern varieties. However, the southern valley is regarded by most potato biologists to be within the region of greatest diversity in Peru (Hawkes 1983). Nevertheless, Tulumayo's higher average underlines the point that modernization has not eliminated diversity. Statistical modeling indicates that the loss of diversity resulting from technology adoption may be asymptotic after an initial period of genetic erosion (Brush et al. 1992). The loss of diversity is neither simply described nor linear. Social reproduction in the Andes is best understood as a syncretic process whereby local and exogenous elements are continually combined (Allen 1988). Likewise, agricultural change in the Andes is not a dichotomous process of the replacement of older technology, but one whereby indigenous and imported technologies are combined into a single mosaic. Thus, fields of modern potato varieties are managed within the sectoral fallow system, and fields of mixed native potato varieties are rotated with European crops, e.g., barley and fava beans. Potato production in these two Andean valleys is not a dual system of production for use with native technology and production for sale with modern technology. Virtually every potato field has elements of indigenous and outside technology, and production of all types of potatoes is used both for consumption and for sale.

Table 8 outlines the major reasons that favor and discourage native and improved potatoes in relation to three factors: consumption, commercialization, and production. This table suggests the complexity of determining the advantages and disadvantages of producing either type. It also shows that there is no single axis on which to select the two types. Cultural identity, culinary quality, risk, yield, and commercial demand interact in the decision. Andean farmers are accustomed to wrestling with complexity of this nature, and they long ago learned that production and use decisions are not simple dichotomies.

Native potatoes are universally acknowledged to be culinarily superior to modern varieties. The first measure for judging taste in both valleys is how a particular variety tastes when cooked in the *watia,* a simple oven constructed of rocks or sod in the field at harvest time. Varieties are also evaluated by how well they taste after boiling or steaming. Give the problems of synonymy, agreement among people on the identity of different tubers, and individual taste differences, no single native variety represents a culinary standard for other potato varieties. The varieties that come closest to this

TABLE 8. Selection criteria for native and improved potato varieties.

	Factors Favoring Selection		Factors Discouraging Selection	
	Native Varieties	Improved Varieties	Native Varieties	Improved Varieties
Consumption factors	good tasting; valued for gifts	lower unit cost	higher unit costs	inferior taste; less suitable for usual cuisine; larger tubers require more fuel
Commercial factors	higher market value; high exchange value	more profitable (good benefit/ cost ratio)	low yield under traditional management	low market value; limited local market
Production factors	don't need new seed; seed readily available	good short-term resistance to specific risks	less resistance to specific risks	new seed required

status are the cosmopolitan, native commercial ones that are found in virtually every household, such as *huayro* in the central highlands and *qompis* in the south. However, I have been frequently told by informants that rare native varieties are equal or superior to these commercial native varieties.

Native potatoes are preferred as a class because they are drier than the improved varieties, which are thought of as insipid and watery *(uno papa)* and suitable for frying or for soups but not for standard boiling. Ritual meals and celebrations and meals for guests emphasize native potatoes. Weismantel (1988) writes that potatoes occupy a primary place in the system of culinary signs and metaphors that comprise Quichua identity in Ecuador. She observes that "White" guests are served meals in which potatoes are minor complements to chicken and rice, while "Indian" guests are served guinea pig and potatoes. Native varieties are favored gift items and are used to strengthen social ties, and some reports refer to them as "gift potatoes" (Spanish: *papas de regalo*) (Mayer 1979). Native potatoes are often expected as part of wages and during reciprocal labor exchange when meals are served. In the extremely tight labor market of Andean agriculture, the offer of *wayk'u papa* as partial payment is a good way to guarantee a supply of workers at critical times. These potatoes likewise are attractive to distant trading partners who bring meat and wool from the *puna* to exchange for potatoes. There is large and active market for all varieties of potatoes between the two valleys and the regional urban and commercial centers, but the internal market for potatoes within the valleys is small and not well developed. Individual households do not trade, barter, or sell significant amounts of potatoes with their neighbors. Farmers speak of the desire to be self sufficient in the different kinds of potatoes. Thus keeping mixed native potatoes is seen as an option that is preferable to specializing in one type and relying on a market to supply mixed types.

While judged to be culinarily superior, native varieties are perceived as agronomically inferior to the modern ones. Native varieties are lower yielding and more susceptible to the major diseases and environmental risks affecting potato production. Table 4 showed that in both the Tulumayo and Paucartambo valleys improved potatoes are concentrated in the lower, *maway* zone. This zone is less subject to frost than the higher zone, but it is more susceptible to some of the most severe threats in Andean potato production: aphids, viruses, drought, and especially late blight *(Phythphtora infestans)*. Zimmerer (1988) points out that modern potato varieties have completely eliminated native varieties in the lower zones of the Paucartambo Valley.

Modern potato varieties depend on regular supplies of fresh seed tubers, since farmers change the seed for these varieties after two or three years. The seed for native varieties is kept for many years, and it is renewed by rotation between fields at different altitudes. Seventy-two percent of the Tulumayo farmers and 79% of the Paucartambo farmers in the sample reported that they never changed native potato seed. Sixteen percent of Tulumayo farmers and 49% of Paucartambo farmers said they never changed improved potato seed. Large farms that are more commercial or farmers with more capital may thus be more able to plant modern varieties than capital-poor farmers. On the other hand, native potatoes are marketed at premium prices, and a household may broaden its economic strategy by producing them for market. This is evident in the large percentage of land devoted to native comrnercial varieties in each valley.

While Table 8 and the preceding discussion explain the persistence of native potatoes, the question "why so much diversity" remains unanswered. This puzzle cannot be cracked by direct inquiry, because the question "why do you grow so many types of potatoes?" is a silly and nonsensical question to Andean farmers. Informants were surprised and baffled by the question. From their point of view, diversity is natural and a given of the Andean ecosystem, rather than something strange or unusual to be explained. They manage one of the most heterogeneous and complex agroecosystems in the world, and diversity within a single crop and within a single field is a logical corollary of the variety of the world around them. From this perspective, the question of diversity may only be asked indirectly by examining why farmers don't eliminate diversity in favor of a single type of potato, improved or native. This question is less absurd to Andean farmers, but it asks them to speculate about something which they don't usually do.

Farmers in the Tulumayo and Paucartambo valleys have not eliminated diversity because they don't perceive any advantage to doing it and because there are advantages to keeping their mixed collections of native potatoes. Improved varieties don't taste very good, so they are not likely candidates to replace native varieties, and no single native variety meets everyone's criteria for best taste or best for exchange, gifts, or sale. Diversity is a pleasure in its own right when sitting down before a bowl of potatoes as the primary food at a meal. It is common for people to eat 20 to 30 potatoes at a single meal, and it is much more interesting if every other potato is a different variety. Diversity is akin to a condiment, like hot peppers, making meals more interesting. Naming often provides for word games that enliven meals. Some names are clearly evoked by the tuber's characteristics: pink, flat, and oval (cow's tongue, *wacapahallum*), cylindrical with eyes clustered at one end (cat's nose, ***mishpasingu***), or a mottled, rounded oval (condor egg, ***condor runtu***). Other names evoke places, perhaps where the variety originated (e.g., ***Curimarca***). This nomenclature is rich in Andean wit, irony, and iconoclasm. We find such folk varieties as "priest's ear" *(kurnpalingling),* as seen through the confessional screen; another is "dog's vomit" or "dog's stomach" *(alcapapanzan)* in Quechua, glossed to "Peruvian flag" in Spanish.

When queried about replacing mixed native varieties with improved, higher yielding ones or selected native types, farmers point to two things that encourage diversity. First, there is no need to make such a simplifying replacement in the diverse Andean landscape. They cultivate potatoes in several fields each year, and in an Andean variant of agricultural involution, they always find space and time for a few native potatoes. Farmers of the Tulumayo valley have reduced this to a very small portion of their fields, but they maintain a high amount of diversity on this small portion. Enough potatoes are produced to satisfy local needs, and the market is often saturated with potatoes during the main harvest. They complain that they lose money on the potatoes that they do sell (Mayer and Glave 1990). Thus there is no incentive to squeeze out the small fields of native potatoes for food or commerce.

Second, the collections of mixed native potatoes are perceived as a resource by farmers who are economically marginalized. Mixed native potatoes are associated with traditional Andean agriculture and culture by subsistence and commercial farmers, by Quechua and *mestizo* farmers, and by urban consumers. Native potatoes are grown in the most marginal of areas by marginalized farmers. Like other material elements of Andean culture, such as weaving, their value has been inverted in the Andean kaleidoscope (Isabell 1978), that at once depreciates and values items of traditional culture. Products of a humiliated group, native potatoes command premium prices in regional markets, such as Cusco and Huancayo, where they have been elevated to the status of an artisan crop. Within farming communities, native potatoes are also appreciated, perhaps as much for their cultural significance as for their superior flavor. They are favored gift items, and in a rural economy that is increasingly short of labor, they are used as added incentives by landowners to attract workers.

Wholesale merchants who purchase native potatoes have a narrow concept of diversity and prefer the one or two varieties that have won widespread appeal and recognition. However, the flow of diverse native potatoes to urban markets is sufficient to bring new native varieties to the attention of consumers and merchants alike. Periodic "booms" in demand for specific varieties are sufficiently common to be an incentive for farmers to keep diversity as a source of seed. The spread of the *huayro* variety from the central highlands to the Cusco region and the local appearance of *olones* (Franquemont et al. 1990) fit this pattern. The difficulty in multiplying seed rapidly and ambiguity in folk taxonomy are reasons farmers prefer to keep their own inventory of varieties rather than relying on exchange or the market place.

CONCLUSION

This paper has explored the persistence of diversity in Andean potato agriculture. The ethnobiology of the potato crop emphasizes diversity at the infraspecific or variety level. Andean categories such as production zones *(maway tarpuy* and *hatun tarpuy)* and types of potato (dry, *miski papa;* watery, *uno papa;* boiling, *wayk'u papa)* all contribute to this emphasis. This case study is representative of several others on the maintenance of traditional crops in centers of agricultural origins in the face of economic and technological change in agriculture (Boster 1985; Brush et al. 1988; Dennis 1987; Richards 1985). These studies document the resilience of traditional crops, like the cultures that have produced and nurtured them.

We might imagine two alternative futures for traditional Andean potatoes from the above analysis. On the one hand, there might be a gradual encroachment of improved and uniform native varieties under the inexorable pressures of population growth and incorporation into regional market systems. The impact of this encroachment is to shrink the area devoted to mixed native varieties, and this impact is evident in the comparison between the Tulumayo and Paucartambo valleys. The small area of mixed native potatoes with its tremendous diversity may be the last remnant of a waning agricultural system, whose replacement is already present. Ultimately, the area of native potatoes might shrink to nothing, thus completing the biological transformation of Andean agriculture that began with the European conquest 500 years ago. On the other hand, the continued presence of traditional potato area and diversity may be interpreted as biological evidence of the tenacity of Andean cultural elements in the technological polyculture that has existed since the European conquest.

Assuming that market incorporation, demographic growth, and technological innovation will continue and increase, the replacement hypothesis is plausible. However, the persistence of diversity in the Tulumayo Valley, at even a higher level per household than in Paucartambo, suggests that the Andean tradition of diversity will survive. The disappearance of traditional crops and of diversity has been predicted by theorists of very different persuasions (e.g., Hawkes 1983; Fowler and Mooney 1990). Like the predicted demise of peasants, the eclipse of diversity is confounded by the complexity of the tropical world and by the actions of the inheritors of ancient farming traditions. Maintaining crop diversity echoes the survival of Latin American peasantry in the face of major structural change (de Janvry et al. 1989). Many factors dampen the predicted erosion of traditional potatoes in the two valleys described here. While the pressures of the adoption of modern varieties, market penetration, and population increase are significant, so too are cultural, economic, and environmental factors that buffer their impact. There is no single axis on which to chart the fate of these genetic resources as farming systems change. What seems to be predictable is that farmers will continue to be active agents in conserving the material base of their Andean agricultural legacy.

ACKNOWLEDGMENTS

This research was supported by funds from the National Science Foundation (BNS 8416724), USAID grant DPE-10680G-SS-8003, and the University of California, Davis. Fieldwork in Peru was conducted in collaboration with Enrique Mayer and Cesar Fonseca, co-principal investigators with Stephen Brush in a project on land use change in the Andes. Z. Huamáan of the International Potato Center and R. Ortega of the National University of San Antonio Abad in Cusco provided useful suggestions. Research assistance in Peru was provided by K. Zimmerer, M. Glave, M. Granados, A. Carbajal, C. Peñafiel, J. Perea, J. Lopez, L. Concha, E. Gudiel, and T. Inca Roca. Mauricio Bellon, Suzanne Vaupel, and Heather Jersild provided valuable assistance and suggestions for the analysis of field data. Hilda Murguia and Ramiro Ortega assisted with the Quechua orthography. Mauricio Bellon, Daniel Mountjoy, Benjamin Orlove, Anne Fitzgerald, Laura Merrick, and Timothy Johns gave useful comments on an earlier draft. Any errors are the author's responsibility.

LITERATURE CITED

Allen, Catherine J. 1988. The Hold Life Has: Coca and Cultural Identity in an Andean Community. Smithsonian Institution Press, Washington, D.C.
Atran, Scott. 1987. Origin of the species and genus concepts: An anthropological perspective. Journal of the History of Biology 20: 195–279.

Berlin, Brent. 1976. The concept of rank in ethnobiological classification: Some evidence from Aguaruna folk botany. American Ethnologist 3: 381–99.

Bertonio, P. Ludovico. 1612. Vocabulario de la Lengua Aymara. Centro de Estudios de la Realidad Económica y Social (reprinted in 1984), La Paz, Bolivia.

Boster, James S. 1985. Selection for perceptual distinctiveness: Evidence from Aguaruna cultivars. Economic Botany 39: 310–25.

Brokensha, David, Michael Warren, and Oswald Werner. 1980. Indigenous Knowledge Systems and Development. University Press of Amer ica, Lanham, Md.

Brunel, Giles R. 1975. Variation in Quechua folk biology. Unpublished Ph.D. dissertation, Department of Anthropology, University of California, Berkeley.

Brush, Stephen B. 1977. Mountain, Field, and Family: The Economy and Human Ecology of an Andean Valley. University of Pennsylvania Press, Philadelphia.

————, Mauricio Bellon, and Ella Schmidt. 1988. Agricultural development and maize diversity in Mexico. Human Ecology 16: 307–28.

————, Heath J. Carney, and Zosimo Huaman. 1981. Dynamics of Andean potato agriculture. Economic Bntany 15: 70–85.

————, J. Edward Taylor, and Mauricio Bellon. 1992. Technology adoption and biological diversity in Andean agriculture. Journal of Develop ment Economics 39: 365–87.

Bulmer, Ralph. 1970. Which came first, the chicken or the Egg-head? Pp. 1069–1091 in Echanges et Communications. Edited by Jean Pouillon and Pierre Miranda. Mouton, The Hague.

————. 1974. Folk biology in the New Guinea highlands. Social Science Information 13: 9–28.

Burtt, B. L. 1970. Infraspecific categories in flowering plants. Biological Journal of the Linnean Society 2: 233–38.

Carter, William E. and Mauricio Mamani P. 1982. Irpa Chico: Individuo y Comunidad en la Cultura Andina. Libreria-Editorial Joventud, La Paz, Bolivia.

Clawson, David. 1985. Harvest security and interspecific diversity in traditional tropical agriculture. Economic Botany 39: 56–67.

De Candolle, Alfonse. 1882. Origine des Plantes Cultivées. Germer Bailliere, Paris.

Dejanvry, Alain, Elisabeth Sadoulet, and Linda Wilcox Yound. 1989. Land and labour in Latin American agriculture from the 1950s to the 1980s. Journal of Peasant Studies 16: 398–424.

Dennis, John V. 1987. Farmer management of rice variety diversity in northern Thailand. Ph.D. dissertation, Department of Rural Sociology, Cornell University. University Microfilms, Ann Arbor.

Dougherty, Janet W. D. 1978. Salience and relativity in classification. American Ethnologist 5: 66–80.

Ferroni, Marco A. 1979. The urban bias of Peruvian food policy: Consequences and alternatives. Unpublished Ph.D. dissertation, Department of Economics, Cornell University, Ithaca.

Fowler, Cary and Pat Mooney. 1990. Shattering: Food, Politics, and the Loss of Genetic Diversity. University of Arizona Press, Tucson.

Franquemont, Christine, Timothy Plowman, Edward Franquemont, Steven R. King, Christine Niezgoda, Wade Davis, and Calvin R. Sperling. 1990. The Ethnobotany of Chinchero: An Andead community in southern Peru. Fieldiana, Botany. No. 24. Field Museum of Natural History, Chicago.

Gade, Daniel W. 1975. Plants, Man and the Land in the Vilcanota Valley of Peru, Vol. 6: Biogeographica. W. Junk B. V., The Hague.

Golte, Jürgen. 1980. La Racionalidad de la Organización Andina. Instituto de Estudios Peruanos, Lima.

Hawkes, J. G. 1947. The origin and meaning of South American Indian potato names. Journal of the Linnean Society, Botany 53: 205–50.

———. 1983. The Diversity of Crop Plants. Harvard University Press, Cambridge.

——— and J. P. Hjerting. 1989. The rotatoes of Bolivia: Their Breeding Value and Evolutionary Relationships. Clarendon Press, Oxford.

Horton, Douglas. 1984. Social Scientists in Agricultural Research: Lessons from the Mantaro Valley Project, Peru. International Development Research Centre, Ottawa.

Huaman, Zosimo. 1986. Conservation of potato genetic resources at CIP (Centro Internacional de Papas). CIP Circular 14: 1–7.

Isbell, Billie Jean. 1978. To Defend Ourselves: Ecology and Ritual in an Andean Village. University of Texas Press, Austin.

Johnson, Allen. 1974. Ethnoecology and planting practices in a swidden agricultural system. American Ethnologist 1: 87–101.

Johnsson, Mick. 1986. Food and culture among the Bolivian Aymara: Symbolic expressions of social relations. Uppsala Studies in Cultural Anthropology 7. Almqvist and Wiksell International, Stockholm.

Johns, Timothy. 1990. With Bitter Herbs They Shall Eat It: Chemical Ecology and the Origins of Human Diet and Medicine. University of Arizona Press, Tucson.

LaBarre, Weston. 1947. Potato taxonomy among the Aymara Indians of Bolivia. Acta Americana 5: 83–103.

Long, Norman and Brian Roberts. 1984. Miners, Peasants and Entrepreneurs: Regional Development in the Central Highlands of Peru. Cambridge University Press, Cambridge.

McArthur, Robert H. and Edward O. Wilson. 1967. The Theory of Island Biogeography. Princeton University Press, Princeton.

McCamant, Kris Ann. 1986. The organization of agricultural production in Corporaque, Peru. Unpublished Masters thesis, Department of Latin American Studies, University of California, Berkeley.

Mallon, Florencia E. 1983. The Defense of Community in Peru's Central Highlands. Princeton University Press, Princeton.

Mayer, Enrique. 1979. Land Use in the Andes. Centro Internacional de la Papa, Lima.

———, and Manuel Glave. 1990. Papas regaladas y papas regalo: Rentabilidad, costos e inversión. Pp. 87–120 in Peru: El Problema Agrario en Debate. Alberto Chirif, Nelson Manrique, and Benjamin Quinandria (editors). Seminario Permanente de Investigación Agraria, Lima.

———, and Cesar Fonseca. 1979. Sistemas Agrarios en la Cuenca del Rió Cañete. Departamento de Lima, Oficina Nacional de Evaluación de Recursos Naturales, Lima.

Murra, John V. 1975. Formaciones Económicas y Políticas del Mundo Andino. Instituto de Estudios Peruanos, Lima.

Ochoa, Carlos. 1975. Potato collecting expeditions in Chile, Bolivia and Peru, and the genetic erosion of indigenous cultivars. Pp. 167–73 in Crop Genetic Resources for Today and Tomorrow. International Biological Programme Vol. 2. Edited by Otto H. Frankel and John Gregory Hawkes. Cambridge University Press, Cambridge.

Orlove, Benjamin S. and Ricardo Godoy. 1986. Sectoral fallow systems in the central Andes. Journal of Ethnobiology 6: 169–204.

Pickersgill, Barbara and Charles B. Heiser. 1978. Origins and distribution of plants domesticated in the New World tropics. Pp. 208–36 in Origins of Agriculture. Edited by Charles A. Reed. Mouton, The Hague.

Quiros, Carlos, Stephen B. Brush, David S. Douches, Karl S. Zimmerer, and Gordon Huestis. 1990. Biochemical and folk assessment of variability of Andean cultivated potatoes. Economic Botany 44 254–66.

Richards, Paul. 1985. Indigenous Agricultural Revolution: Ecology and Food Production in West Africa. Westview Press, Boulder, Colo.

Tapia Nunez, Mario and Jorge A. Flores Ochoa. 1984. Pastoreo y Pas tizales de los Andes del Sur del Perú. Instituto Nacional de Investigación y Promoción Agropecuaría, Lima.

Thomas R. Brooke. 1973. Human adaptation to a high Andean energy flow system. Pennsylvania State University, Department of Anthropology, Occasional Papers in Anthropology No. 7.

Universidad Nacional San Cristobal de Huamanga. 1983. Diagnóstico Técnico Agropecuarío de las Comunidades Campesinas de Arizona, Qas anqay Ayacucho, 1983. In.stituto Inter americano de Cooperación para la Agricultura (IICA), Lima.

Urban Francis and Michael True Blood. 1990. World Population by Country and Region, 1950–2050. U.S. Department of Agriculture, Washington, D.C.

Vavilov, Nikolai. 1926. Studies on the Origin of Cultivated Plants. Institute of Applied Botany and Plant Improvement, Leningrad.

Weismantel, Mary J. 1988. Food, Gender and Poverty in the Ecuadorean Andes. University of Pennsylvania Press, Philadelphia.

Zimmerer, Karl. 1988. Seeds of subsistence: Agrarian structure and genetic erosion in the peasant society of Paucartambo, Peru (Cusco). Ph.D. dissertation, Department of Geography, University of California, Bcrkeley. University Microfilms, Ann Arbor.

———. 1991a. Managing diversity in potato and maize fields of the Peruvian Andes. Journal of Ethnobiology 11:23–49.

———. 1991b. The regional biogeography of native potato cultivars in highland Peru. Journal of Biogeography 18:165–78.

CHAPTER FOURTEEN

Choice of Fuel for Bagaço Stills Helps Maintain Biological Diversity in a Traditional Portuguese Agricultural System

GEORGE F. ESTABROOK

INTRODUCTION

An important reason to study a traditional agricultural system where it has supported a population for hundreds of years is to try to determine, from an ecological point of view, how various aspects of its technology contribute not only to the productivity but also to the sustainability of the system. Because traditional agricultural technology is usually developed empirically over generations, ecological explanations for some of the very specific, but seemingly arbitrary, practices are not always apparent in the oral tradition of the contemporary population, especially when these practices are more related to long-term sustainability than to short-term productivity. It is remarkable how the persistent empiricism of human beings, struggling to make their living in nature, results in practices that make ecological sense, even though they may be codified in ritual or explained in ways that seem superficial or not compelling ecologically. Indeed, local practitioners may have concepts, equally justifiable but very different from those of academics, of what constitutes a useful explanation. This study of a traditional Portuguese agricultural system provides several examples, one of which is an ecological explanation for what initially seemed an arbitrary but nonetheless very specific fuel choice for the brief annual task of distilling a brandy-like liquid, called *bagaco,* from the mass of grape skins, seeds, and pulp that is left over after wine has been made.

In rural villages in Portugal, grapes are harvested in the fall and made into wine. After the fermented wine has been drained from the fermenting vat and casked, alcohol is distilled from the leftover grape skins and pulp by heating them gently over a cool fire. The distillate, called *bagaço* in some regions, is about 40% ethanol and 60% water, plus traces of higher alcohols and impurities. A little of it is drunk, but traditionally most of it is used as a household chemical for treating minor injuries, sterilizing, and cleaning.

The western and southern foothills of the Serra da Estrela (Fig. 1.), the highest range of mountains in Portugal, are made predominantly of Precambrian shale, with occasional quartzite intrusions. This shale easily erodes, producing very infertile clay soil of resedimented ilites high in iron and with low available water capacity (Azevedo and Ricardo 1973), and also producing very deep, steep-sided valleys that alternate with these quartzite peaks and ridges. Paths over the steep, crumbly rock offer poor footing. There is little or no rain in the summer months when temperatures often exceed 30° C. During the winter, temperatures are near 0° C at dawn, rising to near 15° C during the day. Frequent rains raise impassible torrents in the valley bottoms and erode from the hillsides what little soil may have accumulated during the past year.

Human beings have been culturally and economically active in Portugal for thousands of years. However, low overall population densities before the sixteenth century, abundant nearby land that is more level and fertile, the harshness and infertility of these foothills, and the establishment there of Catholic church parishes not before the fourteenth and fifteenth centuries, together suggest that this area had remained largely unoccupied until the fourteenth or fifteenth centuries. Although a discussion of the biological, social, political, and economic factors that may have motivated people to attempt to inhabit this region in the fourteenth century are beyond the scope of the work reported here, it seems plausible that many of the current practices directly observed in this study are based on techniques that have enabled people to inhabit successfully this harsh and infertile area since the fifteenth century. These techniques, and the self-sufficient village economies they supported, have largely disappeared from Portugal now. Refer to Pearson et al. (1987) for discussions of traditional Portuguese agricultural technology, and of the recent social, political, economic, and technological changes that have contributed to its disappearance.

All the details of the agricultural technology that enabled people to thrive in this marginal environment are beyond the scope of the work presented here, but a brief overview of the techniques used to create and maintain soil fertility is relevant. Cultivation of crops occurs on the steep hillsides in narrow terraces that are constructed of dry stone walls that hold the soil level. In winter, these terraces collect soil and water from above and help control water erosion. In the dry summer they facilitate irrigation by streams of water that trickle from slightly rising caves that have been dug above them about 10 m into the soft shale rock, where the shale is still wet from the rains of the past winter. To create fertility in the infertile clay soil in these terraces, large quantities of organic matter are collected, as brush from the hill tops, and mixed with the soil.

Shrubs, mostly heaths and legumes, make up the scrubby vegetation type called *mato,* which occurs in central-interior Portugal on the tops and upper slopes of shale hills. The *mato* on any given place is cut near ground level every four years. *Mato* is cut from somewhere, two or three times a week, all year long, and removed to the village, where it is spread over the floor of indoor, ground level rooms that house goats. After two to four weeks, this old *mato* is removed and replaced with freshly cut *mato.* After its removal, the old cut *mato* is piled up, and at planting time, buried in the soil of the cultivated terraces. Cut *mato,* enriched by goats, is the source of virtually all soil-borne plant nutrients, and much of the soil's available water capacity.

After a plant is cut, it regenerates from a woody root crown (caudex) just below the ground surface. These caudices ramify into an extensive system of fine roots, which penetrate for meters into the soft shale rock below. Although virtually all *mato*

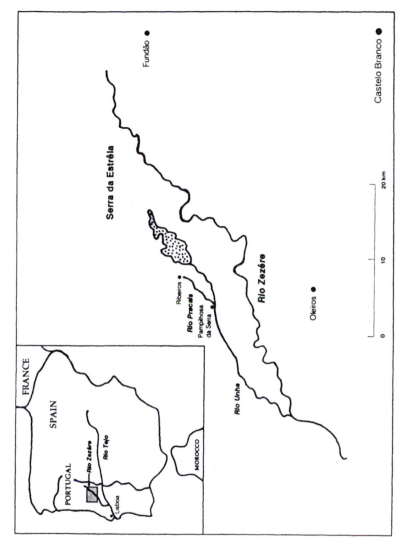

Fig. 1. Map showing the location of the village of Ribeiros, at the headwaters of the Rio Pracais in the south-west foothills of the Serra da Estrela, Portugal. At the town of Pampilhosa da Serra, The Rio Pracais meets the Rio Unha, a tributary of Rio Zezere in the Rio Tejo drainage. The stippled area is an empoundment. Region of map is approximately the rectangle shown on the inserted outline of Iberia.

Table 1. Principle mato species of the region studied.

Scientific name	Common name	Collector Family	Number[1]
Erica arborea L.	*mato negral*	Ericaceae	404
Ulex minor Roth	*tojo branco*	Fabaceae	407
Genista tricanthos Brot.	*tojo negro*	Fabaceae	406
Erica cinerea L.	*urze*	Ericaceae	403
Halimium ocymoidies (Lam.) Wilk. In Wilk & Lange	unknown	Cistaceae	408
Lithodora diffusa (Lag.) I.M.Johnson	unknown	Boraginaceae	401
Caluna vulgaris (L.) Hull	*margarise*	Ericaceae	405
Erica umbellata L.	*negrela*	Ericaceae	402
Chamaespartum tridentatum (L.) P. Gibbs	*carqueja*	Ericaceae	400

[1]All voucher specimens were collected by G. F. Estabrook and are housed at MICH.

species regenerate in this way, the woody caudex of essentially only one, *Erica arborea,* is dug out and burned to distill *bagaço.* The caudex of *E. arborea* burns cool and slow, thus distilling the *bagaço* with a minimum of impurities and water. Pine *(Pinus pinaster),* used inside the houses for cooking and warmth, would burn too hot, but any of the woody caudices of the *mato* species would burn cool and slow. Although the caudices of other mato species *are* occasionally used in conjunction with *E. arborea,* farmers clearly prefer *E. arborea* for still fires. Why principally just this one? They stated that it was used by their parents and grandparents, and that it is the best fuel for this task, but they never offered an explicit, functional or ecological explanation for their preference over other "roots."

Most of the principal *mato* species (Table 1) make distinct contributions, which this study will describe, to soil fertility and to other aspects of the local economy. Therefore, the maintenance of the species diversity of the *mato* is an important objective of this agricultural system. This study will also present species abundance data from plots of *mato* regenerating for differing numbers of years and subjected to different harvesting histories. These data show that Erica arborea, if not held in check, becomes the dominant species and thus reduces species richness and diversity in the *mato.* The choice of the regeneration organ (the caudex) of *E. arborea* as a still fuel eliminates the domination of this species. Elimination of dominance maintains the species diversity in the *mato,* which contributes to the sustainability of this self-sufficient village economy. Grime (1979) discusses in more detail competitive dominance and disturbance-mediated co-existence in stress tolerant plants.

It takes 9–10 ha of regenerating *mato* to supply enough organic matter to create fertility in 1 ha of cultivated terrace. It seems likely that the availability of *mato* may have begun to limit the amount of terrace under cultivation by the beginning of the nineteenth century or earlier. In this situation, all *mato* would have been managed for soil fertility, and thus cut every three or four years. Once the practice of removing a few *Erica arborea* caudices each fall was established, the potential for *E. arborea* to reduce or eliminate other valuable species would no longer be directly observed by the villagers. In the absence of these direct observations, a reason to remove every fall a few *E. arborea* caudices to burn in the brief task of distilling *bagaço* would ensure that the practice happened every year, and thus might serve the local economy better than would a more objectively founded, ecological explanation that did not require a specific action at a specific time.

MATERIALS AND METHODS

The principle area studied is the village group of Ribeiros, located in the Freguesia de Cabril, Concelho de Pampilhosa da Serra, Distrito de Coimbra, Portugal, at about north 40° 06' by west 7° 54'. The village is located near the center of this region of eroded shale foothills, among the branching streamlets (called *ribeiros,* hence the name) at the headwaters of the Rio Pracais, a stream that runs down a deep, steep-sided gully to the Unha river in the Rio Tejo drainage, as shown in Fig. 1. The elevation of the village is 750 m, with the hill tops and ridges rising 100–300 m above the village. Ribeiros is the modern name of the coalescence of three original settlements (Sobra-linho, Melho, and Sanguasuga, located about 1 km apart but separated by deep stream gullies), which, judging from church records, was probably established in the late sixteenth century. It continued to grow steadily, and thrived in the nineteenth and first half of the twentieth centuries, reaching a population peak of approximately 300 in 1940, when the first road capable of carrying a motorized vehicle was built into the area to construct an empoundment (Fig. 1) to generate electric power. By the late 1940s, Ribeiros had begun to lose population rapidly, and by 1988 at the conclusion of this study there were some 25 residents, mostly over 60 years old. Refer to Caldas (1981), Serrao (1982), and Brettell (1986) for a discussion of possible reasons for the near universal demise of northern, interior Portuguese villages since the 1940s.

In the 1980s, preindustrial agricultural technology was still practiced, if incom-pletely, by some of the residents of the villages of the Pracais valley, where I visited briefly in 1980, 1983, and 1984. The steep hillsides surrounding Ribeiros are covered with terraces, some of which may have been originally built over 400 years ago when residents and place names in Ribeiros are first mentioned in church birth records. By the 1980s approximately half of these terraces had been abandoned and about 40% had been planted to apple, fig, and olive within the last decade or so by largely absent owners. The remaining 10% were still in cultivation, mostly in corn, bean, potato, and some rye. In terraces closer to the village, vegetables and herbs are grown. The *mato* is harvested at about one tenth the rate that it was 50 years ago when, according to residents, all terraces were planted with seeds. Because agricultural practices in the village are in decline, much of the *mato* on the surrounding hilltops had not been harvested for varying lengths of time, up to 30 or more years.

I lived in Ribeiros from August until December of 1987. Two married couples among the 21 permanent residents provided me with food and shelter, and introduced

and endorsed me to the other residents. This endorsement was essential for any resident to speak freely with me. The residents consisted of eight married couples, no
single men, and four to six women who were never married or were widows. Except
for the wives of my hosts, the wives of the other six men were essentially not socially
accessible to me. Three of the single women would talk readily and accept my help.

During the first two months of my fieldwork, I observed people at work, took
samples of soil and vegetation, and with the help of a tape recorder and interpreter,
learned the local dialect. During the last three months, I conducted informal interviews on demography, agricultural technology, and economic activities. Typically I
spent half of each day talking either repeatedly to the same 13 accessible residents of
Ribeiros, or to visitors to the village (nine occasions) or to residents of a nearby village
(12 occasions). I talked with people usually as long as they would give me their attention, from a few minutes to often an hour or more. I asked the same things in many
different ways on different days of the same people and also of different people. I
found that whenever different people talked about the same technical subject, their
representations were mutually consistent, never contradictory.

To determine and vouch *mato* species accurately, I collected plants in the *mato*
near Ribeiros. These collections were identified at the herbarium of the Estaçaõ
Agronômica Naçional (LISE), in Oeiras near Lisboa, and named according to *Nova
Flora de Portugal* (Franco 1971, 1984). Voucher specimens were deposited in this
herbarium, and at The University of Michigan Herbarium (MICH).

To calculate the diversity and abundance of the species of plants in the *mato* from
areas subject to different harvesting regimes, I collected samples of vegetation from
four areas (referred to as Areas 1–4) in the *mato*-covered slopes to the north and to the
east of Ribeiros. Area 1, located 130 m above, and 1 km from, Ribeiros, has been
actively harvested for as long as residents can remember. *Erica arborea* caudex is still
taken from here to distill *bagaço*. Area 2 is also still actively harvested, but *E. arborea*
caudex has not been taken from it recently. This area is located 150 m above, and
about 2 km from, Ribeiros. Areas 3 and 4 contain *mato* vegetation that has never been
actively harvested. These areas, located on a nearly level hilltop shoulder, are about
250 m above, and 4 km distant from, Ribeiros. Rye, which grows without irrigation
during the cold, wet winter, had been cultivated here but cultivation was abandoned
about 30 years ago, largely because of the inconvenient distance of the fields from
Ribeiros. *Mato* established spontaneously when this rye plot was abandoned. Area 3
is the eastern part of this shoulder, where above ground *mato* vegetation burned off 8
years ago and has since regenerated. It also contains young pines *(Pinus pinaster)*, all
less than 8 years old. This pine does not survive fires but grows readily from seed
following fires or other disturbance. Area 4 is the western part that did not burn. Its
pines and *mato* are approximately 30 years old.

The residents' description of the history of the vegetation in Areas 3 and 4 is
corroborated by the age of the pines growing in these areas. Pines grow a swirl of
branches from their trunk every year. For at least the first 20 and often up to 30 or 40
years, one can age pines by counting these swirls. Sometimes a few years' swirls will
be universally lost by wind or by a bud worm break out that inhibits the growth of

swirls. This can be checked by counting growth rings. I cut down a 7-year-old sapling, whose rings and swirls matched.

In Area 1 and Area 2, *mato* is cut on a four-year cycle and had been regenerating for the past four years. Individual caudices regenerate growth 10–20 cm in circumference during four years. Areas 1 and 2 have only five or six abundant species. At the scale of a meter square, relative species abundance varies little throughout these areas. So, from an arbitrary one square meter plot in each of Area 1 and Area 2, all vegetation was cut at about 3 cm above the ground, the approximate height at which it is cut by residents when harvested for use. Plants were sorted by species into plastic bags, and removed the next day to Coimbra where the contents of each bag were dried and weighed.

In Area 3, some plants have grown to three times the size of those in Area 1 or 2. Relative species abundance was quite variable at the scale of a square meter, but became more uniform for areas two or three times as large. For this reason, an arbitrary plot 2 m $\times$ 3 m was selected for harvesting. All vegetation was cut as described above and sorted by species. Because of the large amount of vegetation produced on this 6 m2 plot, the quantity produced by each species was weighed wet in the field and approximately 0.5 kg was sealed wet in a plastic bag and removed the next day to Coimbra, where it was weighed and dried and re weighed to determine percent dry weight.

No vegetation samples were taken from Area 4, but the kinds, sizes, and relative abundances of these very large plants were recorded.

To determine the potential of each *mato* species to enrich the soil with mineral nutrients, each plant species was analysed for levels of minerals, including nitrogen and phosphorous, at the Laboratório Agrícola Química Ribelo da Silva in Lisboa.

RESULTS

An account of the history and technology of agriculture in this region, learned as a result of my interviews, archival research, and field observations, was presented above. The results presented here are of three kinds. First, what residents do with and say about the most common species in the *mato* establishes the conspicuous importance of maintaining the biological diversity of *mato* species. Second, the relative abundances of *mato* species measured from plots with different disturbance histories evidences that *Erica arborea* becomes dominant in plots where it is not periodically reduced. Third, the relative abundance among *mato* species of mineral nutrients essential for crops establishes the inconspicuous importance of maintaining the biological diversity of *mato* species for soil fertilization.

Erica arborea is called *mato negral,* which means grey or dark *mato*. Although this study reveals it to be the competitive dominant (Table 2), it is not considered a weed or otherwise undesirable by the village farmers. Its woody caudex is genuinely valued as a fuel, and its foliage is also valued as goat forage and bedding. Like all the harvested *mato,* it is spread over the ground inside the goat houses, where it is enriched by goat urine and excrement before it is finally added to the soil.

TABLE 2. Above ground accumulation in three areas of *mato*. Dry weight (gm) of accumulation per m² precedes average accumulation per year for each species.

Areas	Area 1		Area 2		Area 3	
Size, age	1 m²	4 yr	1 m²	4 yr	6 m²	8 yr
Species						
Erica arborea	103	26	222	56	1,702	213
Ulex minor	—		347	87	882	110
Genista tricanthos	—		104	26	590	74
Erica cinerea	—		163	41	35	4
Halimium ocymoides	—		12	3	7	1
Lithordora difusa	5	1	—		3	0
Caluna vulgaris	30	8	241	60	63	8
Erica umbellata	256	64	—		—	
Chamaespartum tridentatum	816	204	198	50	—	

Ulex minor is called *tojo branco*, which means white *tojo*, even though it is covered with green leaves and prickers all year long. *Genista tricanthos* is called *tojo negro*, which means black *tojo*. It has green leaves in the winter that fall in the dry season, leaving a dark brown thorn scrub that not even goats will eat. Both *tojos* prick the hands of *mato* harvesters, making harvesting unpleasant and difficult, but these plants are nonetheless harvested, included in goat bedding, and finally buried in the soil. Beyond repeating their preference for *mato negral*, residents did not say why the regeneration organs of *tojo branco* and *tojo negro* are not dug up and burned in stills.

Erica cinerea is called *urze*. It is valued for goat forage, although I rarely saw goats eating it, and highly valued for goat bedding. Except from the thorny *tojos*, there was nothing superficially apparent to set *urze* apart from the other cut *mato* spread on the floor in goat houses.

Halimium ocymoides and *Lithodora difusa* are called *mato* plants by residents, but did not have more specific names that anyone remembered. Neither did residents describe specific uses for them. These species make up a very small percentage of the *mato*.

Caluna vulgaris is called *margarise* by the residents of Ribeiros. This species, one of several known as heather, is common throughout northern Europe as well. In Ribeiros, its floral display in August and September is spectacular. Its prolific nectar production is recognized, and in order to increase the amount of honey collected by village bee keepers, *mato* is harvested less frequently during the flowering season of *margarise*.

Erica umbellata is called *negrela*, a diminutive *negral*. Its caudex is not taken for fuel, and it is readily excluded by its more aggressive congener, *E. arborea*. Although *urze* is explicitly recognized, all three *Ericas* are valued as goat bedding.

Chamaespartum tridentatum is called *carqueja* here and over most of northern Portugal. It is highly valued as goat forage. The stems are only slightly lignified, and the goats eat much more of it than of the other *mato* species. Like all harvested *mato*, it becomes part of the goat pen bedding before being added to the soil.

TABLE 3. Concentration (percent dry weight) of nitrogen (N), and phosphorous (P) in samples of *mato* species from study areas, and in a homogenized sample of old cut *mato* removed from the floor of a room housing goats.

	N	P
Erica arborea	0.86	0.055
Ulex minor	0.64	0.140
Genista tricanthos	1.24	0.101
Erica cinerea	0.64	0.160
Halimium ocymoides	0.59	0.080
Lithodora difusa	0.63	0.096
Caluna vulgaris	0.58	0.098
Erica umbellata	0.90	0.055
Chamaespartum tridentatum	0.48	0.100
Old *mato*, homogenized	1.44	0.377

Table 2 presents the total and approximate annual above ground accumulation, in dry weight, of each species at each of Areas 1, 2, and 3. Area 4 was densely dominated by *E. arborea*, which had grown, true to its name, into gnarled trees, 2–3 m high, overtopped with 30-year-old pines.

Table 3 presents concentrations, in percent dry weight, of nitrogen and of phosphorous, in samples of *mato* species collected from the study areas, and in old cut *mato* removed from the floor of a room used to house goats. For both of these plant nutrients, the concentrations vary among the species by a factor of more than 2.5. Nutrient levels are clearly increased in *mato* that has been on the floor where goats are housed.

DISCUSSION

For the last 500 years or more, growth of plants of the *mato* has been essential for the maintenance of soil fertility in the Pracais valley and throughout central interior Portugal. The *mato* species play different and complementary roles to support the lives of the local people. Sugar production, fuel, goat forage, and soil fertility have been mentioned here. Thus, maintaining the species diversity of the *mato* is of genuine, immediate economic value to the residents. Some of their traditional practices can be understood by observing and interviewing the people who employ them. Other dimensions of this understanding are suggested by evidence revealed by the decline or discontinuance of these practices, by experimentation, and by laboratory analysis.

Mato negral is one of the many useful plants of the mato, but its competitive superiority would reduce species diversity if were not somehow controlled. The utility of its caudex (the regeneration organ) as a distilling fuel is the stated reason for digging up caudices every fall, even though the caudex of any *mato* plant would work well in a still fire. Over the past 100 years or more, people may have forgotten that this practice helps maintain *mato* species diversity because, when all the mato was being cut and properly managed to maintain both soil fertility and diversity, *mato negral* never had a chance to reveal its dominance. This more ecologically and observationally founded understanding of dominance reduction remains implicit in the traditional preference for *mato negral* caudex as the still fuel. It is much more important to the local economy to practice the appropriate activities at the right time than to explain them objectively as long term ecological phenomena.

The residents of the Pracais valley often do explain their technology in very objective terms and with sound observational bases. Their explanation of irrigation technology and the factors that determine the height, width, and frequency of dry stone retaining walls for cultivated terraces, are two examples. Here, scientific explanations incorporate what people need to do to create and maintain these structures. Thus to participants in this self-sufficient economy, an important part of the utility of an explanation is to help people remember what to do.

Results of this study provide two other examples of local distinctions or explanations that seem to serve primarily to instruct people what to do or value, but that also have compelling scientific explanations of longer term effects. The naming of the three different species of *Erica* that occur in the *mato* provides one example. All three *Ericas* look similar enough to be considered congeners by taxonomists; indeed two of them, the large and small *negral*, are given similar names by residents even though they must be distinguished when it is time to distill *bagaço*. Residents give *urze*, *Erica cinerea*, separate folk generic status and value it highly as goat bedding, even though they give no compelling reasons. When the cut branches of *urze* are spread on the floor of the goat pen with those of other *mato* species, they cannot be readily distinguished and the goats do not seem to treat them differently. Residents do not know that *urze* branches, in comparison to those of the other *mato* species, have the highest phosphorous concentration. As Table 3 shows, *urze* has more than twice the phosphorous of most other *mato* species (only *Ulex minor* has comparable, but lower, levels), and three times the phosphorous of the other two *Ericas*. Because traditional practice is to use and value this species for goat bedding, which ultimately becomes soil enrichment, soil phosphorous levels are more effectively maintained. The ancient sedimentary ilite minerals in the shale-derived soils of central interior Portugal are especially poor in phosphorous and rich in iron (Azevedo and Ricardo 1973). Iron tends to chelate phosphorus so that it can not be taken up by plants. The release of phosphorous from decaying organic matter occurs at a slow enough rate that it can be taken up immediately by growing crop plants and not lost to the iron in the soil. Thus, organic matter has probably always been an essential source of phosphorous for this agricultural system. It is not surprising that hundreds of years of agricultural tradition in this region has distinguished the plant that is the best organic source of phosphorous from other members of its genus, and valued it as goat bedding, even though as goat bedding per se it has no special value.

The second example of an explanation that seems not to have an observational basis, but that is preferred by villagers because it helps people remember what to do, is provided by the concept of the goats' bed. Like valuing *urze* for goat bedding and removing occasional *Erica arborea* caudices for still fires, the important consequence of spreading *mato* as goat bedding is not immediately apparent, and so an explanation that requires the appropriate activity is created. Residents spent about a quarter of their total economic effort cutting *mato*, hauling *mato*, spreading it out in goat pens to make a "bed" for goats, removing it from goat pens, piling it in heaps, and finally carrying it to cultivated terraces to dig into the soil before a new crop is planted. Although this effort is essential for the maintenance of soil fertility, it was always explained primarily as providing food or bed for goats. Goats feed as foragers grazing at large during the day, and on weeds and thinnings pulled from the cultivated terraces and given to them, along with occasional rations of grain, when they return to their pens in the evening. Except for *carqueja*, the goats ate very little of the cut *mato*, all of which was spread out below them to make their "bed." Even *tojo negro*, leafless, spiny wands of dense wood that goats won't eat, is included in this "bed." The goats stand up, rarely lying on their thorny bed of sticks and twigs. Why is cutting and carrying *mato* explained as a means of providing food and bedding for goats, when residents are fully aware that their goats eat very little of it and rarely lie on it? Why is it not explained as a means of maintaining soil fertility, the need for which the residents are also fully aware? Spreading *urze, tojo negro,* and the rest of the cut *mato* in goat pens before adding it to the soil raises the ratio of nitrogen to carbon in cut *mato* (Table 3). When this old cut *mato* is buried in soil, the higher N/C ratio provides a microenvironment in which the balance of microbes is shifted towards more effective decay organisms that can decompose *mato* and release its nutrients during one growing season (Griffin 1972). In fact, no residual sticks or twigs were evident in the soil at the time of the corn harvest even though 7–10 metric tons dry weight per hectare of *mato* (mostly sticks and twigs) had been added at the time of corn planting. Effective, rapid decay of the dense woody branches of *Genista tricanthos,* which might otherwise decay more slowly than the fruticose twigs of some other *mato* species, is especially important because this species is highest in nitrogen, substantially higher than other species of *mato* (Table 3). Thus it is important for soil fertility to leave the caudices of the slow growing *tojo negro* in the ground, to include its dense, spiny branches in the harvest of cut *mato* and especially to spread them out in the goat pens. Chemical analyses and microbial ecology are not evoked by residents to explain why they include inedible thorns in the "food" and "bed" of goats, but the consequences of their traditional agricultural practices are clear. Feeding and bedding goats is an explanation that reminds farmers what to do next, especially when the long term consequences of the activity are important, but not immediately apparent. This more proximal, but apparently less correct explanation, thus may serve a self-sufficient village economy better than would a more ultimate, and apparently more correct, one.

     Other authors have discussed aspects of some of the ideas presented here. Brush (1986) documents the maintenance of the biological diversity of surrounding areas by farmers practicing traditional methods. Brush (1992) also discusses the specific case of the persistent, deliberate maintenance within individual fields of high potato cultivar diversity by Andean farmers even following the introduction and acceptance of new potato varieties bred by Green Revolution techniques. He lists some of the reasons why farmers might preserve this diversity: taste, interest, agronomic factors, economic opportunity, and prestige or social status, and observes that not a single ecological reason was given by farmers. Zimmer (1991) also discusses the maintenance within individual fields of high potato cultivar diversity by Andean farmers who have *not* accepted Green Revolution varieties, and describes prestige or social status as the most compelling proximal motive. Although neither author demonstrates, or even hypothesizes, a long term ecological effect of the maintenance of high potato cultivar diversity beneficial to these self-sufficient agricultural economies, attributing proximal prestige to those who maintain diversity would stimulate the practice and produce the ultimate benefit, if it did exist.

There are many examples of the use of specific foods or medicines where the preventative or healing effects are known by practitioners who cannot explain, in scientific physiological or chemical terms, how they work. Kuhnlein (1981), Johns (1981), and Timbrook (1987) provide examples. Even though explanations for these practices may incorporate spiritual or magical concepts, by and large these food and medicinal practices are efficacious and people *do* understand the basic purpose for them, namely to maintain or restore health. These authors do not give examples of less relevant or somewhat artificial reasons, such as the examples of bedding goats or choosing still fuel discussed here, that maintain advantageous practices because they evoke appropriate activity.

Concepts of utilitarian explanations and distinctions have been explicitly discussed by some authors. Alcorn (1981), in discussing Huastec perception of botanical resources, mentions invisible technology that not only enables plant use but also manages the plant resource, but gives no examples. Invisible technology may refer to parts of Huastec explanations with little or no observational basis that function to stimulate timely activity, with long term resource management effects not accounted for by the explanation.

Hays (1982) suggests that distinctions among kinds of organisms made in self-sufficient agricultural economies may result in differential behavioral or attitudinal responses to the organisms distinguished with consequences that are useful or beneficial, even when the benefit cannot be described by those making the distinction. If the distinction is made, then the benefit is enjoyed, not because of the explanation but because of the behavior it elicits. The distinction of the phosphorous rich *urze,* whose name differs from *neqral* and *negrela,* the other two *Ericas,* would seem to be an example of this phenomenon.

The procedural, ritualized, unsubstantiated, or seemingly irrelevant explanations that elicit timely or appropriate behavior in self-sufficient farming communities may describe practices that represent a deeper ecological or natural wisdom. The wisdom of these practices (if not of their explanations) may transcend the short term, production orientation of modern agricultural technology, whose development has been in part motivated by the desire to convert natural resources to cash profits as fast as possible. It is becoming clear that many modern agricultural practices cannot be sustained without decimating the very natural resources on which productivity depends. Studying, recording, and understanding the human ecosystem in the Pracais valley, an ecosystem based on practices that for centuries have sustained agricultural production on poor soils, is especially relevant to the present challenge of developing technology for sustainable agriculture to ensure the future well-being of people. Some aspects of this preindustrial technology were still available through the memory and activities of the aging residents of the Pracais valley. However, some access to the understanding of how things worked, and especially why things worked, is made available to us by studying the present breakdown of their traditional system. For these reasons, studies of preindustrial agricultural systems should be undertaken with any available evidence of how and why these past technologies were successful.

ACKNOWLEDGMENTS

Dra. Graziana Goncalvez Engles, with her husband Prof. Horst Engles, first took me to the Pracais valley in 1980, where I saw that effective traditional agricultural technology was still practiced. I am grateful for the Engles' help in 1987, when I made an intense study of this technology. I thank the residents of Ribeiros whose trust and interest made this work possible, and especially João de Santos who gave me shelter, and Maria Crina who gave me food. I thank Pedro Nunes for his help with the local dialect. Dr. José Sovral Dias, director of the Laboratorio Química Agrícola Ribelo da Silva, and his staff helped perform the chemical analyses of soils and vegetation. Personal support and encouragement by him and his family are gratefully acknowledged. The friendship and advice of Dr. Manual Bravo Lima, Chief of the Herbarium at the Estaçaõ Agronômica Naçional in Oeiras, and the help of his staff member, Dra. Isabel Saraiva, with the identification of plants, were very valuable. The sabbatical program of the University of Michigan made possible my continuous presence in Portugal for six months in summer and fall of 1987.

LITERATURE CITED

Alcorn, Janis B. 1981. Factors influencing botanical resource perception among the Huastec: Suggestions for future ethnobotanical enquiry. Journal of Ethnobiology 1: 221–30.

Azevedo, Ario Lobo and Rui Pinto Ricardo. 1973. Caracterização e Constituição do Solo. Terça ediçao. Fundaçao Gulbenkian, Lisboa.

Brettel, Caroline B. 1986. Men Who Migrate, Women Who Wait: Population and History in a Portuguese Parish. Princeton University Press, Princeton, N.J.

Brush, Stephen B. 1986. Genetic diversity and conservation in traditional farming systems. Journal of Ethnobiology 6: 151–16.

——— 1992. Reconsidering the green revolution: Diversity and stability in cradle areas of crop domestication. Human Ecology 20:145–67.

Caldas, João Castro. 1981. Caseiros de Alto Minho: Adaptaço e declinio. A Pequena Agricultura em Portugal 7/8: 203–16.

Franco, João Do Amaral. 1971, 1981. Nova Flora de Portugal. Volumes I e II. Sociadade Astória, Lisboa.

Griffin, D. F. 1972. Ecology of Soil Fungi. Syracuse University Press, Syracuse, N.Y.

Grime, J. P. 1979. Plant Strategies and Vegetation Process. John Wiley and Sons, Chichester, U.K.

Hays, Terence E. 1982. Utilitarian/ adaptionist explanations of folk biological classification: Some cautionary notes. Journal of Ethnobiology 2: 89–94.

Johns, Timothy. 1981. The añu and the maca. Journal of Ethnobiology 1: 208–20.

Kuhnlein, Harriet V. 1981. Dietary mineral ecology of the Hopi. Journal of Ethnobiology 1: 84–94.

Pearson, Scott R., Francisco Avillez, Jeffery W. Bentley, Timothy J. Finan, Timothy Josling, Mark Langworthy, Eric Monke, and Stefan Tangerman, (eds.). 1987. Portuguese Agriculture in Transition. Cornell University Press, Ithaca, N.Y.

Serrão, Joel. 1982. A Emigração Portuguesa. Quarta edição. Livros Horizonte, Lisboa.

Timbrook, Jan. 1987. Virtuous herbs: Plants in Chumash medicine. Journal of Ethnobiology 7: 171–80.

Zimmer, Karl S. 1991. Managing diversity in potato and maize fields of the Peruvian Andes. Journal of Ethnobiology 11: 23–49.

Contact Authors

JANIS B. ALCORN, World Wildlife Fund, 1250 24th Street NW, Washington, D.C. 20037.

M. KAT ANDERSON, Natural Resources Conservation Service, Department of Environmental Horticulture, University of California, Davis, Calif. 95616.

CECIL H. BROWN, Department of Anthropology, Northern Illinois University, DeKalb, Ill. 60115.

STEPHEN B. BRUSH, Department of Human and Community Development, University of California, Davis, Calif. 95616.

ROBERT A. BYE, JR., Instituto de Biología, Universidad Nacional Autónoma de México, Apartado Postal 70-614, México, DF 04510 México.

GEORGE F. ESTABROOK, Department of Biology, University of Michigan, Ann Arbor, Mich. 48109.

RICHARD I. FORD, Museum of Anthropology, University of Michigan, Ann Arbor, Mich. 48109.

CATHERINE S. FOWLER, Department of Anthropology, University of Nevada, Reno, Nev. 89557.

EUGENE S. HUNN, Department of Anthropology, University of Washington, Seattle, Wash. 98195.

TIMOTHY A. JOHNS, Center for Indigenous Peoples' Nutrition and Environment, Macdonald Campus of McGill University, 21,111 Lakeshore, Ste-Anne-de-Bellevue, Que., Canada, H9X 3V9.

PAUL E. MINNIS, Department of Anthropology, University of Oklahoma, Norman, Okla. 73019.

BRIAN MORRIS, Goldsmiths College, University of London, New Cross, London, SE14 6NW England.

GARY P. NABHAN, Arizona-Sonora Desert Museum, 2021 North Kinney Rd., Tucson Ariz. 85743.

JAN TIMBROOK, Santa Barbara Museum of Natural History, 2559 Puesta del Sol Rd. Santa Barbara, Calif. 93105.

NANCY J. TURNER, School of Environmental Studies, University of Victoria, B.C., Canada V8W 2Y2.

ROBERT A. VOEKS, Department of Geography, California State University, Fullerton, Calif. 92834.

Index

Breinigsville, PA USA
08 February 2011
255063BV00002B/1/P

9 780806 131801

Ship To:

Tsilat Musie
5484 Gardenbrooke St
Columbus, OH 432355813 USA

Ship From:

TEXTBOOKSNOW-AMAZON
8950 W PALMER ST
RIVER GROVE, IL 60171

Date: 08/22/2013

SKU	Qty	Condition	Title
4835898U	1	Used	Ethnobotany
		9780806131801	Refund Eligible Through= 9/25/2013

Page 1 of 1

Return Information (cut and attach to the outside of return shipment)

Order #: 111-0924882-8016258

DM69198

TEXTBOOKSNOW-AMAZON
8950 W PALMER ST
RIVER GROVE, IL 60171

(Attn: Returns)

Order #: 111-0924882-8016258

	Price	Total
	$ 7.09	$ 7.09

Sub Total	$	7.09
Shipping & Handling	$	6.99
Sales Tax	$	0.00
Order Total	$	14.08

Order #: 111-0924882-8016258

Refund Policy: All items must be returned within 30 days of receipt. Pack your book securely, so it will arrive back to us in its original condition. To avoid delays, please use the return section and label provided with your original packing slip to identify your return. Be sure to include a return reason. For your protection, we suggest using a traceable, insured shipping service (UPS or Insured Parcel Post). We are not responsible for lost or damaged returns. Item(s) returned must be received in the original condition as sold and including all additional materials such as CDs, workbooks, etc. We will initiate a refund of your purchase price including applicable taxes within 5 business days of receipt. Shipping charges will not be refunded unless we have committed an error with your order. If there is an error with your order or the item is not received in the condition as purchased, please contact us immediately for return assistance.

Reason for Refund/Return:
Condition   Incorrect Item Received   Incorrect Item Ordered   Dropped Class   Purchased Elsewhere   Other
Contact Us: For customer service, email us at customerservice@textbooksNow.com.

We are in the process of relocating to our new Aurora Illinois Distribution Facility. You may receive orders shipped from one or both River Grove and Aurora locations until our move is complete. Some orders may be split with a portion fulfilled from our two locations - generating two shipments, each having its own packing slip, but consolidated into a single invoice or charge to your account, whichever is applicable.